MAIN CURRENTS IN
NINETEENTH CENTURY
LITERATURE

GOETHE

MAIN CURRENTS IN NINETEENTH CENTURY LITERATURE

BY

GEORGE BRANDES

IN SIX VOLUMES ILLUSTRATED

VI

YOUNG GERMANY

HASKELL HOUSE PUBLISHERS Ltd.
Publishers of Scarce Scholarly Books
NEW YORK, N. Y. 10012
1975

HASKELL HOUSE PUBLISHERS LTD.
Publishers of Scarce Scholarly Books
280 LAFAYETTE STREET
NEW YORK. N. Y. 10012

Library of Congress Cataloging in Publication Data

Brandes, Georg Morris Cohen, 1842-1927.
  Main currents in nineteenth century literature.

  Translation of Hovedstrømninger i det 19de aar-
hundredes litteratur.
  Reprint of the 1923 ed.
  CONTENTS: 1. The emigrant literature.--2. The
romantic school in Germany.--3. The reaction in France.
[etc.]
  1. Literature, Modern--19th century--History and
criticism. 2. Naturalism in literature. 3. Romanticism. I. Title.
PN766.B7 1975   809'.034   72-3577
ISBN 0-8383-1574-7

Printed in the United States of America

CONTENTS

v

LIST OF PORTRAITS

" *Si l'artiste ne se précipite pas dans son œuvre, comme Curtius dans le gouffre, comme le soldat dans la redoute, sans réfléchir ; et si, dans ce cratère, il ne travaille pas comme le mineur enfoui sous un éboulement ; s'il contemple les difficultés au lieu de les vaincre une à une, l'œuvre reste inachevée, elle périt au fond de l'atelier, ou sa production devient impossible, et l'artiste assiste au suicide de son talent.*"--BALZAC.

YOUNG GERMANY

I

THE POLITICAL BACKGROUND

FROM the days of the Holy Alliance onward, the spirit of systematic reaction brooded over the German countries— a reaction which dated from the Congress of Vienna, and had its centre in Austria. Its most typical representative, Metternich, a pupil of Talleyrand, a less adroit but far more mischievous man than his master, hoped to extend it to the whole of Europe. Everything that had been shaken, loosened, or overturned by the Revolution or by Napoleon was to be repaired and re-established. In the struggle with the great enemy they had been obliged at last to resort to every possible method, had been forced to appeal to the people instead of simply commanding, to appeal to their sentiment in place of their allegiance, and even to promise a thing as contrary to all cabinet policy, as youthfully revolutionary, as "the regeneration of Germany." There had been, it is true, a very noticeable difference between the Austrian and the Prussian watchwords. "Justice and Order," "Order and Peace," were the cues of the Austrian proclamations ; those of the Prussian were "The Nation," "Freedom and Honour," "Germany." Still both of the great German States had made more concessions to the spirit of the times than at all suited the ideas of their leading statesmen. And no sooner was the enemy driven off, the heir of the Revolution crippled, and "the war of freedom" ended, than it became their object to put an end to the freedom as they had put an end to the war.

The generation that had grown up during the war with

A

France had expected to see a united Germany arise as the result of victory. As far back as 1812, Stein had sketched a plan for the reunion of the scattered parts of the former German Empire, and Arndt and Görres had given expression to the same idea. But the Peace of Paris, in 1814, decreed: "The German States shall be independent, and united by a federative league;" and herewith all hopes of unification were dashed to the ground. Almost a generation passed before the people were again animated by the thought. In place of the unified State arose the German Confederacy, *der deutsche Bund*, or, as Jahn called it, *Bunt*, a many-coloured harlequin's garb for the nation; and the disappointment was a bitter one.

The dream of freedom shared the fate of the dream of unification. To animate their peoples in the struggle with Napoleon, several of the princes had promised them constitutional government. Of the larger States, only Bavaria, Baden, and Würtemberg, the former members of the Napoleonic Rhenish Confederacy, kept these promises. Bavaria and Baden received constitutions in 1818; Würtemberg, where for once the king was more liberally minded than the estates, in 1819; and in little Saxe-Weimar, Karl August, the pioneer of political freedom in Germany, had given his people a free constitution and inaugurated a Parliamentary idyll as far back as 1816.

All this, however, was of small significance in view of the fact that Austria, after, as well as before, the Peace, represented the reactionary principle, and that Prussia, with a population more inclined than any of the others to political activity, adhered unhesitatingly to the Metternichian principles.

Yet the Prussian people not only desired a constitution, but possessed a right to it. They had it in black and white. In an edict of 1810, the Chancellor, Prince Hardenberg, the restorer of the power of Prussia, had held out the prospect of representative government. During the war with Napoleon the promise had been repeated, and finally, in an ordinance of the 22nd of May 1815, a formal promise had been made to the people, a clear intimation of the king's intention to appoint without delay a committee whose task it should be to prepare the draft of a constitution. But as the Metternichian principles gained ground, the realisation of this plan was postponed. When Görres ventured to present to Hardenberg an address from the Rhine provinces, in which the King of Prussia was reminded of his promise, the only answer he received was, that the king who had given the promise had also, in his wisdom, reserved the right to judge of the proper time for its fulfilment. On several later occasions the king declared himself to be bound by his promise, but at the same time always insisted that the question of time must be left to his fatherly care to decide. And meanwhile full twenty-five years passed—the rest of the king's life.[1]

The object of the Powers was to eradicate every trace of the Napoleonic administration. In Hanover, for example, the *Code Napoléon*, with its public, verbal judicial proceedings, was abolished, and the old inquisitional system of the sixteenth century, with its secret modes of procedure, was re-established. The peasants, who had been liberated by the French, had to return to serfdom and villenage. The principle of equality before the law was set at naught, the aristocracy re-acquiring the political and social privileges which they had possessed in the eighteenth century.

And just as the first germs of a freer political life were ready to sprout in South Germany, an event occurred which gave the signal for much stronger, much hastier reaction, one symptom of which was the employment of the most violent measures in the repression of unimportant and innocent expressions of popular feeling. This event was the assassination of Kotzebue, or, to be more correct, the enthusiasm for the assassin which his deed awakened throughout Germany, then suffering from oppression and espionage.

The strong national feeling and the enthusiasm for freedom which had asserted themselves during the conflict with France, had in the years following on that

---

1 Biedermann: *Dreissig Jahre deutscher Geschichte.* Prutz: *Zehn Jahre*, i. and ii.

conflict given birth to two movements among the youth
of Germany, to which the attention of the Governments
were now directed—the gymnastic and the student movement (Turnwesen and Burschenschaftswesen).

Jahn, the populariser of gymnastics, who succeeded
Fichte in the favour of the youth of Germany, opened the
first school of gymnastics in Berlin. He had belonged
to Lützow's free-lance Jaegercorps, was a German of
Germans and a hater of the French, and went about with
his long, unkempt grey hair hanging over his shoulders,
bare-necked, his broad shirt-collar thrown wide open, and
a thick, knotted stick in his hand. In the course of the
holiday excursions which he made with his pupils, whenever they came upon a French sign-board or met a
fashionably-dressed man, they would draw up round the
object of their detestation, bawling: "Oh! Oh!" On these
excursions the strictest temperance in food and drink was
observed; they lived chiefly on bread and water, and
bivouacked at night under the open sky. From round
the fire rose the strains of the worthy Massmann's beautiful
Turnerwanderlied:

> "Stubenwacht, Ofenpacht,
> Hat die Herzen weich gemacht,
> Wanderfahrt, Turnerart
> Macht sie frank und hart." [1]

This Massmann, who, besides being one of the leaders
of the gymnastic movement, was one of the founders of the
students' unions (Burschenschaften), is the same who figures
so frequently as scapegoat in Heine's poems and prefaces. [2]

Jahn soon became the object of the most ardent admiration, not only on the part of immature youth, but of men
of note and of public bodies. Poets inscribed their verses
to him; a philologist like Thiersch dedicated his *Pindar* to
him, and compared German to Greek gymnastics; two

---

[1] Soul and body lose their strength
Cowering idle by the stove,
Free beneath the open sky
Must the hardy gymnast rove.

[2] *Wintermährchen*, Kap. xi.; *Lobgesänge auf König Ludwig;* preface to *Romancero.*

universities invested him with an honorary degree. He himself was a most loyal subject, but it was the fashion among his long-haired, bare-necked gymnasts with the unbleached linen jackets to jeer at the army, especially at the dandy officers of the guard. They raved, too, against abstract enemies; among their rules was one for the assassination of the enemy of the good cause; they were to aim with a dagger at his eyes, and, when the victim covered his face, to strike at his heart.

This movement emanated from Berlin, the student movement from Thuringia. The latter began as a sort of semi-national, semi-Christian enthusiasm, and aimed among other things at the reform of the low standard of manners and morals among the students. Originating in one of the small States of Germany, it took for its programme that famous song of Arndt's which declares the whole of Germany to be the German's fatherland.

Amongst the Jena professors a certain Fries had most influence among the students, the same Fries who, in the preface to Hegel's *Philosophy of Right,* is loaded with invective as being the representative of shallowness. He was a violent Liberal, who had said that Hegel's new theories did not grow in the gardens of science, but in the hotbeds of servility; and under his fostering care the endeavour after unity and abstract liberty spread amongst the youth of the universities. The banner of the Burschen was black, red, and gold, said to have been suggested by the colours of the uniform of Lützow's Corps, black, with red facings and gold buttons.

The Reformation commemoration-festival in 1817 first drew general attention to the gymnastic and student societies (Turner and Burschen). It had suggested the idea of a meeting at the Wartburg of delegates from all the German student unions. In a pamphlet published on the occasion of the festival by Karl Sand, he names as the three enemies of German nationalism from time immemorial, Roman imperialism, monasticism, and militarism. On the 18th of October, five hundred students, headed by several professors, marched up from Eisenach to the Wartburg, where they dined in the Knights' Hall, placed at their disposal by the liberal Karl August. After the repast the gymnasts gave a display of their agility for the benefit of the astonished natives. In the evening great bonfires were lighted, and then Jahn proposed that, following the example of Luther, who had burned the Papal Bull, they should burn what the enemies of the good cause had written. Massmann feelingly expressed his approval of the proposal, and bundles of old printed paper were produced, on which were inscribed the titles of the detested books written by the enemies of the gymnasts. There were three by the notorious Schmalz, the first Rector of the University of Berlin, the Police Statute Book of the equally notorious Prussian Minister of Justice, Herr von Kamptz, the *Code Napoléon*, Kotzebue's *Deutsche Geschichte*, Haller's *Restauration*, &c., &c. The last things thrown into the flames were a Uhlan's corset, a queue, and a corporal's baton.

When Fries in high-flown language bade the students farewell, he particularly impressed on them that they had been in the country of German liberty, liberty of action and of thought : " Here there is no standing army," &c. ; an expression rendered more absurd by the fact that the army of Weimar consisted of a number of worthy artisans, who at times, in consideration of a small payment, appeared as hussars, with high riding-boots and spurs, but without horses. In Hegel's preface to the *Philosophy of Right* he remarks, *à propos* of this speech, that Fries was not ashamed, on the occasion of a notorious public demonstration, to say of the constitution of the State that it was from below, from the people, that life would come, if true public spirit prevailed ; that only by the sacred chain of friendship could a community, a society, be inviolably united. Hegel calls this the very hall-mark of shallowness, this melting down of the elaborate architecture of a rationally designed state into " a broth of feeling, friendship, and enthusiasm."

Massmann published an account of the festival, in which he described how night still brooded over Germany, but proclaimed that the blood-red dawn was about to break.

Metternich succeeded in persuading both Prince Harden-

[1] Treitschke : *Deutsche Geschichte*, ii. 383-443.

berg and the Emperor Alexander to bring pressure to bear
on Karl August in the matter of this festival, and ever afterwards Karl August's nickname at the court of Vienna was
" der Altbursche."

Amongst the books burnt in effigy at the Wartburg were
some of Kotzebue's. Kotzebue was publishing at this time in
Weimar his *Litterarisches Wochenblatt*, a journal which flattered
Russia and made merry over the youth of Germany. Little
as Goethe generally sympathised with youth, he rejoiced with
them, for once, at the insult offered to his old enemy.[1]

As Councillor of the Russian Legation, Kotzebue from time
to time sent communications to St. Petersburg, and was consequently supposed to be a Russian spy. It is probable that
his communications were no more than harmless reports on
literary matters, but, be this as it may, in the eyes of the
students, he was Beelzebub—Beltze- or Kotze-bue. At the
University of Giessen at this time, under the leadership of three
brothers Follen, fanatical Republicans, a species of Radicalism
had developed, which gloated over the idea of the assassination of tyrants and their instruments. In the students' songs
such expressions occurred as : " Freiheitsmesser gezückt !—
Hurrah ! den Dolch durch die Kehle gedrückt." (Draw freedom's knife from its sheath !—Hurrah ! Thrust the poniard
into the throat.) Karl Follen, the leading spirit, had completely under his influence that young, narrow-minded mystic,
Karl Sand, who had the image of Jesus constantly before his
eyes, and who, on the 23rd of March 1819, drove his poniard
into old Kotzebue's neck. On a strip of paper which he left
lying beside the corpse, was, amongst other writing, this line
by Follen : " You, too, may be a Christ."

It was perfectly clear that this murder, committed in a
moment of religious exaltation, could not be laid to the
charge of the Liberal youth of Germany ; nevertheless, and

---

[1] Epigram :

" Du hast es lang genug getrieben,
 Niederträchtig vom Hohen geschrieben.
 Dass du dein eignes Volk gescholten,
 Die Jugend hat es dir vergolten."

Thou hast long enough had thy way, long enough reviled what is great ; youth
now requites thee for the insults offered to thine own nation.

more especially as Sand became a species of saint in the popular estimation, Metternich and Gentz, the Emperor of Austria, the King of Prussia, and the Czar, who was irritated by this expression of Russophobia, took united action, and the Resolutions of Karlsbad were passed—provisional, exceptional legislation for the universities, the "demagogues," and the press. Thus a censorship of the German press came into existence, answering to that prevailing in Russia now. Gentz was not mistaken when he called this the greatest retrograde movement that had taken place for thirty years.

Under the pretext of combating a great revolutionary party, which they knew did not exist, the Governments began a war of persecution against what was then called Liberalism. Even the professor of theology at the University of Berlin, De Wette, was dismissed, because he had written a private letter of condolence to Sand's mother, which was seized and opened by the police. The reaction went the length of attacking the men who represented the German national feeling which had arisen during the war. Jahn was arrested, first confined in a fortress, and then sent to live in a small town under police supervision. Arndt was entangled, as a "demagogue," in a criminal case, and lost his appointment. Görres, who was dismissed, escaped over the frontier.

In Prussia the censorship was not only exercised in the case of books and newspapers printed in the country, but extended to foreign printed matter. All German newspapers published in England, France, or Holland were forbidden. The whole stocks of some publishers, Brockhaus, for example, were subjected to a special censorship, on account of one or two pamphlets published by them. At all the universities trusted agents of the Government were appointed to watch over the disposition of the students and the lectures of the professors. All gymnastic and student societies were put down. The so-called old German dress, and the black, red, and gold colours were forbidden. The police especially distinguished themselves in the carrying out of these last prohibitions; they hunted coats, caps, tassels, ribbons, and pipe-bowls, and any man caught wearing a straw hat, a red waistcoat, and a black coat was imprisoned on a charge of high treason.

Some Marburg students in the Twenties had ordered foils from a manufactory in Solingen, and it was reported that the usual trade-mark, " Prince," was wanting on these particular foils. The government of Hesse-Cassel instituted an inquiry for the purpose of discovering if the omission had been ordered by the students. To the great annoyance of the police, no cause for accusation was found. " I am sorry for your statesmen," said the French Minister, Comte de Serre, to the famous Niebuhr about this time ; " they are making war on students."

A specially keen look-out was kept for prohibited combinations among students. When Arnold Ruge was imprisoned, Herr von Kamptz set the whole police on the chase after a walking-stick belonging to him, on which the names of some Jena students were carved, the *corpus delicti* being finally confiscated in Stralsund. Ruge was tortured by long pauses between his examinations, having to spend the intervals in a cell where life was rendered unendurable by vermin. Fritz Reuter had to expiate the crime of having "worn the German colours in broad daylight" by imprisonment, first in a miserable hole in Berlin, and after having been condemned for high treason, in dirty fortress cells. A youthful political offender in Bavaria was sentenced to fortress-imprisonment for treason on an indictment of which one of the gravest clauses was that something resembling a German prince's robe had been found in his room. Chiefly at the instigation of Austria, thousands of young Prussians were either imprisoned or driven into exile. In short, the Liberal middle-class youth of the Germany of those days was as unprotected by the law and as much persecuted as are, in our days, the Socialistic youth of the fourth estate of the same country, or the Liberal youth of Russia.

Political and religious reaction went, as usual, hand in hand. In the year 1821, the Prussian Government concluded a concordat with the Pope, which gave the Roman Catholic Church an influence in Prussia such as would have been unimaginable under Frederick the Great. In the following year a new liturgy, more nearly resembling the Roman, was introduced into the Protestant Church. And it is exceedingly significant that the word Protestantism now fell into disrepute. By a Ministerial decree of the year 1821, the terms Protestant and Protestantism were forbidden in Prussia ; the censors received orders not to pass these words, but to substitute the word Evangelical.

The sadness that takes possession of all progressively inclined minds during long and apparently hopeless periods of reaction now weighed upon the spiritual *élite* of Germany. But the great majority fell a quick prey to carelessness and political indifference. With the reaction, at first forced on them from without, they soon familiarised themselves. Many began to be of opinion that a representative constitution, such as had been promised to Prussia, was a thing of no value. Others felt it deeply that Prussia, which had made such sacrifices in the war with Napoleon, had not succeeded in obtaining a constitution, while the South German States, which had to the last made common cause with the enemy, had long enjoyed popular government and the privilege of Parliamentary debate ; but they concealed their shame under a mask of contempt for these skirmishers, a contempt that had a strong family resemblance to envy and anger. It was malevolently pointed out that the Bundestag, in which Austria and Prussia predominated, took good care that the trees of the South German Parliamentary system were well pruned down. The various Governments had, moreover, succeeded in bringing such opposition as arose in the South German States into disrepute. Ministers often succeeded in preventing an election that was objectionable to them ; they also won over opponents by direct bribery or fear of dismissal ; and they had always the final resource, to which they frequently resorted, of completely disregarding the oppositionist resolutions of the Chambers. As the power was in the hands of the Governments, it lay in the nature of things that the proceedings of the Parliaments, up to 1830, were of no serious interest.

The German press had never occupied a high position. All discussion of State matters being now prohibited, it had

to confine itself, as regarded politics, to the simple chroni-
cling of facts, and to fill its columns with court news,
accounts of storms and floods, the birth of marvellous
monsters in the animal, and the appearance of new stars in
the theatrical, world.

The cultivated classes sought a kind of compensation for
their exclusion from politics in a frantically exaggerated
interest in the theatre.   Never had the adoration of a prima
donna or a ballet-dancer been carried to such an extreme.
In the Berlin of the Twenties every other interest was
swallowed up in the question of the superiority of German
or Italian music.   People thought of nothing but the rivalry
between Spontini and Weber.   When Börne came to Berlin
in 1828, the public mind was so engrossed with the famous
singer, Henriette Sontag, that no one remembered anything
about Börne, except that he had written an article on her.
In his *Letters from Paris* (in " Härings-Salat ") he gives a
witty and yet veracious account of how he was met and
saluted everywhere with the cry : " This is the man who
wrote about Sontag ! "   Even in 1832, everything—the agitation in France, the Polish defeat, sympathy with the exiled
Poles—everything was forgotten in the enthusiasm for the
feet of the great *danseuse* Taglioni, which were then setting
out on their triumphal progress through Europe.   The chief
representative of the reactionary spirit in Prussia, the Hof-
marschall and future diplomatist, General Theodor Heinrich
von Rochow, writes in May 1832 to von Nagler, the
Postmaster-General : " She is to dance, consequently there
is great rejoicing, and occupation in abundance. . . .
Taglioni's mimetic grace has dispelled the threatening signs
of the times." [1]   The word occupation here is significant.
The performance did not merely please, it occupied.[2]

As regards literature, the generation of that day luxuri-
ated in an idolisation of the octogenarian Goethe, which

[1] " Sie wird tanzen und somit ist grosse Freude und Beschäftigung vollauf . . . die
Mimik der Grazien der Taglioni haben die drohenden Zeichen der Zeit verdrängt."

[2] " Preussen und Frankreich zur Zeit der Julirevolution.   Vertraute Briefe des
Generals von Rochow, herausgegeben von E. Kelchner und K. Mendelssohn-
Bartholdy."

accepted everything that the aged master wrote or said as
wisdom, and beauty, and inspired poetry. All his life long
he had had to struggle against hatred and misunderstanding;
now the reverence for him verged on the ridiculous ; in
Berlin it verged on idiocy.[1]   In Zelter's *Letters to Goethe* he
writes, on the subject of the latter's *Elpenor :* ." Posterity
will not believe that the sun of our days beheld the forth-
coming of such a work." [2]   All those who had obstructed
Goethe's path so long as his name still belonged to combatant literature, became his votaries from the moment that
that name conveyed undisputed authority, and could be
employed as a sort of Conservative and national emblem.
Otherwise literature languished.   The day of romantic
poetical fancy was at an end—Raupach and Müllner ruled
the stage, Clauren fiction.   Light literature sank deeper and
deeper into the slough of vulgarity and pruriency.

[1] A certain Geheimrath Schulz, of the Berlin " Wednesday Society," addressed
the following birthday poem to Goethe : " Ich wollt, ich wär ein Fisch—so wohlig
und frisch—und ganz ohne Gräten—So wär ich für Goethen—gebraten am Tisch—
ein köstlicher Fisch.   (I would I were a fish—lively and fresh—and without any
bones—Then I should be for Goethe—fried for his table—a delicious fish.)

[2] Die Nachwelt wird es nicht glauben, dass die Sonne unsrer Tage ein solches
Werk hervorgehen sah.

II

PHILOSOPHY AND REACTION

GERMAN philosophy, all the branches of which shot out vigorously after the flood of Romanticism had fertilised the ground with its deposit, at the same time changed colour. Through the unpropitiousness of circumstances, it became farther removed from reality than heretofore, though more closely bound up with existing conditions.

Hegel is the great example. In March 1819, Karl Sand murdered Kotzebue; on the 22nd of October of the preceding year, Hegel entered on his professorial duties at the University of Berlin. From the programme which he gave his audience in his opening address, it could be clearly deduced that Hegel's philosophy and the Prussian State in its existing form were closely connected; for the said philosophy was based on the omnipotence of the Idea, the State on the power of intelligence and culture. Of the fact that Prussia, allowing herself to be led by Austria, was at this very time proving false to her character and traditions by entering on a policy of spiritual and political reaction, no account was taken. Yet the Resolutions of Carlsbad were already drafted, and it was Prussia that took the initiative in issuing all the petty tyrannical regulations which soon placed the whole of Germany under police surveillance. But the sentimental politics of the students were as obnoxious to Hegel as sentimental philosophy ; the Wartburg rendezvous was to him a piece of romantic foolery, and Sand's poniard-thrust an abomination. In the preface to the *Philosophy of Right*, the first and most important work he produced in Berlin, he not only condescended to defend the persecution of the demagogues, but demeaned himself by playing police agent, and denouncing his former colleague, Fries, to the Governments : " It is to be hoped that neither office nor title will serve as a talisman for principles destructive both of morality and public order." From this time onward Hegel became the philosophic dictator of Germany. He ruled from Berlin over the whole domain of German thought.

Yet in this same philosophy, even in a work with such a pronounced Conservative tendency as the *Philosophy of Right*, there existed a portentous ambiguity. As early as in the above-mentioned notorious preface we find the proposition which was to become the classic motto of the age, which was first appropriated eagerly by the Conservatism of the Restoration period, and then used as a battering-ram by Hegel's younger disciples. It is in larger print than the rest, in two lines :

> " What is rational is real,
> What is real is rational."

What does this mean ? Hegel goes on to explain that when reflection, feeling, or whatever other form the subjective consciousness may assume, regards the present as vanity, it is itself false, finds itself in emptiness. But, on the other hand, the doctrine that the idea is a mere idea or figment, philosophy meets with the assertion that nothing is real except the idea. What is all-important is to recognise that which is eternal in the present, temporal, transient ; in other words, in this case, not to construct a state, but to understand the state as it exists.

Hegel's biographer, Haym, rightly says that not even the doctrine of divine right is so dangerous as this, which declares everything existing to be sacred. But, on the other hand, it may with equal right be maintained that not even the destructive ardour of the youthful revolutionaries went so far as this doctrine, which grants reality only to what is rational, and to all else nothing but a mock reality, which can and should be defied, disregarded, overturned, exploded. Hence Robert Prutz could say of this same proposition that by it all doubt was removed, the old God of darkness hurled into the abyss, and a new, eternally reigning Zeus, the idea that comprehends itself, man as a thinking being, raised to the throne.[1]

[1] Haym : *Hegel und seine Zeit*, p. 365 ; R. Prutz : *Vorlesungen über die deutsche Litteratur der Gegenwart*, p. 259.

The interpretations of Hegel's philosophy that soon appeared were many and widely different, but the kinship between his doctrines and Goethe's poetry was felt by all the initiated. Hegel became the strongest ally of the little circle of Goethe votaries in Berlin, and the two men, known as the absolute poet and the absolute philosopher, were the objects of a common veneration. The orthodox Hegelian even saw a significant coincidence in the circumstance that Hegel was born on the 27th of August and Goethe on the 28th. In the Twenties, the faithful gathered round the festive board on the evening of the 27th of August, drank the toast of the master in the kingdom of thought, and called to mind the saying in the preface to the *Philosophy of Right* about the owl of Minerva, which begins its flight only when the shades of night are gathering. " But as soon as the midnight hour had struck, an orator rose to proclaim the glad tidings that Apollo, the God of day and of song, was now in his sun-chariot, ushering in the 28th, the glorious day." [1]

The patriotism which in 1813 had driven the enemy out of the country, contained two radically different elements, a historical, retrospective tendency, which soon developed into Romanticism, and a liberal-minded, progressive tendency, which developed into the new Liberalism. When the reaction came, it sought support in many of the theories of Romanticism, and finally took the whole movement into its pay. Men like Görres, Friedrich Schlegel, and others, passed from the camp of Romanticism into that of reaction.

The freedom-loving group had, of course, during the wars with Napoleon, shared the Romanticists' hatred of France. But when their sympathies came to take the shape of wishes and demands (for liberty of the press, constitutional government, the franchise, &c.), the hatred of France inevitably evaporated. And the stronger the reaction became, the more keenly were all eyes turned to that neighbouring country which possessed Parliamentary government. The heroes of French Liberalism were soon men of great consequence in the estimation of the German Liberals ; indeed

[1] Treitschke : *Deutsche Geschichte*, iii. 686.

at a distance they seemed of more consequence than they did at home.   In Germany, after the victory over Napoleon, as after the great defeat, quietness was the first duty of the citizen.[1]   All was obedience and silence.   And the result was what it usually is when a highly gifted but unenergetic people are incapable of throwing off a yoke; its pressure generated self-contempt, and the self-contempt a kind of desperate wit, of chronic " gallows-humour "; the better sort developed a real passion for solacing themselves with derision of their own impotence.   The observation of existing con- ditions gave constantly recurring occasion for irony directed against themselves—against visionary Romanticism, the spirit of patience and submission in the domain of politics, ortho- doxy and pietism in the domain of religion.   Caricature-like developments of political life, religion, and poetry incited to sarcasm, that sometimes ruthlessly wounded patriotic feeling, sometimes assumed a frivolous tone which, taken in connection with the French leanings of Liberalism, was, or inevitably seemed to be, more French than German.

[1] " *Die erste Bürgerpflicht ist Ruhe.*" These words occur in an official notice posted in the streets of Berlin after the defeat of Jena.

CHAMISSO

III

SPIRIT OF THE OPPOSITION

THE most notable of the freedom-loving poets and prose authors of the period are embodiments of some of the shades of opinion which have been alluded to. Adalbert von Chamisso, who, by virtue of his famous prose tale, *Peter Schlemihl*, and certain of his qualities, belongs to the German Romantic School, while in other respects he approaches more nearly to the French ideal of thought and writing, is, in some of his most characteristic poems, and even in his epigrams, a mouthpiece of the grief of the better sort over the steadily growing politica land social reaction. As early as 1822, in his poem, *Die goldene Zeit* ("The Golden Age"), he ridicules an age in which that man is a Jacobin who has openly expressed his belief that 2 and 2 make 4; in the *Nachtwächterlied* ("Watchman's Song") he scoffs at the power of the Jesuits; in *Joshua* and *Das Dampfross* ("The Steam Horse"), at those who have robbed time of its secret, and learned how to force it backwards day by day; in *Das Gebet der Wittwe* ("The Widow's Prayer") he gives a darkly pessimistic picture of the heartless rule of the powers that be, with its complete indifference to the fate of the common people; finally he sums up his view of the times in this bitterly humorous quatrain, which greets us sadly in the form of a four-part catch:

KANON.

" Das ist die Noth der schweren Zeit!
Das ist die schwere Zeit der Noth!
Das ist die schwere Noth der Zeit!
Das ist die Zeit der schweren Noth!"[1]

---

[1] This is the need of these hard times!
These are the hard times of need!
This is the hard need of these times!
These are the times of hard need!

Count August von Platen-Hallermünde, whose youthful efforts were Romantic, both in their choice of subject and in their imitation of the forms of the Spanish drama, afterwards waged systematic war with Romanticism. Its latest developments in Germany he holds up to ridicule, without possessing enough of critical tact to discriminate between the authors who did and those who did not belong to the Romanticist group. He quits the literary drama to cultivate the political lyric muse, as he gradually arrives at the conviction that the pitiable condition of public affairs is also at the bottom of the German people's lack of appreciation of power and style and form in poetry. He finds life in Germany impossible to endure, and seeks, under the sunny skies of Sicily, amidst its reminiscences of antiquity, to forget the heavy atmosphere and the political abuses of his Northern home. But he cannot completely distract his thoughts from the ignominy there. He writes his Berlin national song, which begins with the chorus:

> " Diesen Kuss den Moscoviten,
> Deren Nasen sind so schmuck ;
> Rom mit seinen Jesuiten
> Nehme diesen Händedruck ! " [1]

We find also the following bitter outburst of national self-contempt, written in wrath over the maltreatment of his poems by the censor :

> " Doch gieb, o Dichter, dich zufrieden,
> Es büsst die Welt nur wenig ein ;
> Du weisst es längst, man kann hienieden
> Nichts Schlechtres als ein Deutscher sein." [2]

Romantically as Platen's adversary, Heinrich Heine, starts, the modern spirit soon makes itself perceptible in his prose. Even before he touches on the subject of politics proper, he amuses himself, in his *Reisebilder*, by making taunting allusions to German conditions and to the way in which German stolidity accommodates itself to them.

[1] This kiss is for the Muscovites, with their handsome noses ; this hand-clasp for Rome with her Jesuits.

[2] Console thyself, O poet ! 'tis but little the world loses ; thou hast long known that on this earth a man can be nothing worse than a German.

And the love of liberty, abstract, political liberty, was all along the true passion of Ludwig Börne, who long appeared to occupy himself with purely æsthetic matters, being known for whole decades only as a dramatic critic and writer of short stories.

That these authors found readers and admirers bears witness to the fact that the thinking part of the German people at the end of the Twenties was laying aside its faith in authority in the domain of politics as well as in general intellectual matters. At this time the persecution of the students' unions (Burschenschaften) was being carried on with the utmost ardour. They were broken up everywhere. But they formed again at once, and in one German State, Bavaria, after the accession of King Ludwig, they were actually sanctioned by the police. The divisions that occurred among them show the directions of the various currents of public opinion at that time. In Erlangen, after 1827, there were three unions, at feud with each other—Teutonia, Arminia, and Germania.

Teutonia was the organ of pure Romanticism, of religious mysticism, and declared that politics in no way concerned it. Arminia's principles were strict morality and the pursuit of science ; it aimed at the reformation of the conditions of public life, and also at the unity and liberty of Germany. Germania answered to the Radical tendencies of the day. It dropped the older *Tugendbund's* requirement of strict morality, emancipated itself from the rule of authority, including authority in the matter of religion, and declared the belief that its aim—which in the case of this union also was the unity and liberty of Germany—could only be attained by revolution. Though it was essentially a political organisation, it would be ridiculous to call it an important and dangerous one.

These three main movements were soon represented at all the German universities, and significantly enough, it was, as a rule, the one represented by Germania, which had the greatest influence.

IV

INFLUENCE OF THE REVOLUTION OF JULY

In 1830, while things were in this state of stagnation, oppression, and ferment, the news of the Paris Revolution of July arrived, and acted upon public feeling in Germany like an electric shock. All eyes were turned towards Paris, and among thinking people real enthusiasm was felt.

The effect was perhaps most plainly observable among the quite young men.

Two months before the Revolution, Karl Gutzkow, then nineteen, had, as he himself has told us, no understanding whatever of European politics. He neither knew who Polignac was, nor what it meant to violate *la Charte* (the French constitution). He only knew that in spite of all the persecution of the German student unions (Burschenschaften), they were still alive, and that the object to be attained was the unification of Germany. If he thought at all of upheavals which might hasten the march of events, he looked for them rather from the direction of Erlangen or Jena than from Paris ; at the utmost he conceived it possible that a troop of returning Philhellenes landing armed at Stralsund, might take forcible possession of the town and call the Pomeranian militia (Landwehr) to arms, and that the peasants, driven to it perhaps by famine, might join in the revolt.

At this time the French author, Saint-Marc Girardin, had come to Berlin to study the German language, the Prussian school system, and also the University theology as represented by Schleiermacher and Neander, and the Pietism emanating from Halle. As a contributor to the *Journal des Débats*, he received his newspaper regularly from Paris, and with the eager interest of the aspirant to office, followed the progress of the Opposition in France. Gutzkow gave him a German lesson daily ; they read one of Kotzebues' comedies, which the Frenchman preferred as practice to Goethe or Schiller, but they invariably drifted into political discussions. Gutzkow made no attempt to conceal from Saint-Marc Girardin the slight general significance he attached to the French constitutional struggle, openly ascribing a greater influence on the course of history to the student union in Jena than to the Chamber of Deputies in Paris. Girardin smilingly gave a polite answer. From time to time these conversations were interrupted by Eduard Gans, the famous Prussian professor, Hegel's most renowned disciple in the faculty of law, Varnhagen's and Heine's friend, who in fluent French joined in the political argument, and made a great impression on Girardin by his woolly black hair and his whiskers. Gutzkow, who had heard the fashionably dressed, subtle and sarcastic professor ridicule the student movement from his professorial chair, and laughingly confess that he too once on a day, on the banks of the Saale, had deliberated upon the best means of helping Germany to an imperial crown, entreated the French politician not to believe that the youth of Germany thought with Gans. "I am quite aware of it," answered Girardin, "you intend to liberate the world with Sanscrit."

On the 3rd of August 1830, the king's birthday was celebrated with song and speech in the great hall of the Berlin University. The students stood crowded together in front of the barrier behind which sat professors, officials, and officers of high rank. The famous philologist Boekh was the orator, and from the gallery above his head songs were sung by the University choir, under the leadership of Music-Director Zelter, Goethe's correspondent. The Rector of the University, Professor Schmalz, with queue and sword, went from chair to chair, exchanging a few words with the most honoured guests. But Gans, excited and impatient, passed round letters from Friedrich von Raumer, who had just come from Paris. The Crown Prince, afterwards Frederick William IV., sat and smiled ; but all knew that a few days ago in France a king had been dethroned. It was as if the thunder of the barricade cannonade were booming through the festive hall. Boekh's speech on the subject of the fine arts did not succeed in arousing attention, and when Hegel read from the chair the names of the prize-winners of the year, no one except the medallists listened. Gutzkow did hear with one ear that he had taken the prize in the faculty of philosophy, but with the other he heard of a people that had deposed a king, of cannonades, of thousands fallen in the fight. He was oblivious to the congratulations offered him ; he did not even open the case which contained the gold medal with the king's portrait ; he had forgotten the hope of a professorship which he had connected with the thought of winning this medal ; he stood dazed, thinking of Saint-Marc Girardin and his prophecies, and of what he himself had prophesied of the German Burschenschaft. Then he rushed off to a confectioner's shop in Unter den Linden, and for the first time in his life read a newspaper with avidity. He could hardly await the publication of the official gazette that evening ; not because he was impatient to see his name in the list of medallists; all he wished was to know the state of matters in Paris, whether or not the barricades were still standing, whether France was to come forth from Lafayette's hands a republic or a monarchy. "Science lay behind me," he writes, "history before me." [1]

And Gutzkow is a type of the youngest generation of the Germany of that day—the young men of twenty.

Almost simultaneously with Karl Gutzkow's political awakening, there occurred a memorable misunderstanding in the study of the octogenarian Goethe. A visitor, greeted by the old man with exclamations of joy over the great event in Paris, at first believed that he meant the Days of July, and only gradually came to understand that he was talking of the decision of the scientific dispute between Cuvier and Saint-Hilaire in favour of the latter. This famous mis-understanding has long enough been regarded as only a symptom of Goethe's limitation in matters political ; it is

---

[1] Karl Gutzkow : *Das Kastanienwäldchen in Berlin.—Rückblicke auf mein Leben* p. 7.

but fair to point out that the anecdote is also an indication
of the old sage's justifiable indifference to over-estimated
political events. The scientific dispute was, by reason of
the idea involved, and its transforming effect on the spiritual
map of the world, a weightier matter than the French
Revolution of July. Does not Saint-Hilaire's theory of the
"unity of plan" herald *The Origin of Species!* But the
picture of the overwhelming effect of the French political
catastrophe on the youngest generation stands out all the
sharper against the background of Goethe's impassibility.[1]

The impression made on eminent individuals belonging
neither to the youngest nor the oldest generation was very
deep.

The most intellectual and open-minded woman of the
day, the most distinguished of Goethe's female admirers,
Rahel, who by this time was sixty, was in entire sympathy
with the Revolution. To her, as a woman, the social side
was of more interest than the political. Saint-Simonism
takes strong hold upon her ; her marvellously youthful mind
perceives its possibilities, and in the events of July she sees
the beginning of the triumph of its social theories.

To the reviving, inspiriting impression of the Revolution
of July was now added another, which gave a sharp edge
to the passionate political feeling of the younger generation
—the impression, to wit, made by the outbreak of the
Polish revolt. It is most plainly observable in the case of
Platen, who in wild excitement addresses a poetical adjuration to the Crown Prince of Prussia (said to be the most
favourably disposed) to take the part of unhappy Poland,
and also writes the *Polenlieder*, the only poems of his that
rise to the height of passion, proud songs of liberty, full
of outspoken scorn of the autocrat who was worshipped at
the German courts as an almighty being, and of those
who allowed themselves to be bribed and bought with his
roubles.

On Ludwig Börne's mind the news of the Revolution of
July acted with the effect of a flash of lightning.

In the summer of 1830 he was at the watering-place of

[1] *Cf.* Emil Kuh : *Biographie Fr. Hebbels*, i. 437.

Soden, near Frankfort-on-Main, recovering from a long bout of rheumatic fever and repeated attacks of hemorrhage. His *Journal* shows that his political hopes were almost extinguished, his desires stifled. A soul like his, whose aspiration after liberty was a passion, whose hunger and thirst after righteousness consumed his vital force, was unable permanently to bear the heavy weight of political reaction.

He was now forty-four, and since the time of the War of Liberation, that is to say as youth and grown man, had had experience of nothing but the triumphs of baseness and its persecution of all rectitude, all freedom of opinion. He had never been able to lift his eyes from the sheet of paper he was writing on, without seeing pallid fear of every great passion, of ideals, of youth itself, enthroned in high places, side by side with the animal instinct of self-preservation and animal self-indulgence— the Metternich and Gentz principle. He had given up none of the convictions of his youth and manhood, but the world to him was draped in mourning weeds. He had the feeling in Germany of sitting at the bottom of the sea, a diving-bell providing him with just enough air to keep him from suffocation. In Paris he had breathed fresh air. There the light of the sun, human voices, the sounds of life had enraptured him. Now, down among the fishes, he shivered with cold. He suffered the most terrible ennui. The stillness made him ill ; the narrowness of everything galled him to the quick.

He describes himself as one of those natures which cannot in the long run endure the "solo music" of existence. "Symphonies of Beethoven or thunder-storms" were a necessity to him. He was one of the people who feel themselves out of place in a box at the theatre, who sit from choice in the pit, in the middle of the crowd.

It seemed to him as if in Germany the bullion of life were minted underground, in the silence of midnight, like counterfeiters' coin. Those who worked did not enjoy, and those who enjoyed, who in the light of day set the money in circulation that had been coined in fear and trembling in the darkness, did not work. In France a man of health and spirit lived a life like that of a king's messenger, who is sent with despatches to foreign towns, never twice to the same place, and who on his long journeys sees and enjoys life in its most different developments; in Germany he lived like a postilion, who is always taking the same short journey back and forwards between two post-houses, receiving a miserable tip from fortune for his trouble. The postilion was perfectly able to take the journey in his sleep; he knew every stone on his ten miles of road; and this in Germany was called thoroughness; but Börne, sitting in the little hotel in Soden, watching the geese fighting in the yard, and studying the jealousy of the turkey-cocks and the coquetry of the turkey-hens, was not grateful for the opportunity of remarkable thoroughness afforded him.[1]

When the news reached him that Polignac's ministry had issued the famous ordinances, had violated the constitution, he cried, anticipating all the consequences of this step: "And God said, let there be light!"

The news of the Revolution of July followed. Every day he awaited the hour of the arrival of the newspaper with impatience; he walked out the country road, on the look-out for the mail; if it delayed too long, he went all the way to Höchst, where the papers came from. Soon he felt unable to remain in Soden. He returned to Frankfort, and astonished, electrified his environment by his fire. The silent, invalid-looking Börne was unrecognisable; a miracle seemed to have happened; he was young and strong again. All his old dreams seemed to have become realities, and everything in him that he had been forcibly keeping down sprang up again like a spring when pressure is removed.

Frankfort did not long satisfy him; presently we hear of him in Paris.

On the 7th of September he writes from Strasburg: "The first French cockade I saw was on the hat of a peasant who passed me in Kehl coming from Strasburg. It seemed to me like a little rainbow after the flood of our time, a sign of peace from a reconciled God. But when the bright tri-coloured flag greeted my eyes—oh! words

---

[1] *Aus meinem Tagebuch.* Soden, May 22, 1830.

cannot express my emotion. My heart beat so violently that I was on the point of fainting. . . . The flag was on the middle of the bridge, its staff rooted in French ground, but part of the bunting waving in German air. Ask the first Secretary of Legation you meet if this is not a breach of international law. It was only the red stripe of the flag that fluttered over our native soil. And this is the one colour of French liberty that will be ours. Red, blood, blood—and alas! not blood shed on the battlefield."

Börne is here only the mouthpiece of a feeling which had taken possession of most of the many in Germany who were susceptible of enthusiasm. The heroism shown by the French students, polytechnicians, and working men during *les trois jours glorieux* was admired as much as in France itself, and doubly admired as the proof of an energy which the German people appeared to have lost. There was a universal inclination to drift into exaggerated contempt of their own want of political aptitude and insight, their own want of ability to act at the decisive moment.

Thus powerfully did events act upon characters like Börne, and upon the enthusiasts who were to be found in greatest numbers in the scholarly class. Let us complete the picture by observing their effect on the men of the reaction.

Gentz, who had at first exulted over Charles X.'s energy, grew anxious as the *coup d'état* approached. " I look upon the ordinance against newspapers and books," he writes, " as a tremendous venture, of the success of which I am as yet by no means assured. . . . Such weapons ought to be played with only by people who are sure of their strength and of the means at their disposal. To venture into such regions means ruin for men like Polignac and Peyronnet."[1]

As soon, however, as the first alarm had subsided, he and his spiritual kindred set to work to take advantage of every mistake made by the Liberals. Wisely turned to

---

[1] " Die Ordonnanz gegen die Zeitungen und Bücher betrachte ich als ein kolossales Wagstück, dessen Ausführbarkeit mir noch nicht recht einleuchtet. . . . Mit solchen Waffen darf man nur spielen, wenn man seiner Kraft und seiner Mittel gewiss ist. Leute wie Polignac und Peyronnet, wenn sie sich in diese Regionen versteigen, gehen zu Grunde."

account, the after - effects of the Revolution of July in Germany, by the occasion they gave for ruthless repression and persecution, censorship, and imprisonment, might lame the German Liberal movement for many a day ; might (as Metternich said a few years later of the Hambach Festival) make the anniversary of the Revolution a day of rejoicing for the good instead of for the bad. And only a year later, Gentz, who at times had seen the future in a very dark light, was able to write : " Away with all gloomy forebodings now ! We are not to die, Europe is not to die, and what we love is not to die. I am proud of never having despaired."[1]

Metternich had enough literary taste to admire Börne, and Gentz was a fanatical Heine enthusiast. Before the Revolution of July it was still possible to look upon Heine as essentially the poet of unhappy love and the poetical humorist, with a touch of blasphemy and frivolity.

In the summer of 1830 Heinrich Heine was at Heligoland, dreaming on the shore, gazing out to sea, listening to the plash of the waves. He had given up all hope of better times. He occupied himself with reading the few books he had taken with him—Homer, the Bible, the history of the Lombards, and some old volumes on witches and witchcraft. He could hardly himself believe that he had quite lately been the editor of the *Politische Annalen* in Munich. Two days after the Revolution of July had taken place, but before the news of it had reached Heligoland, he wrote, in one of his letters from that island, that he had now determined to let politics and philosophy alone, and to devote himself entirely to the observation of nature and to art ; that all this torture and trouble was to no purpose ; that however great sacrifices he might make in the general cause, they would be of little or no avail ; the world, doubtless, did not stand still, but it moved in a circle, with no result whatever ; when he was young and inexperienced, he had believed that even if the individual perished in the war of

---

[1] "Nun fort mit allen schwarzen Gedanken ! Wir sterben nicht, Europa stirbt nicht, was wir lieben stirbt nicht. Wie viel bilde ich mir darauf ein, nie verzweifelt zu haben."

human liberation, the great cause would be victorious in the end ; now he recognised the fact that humanity, like the ocean, moved according to fixed laws of ebb and flow.

Even if these expressions have been strung together at a later period, even if the letters are not genuine, but a fragment of memoir inserted later, for the sake of contrast, in the book on Börne,[1] they will undoubtedly give us a correct picture of Heine's mental attitude at that time.

On the 6th of August he writes: "I was sitting reading Paul Warnefried's *History of the Lombards*, when the thick packet of newspapers, with the warm, glowing-hot news, arrived from the mainland. Each item was a sunbeam, wrapped in printed paper, and together they kindled my soul into a wild glow. I felt as if I could set the whole ocean, to the very North Pole, on fire, with the red heat of enthusiasm and mad joy that glowed within me." It was all like a dream to him ; the name Lafayette especially was like the echo of one of the stories of his earliest childhood ; he could hardly believe that the man who had ridden in front of the grandfathers of the present generation in the American War of Independence was once more on horseback, the hero of the nation. He felt as if he must go to Paris and see it for himself.

He writes with a passionate fervour, which he soon feels obliged to temper with a touch of self-contempt: "Lafayette, the tri-colour flag, the Marseillaise. . . . It intoxicates me. Bold, ardent hopes spring up, like trees with golden fruit and with branches that shoot up wildly, till their leaves touch the clouds. . . . My longing for rest is gone. I know once more what I desire, what I ought to, what I must, do. . . . I am the son of the Revolution, and again I take into my hand the charmed weapons, over which my mother spoke the magic spell. . . . Flowers, flowers ! that I may crown my head for the death struggle. And the lyre, too; give me the lyre ! that I may sing a song of battle. . . . Words like flaming stars, that shoot down from the sky, set palaces on fire, and illuminate huts. . . . Words like burnished javelins, that whirr up into the seventh heaven and

---

[1] Heine : *Sämmtliche Werke*, XII. 80.

transfix the pious hypocrites who have insinuated themselves into the holy of holies. . . . I am all gladness and song, all sword and flame, and quite possibly mad."

Among other things, he tells how the fisherman who some days later rowed him out to the sandbank from which they bathed, told him the news smilingly, with the words : " The poor people have won the victory." Heine expresses his astonishment at the correct instinct of the common man. And yet the exact opposite was the real state of matters ; it was the rich people who in the end were and remained the victors.

But an utterance such as the last quoted suffices to show the light in which German authors regarded the Revolution of July. It inspired in them the same religious emotion with which forty years previously the leading spirits of the Germany of that day had regarded the great Revolution. It was not to them the result of the strength of the Liberal bourgeoisie, and of their ability to persuade the lower classes to work and shed their blood for them ; it was the general signal for the political, economical, and religious emancipation of humanity. It was the great deed that with one blow freed all nations from the yoke, all minds from oppression.

In 1847 one of the foremost of the Radical writers of the Forties, Robert Prutz (at the time of the Revolution only fourteen), gave an excellent reproduction of the impression it created. " For fifteen years," he says, " it had seemed as if the eternal generative power of the world's history were paralysed. For fifteen years they had been building and cementing, holding congresses, forming alliances, spreading the net of police supervision over the whole of Europe, forging fetters, peopling prisons, erecting gallows—and three days had sufficed to overturn one throne, and make all the others tremble. It was not true then, after all, what the sovereigns had boasted, what the court romanticists had said and sung." [1] The millennial reign of the Holy Alliance had lasted fifteen years. It seemed as if a new spring must be at hand in the political and intellectual life of the German people.

[1] R. Prutz : *Vorlesungen über die deutsche Litteratur der Gegenwart*, 270, 271.

V

INFLUENCE OF BYRON

THE classical literature of Germany in the end of the eighteenth and the early years of the nineteenth century was in subject or form imitative of the antique ; the Romantic literature which followed swore allegiance to the Middle Ages ; both stood aloof from surrounding actualities, from the Now, from existing political or social conditions ; neither directly aimed at producing any change in these. The ideal floated in the deep blue ether of Greece or in the Catholic sky of the Middle Ages. Now it was resolutely dragged down to earth. The modern ideal, an ideal which contains no mythic element, manifested itself to the dreamers and the workers. And with a haste, a violence, that too often made prose journalistic, poetry only lyric or quite fragmentary, the opposition poets and prose writers set to work to draw all modern life into the sphere of literature. From the fact of this inclusion, this appropriation, taking place when things were on a war footing, wit and satire became more prominent powers than they had ever been before in Germany ; and the mood and inspiration of the " Sturm und Drang " period seemed to have revived, so far as aggressive defiance of the established was concerned. It was a strong craving for liberty that first induced Heine and Börne to strike out a new path in German literature, and afterwards inspired the writers who followed them, and were known by the vague name of " Young Germany."

But there was one great man who, foreigner though he was, influenced German intellectual life by his personality, writings, and actions more than any of the famous men of the past. This was Lord Byron. It was long before men's eyes in Germany were opened to his artistic weaknesses and deficiencies. Gutzkow alone, about the year 1835, begins to criticise him discerningly. But the Byron whom Goethe had admired and shown favour to (though principally because of that in him which the old master attributed to his own influence), Byron, with his contempt for the real negation of liberty that lay concealed beneath the " wars of liberty " against Napoleon, with his championship of the oppressed, his revolt against social custom, his sensuality and spleen, his passionate love of liberty in every domain, transfigured by his death as a liberator, seemed to the men of that day to be an embodiment of all that they understood by the modern spirit, modern poetry.

Wilhelm Müller, the poet of the *Griechenlieder*, sings of him with fervent enthusiasm :

" Siebenunddreissig Trauerschüsse ? Und wen haben sie gemeint ?
Sind es siebenunddreissig Siege, die er abgekämpft dem Feind ?
Sind es siebenunddreissig Wunden, die der Held trägt auf der Brust ?
. . . . . .
Siebenunddreissig Jahre sind es, welche Hellas heut beweint !
Sind' die Jahre, die du lebtest ? Nein um diese wein ich nicht :
Ewig leben diese Jahre in des Ruhmes Sonnenlicht,
Auf des Liedes Adlerschwingen, die mit nimmer müdem Schlag
Durch die Bahn der Zeiten rauschen, rauschend grosse Seelen wach.
Nein, ich wein um andre Jahre, Jahre die du nicht gelebt,
Um die Jahre, die für Hellas du zu leben hast gestrebt :
Solche Jahre, Monde, Tage kündet mir des Donners Hall,
Welche Lieder, welche Kämpfe, welche Wunden, welchen Fall !
Einen Fall im Siegestaumel auf den Mauern von Byzanz,
Eine Krone dir zu Füssen, auf dem Haupt der Freiheit Kranz ! "[1]
. . . . . .

Byron's pride and his contempt for political slavery meet us again in Platen ; his aristocratic tone, his antipathy to prejudice, his taste for travel, his love of animals and of nature, his charm and his irony, live again in Prince Pückler.

[1] What mean these thirty-seven minute-guns ? Do they tell of thirty-seven victories ? of thirty-seven wounds on the hero's breast ? . . . They are thirty-seven years, that Greece is mourning to-day. Are they the years of thy life ? Nay, over these we do not mourn ; these live for ever in the sunlight of fame, borne upon the eagle wings of song, whose tireless beat resounds down the ages, awakening great souls. 'Tis other years I weep, the years thou wouldst have lived for Greece. 'Tis of these years and months and days that the volley's thunder speaks to me. What songs, what struggles, what wounds, what a fall ! A fall in the intoxicating moment of victory, on the walls of Byzantium, a crown at thy feet, on thy brow the wreath of liberty !

How enormously he influenced the formation of Heine's poetical ideal needs no insisting on, so forcibly does it strike every one who is familiar with the development of the modern literature of Europe. But it is both remarkable and instructive to observe the light in which he was looked upon by Börne, the first pioneer of the new German literary movement, a fundamentally different character from the English poet. One would naturally imagine that the vain, frivolous sides of Byron's personality would repel him, as these same qualities did in the case of Heine. Far from it. Note the expressions he employs in writing about him (*Briefe aus Paris*, No. 44) after reading Moore's *Life of Byron*. He calls the book wine that sends a glow of warmth through the poor German wayfarer, shivering on his journey through life. He feels almost ill with envy of such a life :—

"Like a comet that submits to no rules and regulations of the star community, Byron wandered through the world, wild and free ; came without welcome, departed without farewell, preferring solitude to the thraldom of friendship. His feet never touched the dry earth ; through storm and shipwreck he steered undauntedly onwards, and the first harbour he came to was the grave. Oh, how he was tossed about ! But what islands of bliss did he not discover ! . . . His was the kingly nature . . . he is king who lives as he lists. When I hear people say that Byron only lived for thirty-seven years, I laugh ; he lived for a thousand. And when they pity him because he was so melancholy ! Is not God melancholy ? Melancholy is God's gladness. Is it possible to be glad when one loves ? Byron hated men because he loved mankind, hated life because he loved eternity. I would give all the joys of my life for a year of Byron's sorrows."

We observe not only that Börne takes everything about Byron seriously, but that he is quite unconscious of the same self-indulgent temperament in Byron which repelled him so strongly in Goethe. And it is still more surprising that Börne should consider his own nature to be akin to Byron's. He writes :—

"Perhaps you ask me in surprise how such a beggarly fellow as I come to compare myself with Byron ; in which case I must tell you something that you do not know. When Byron's genius on his journey through the firmament first came to this earth, he stayed for a night with me. But the lodging was not to his mind ; he left again at once, and took up his quarters at the Hotel Byron. I sorrowed over this for many a year, grieved over my insignificance, my failure. But that is past now ; I have forgotten it, and live contented in my poverty. My misfortune is that I was born in the middle class, for which I am not suited."

Words such as these bear striking witness to the magic power which the shade of Byron still exercised over the minds of the leaders of literature.

VI

VALUE OF THE NEW LITERATURE

IT was under the conditions and influences just described that the German opposition literature of 1820 to 1848 came into being. In surveying such a large group of intellectual productions, we naturally look upon them in the first instance as being, taken generally, a series of documents which inform us how the people of that country and that time thought and felt, what were the developments of their civilisation, what their hopes, their wishes, their philanthropy, their devotion to liberty, their sense of right, their ideal of good government, and, finally, what their taste was —that is to say, in what manner an author required to write who wished to be read and to awaken real interest.

Our historical curiosity on these points being satisfied, there next involuntarily arises the question of the actual value of the literature. In the case of philosophical writings this question turns mainly upon the measure of new truth they contain ; or if, as is too often necessary, we are obliged to regard them chiefly in the light of productions of the imagination, it turns upon the scope and suggestiveness of their hypotheses. In the case of poetry and fiction, and also to a certain extent in the case of the allied historical and descriptive writings, the question of their value is the same as the question of their beauty ; for by beauty we mean artistic worth.

It is a well-known fact that out of a very large number of authors only one or two continue to be read after the lapse of a few generations ; out of an enormous number of works there is only one here and there that people continue to make their own. Of the writers of the period under consideration, very few are known and read to-day out of Germany; in Germany of course a considerably greater number; still, comparatively few of the productions of that day are in the hands of the general reading public.

The first rough criticism is thus the work of time; after the lapse of so many years, such and such an author does not sell, whilst another is perpetually coming out in new editions. But it is no absolute proof of the worth of a writer that he long continues to have a wide circle of readers. It does not prove that his place is among the best, only that he is among the most approachable, the most entertaining. A high degree of culture, or of refinement of mind, may stand in the way of a wide circulation, though they ensure lasting fame.

At the present day, out of Germany, only two of the philosophical writers of that day, Feuerbach and Schopenhauer, are still read, the former little, the latter much; but it was at a later period that Schopenhauer began to influence men's minds, and both these thinkers are read less for the sake of their matter than for their original, daring style. Of the poets, only Heine is much and steadily read out of Germany. In Germany he is looked on and judged as the stinging-nettle in the garden of literature; he stings the historians' fingers and they curse him. In histories of literature and magazine articles his prose is described as old-fashioned and his poetry as artificial; yet his works, now that the copyright has expired, are republished in innumerable editions. Both in and out of Germany he is as much sung as read. His poems have given occasion to more than 3000 musical compositions. In 1887 the solo-songs alone (leaving out of account the duets, quartettes and choruses) numbered 2,500. Hueffer has counted one hundred and sixty settings of "Du bist wie eine Blume," eighty-three each of "Ich hab' im Traum geweinet" and "Leise zieht durch mein Gemüth," seventy-six of "Ein Fichtenbaum steht einsam," and thirty-seven of "Ich weiss nicht was soll es bedeuten." Amongst these compositions are many of the most beautiful songs of Schubert, Mendelssohn, Schumann, Brahms, Robert Franz, and Rubinstein— very few of which the poet himself can have heard. Of all the German lyric poets Heine is the one whose songs have been most frequently set to music. After him, with his 3000 compositions, comes Goethe, with about 1700; the others follow far behind.

Out of Germany Heine's fame not merely lives unassailed, but is steadily growing and spreading. In France he occupies men's minds as if he were a contemporary. He is the only foreign poet whom Frenchmen regard as one of their own, one of their greatest. No other foreign author is so frequently mentioned in the French literature of our own day, and none is named with greater admiration, not even Shelley or Poe. Edmond de Goncourt makes use of the strong expression, that all modern French writers when compared with Heine remind him of commercial travellers; and Théophile Gautier said that the Philistines sought to drag the stones to build a pyramid above Heine's grave.

A question that is constantly cropping up in one civilised society or another is: What works should be included in a library of the hundred best books? The answers of course vary very much. But in all Romanic and Slavonic countries, Heine's name is sure to be one of the first on the lists. On English lists there are usually ninety English books and ten foreign, but Heine's name is certain to be among the ten. The belief that it is possible to find a hundred books which would be the best reading for every one, a belief which has its origin in the Protestant notion of there being one such great book, is of course childish, and the question interesting only in so far as it shows what an entirely impersonal ideal of culture exists in the mind both of the questioner and of those who naïvely set themselves to answer his question. It is instructive, however, à propos of Heine, to notice the results in certain specific cases. No small astonishment was expressed in Germany a few years ago, when a great number of English lists were published, and Heine was found in them all— a distinction shown to no other German author, for there were lists which contained no book by Goethe.

This universal fame is not, however, founded on Heine's merits alone, but also on the fact that much of his writing demands only the very slightest amount of culture for its comprehension, and of refinement of mind for its enjoyment ; the latter quality being indeed rather a hindrance to the enjoyment of some of it. Still its main foundation is the fact that, after all, his talent was, in its way, the most eminent of that period.

If, then, the value of a literary work of art is evidenced by its power of resistance to time, and its attraction for foreign readers, and yet these qualities form no proper criterion of its value, how are we to gauge it ? By the originality and vigour of the spiritual life and of the emotion of which the work is an expression, together with its power of impressing these characteristics on the reader. All art is the expression of some emotion, and has for its object the production of emotions. The deeper a signet gem is cut, the sharper, the clearer are the outlines in wax. The deeper the impression in the soul of the artist, the clearer, the more forcible is its artistic expression. The emotions of the artist differ from those of other men only in this, that they leave in his memory that species of impression, which, when he reproduces it, infects listener or reader.

The questions to which any work provides us with answers are such as the following : How far-sighted was the author ? How deeply did he penetrate into the life of his time ? How characteristically did he feel joy, or grief, or sadness, or love, or enthusiasm, or cynicism ? We say : So great was the horror, or disgust, inspired in him by stupidity or wickedness ; so sharply or wittily did he revenge himself and us on contemptible stupidity or worthlessness. From the best we receive an impression of high-mindedness or greatness, of love of truth or love of beauty ; in the case of inferior men we suffer from deficiency in understanding, in depth of feeling, in sense of beauty, or in strength of character.

Now the literary group under consideration includes no creative minds of the highest, and only one of very high rank, namely Heine. It bequeathed to posterity little that was tangibly great. It denied, it emancipated, it cleared up, it let in fresh air. It is strong through its doubt, its hatred of thraldom, its individualism.

In Germany, especially in North Germany, it has never stood so low in general estimation as at the present day. Those writers who, about the year 1830, made war upon all the forms of tyranny which weighed upon the German-speaking peoples, have in our days been overtaken by an unpopularity which shows no signs of decrease. .

The explanation is simple. The younger generation of the Germany of to-day, which has the unification of the Empire behind it—that unification which to the men of 1830 was a fantastic hope—and which has seen Germany put forth its united strength in prompt, universally successful action, that generation takes little interest in the old dreamy speculations as to how the unification was to be brought about, and is bored by these old writers' everlasting ridicule of German sleepiness and inactivity, German pedantry and theorising, now that results have shown how practical and how resolute the flouted Germany could be when an opportunity was offered her.

More especially since the Franco-German war, the writers who half a century ago were always praising France at the expense of Germany, or maintaining that liberty would bring to Germany those blessings which actually came to her through Bismarck, have been placed under a sort of ban. They are looked on as bad patriots and foolish prophets. Only a small minority are able to perceive how powerfully that very indignation, that scorn for the contemptible existing conditions, helped to bring on the change and improvement that followed. And still fewer in number are those who read in the literature of the Thirties and Forties a living reproach for betrayed or forgotten ideals, and who, as they turn over the leaves of these old books, ask themselves sadly what, in the new order of things, has become of the best that these men fought for.

VII

BÖRNE

OF the authors who in those days stood in the foremost rank, Ludwig Börne is now almost the most neglected. The subjects on which he wrote are obsolete, and none but those interested in the personality of the writer read his short prose pieces in the form of newspaper articles or letters, for the sake of the style, or of the spirit in which the subject is treated. It was in the later years of his life that Börne first really made a name for himself by his *Letters from Paris;* and the abstract hatred of princes and the republican faith which find expression in these letters are entirely out of place in the young Empire of to-day. No personality could be more utterly out of keeping with the new order of things. Where the idea of the State is by slow degrees becoming all-powerful : where, from above, despotically socialistic, it seeks to restrict initiative, transforms as many citizens as possible into paid officials, and gives the paid official precedence of the simple citizen, and from below, revolutionarily socialistic, strives with all its might to restrict individual freedom of action : there markedly self-reliant characters inevitably disappear, and the rugged, independent individuality seems something illegal, something which no one can accept as a model of culture. Börne's was just such an angular individuality and perfectly independent character.

In the German middle-class of to-day, speaking generally, the only task that seems worthy of a man is to build up, to forward, to strengthen or remould the already acquired. The iconoclastic tendency of Börne's mind at once alarms. The fire which warmed his age and generation is to the new generation that of a Don Quixote who charges with his lance at fortress and castle walls. And yet Börne, too, had a hand in the production of the iron architecture of the new

Iron Age of Germany.　His fire melted the ore out of which
the new pillars of society have been cast.

Perhaps nothing has injured Börne more in the estimation of the present generation than his violently prejudiced
denunciation of Goethe.　Goethe, as productive and intelligent spirit, is so great, and his temperament and personality
are so unique, that in our own day a man's judgment of
him gives a valuable clue to that man's mind and character.
And although in those days there were quite a number of
writers, not only belonging to the clerical party, but also
among the opposition, who detested Goethe, there can be no
doubt that Börne gave clear proof of narrow-mindedness by
the manner in which he wrote of the venerable old man in
Weimar, by the nature of his protests against the general
belief in Goethe's greatness as a man and as a poet.

But in order to understand how it came about and
what it signified that a revolutionary political moralist
like Börne entertained a feeling of positive hatred and of
lasting and lively resentment towards the greatest genius
in all German literature, it is necessary that we should
understand how, from his very birth, Börne's fate placed him
in a position of antagonism to the great man whom he was
driven to judge by an alien and therefore a false standard.

Goethe and Börne were natives of the same town, born,
one thirty-seven years after the other, in Frankfort-on-
Main.　Frankfort was an old imperial fortified city, with
gates and towers which indicated the boundaries of the
town in earlier days, and an outer circle of gates, towers,
walls, bridges, ramparts and moats round the new town.
It was a fortified place enclosing smaller fortifications in
the shape of monastic buildings and castle-like mansions.
There was something unalterable about the town, which
was surrounded by a sort of halo of ancient, venerable
independence.　It was a patrician republic, in which a
stranger was practically without the pale of the law.
Woe to him if he engaged in a law-suit with a Frankfort
citizen in a Frankfort court of justice, though it might be
clear as noon-day that he was in the right!　The ruling
families formed an exclusive coterie, and their social inter-

LUDWIG BÖRNE

course was marked by much old-fashioned ceremony. No one dreamed of the possibility of tampering with any of the old political or social institutions of the city. The authorities had no spirit of enterprise, the inhabitants no feeling that change of any kind was possible. Such a thing as political cohesion with the rest of Germany was unthought of. In the Germany of that day each town, and in the town each quarter, was a little world by itself.

Goethe was a young patrician. His father was an Imperial Councillor (*kaiserlicher Rath*). As soon as the young man had acquired a thorough knowledge and understanding of his native town, it must have seemed to him that fate could not possibly have any other lot in store for him but that of a prosperous Frankfort citizen. For the town enthralled him; its best families took possession of the handsome, gifted youth, their women made much of him, their tradition bound him. There was nothing to attract him to the larger towns, Vienna or Berlin, which were then practically as far from Frankfort as Rome and St. Petersburg are in our days. Fate appeared to have destined him to become in due time a lawyer, paterfamilias, public official, house-owner, and literary notability in his native town.[1]

Goethe's actual evasion of this fate was, as every one knows, mainly due to the fact which calls down Börne's wrath upon him, that he became the retainer of a prince, that the Duke of Weimar gave him an important appointment at his little court.

Börne, too, was born in Frankfort-on-Main, but in the Jews' quarter. In his day it was a misfortune to be born a Jew in Germany; for there, as elsewhere, the Jews had none of the rights of citizens. But it was a special misfortune to be born a Jew in Frankfort-on-Main. In other large towns, the position which Jews by this time took in society to a certain extent counterbalanced their political disqualifications. Both in Vienna and Berlin many Jewish houses were frequented as centres of liberal-minded culture and brilliant wit. Jewesses of

[1] Hermann Grimm : *Goethe.*

genius like Rahel, charming Jewesses like Henriette Herz, Baroness Grotthuis, Baroness Arnstein, the Prince of Reuss's consort, and many others, were soon to become leaders of society in the capitals of Prussia and Austria. But in Frankfort, in every walk of life, the barrier between the religions was an impassable one.

All Jews were compelled to live in the narrow, mean, over-populated Judengasse, which was their only place of abode for 334 years, from 1462 onwards. The contrast we read of in novels between the outward meanness and inward splendour of the Ghettos did not exist here ; the interiors of the houses corresponded to their exteriors ; in the small, dark rooms no display of splendour or of taste was possible. A few years ago we had the best of all opportunities of judging of the kind of life the inhabitants of the Judengasse must have lived. One side of the street was pulled down, and a single stunted row of deformed, hunchbacked, cramped, startled-looking houses, in which great gaps had already been made by the axe of the leveller, was exposed to the full light of day, from which their little blinking bull's-eye windows gave them the appearance of shrinking.

As soon as it began to grow dark, all the inhabitants of the Ghetto were locked in. When they walked through the streets or round the ramparts in the day-time, they dared not set foot on the pavement or foot-paths, but had to keep to the middle of the road. They were obliged to take off their hats and make a low bow to every passer-by who called : "Mach mores, Jud'!" In order to prevent their too rapid increase, only fourteen couples were permitted to marry each year. Although even at that time a large proportion of the Frankfort Jews, with Rothschild at their head, were wealthy, a strong society barrier existed between the religions. They were even separated in the Masonic Lodges, which are consecrated to "brotherly love" and the worship of "the highest Being."

It is clear that such a condition of things must have had a strong influence on a receptive young mind.

On the 6th of May 1786, in house No. 118 of that

Judengasse which has now disappeared, there was born to the " Jew merchant Jakob Baruch " a third son, the same who in 1818, shortly before his baptism, exchanged the name Juda Löw Baruch, given him at his birth, for that of Ludwig Börne. The family stood in very high estimation. Börne's grandfather was a rich and remarkably benevolent man. He built and fitted up a synagogue for the community at his own expense. He was the business agent at Neckarsulm of the Teutonic Order, and was thence transferred, on account of his ability and honesty, to Mergentheim, the headquarters of the Order, where he took up his residence. An Electorship becoming vacant, he did such good service, in the course of the election, to the House of Hapsburg, that Maria Theresa with her own hand signed a document promising all sorts of privileges to him and his descendants if they should at any time take up their abode in Austria.

This man's son, Jakob Baruch, inherited, it seems, his father's ability and sagacity without his orthodox religious faith. He was a clever man of business, with considerable diplomatic talent, much esteemed at courts and by high officials for his knowledge of human nature, his clear-sightedness and coolness ; a cold, prudent man, to whom life had taught the lesson that the best thing those in his position could do was to live quietly and thus avoid exciting hatred. He held enlightened opinions on religious subjects, and the wearisome Jewish ceremonial, which, chiefly for his father's sake, he felt obliged to observe with all his household, was a burden to him personally. It was not till late in life that he tried to emancipate himself. Being a rich man's son, he had received a fair education ; it is said that he was at the same school in Bonn as Prince Metternich ; but his cautiousness led him to give strict orders to his own son's one tutor to confine himself to the old Jewish course of instruction—the Bible, the prayer-book, and the Talmud.

The boy was quiet and shy. As he was the one of her children his mother cared least for, and was constantly in disgrace with the tyrannical old servant, his home-life was one of severe discipline, his father too, no doubt with the best of intentions, checking every manifestation of independence in thought or action. One result of this was, that when he first came into contact with the outer world, his emotions blunted, his intellect doubly keen, he looked at everything from the purely intellectual point of view. A thing was stupid or not stupid, and that was all.[1]

The religious observances of his home and of the synagogue aroused in the boy a feeling of aversion as dead ritual ; the religious instruction he received at home made as little impression on him as his attendance at the synagogue. Certain prayers, as, for instance, the prayer for the reinstitution of sacrificial worship, displeased him, in spite of his boyish orthodoxy. To the horror of those about him, he said : "That is a stupid prayer."

His learning was mere committing to memory, his teacher not believing himself what he taught ; and it was all quickly forgotten. As a grown man, he did not know a single word of Hebrew, had no understanding whatever of Jewish customs, and no affection even for the Old Testament, of which Heine was such an enthusiastic admirer. The man who himself reminds us of an Old Testament prophet, has not one allusion to the prophets in all his writings. From time to time, indeed, with complete indifference, and merely as a well-known illustration, he refers to some Bible narratives ; but as Steinthal acutely observes, he quotes even such a passage as Samuel's republican warning against the establishment of a kingdom, which one would expect to excite his every sympathy, as if he were quoting one of Æsop's fables.[2]

Schiller's essay, *The Mission of Moses*, was the first hint of a rational conception of religion that reached the boy. It made a deep impression on him, and shook his faith. Naïvely simple as the essay is, with its implicit trust in the historic accuracy of the Bible narrative, it yet inevitably produced a revolution in the mind of the youthful reader, who now for the first time saw the most important

[1] Gutzkow: *Börne's Leben.*—M. Holzmann : *Ludwig Börne. Sein Leben und Wirken.*

[2] Steinthal: *Ludwig Börne. Illustrirte deutsche Monatshefte,* Juni 1881.

events in the life of his people and of their lawgiver divested
of every miraculous element, Providence itself being superseded by "destiny."

Various anecdotes exist, illustrating the awakening of the
spirit of criticism in the boy, and the play of the different
forces which formed his character. One day, when it was
raining heavily and the road was inch-deep in mud, he was
walking with his tutor outside the gates of the town. "Let
us walk on the footpath," said Börne. "Do you not know,"
answered the teacher, "that we are forbidden to do that?"
The boy's reply, "no one sees us," gave the tutor an opportunity for a moral exhortation, with remarks on the sacredness of law. "That is a stupid law," said Börne.

The tutor was careful to avoid occasions of exciting
bitterness in the child. But there were so many. No Jew
was allowed to be present at any open-air public amuse-
ments, not even at a balloon ascent. On all festive occasions,
as, for instance, when the town was decorated for the reception of royal guests, the Jews were shut up in the
Judengasse; on the day of the coronation of Leopold II.
some of their leading men ventured out, but were at once
arrested and taken to the guard-house. They were prohibited from entering most of the hotels, and from setting
foot in any public grounds or open spaces. The general
rule was: Where there is green grass, no Jew must be
seen. On Sundays the gates of the Judengasse were locked
at four o'clock in the afternoon, and the sentry allowed no
one to pass out except persons taking letters to the post-
house or going for medicine to the apothecary's. Little
Börne used to say: "I only don't go out because the
sentry is stronger than I am." Yet when the boy, who early
showed signs of a distinctly benevolent disposition, was
accosted one day by two beggars, the one a Jew, the other
a Christian, it was to the latter he gave all the money he
had in his pocket. "Why do you not give the preference
to one of your own people?" asked the tutor. "Because
it is written in the Proverbs of Solomon that we are to
heap coals of fire on our enemies' heads." The conscientious tutor would not hear of this reason: "it was based on

the false assumption that the Christians are the enemies of the Jews."

It is easy to understand that such impressions, received in childhood, must have caused Börne's ancestry to weigh more upon his mind than it would have done under normal conditions. And even if he could have forgotten it, the frequent humiliations experienced in his youth, and in later years the perpetual allusions to his nationality made both by his opponents and his champions, would have constantly reminded him of it. With reference to these perpetual allusions he writes in *Briefe aus Paris* (Feb. 7, 1832): "It is like a miracle! The thing is always happening, and yet is always new to me. One set of people reproach me with being a Jew ; another set forgive me for it ; a third go the length of praising me for it ; but they one and all think of it. It is as if they had been conjured into this magic Jewish circle ; none of them can get clear of it. And I know quite well what is the evil spell. These poor Germans! They live in the basement, weighed down by seven stories of higher ranks, and it eases their perturbed minds to talk of human beings who live even lower down than they do, right down in the cellar. The fact that they are not Jews consoles them for not even being court-councillors (*Hofräthe*)."

It cannot, however, be asserted that Börne was peculiarly sensitive on the subject of his Jewish extraction. He often declaimed with the greatest indignation against the oppression of the unfortunate inhabitants of the Ghettos, but he could not do what many expected of him, could not advocate the emancipation of the Jews with greater warmth than other kindred causes. A pursuit of liberty with only that end in view he looked upon as one-sided and egoistic.

Moreover, the Jews inspired him with a feeling of dissatisfaction, of aversion, originating in the antipathy which Frankfort commerce, consisting chiefly in banking business, early awoke in the born poet and idealist. It horrified him to hear a Frankfort merchant speak with the same enthusiasm and ardour of Rothschild or the Austrian loan, with which "a lover of art would speak of a Raphael." In 1822 he wrote: " My aversion from traders and Jews, as such, has reached a climax, now that I have got away from Frankfort, and see what it really means to enjoy life." Börne was by no means incapable of appreciating great commercial undertakings from the æsthetic as well as the practical point of view. Not many years later, the exchange and the harbour of Hamburg excite his lively admiration. But the Frankfort merchants, Rothschild among them, appeared to him, with their speculations in government stock, to be connected with what he abhorred above everything—the dismembered state of Germany and the Metternichian principles. His writings abound in thrusts at "the ennobled German Jews, who are on terms of the most familiar intimacy with all the ministers and royal mistresses," and in consequence look with complete indifference on the Poles' struggle for liberty. Rothschild especially is to him the symbol of evil: "The government could not be more despicable if Rothschild the Jew were king, and had formed a ministry of bill-brokers. . . . Rothschild will stand till the last day of kings. What a day of reckoning! what a crash!" In his bitter hatred of him he goes so far as to call it a disgrace to the Jewish nation when Rothschild is sentenced in Paris to two days' imprisonment for declining, in spite of repeated warnings, to have his cabriolet numbered. Börne had, of course, no personal enmity to the man, but he detests him as "the great broker of all those State loans which give monarchs the power to defy liberty." Being firmly persuaded, after the Revolution of July, that another great revolution was close at hand, he mistakenly considers it stupid of the Jews to curry favour with those in power throughout Europe. But he is right when he calls them "stupider than cattle" for imagining that in the event of a threatening revolution they will be protected by the governments.

With sound political judgment he perceives, what events in Russia have confirmed, that it is exactly at such a time that those in power will deliver them up to the tender mercies of popular hatred in order to escape themselves. [1]

The fact of Börne's being born without the pale of

[1] L. Börne: *Gesammelte Schriften.* *Reclam.* Leipzig. III. 112, 129, 167, 173, 209, 244, 259, 313.

Christian society did not produce in him any excessive
sympathy with his co-religionists ; but the severe discipline
of his joyless childhood, the coldness of his parents, the
aversion aroused in him by the cupidity, cowardly caution,
and other vices generated by oppression which he observed
in those around him, all contributed to forge a spirit that
could never be bent, softened, or broken—a character on
whose adamantine firmness neither flattery nor threats made
the smallest impression. The severity of this character of
ermine-white purity, a severity born of the burning love
of justice, at times clad itself in the garment of humorous
irony, at times in that of scathing ire. As a writer Börne
was for Germany much what Paul Louis Courier was
for France, that is to say, a political tribune, as satirical
and as liberty-loving as the Frenchman, less clear-sighted
in matters of the day, but with more feeling, more imagination, an all-round richer nature.[1]

For in Börne's case firmness of character did not preclude gentleness of disposition. The weak, always rather
sickly boy, who grew up in a sunless street, shut off from
fresh air and from nature, was tender-hearted. The germ
of tenderness in his nature was perhaps first developed by
reading that German author who exercised most influence
on the formation of his opinions and his style—Jean Paul.
It is from Jean Paul, his best comforter in the dark days of
his youth, that Börne, the author, is directly descended.

To him Jean Paul was the poet of those who are born
in obscurity. He loved him as the spokesman of those who
suffer wrong. He saw in him a priest of justice, an apostle
of mercy. His famous commemorative oration gives us
some idea of his youthful enthusiasm, and at the same time
shows what it was in Jean Paul's style that he endeavoured
to make his own. Real emotion makes itself felt through
the artificial antitheses in such a passage as this :—

"We will sorrow for him whom we have lost, and for
those who have not lost him. For he did not live for all.
But the time is coming when he will be born for all, and
then all will mourn for him. He stands with a patient

[1] See *Main Currents*, iii. chap. xiii.

smile at the gates of the twentieth century, waiting till his
lagging people overtake him.   Then he will lead the tired
and the famishing into his city of love."

And there is clever character-drawing in such lines as
the following :—

" In countries the towns only are counted ; in towns, only
the towers, the temples, and the palaces ; in houses, their
masters ; in nations, parties ; and in parties, their leaders.
. . . By narrow, overgrown paths Jean Paul sought out the
neglected village.   In the nation he counted the human
beings, in towns the house-roofs, and under every roof each
heart."

It was possibly Jean Paul's political attitude which first
brought Börne under his spell.   Jean Paul early took his
place in German literature as the inheritor of Herder's
cosmopolitan sentiments and doctrines.   Herder had persistently exalted love of humanity, at the expense of patriotism
and national antipathy.   Jean Paul continued to proclaim
the common brotherhood of man.   All his writings were,
moreover, pervaded by a general spirit of political liberalism, resembling that formulated in the Declaration of the
Rights of Man, which had electrified him ; and he treats
of sovereigns, courts, and the great world generally, in a
tone of sustained irony.   At times he regards as close at
hand a coming golden age, in which it will no longer be
possible for nations, but only for individuals, to sin, and
from which the spectre of war shall have disappeared ; at
other times he relegates it to a very far off future ; but the
rapidity of what was and is called *historic progress* induced
both him and his disciple to imagine that universal brotherhood was not very distant.

It was, however, not only his grand conception of the
future that made Jean Paul so attractive to Börne, but also
the idyllic and satiric qualities of his talent.   Börne adopted
some of his comical names of places (*Kuhschnappel Flach-
senfingen*), and as a young man imitated his humorous style.
Many of the short tales and sketches contributed to periodical
literature—the comic *Esskünstler am Hoteltisch, Allerhöchstdie-
selben, Hof- und Commerzienräthe, Die Thurn und Taxissche*

D

Post (the postal system of the day), &c. &c.—are in Jean Paul's manner, though Börne keeps closer to reality both in his facts and his local colouring than Jean Paul does. Börne attacks State, Church, executive, manners, and customs in Jean Paul's farcical fashion ; but he has not his predecessor's stores of observation to fall back on, and does not approach him in variety of knowledge.

By way of compensation, his style is in many ways superior to Jean Paul's.

Börne, who was not gifted with any profound artistic feeling, or delicate appreciation of style, admired the inartistic in Jean Paul as being unartificial. He did not feel that the profusion of imagery was collected from here, there, and everywhere, and was seldom the natural outgrowth of the subject it adorned. That Oriental wealth of simile, that flowery luxuriance of language, pleased his taste as being poetical ; and the want of harmony in the periods, the heavy ballast of the innumerable parenthetic clauses, were to his ear only evidences of the naturalness of the style. To him, too, Goethe's plastic art was only coldness, while the impersonal style of Goethe's old age was a horror. When he read Jean Paul's works, the living, restless ego in them came forth to meet his own warm-hearted, passionate ego.

He unconsciously remoulded Jean Paul's style on the lines of his own individuality, that individuality which discloses itself in his earliest letters, and whose distinguishing traits were modified or developed, but never altered. There were no wildernesses, no primeval forests in his mind, as there were in Jean Paul's. He did not think of ten things at a time, all inextricably entwined. No ; in his case both fancy and reasoning-power were clear, and concise in expression. His acquaintance with Johannes von Müller's works early produced a propensity for pithy, Tacitus-like brevity. From the first there was a half French, half Jewish tendency to antitheses and contrast in his style. He loved symmetry of thought and symmetry of language ; his spiritual *tempo* was quick ; as a writer he was short-winded. Hence short, sharp, strong sentences following each other at a gallop ; no rounded periods. Metaphors abound ; yet they are not so numerous as to jostle each other out of place, and all are apt and suggestive; he did not ransack note-books for them, like Jean Paul; they presented themselves in modest abundance. He employed similes freely; but in his clear-headed fashion he arranged them almost algebraically in his sentences, so that they produce the effect rather of equations than of scattered flowers.

By degrees his decidedly marked individuality took shape in a decidedly individual humorous style. Jean Paul's humour spreads itself throughout lengthy and discursive investigations, narratives, romances; not so Börne's. He was never able to produce a political, poetical, critical, or historical work of any length; he could not write books, only pages. His was an essentially journalistic talent.[1] And this determines the character of his humour.

Playful humour was his, but also that sarcastic wit which stings like a lash, and yet thrills and touches by an indirect appeal to the feelings; his that bitterness of complaint and accusation which assumes the conciliatory form of an attempt to comfort; and that melancholy, which with a smile and a whimsical conceit rises above time and place. But something similar to this might be said of other great humorists. What distinguishes Börne (from Sterne, Jean Paul, and others) is, in the first place, the strength, the violence of the reaction produced in him by all the occurrences of the day which came within the bounds of his horizon. A comparatively trifling incident in real, and especially in public, life is sufficient to set all the chords of his being in vibration. The second peculiarity is that all occurrences directly act upon one and the same point in his spiritual life, that passion for liberty which was born of the keenest sense of justice. One of his critics, Steinthal, explains in a masterly manner the connection between this fact and the fact of his inability to produce a great work. He never thought systematically, never combined with each other all the many things that one after the other occupied and affected his

---

1 "Was jeder Morgen brachte, was jeder Tag beschien, was jede Nacht bedeckte, dieses zu besprechen hatte ich Lust und Muth."

What each morning brought, each day's sun shone on, each night covered—that was what I had the desire and the courage to discuss.

mind, but looked on each separately in its relation to the centre point of his being.[1] His humour brought the miserable reality into juxtaposition with the ideal demand of his intellect; but he gave no picture of the different elements of reality, he merely focussed them.

Given such a state of matters, it is easy to understand how inevitable it was, not only that Börne should place Schiller high above Goethe, but also that he should consider Jean Paul to be greatly Schiller's superior. And it is highly characteristic that what he objects to in Schiller is not his purely poetical shortcomings, but his want of moral idealism. We are accustomed to think of Schiller as unassailable on this point, but to Börne's ruthless severity of moral requirement he is not so. Börne's pronouncement on the character of Wilhelm Tell is especially enlightening. To him Tell is nothing but a Philistine—a good citizen, father, and husband, but a man the essence of whose character is submissiveness. He did not appear at the Rütli, that meeting-place of the elect, to take the oath ; he had not the courage to be a conspirator. His words:

> " Der Starke ist am mächtigsten *allein* "—
> (The strong man is strongest alone)

are to Börne the philosophy of weakness; a man who has only the strength necessary to get the better of himself, is strongest alone, but he that has strength to spare after gaining the mastery over himself, will rule others also. The critic reviews Tell's actions one by one. Tell does not uncover to the hat on the pole, but his is not the noble defiance of the lover of liberty ; it is only Philistine pride, a mixture of a sense of honour with fear ; he passes the pole with his eyes cast down, that he may be able to say he has not seen it. And when Gessler calls him to account, he is humble—so humble that we are ashamed of him ; he says the omission was accidental, and shall not occur again.

---

[1] "Im Centrum seines Geistes trafen unzählige Strahlen zusammen, nur dass dieselben durch keine Peripherie verbunden waren."

Countless rays were focussed in the central point of his mind, but no periphery united these rays.

The famous apple incident arouses no admiration in Börne. A father may dare everything for his child's life, but he has no right to hazard that life. Why did Tell not shoot the tyrant at once instead of beseeching like a woman with his reiterated " Lieber Herr! lieber Herr! " ? He deserved to have his ears boxed. And when the governor, in the storm on the lake, trusted himself to him, as enemy trusts enemy, was it not treachery and a knavish trick on Tell's part to leap on shore, push the boat out into the lake and leave him to the mercy of the storm ? Börne finds strong cause of offence in the speech :

> " Ich aber sprach : Ja, Herr mit Gottes Hilfe
> Getrau ich mir's, und helf uns wohl hindannen.
> So ward ich meiner Bande los und stand
> Am Steuerruder und *fuhr redlich hin*." [1]

" How," exclaims the critic, " are we to explain such Jesuitry in the simple-minded man ? It is inconceivable to me, too, that any one can consider Tell's next action moral, much less beautiful—he lies in safe ambush, and kills his enemy, who has no idea that he is in danger."

No one can be surprised that a man in whose spiritual organism the sense of justice was so sharply, so intensely developed that it almost took the place of the æsthetic sense, should be wanting in the organ of appreciation for Goethe, whose craving for justice was undoubtedly less developed.

In 1802, after one or two years' residence with a professor at Giessen, young Börne was sent to Berlin, his father being obliged to give in to his desire to study, although on account of his religion this could only lead to his becoming a doctor, a profession for which as yet he showed no turn whatever. He boarded in the house of the famous physician and Kantian, Marcus Herz, whose public lectures on philosophy had drawn such crowded and influential audiences, that the appointment of Professor of Philosophy was conferred on him before any University of Berlin existed. Herz was an eminent physician, a clear thinker, and a good orator ; a friend of Lessing, whose

[1] So I said : Yes, my Lord, with God's help I can do it, can bring us all safe to land. Then I was unloosed, and took the helm and *steered honourably onward*.

poetry he valued as highly as his critical writings. Hence
the mysticism of the Romantic school, more especially
Hardenberg's, was to him both meaningless and obnoxious.
As he died in 1803, his influence on young Börne's development was inconsiderable. All the more powerful was
the impression made on the youth by Herz's famous wife,
Henriette, *née* Lemos. She was seventeen years younger
than her husband, to whom she was betrothed, without
her consent being asked, at the age of twelve. Remarkably
beautiful, mistress of many languages, admired by numbers
of the most eminent scientific men and authors of the
day, she made her house one of the most frequented,
most talked of, most looked up to in Berlin. She was
thirty-eight, Börne sixteen, but this naturally did not prevent
the young man from at once falling violently, though hope-
lessly, in love with the most beautiful, most distinguished
woman it had been his lot to meet.

The charming Henriette presented in outward appearance, as well as in character, a marked contrast to her
little, clever, ugly husband ; she was a faultless beauty, tall
and stately as Queen Louise, with the small head we see on
Greek statues. She went by the name of the Tragic Muse
or the Beautiful Circassian. She was worshipped by Wilhelm
von Humboldt, by Mirabeau, by Schleiermacher, and after
her husband's death she was surrounded by a bevy of men
of position, who all wooed the fair widow in vain. She
refused all offers, in spite of her poverty rejected even the
hand of the richest noblemen in Germany, and took the
place of governess to the future Empress of Russia. She
was as severely virtuous as she was intoxicatingly beautiful.
She was on terms of intimacy with more than one man, but
always within the strict bounds of friendship.

In her circle a line was drawn between the admissible
coquetry which aims at enthralling the whole man, and the
inadmissible, which only aims at enthralling his senses. She
herself belonged to the dangerous class of virtuous flirts.
Of a passionless temperament and much addicted to sentimental moralising, she founded in her younger days a
"Tugendbund" (league of virtue), in which Wilhelm von

Humboldt played the principal part, and of which old and young, known and unknown men, were members. They called each other Thou, wrote long letters to each other in foreign languages or in Greek or Hebrew characters, exchanged rings or silhouettes, aimed at each other's "moral development," desired "to attain happiness by self-devotion" (unencumbered by duties, for self-devotion knows no duties), and ignored the rules and regulations of conventional propriety—but in all chastity and honour. Rahel laughed at them, and would have nothing to do with the league.

The letters the members of the league exchanged bear a strong resemblance to those which passed a little later in Denmark between Kamma Rahbek and Molbech. They were absorbed in their own feelings, but in constant self-examination, thereby naturally depriving their feelings of all freshness. Friends of different sexes explained to each other in interminable letters, with written tears, how they mutually supplemented and developed one another. They tore themselves up into lint, and contemplated themselves in this unravelled condition ; they did not collect themselves for each other's benefit, but spun themselves out. They put their inner man under pressure till the result was a liquid—tears, heart's blood, or such like—and this they poured into the bosom of a like-minded friend, without themselves becoming in any way more remarkable or original under this treatment.

The beautiful and noble Henriette Herz herself was less an original personality than what the Germans call an "Anempfinderin." From the remarkable men with whom she came in contact, she seldom assimilated more than what she picked up from a surface knowledge of their ways and doings. What brought her particularly into notice was the tender friendship existing between her and Schleiermacher. It was much talked about in Berlin, but with no insinuation of evil. The contrast was too striking between the "Tragic Muse" and little Schleiermacher, whose distinguished head was set upon a fragile, slightly deformed body. People smiled good-naturedly when they saw the little pastor coming out of Henriette's house in the evening with a lantern fastened to the button of his coat, or when they met him in the daytime hanging on the arm of his majestic Melpomene. A caricature appeared, in which she was represented carrying him—the jewel, as he was called—in her hand, like a parasol.[1]

Even if young Börne had been the fresh, red-cheeked youth he was not, he would hardly have made much impression on his proud, spoiled foster-mother. At first she did not even understand what was the matter with the young man, whose passion—described in his own memoranda —was a real school-boy worship, of the kind produced at his age by half-conscious instinct and exaggerated ideas of the perfection of woman. One or two attempts which he made, through the medium of the servant, to procure arsenic from an apothecary's, opened Henriette Herz's eyes to the position, and she did her best, by an admixture of kindness with strictness, to bring him to reason.[2] That she was not quite insensible to his adoration, or quite innocent of a certain amount of coquetry, which masqueraded in this case as motherliness, is shown by the following little incident. Börne had taken her to be between twenty-eight and thirty, but at the dinner-table, on the 3rd of December 1802, she told him that she was thirty-four. In the evening she added two to this figure, but she never acknowledged more than the thirty-six, and on the 5th of March 1803, Börne still supposes this to be her age. So the charming "Frau Mutter," as she allowed him to call her, made herself two years younger than she was. Naturally he continued to love, to admire, to despair, to suffer the pangs of hell because of her indifference, and to feel the bliss of heaven when she smiled at him or said a friendly word; also to be so suspicious, bitter, unreasonable, and capricious that at last it became necessary to send him away.

He went to Halle to continue his studies there. As he was leaving he handed her the diary of his emotions—she had, it seems, advised him to pour forth his sorrows on paper—and a number of passionate letters addressed to herself. He continued to write to her from Halle with un-

[1] Karl Hillebrand: "La société de Berlin," in *Revue des Deux Mondes*.
[2] Fürst: *Henriette Herz*, p. 185.

changeable devotion and passionate longing, but in absence he soon so far recovers himself as no longer to be entirely absorbed in the sifting of his own feelings; we presently have calm and entertaining criticism of his surroundings, and a certain dignified self-esteem, combined with self-criticism. In these letters we already notice the characteristic combination of enthusiasm for ideas, indignant denunciation of slavishness, and sharp satire. They give us an understanding of Börne's real nature—a temperament to which licentiousness presents as little temptation as does drink, a soul that suffers under weakness of body, suffers from the inward conflict that ensues where there is courage without power, love that meets no return, undefined longing to do great deeds without any definite aim. Here and there we come upon a threat of what, when once his powers are matured, awaits the Philistine crowd that now smile at him—upon a wrathful presentiment of future humiliations, and fiery projects of revenge on those who, as he already knows, will shamelessly revile him because of his birth, and torture him by calling his reserve cowardice.[1] It is plain that one result of young Börne's stay in Berlin has been the maturing of his emotional life, and also that his intellectual powers have been stimulated by his being brought into contact, in Marcus and Henriette Herz's house, with the most eminent men of the day.

Börne was studying at Halle when the battle of Jena was fought. Shortly afterwards that university was suppressed by Napoleon, and he went to pursue his studies at Heidelberg, full of patriotic rancour against the French, to which he gave vent in a pamphlet which the censor refused to pass. Whilst one result of Napoleon's triumphal progress was the expulsion of the students from Halle, another was a complete revolution in the political conditions of Börne's native town. In 1806 Dalberg, as " Prince-Primas " of the

---

[1] *Briefe des jungen Börne an Henriette Herz*, 164, 167. " O, wenn ich dies bedenke, wie ein Sturm braust es in meinem Innersten, es möchte die Seele aus ihrem Wohnhaus stürzen, und sich den Leib eines Löwen suchen, dass sie den Frechen begegnen könnte mit Klauen und Gebiss."

Oh, when I think of this, a storm rages within me ; the soul struggles to burst from its lodging, that it may find for itself the body of a lion, and rush upon the shameless ones with claws and teeth.

newly formed Rhenish Confederation, took possession of Frankfort-on-Main. One of his first acts was to impr ove the position of the Jews, and in 1810 Napoleon issued an ordinance removing all burdens resting upon them and upon serfs. In 1811 the Jewish community in Frankfort received the full rights of citizens, in consideration of a sum of 440,000 guldens, which was paid up by the following year. The first result of all this, as far as Börne was concerned, was that he gave up the study of medicine, which he had taken to unwillingly, and only because he was debarred from every other, and entered on that of political economy and jurisprudence, as opening the way to a government appointment. In 1818 he took the degree of Doctor of Philosophy.

His father, who had been extremely dissatisfied with his want of application as a student, and with being constantly called on to pay small debts, and who was now no less dissatisfied with him for throwing up the study of medicine, insisted that he should begin to support himself, and procured for him a small post in the Frankfort police establishment, an appointment which contrasts comically with the position which he afterwards took as an author.

He was appointed "Aktuarius," sat in the old, dark Römer building, examined passports and journeymen's certificates, entered minutes, and on state occasions, dressed in uniform and wearing a sword, represented local authority.

But he had also by this time made his *début* as a writer. He contributed to a Frankfort daily paper articles crammed with primeval German rhetoric, defying the mighty Corsican with a patriotic enthusiasm which he at times allows to run away with common sense. They are appeals to the youth of Germany, and passionate expressions of blind, loyal faith in the rulers of Germany.[1] He is absolutely hopeful of the result of "the war of liberation."

[1] "Aber lasst uns nicht, männernde Jünglinge, unsere Kraft vergeuden, sondern die Lust in keuscher Ehe umarmen, damit sie fruchtbar und unsterblich werde . . . Es ziemt uns nicht, uns keck in den Rath der Fürsten einzudringen; sie sind besser als wir."

But let us not squander our strength, O youths who are becoming men; let us embrace joy in chaste wedlock, that she may become fruitful and immortal . . . It becomes us not audaciously to thrust ourselves into the counsels of princes; they are better than we.

He had no foreboding that he himself would be one of the first victims of victory. Hardly had the Emperors of Russia and Austria and the King of Prussia entered Frankfort, when the seven years' rule of Prince Dalberg came to an end. The Grand Duchy of Frankfort was blotted from the list of States, and the old constitution came into force again. The citizenship which the Jews had acquired at such a high price was simply taken from them again, of course without the return of the money. "It was," writes Karl Gutzkow, "as if the couriers who rushed back and forwards between Vienna, where the Peace Congress was sitting, and the other German towns where reactionary congresses were being held, tore furrows in the blood-manured soil of Germany, in which the ruling powers dared to sow the seed of the old prejudices and privileges."

The fall of the French power deprived Börne of his appointment, and his brothers in misfortune of their rights as men ; he was impersonal enough in his way of looking at things to consider the foreign rule a disgrace from first to last.

It is not surprising that Goethe's indifference to this, as to other results of the great reaction, strengthened Börne's hatred for a personality that appeared great upon no side accessible to him. In his notice of Bettina's book, *Goethe's Briefwechsel mit einem Kinde* ("Goethe's Correspondence with a Child")—perhaps the most misleading criticism he ever wrote—Börne says : "What made Goethe, that greatest of poets, the smallest of men ? What entwined hops and parsley in his wreath of laurel ? What set a night-cap on his lofty brow ? What made him a slave of circumstances, a cowardly Philistine, a mere provincial ? He was a Protestant, and his family belonged to the ruling class in Frankfort, from among whom its senators were chosen. At the age of sixty, at the zenith of his fame, with the incense-clouds under his feet separating and sheltering him from the base passions of the valley-dweller, it angered him to hear that the Frankfort Jews demanded the rights of citizens, and he foamed with rage at the ' humanitarian twaddlers' who championed their cause."

It was his relations with the great ones of the earth that Börne could least of all forgive Goethe.

He overlooked the fact that the generation that lay between him and Goethe meant a complete change in the position of the author towards men of rank and the public generally. In Germany in the eighteenth century authors did not live on their works, but on their dedications. Poets were obliged to seek the favour of a high-born patron, to educate young noblemen, or accompany young princes on their educational tours. Wieland accepted money in return for his dedications ; Schiller gladly accepted the assistance which the Duke of Augustenburg procured for him from Denmark. In the end of the eighteenth century, kings, princes, and the aristocracy generally, took a true and keen interest in philosophy and poetry, in all the new truth and beauty ; they sought the acquaintance of authors, and associated with them as with their equals. With the French Revolution these admirable relations came to an end, but Goethe's position dated from before the Revolution.

Börne blinded himself with gazing at disconnected expressions of Goethe's veneration for rank. Somewhere or other he copies this passage from Goethe's diary : " I afterwards had the unexpected happiness of being permitted to pay my homage to their Imperial Highnesses the Grand Duke Nicholas and his consort, in my own house and garden. The Grand Duchess graciously allowed me to write some lines of poetry in her elegantly splendid album." Börne adds : " This he wrote in his seventy-first year. What youthful power !" The older Börne grew, and the more he developed, by his own conscious volition, into a simple incarnation of political conviction, into a being of whose feelings, talents, and wit political conviction had taken possession, to whom it had become a religion, with all the outward expressions of religion, faith, worship, fanaticism —the more unworthy and contemptible did Goethe's rôle of spectator of the political struggles of the day appear to him. Elsewhere he writes : " I have finished Goethe's journal. No drier or more lifeless soul exists in the wide world, and nothing can be more comical than the simplicity

with which he lays bare his own callousness. . . . And
these are the consuls chosen by the German people—Goethe,
who, more timid than a mouse, burrows in the ground, and
gladly dispenses with light, air, liberty, everything, so long as
he is left in peace in his hole gnawing at his stolen bacon ;
and Schiller, more noble, but equally faint-hearted, who seeks
refuge from tyranny above the clouds, where he vainly cries
to the gods for aid, and, dazzled by the sun, loses sight of
the earth, and forgets the human beings whom he intended
to help.   And meanwhile the unhappy country, without
leaders, without guardians, without advisers, without protectors, falls a prey to its kings, and the nation becomes a
byeword among nations."

From the summer of 1818 onwards, Börne, who till
then had only published an occasional pamphlet, appears as
an independent journalist, publisher of the *Die Wage* ("The
Balance "), most of the articles in which he wrote himself.
He was the first German journalist in the grand style, and
first to make the periodical press of Germany a power.   The
possessors of the now rare numbers of that old epoch-
making magazine "of politics, science, and art," look on
them as treasures.   Its success is to be ascribed to its publisher and chief contributor's lively style and apt wit.   It
treated of politics, literature, and the drama, and had on its
staff men like Görres (before his conversion) and Willemer,
Goethe's rationalistic, liberal-minded friend ("Suleika's"
husband) ; but whatever the subject under treatment might
be, it took a political colouring from the manner in which
it was approached.   For three months of the four years
during which Börne continued to publish *Die Wage*, he was
also editor of the daily newspaper, *Zeitung der freien Stadt
Frankfurt*, a position he had to give up because of the constant annoyance to which he was subjected by the censorship.   He afterwards edited another daily paper, *Die
Zeitschwingen;* but this was suppressed, and its editor
sentenced to a short imprisonment.   Börne now paid his
first visit to Paris, whence he for a time wrote letters for
Cotta's various periodical publications ; but by 1822 he was
again in Germany, where a long and dangerous illness soon

swallowed up all his savings, and compelled him to apply to his father for assistance.

His father was exceedingly dissatisfied with him. All his other children did him credit, he said ; but this son, now unable to support himself, had had a most expensive education, and what was there to show for it ? He could do nothing but write articles with a tendency highly disapproved of by his (the father's) patron, Prince Metternich, in Vienna. What was the good of making enemies for himself ? of attacking the great ? Was it becoming in his position of life ? What position, indeed, did he suppose himself to occupy, seeing he allowed himself such liberty of speech ? By this time he might have been a doctor in good practice, or a barrister, and counsel for Rothschild ; instead of which he elected to be a hack writer for periodicals, spending the trifle he got for his articles on travelling, and closing every avenue to success by his impious attacks on those in authority.

And Börne's father had sufficient political sagacity to be aware that it was quite unnecessary for his son to be either a doctor or an advocate in order to find lucrative employment. He knew very well where Herr von Gentz's and Herr Friedrich von Schlegel's bank-drafts came from. And besides, had not his son Maria Theresa's promise to fall back on ?[1]

From the very commencement of Börne's career as a journalist, his talent had attracted the attention of the great reactionaries. On the 18th of May 1819, Rahel writes that Gentz has recommended *Die Wage* to her, as containing the cleverest, wittiest writing of the day, the best of its kind since Lessing's time. Börne's father was perfectly aware that Herr von Gentz praised his son's style, and Prince Metternich his grasp of politics.[2] So he privately

---

[1] Karl Gutzkow: *Börne's Leben. Ges. Werke*, xii. 328, 329.

[2] Metternich was even acquainted with the later, quite revolutionary letters from Paris. On the 26th of January 1834, Princess Mélanie Metternich writes in her diary : " I spent the early hours of the evening with Clemens, to whom I read Börne's *Letters from Paris*. They are of course as malicious as possible, but the style, with its dæmonic extravagance, is remarkably clever." (Metternich's *Posthumous Papers*, v. 545, quoted by Holzmann.)

set to work to secure an advantageous sphere of operation for him on the sunny side of society. Before young Börne was told anything about it, Metternich had eagerly come forward with the most liberal proposals : The young man was to live in Vienna with the title, position, and emoluments of an Imperial Councillor (kaiserlicher Rath), and with no claim made on him for any service in return. Everything he chose to write was to be entirely exempt from censorship ; he should be his own censor. And if, in the course of a few months, he should elect to give up his appointment, he was to be free to do so. In such a position he would have the very best opportunity of working for the cause of progress and humanity.

His father wrote : " Dear Louis ! I beg of you to read this letter as carefully as I have read it. Believe me, the independence you prize so highly is an uncertain possession ; will you, can you retain it ? Why should not you, too, at last think of making a settled position for yourself ? . . . On what is your present bliss founded ? Surely not on the 500 francs (Cotta's monthly payment) ? Make up your mind, for the sake of your future, to take a journey to Vienna at my expense ; I beseech of you not to throw away this chance of success. . . ."

Börne refused everything point blank, refused to hold any communication with those in power.[1] Goethe might allow himself to be appointed Privy Councillor at a court, but he, Börne, would not. And yet the temptation must have been greater in the case of the born plebeian, who had had to take off his hat at the bidding of every passer-by, than it was in the case of the great patrician. In reading the hard, contemptuous, and unjust words which Börne wrote of Goethe, we must not forget that behind these words there was a man who would not do what Goethe did.

Börne was devoid of artistic sense in the strict acceptation of the term. He frankly confessed the fact himself, and, moreover, betrays it in his intolerance of those to

[1] He writes to his father : " Gentz, too, was doubtless a Liberal to begin with, but he could give securities for a sincere conversion which I cannot give. He had been sold to England for many years before he took service with Austria. He is sensual, extravagant, the most dissolute man in the country. . . ."

whom it is a matter of indifference what the artist represents, but all-important how he represents it. Artists and
connoisseurs of this type are utterly repugnant to him. It
disgusts him that any man can prefer a painting of still life
to a painting of a Madonna. His natural bias towards the
lofty, the sublime, the divine, leads him to demand these
qualities in art, and to declare frankly that all works of art
in which these qualities are wanting, are to him simply daubs
or monstrosities.[1]

We cannot agree with Steinthal when he says that Börne
was at home in every domain of culture, every sphere of
artistic production ; for that very branch of art to which the
name art is more specially applied, was a sealed book to
him. This naturally did not prevent his writing much that
is sensible and instructive about works of art ; but what he
wrote is not art criticism.

Börne has been often and much praised for his energetic
condemnation of the German fatalistic tragedies (*Schicksalstra-
gödien*) which began in his day to take possession of the stage
and to confuse men's minds. But it is to be observed that it
is not as æsthetically reprehensible that he objects to them ;
he looks at the matter from the moral or religious point of
view. The belief that a certain date, say the 24th of February,
is peculiarly fraught with fate for any family, is stupid and
futile. It has no connection whatever either with the belief
of the ancients in an inevitable, pre-ordained fate, or with
the Christian belief in an omniscient Providence, or with
the modern determinist theory of cause and effect, which
has undermined the earlier belief in so-called freewill. But
to Börne the belief in question is an unreasonable one
only because it is a confusion of two theological systems.
His chain of reasoning is this : death is either a loving
father, who takes his child home, in which case fate is not
tragic, or a Kronos, who devours his own children, in which

---

[1] " A frog, a cucumber, a leg of mutton, a Wilhelm Meister, a Christ—it is all
the same to them ; they actually forgive a Madonna her holiness, if she is well
painted. So am not I, and never was. In nature I have always sought God, God
only, and in art the divine ; and where I did not find God, I saw nothing but miserable botch-work. History, men, and books I have judged in like manner—
unfortunately ! "

case it is unchristian.[1]   As if that were any objection !   It might still be extremely poetical.

Börne is so clever and clear-headed that his opinion as to the worth or worthlessness of the many dramas it falls to his lot to criticise is almost always correct. He thoroughly enters into the spirit of Oehlenschläger's *Correggio*, and is full of indulgence for the weaknesses of the play, but quite oblivious to its scenic effect. He shows thorough appreciation of dramatists like Kleist and Immermann and young Grillparzer. But when he begins to give his reasons for blame or praise, the inartistic temperament invariably betrays itself, and he frequently displays all the many prejudices of the idealist. He is undoubtedly justified in his unfavourable opinion of Iffland's *Die Spieler* ("The Gamblers"), for instance. But the justification he offers is most peculiar : "What has gambling to do on the stage ? " he cries ; " one might as well dramatise consumption in all its different stages." There is only this difference, one would imagine, that consumption is a physical ailment, gambling a vice. His position is one that is characteristic of idealism, namely, that there is no need to go to the theatre to see what we can see at home. He gives as examples poverty, debt, a faithful wife's patient endurance of hardships ; and instead of remarking on the dull, inartistic spirit in which such things are represented, he exclaims : " Are these such rare sights that we should pay money to see them ?   On the stage, humanity ought to be raised a step above its common level." And he goes on to explain that it was for this reason the Greek and Roman tragedians had recourse to mythic fable, and to maintain that the modern dramatist ought to represent the real characters of ancient days ; or, if nothing will serve him but to grapple with the present, that he must only venture to reproduce its passions. We perceive that Börne is possessed by the naïve belief that the

[1] " I have never been able to understand their conception of fate, their confusion of the antique with the Romantic idea, their Christian paganism. Death is either a loving father, who comes to fetch his child home from the school of life, in which case fate is not tragic ; or he is the cannibal Kronos, who swallows his own children, in which case it is unchristian. Your fate is a hermaphrodite, unable either to beget or to bring forth."

E

" classic " characters of olden times stood on a higher level than the human beings of to-day ; and that he does not understand how every-day reality, properly treated, can be refined into art.

A still stronger proof than these academic utterances of Börne's inability to appreciate simple, primitive poetry, is his indifference to the Old Testament.　In a letter to Henriette Herz, written in his nineteenth year, we come upon a passage of absolutely alarming sterility, dry and senile as a joke on the Pentateuch by Voltaire—and this after Goethe : " It has always appeared to me as if it had been the intention of the old Jews, from Abraham down to Solomon the Wise, to parody the history of the world.　Read Joshua or the Book of Kings, and you will at once be struck by their resemblance to Blumau." [1]　A comparison between these venerable compilations of memorable legends and historical events and a clumsy German parody of Virgil's *Æneid* could only be instituted by a critic who, devoid of all appreciation of antique literary form, set himself to find in every work some modern sentimental, religious, or political moral.　It is quite of a piece with this that Börne should end by blindly admiring the vague, half Biblical, half modern unctuous pathos of Lamennais' *Paroles d'un Croyant.*

[1] *Briefe des jungen Börne,* p. 143.

VIII

BÖRNE

But for this lack of poetic-artistic understanding, it would be difficult to explain how Börne came to take the share he did in the reaction against Goethe which was set on foot by some of the leading men of the day. For, though he had a quite individual, spontaneous animosity to Goethe, Börne was certainly not the originator of the reaction, which was in full swing before he took any part in it. About the time when the Pietists were gloating over Pastor Pustkuchen's parody of the *Wanderjahre*, with its attack on the impiety of Goethe, the pagan, progressive, youthful politicians were beginning to approve of investigations into Goethe's political convictions, which measured them by the very latest standard and made him out to be an "aristocrat," with no feeling for the people, and in reality with no genius.

The first writer of any note who perseveringly and fanatically devoted himself to the systematic disparagement of Goethe was Wolfgang Menzel (born in 1798), a man who before the age of thirty had made his name famous and feared by the help of a certain coarse literary ability, tremendous self-assurance, and the severity of his creed as a Liberal, Nationalist, and moralist. Like Börne, he was originally a disciple of Jean Paul. But his *Streckverse* (1823), which were much admired in their day, and which are unmistakable imitations of that master, carry Jean Paul's peculiar kind of humour to the verge of caricature. Things that have no natural connection whatever with each other are forced into juxtaposition to produce an aphorism, in much the same manner as totally unconnected ideas are coupled together in a pun. He writes: "All Saints' Day

comes before All Souls'; the prophets reach heaven before
the people." "The religion of antiquity was the crystal-
matrix of many resplendent gods ; the Christian religion is
the mother-of-pearl that encloses one god only, but one
beyond all price." "This mortal life is a bastinado."
"Every church bell is a diving-bell, beneath which the pearl
of religion is found."[1]

In his periodical, *Deutsche Litteratur*, he began, in 1819,
an attack upon Goethe, which he carried on with insane
conceit and immovable faith in the justice of his cause. He
first tried to undermine the admiration of the reading world
for Goethe's originality, examined his works with the aim of
discovering imitations or plagiarisms, and demonstrated
the existence of foreign influence everywhere throughout
them.

In his first connected work on the history of literature,
Die deutsche Litteratur, which was published in 1828, in two
parts, he calmly accuses Goethe of having flattered all the
prejudices and vanities of his time. He declares him to be
possessed of nothing more than great descriptive ability, great
"talent," which is a thing unattended by inward conviction,
"a hetaira, who is at every one's beck and call." Goethe
has always, he declares, swum with the stream, and on its
surface, like a cork; he has ministered to every weakness and
folly that happened to be in fashion ; under the fair mask of
his works a refinement of sensuality lies concealed; these
works are the blossom of that materialism which prevails in
the modern world. Goethe has no genius, but a very high
degree of "the talent for making his readers his accomplices,"
&c., &c.[2] Heine, who was uncritical enough in his review
of the book to praise both it and its author—praise which he
was soon to regret—would have nothing to say to Menzel's
doctrine that Goethe's gift was not genius, only talent. He

---

[1] "Allerheiligen geht vor Allerseelen, die Propheten haben den Himmel eher als
das Volk.—Die Religion des Alterthums war die Cristalmutter vieler glänzenden
Götter, die christliche ist die Perlemutter eines einzigen aber unschätzbaren Gottes.
—Das Erdenleben ist eine Bastonade.—Jede Kirchenglocke ist eine Taucherglocke,
unter welcher man die Perle der Religion findet."

[2] Menzel : *Die deutsche Litteratur*, ii. pp. 205-222.

expresses the opinion that this docrine will be accepted by few, "and even these few will confess that Goethe at times had the talent to be a genius."[1]

Menzel continued the cannonade in his numerous contributions to periodicals, and in a new, very much enlarged, edition of his work on German literature. He convicts Goethe of three distinct kinds of personal vanity and six kinds of voluptuousness ("dreierlei Eitelkeiten und sechserlei Wollüsteleien"). He analyses his works, great and small, one by one, measures them by his own patriotic standard, and declares them to be despicable. *Clavigo* he condemns, because Goethe makes Clavigo desert Marie. That he afterwards makes him die by the hand of her brother goes for nothing, in fact is only an additional cause of offence to Menzel, who knows that in real life Clavigo lived on happily, which make his death on the stage a mere *coup de théâtre*.[2] To find sufficient immorality in the play, the critic must, we observe, take advantage of his knowledge of circumstances that do not concern it. *Tasso* is to him Goethe's *Höflingsbekenntniss* ("Confessions of a Courtier "), in which he betrays the vanity of the *parvenu*, to whom the high rank of a woman is an irresistible attraction.[3] The reader will have no difficulty in imagining for himself all the moral reflections for which Menzel finds occasion in *Die Mitschuldigen*, in *Die Geschwister*, where "voluptuousness casts sidelong glances at the pretty sister," in *Stella*, where it craves the excitement of bigamy ("nach dem Reiz der Bigamie gelüstet "), and in the *Mann von fünfzig Jahren*, which is the special object of his indignation.

---

[1] Heine: *Sämmtliche Werke*, xiii. 265.

[2] "Der Dichter . . . fühlt zwar, dass das Schicksal in's Mittel treten müsse, und lässt den Verräther durch eine rächende Bruderhand fallen ; wie vielmehr muss uns dieser Theaterstreich indigniren, wenn wir wissen, dass der berühmte Liebhaber in der Wirklichkeit fortgelebt, um das Unglück zu beschreiben, welches er angerichtet."

The poet . . . it is true, feels that destiny ought to intervene, and therefore the betrayer falls by the brother's avenging hand ; but this *coup de théâtre* only arouses more indignation in us, who know that in real life the famous lover lived on happily, to describe the misfortunes of which he had been the author.

[3] " Die Eitelkeit des Emporkömmlings, die in den Frauen zugleich das Vornehme, das Königliche, begehrt."

The vanity of the *parvenu*, who is not attracted simply by women, but also by their position, their royal birth.

Even *Wilhelm Meister* is to Menzel only an expression of the shamefully light esteem in which Goethe held true virtue, and the strong attraction which the outward conditions of rank possessed for him.[1] *Die Wahlverwandschaften* he regards as the type of "the novel of adultery," which takes for its theme the desire of voluptuousness after untried sensations ("die Wollüstelei, die das Fremde begehrt"). *Die Braut von Korinth* is simply the expression of the voluptuousness whose desire is set on corpses, "die sogar noch in den Schauern des Grabes, in der Buhlerei mit schönen Gespenstern einen *haut goût* des Genusses findet"—(which even amidst the horrors of the grave finds a *haut goût* of sensual enjoyment in intercourse with beautiful spectres).

Where it is impossible to bring an accusation of immorality, Menzel returns to his accusation of want of originality. It is not only its glorification of middle-class Philistinism that stamps *Hermann und Dorothea* as an inferior work, but also the direct imitation of Voss's *Luise*. According to Menzel, Goethe showed real originality only in *Faust* and *Wilhelm Meister*, because in these two works he copied himself. In his youth he borrowed from Molière and Beaumarchais, from Shakespeare and Lessing, and his later iambic tragedies are "the fruits of his rivalry with Schiller." Added to all this, he was, God knows, no patriot.

Let us compare Börne's attacks on Goethe with Menzel's, and we shall find, in spite of similar extravagance of expression, this great difference, that Börne does not attempt to judge, still less to condemn Goethe's great works, nor does he condescend to accusations of sexual immorality; he invariably confines himself to attacking Goethe in his political relations. Saint-René Taillandier correctly observes that Börne gave expression to everything that was rankling in his heart when he took as motto for his review of Bettina's

---

[1] "Geadelt zu werden, im Reichthum zugleich den *haut goût* der Vornehmigkeit in behaglicher Sicherheit zu geniessen, war ihm für dieses Leben das Höchste."

To be ennobled, to enjoy in comfortable security not only wealth, but the *haut goût* of rank, was his ideal in this life.

Goethe's Briefwechsel mit einem Kinde ("Goethe's Correspondence with a Child"), these words from *Prometheus :*—

> ' Ich dich ehren ? Wofür ?
> Hast du die Schmerzen gelindert
> Je des Beladenen ?
> Hast du die Thränen gestillet
> Je des Geängsteten ? " [1]

Though he could only appreciate those of Goethe's works in which the fire of youth was perceptible, his attacks are not based on contempt for the other works, but on the fact that Goethe, so highly favoured in the matter of ability and of social position, never thought of devoting that ability, that position, to the improvement of the existing conditions of life in Germany. It is easy to cull foolish passages conceived in Menzel's strain from Börne's works. In his Journal of 1830, for instance, he writes of Goethe's luck in having succeeded in imitating with his talent the handwriting of genius for sixty years without being detected ; and in another place he calls Goethe the rhyming, Hegel the rhymeless, thrall.[2] But to understand these wild and regrettable outbursts, we must make ourselves acquainted with Börne's bill of accusation against both Goethe and Schiller.

He started from the premise (in all probability quite a false one) that Goethe, by making timely and energetic protest, could have prevented the Resolutions of Karlsbad, could have secured the liberty of the press and the other spiritual rights of which the reaction had deprived the German nation. In any case, whatever the results might have been, he was firmly convinced that it was Goethe's duty to have protested. Instead of this, what happens ? "Geheimrath von Goethe, the Karlsbad poet," as Börne, knowing that he goes there every year to drink the waters,

---

[1] *I* honour thee? Wherefore? Hast thou ever lightened the burden of the heavy laden ? ever stayed the tears of the distressed ?

[2] " Welch ein beispielloses Glück musste sich zu dem seltenen Talent dieses Mannes gesellen, dass er sechzig Jahre lang die Handschrift des Genies nachahmen konnte und unentdeckt geblieben ! . . . Goethe ist der gereimte Knecht, wie Hegel der ungereimte."

satirically nicknames him, subscribes himself *servant* among other servants of his Prince ("wir sämmtlichen Diener"); confesses in his *Tag- und Jahres-Hefte* that he wrote his stupid little play *Der Bürgergeneral* (the whole plot of which hinges on the stealing of a pail of milk from the peasant Martin), with the intention of ridiculing the French Revolution ; also confesses that, far from taking Fichte's part when that philosopher was accused of teaching atheism in the University of Jena, he was much annoyed at the vexation caused to the court by the outside interference which Fichte's utterances provoked.[1] Another cause of offence was the way in which, when Oken's *Isis* was published, Goethe bewailed the peaceful times brought to an end by the establishment of the liberty of the press in Weimar, "the further consequences of which every right-thinking man with any knowledge of the world foresees with alarm and and regret."[2] And the same feeling of disappointment and mortification was aroused in Börne when he read that Schiller, whom he highly esteemed, had at the very crisis of the French Revolution declared in his announcement of the new periodical *Die Horen*, that from this publication everything in the nature of criticism of the government, of religion, or of the political questions of the day, would be expressly and strictly excluded.[3]

We must bear all this in mind when we read Börne's flaming denunciations—ablaze with a passion for liberty that forgets to be just—of Schiller and of Goethe, his lament that in their correspondence these two greatest minds of Germany show themselves so small that nothing at all would be better ("so Nichts sind—nein weniger als Nichts, so wenig"), and that they actually are what he, the confirmed democrat, considers the worst thing possible, a pair of confirmed aristocrats. He sees in Schiller a

---

[1] "Fichtes Äusserungen über Gott und göttliche Dinge, über die man freilich besser ein tiefes Stillschweigen beobachtet."

Fichte's utterances on the subject of God and things divine, on which it is undoubtedly better to preserve unbroken silence.

[2] L. Börne: *Gesamm. Schriften* iii. 216, 217, 222.

[3] "Vorzüglich aber und unbedingt wird sich die Zeitschrift Alles verbieten, was sich auf Staatsreligion und politische Verfassung bezieht."

worse aristocrat than Goethe, for Goethe's partiality is
merely for the upper classes of society, whereas Schiller
will associate with none but the *élite* of humanity. It
is Börne's belief that Goethe might have been the Her-
cules who should cleanse the Augean stables of his country;
but he rather elected to fetch the golden apples of the
Hesperides, and to keep them for himself.[1] He compares
him in his own mind with the great productive spirits of
other countries; with Dante, who championed the cause of
justice; with Alfieri, who preached liberty; with Montesquieu,
who wrote the *Lettres Persanes;* with Voltaire, who dared
everything and gave up all his other occupations to assist
a persecuted man, or to vindicate the memory of one who
had been unjustly condemned to death; with the republican
Milton; with Byron, whose life was one struggle against
tyranny, intelligent or unintelligent—and he summons him
before the judgment seat of posterity. "That terrible,
incorruptible judge will say to Goethe: A mighty mind was
given to thee, didst thou ever employ it to oppose baseness?
Heaven gave thee a tongue of fire, didst thou ever champion
justice? Thou hadst a good sword, but it was drawn to
defend thyself alone." [2]

We cannot deny that Börne has pointed to real flaws
in Goethe's greatness, and to real limitations in his nature,
even though we know that some of his qualities were bought
at the price of these defects, and that a certain limitation
was inevitable if the many-sidedness of his genius was not
to be its bane. It was not for him to do what Börne
required of him. Still we must understand the proportion
of justice there is in Börne's attacks, to be able to forgive
him this violent and foolish expression of resentment against
Goethe during those years when the hopes of the Liberals
in the results of the Revolution of July were receiving their
double death-blow, from the subjection of the French
Government to the power of the great financiers, and from
the suppression of the Polish revolt. He is now more
bitter and violent than ever. He calls Goethe a prodigious

[1] Börne: iii. 536, 572.
[2] Ibid., 573.

obstructive power, compares him to a cataract on the eye of Germany, and expresses the opinion that not until the old man of Weimar dies will German liberty be born.   (Nov. 20, 1830.)[1]

It was on the 1st of October 1831, after whole days spent in despair over events which conveyed the impression, specially painful to this obstinately hopeful man, that France was lost and the reaction victorious, that his anger reached boiling-point.   He took up Goethe's *Tag- und Jahres-hefte*, and was horrified by its author's "apathy."   Goethe tells how, when he was with the army in Silesia in 1790, he wrote one or two epigrams, and how later, at the royal headquarters in Breslau, he lived the life of a hermit, completely engrossed in the study of comparative anatomy.   He adds that what originally led to his taking up this study was his finding a half-cloven sheep's skull one evening in Venice on the sand-hills of the Lido.

"What!" writes Börne, "Goethe, a highly gifted man, a poet, in the best years of his manhood . . . to be in the council of war, in the camp of the Titans, on the very spot where, forty years before, the audacious yet sublime war of kings against their peoples began, and to find no inspiration in these surroundings, to be moved to neither love nor hatred, neither prayer nor curse, to nothing but a few epigrams, which he himself does not consider worth offering the reader.   And with the finest of regiments, the handsomest of officers passing in review before him, he finds nothing better to turn his attention to than comparative anatomy!   And walking by the sea-shore in Venice— Venice, that *Arabian Night* in stone and mortar, where everything is melody and colour, both nature and art, man

---

1 "Dieser Mann eines Jahrhunderts, hat eine ungeheure, *hindernde* Kraft! er ist ein grauer Staar im deutschen Auge. . . . Seit ich fühle, habe ich Goethe gehasst; seit ich denke, weiss ich warum. (20 November 1830.) Es ist mir als würde mit Goethe die alte deutsche Zeit begraben; ich meine an dem Tage müsse die Freiheit geboren werden."

This man of a century possesses a prodigious *obstructive* power! he is a cataract on the eye of Germany. . . . Ever since I could feel, I have hated Goethe; ever since I could think, I have known why. (20 November 1830.)   I feel as if the old German era will be buried with Goethe, as if liberty must be born on that day.

and state, past and present, liberty and despotism ; where even tyranny and murder merely clank like the chains in some gruesome ballad (the Bridge of Sighs and the Council of Ten are scenes from Tartarus)—Venice, towards which I turn my longing eyes, but cannot turn my steps, because the Austrian police lies in wait like a serpent at the city gates and repels with the terror of its poisonous gaze—there, after sunset, when the red glow of evening was spread over sea and land, and the waves of crimson light broke upon the man of stone, and imparted their colour to his eternal greyness ; when, perhaps, the spirit of Werther came upon him, and he felt that he still had a heart, that there were human beings around him and a God above him ; and the beat of his heart, the apparition of his dead youth terrified him, and he felt the hair standing up on his head—he behaved as usual, escaped from his terrors, avoided all disagreeable reflection, by creeping into a cloven sheep's skull and hiding there till night and coldness once more descended upon his heart ! And I am to honour that man ! to love that man ! I would sooner throw myself in the dust at the feet of Vitzli-Putzli, sooner lick the spittle of the Dalai Lama !"

Certainly Börne ought to have honoured this man, and for the very reason for which he despises him. For perhaps at no time was he more clearly worthy of all honour. Börne, by his own showing, would, like the ordinary tourist in Venice, have spent himself in vague moonlight and sunset romancings on the subject of the Bridge of Sighs, the terrors of tyranny, the blessings of liberty, and all the melody and colour—Goethe gazed at his sheep's skull. What was there remarkable about it ? It was split ; and with his naked eye, that seeing eye which pierced into the deepest recesses of nature, into the innermost workshop of life, whence issue all its various forms, Goethe *saw* the great truth, which he had already suspected, that all the bones of the skull were in reality metamorphosed vertebræ, thus making a discovery in the science of osteology that was closely connected with one he had already given to the world in his work on the *Metamorphosis of Plants,* and founding philosophic anatomy, as he had already founded philosophic botany. Börne did not perceive that this man, whose life-work is one of the foundation-stones in the edifice of the modern world, in this particular instance, with his intuition of the unity underlying all variety of form, in his divine simplicity, resembles one of the fathers of ancient science, a Thales or a Heraclitus.

Börne's attacks on Goethe do not come under the same category as Menzel's. They are never malicious, much less base. Though they certainly now and again hit some vulnerable spot in the great man, they throw more light on Börne's own nature than they do on Goethe's; and, even where they most clearly show the limitation of his intelligence, they witness to the purity of his character. They have been powerless to affect men's admiration for Goethe's genius. It would be as foolish to judge Goethe by the false political standard set up by Börne in 1830 as to judge Börne himself by the false German standard of 1870, which those do, who say of him, what he said of Goethe, that he was no true patriot. It was natural, nay inevitable, that Börne should undervalue Goethe. It is possible to understand his want of understanding without sharing his dislike. And it is possible to do full justice to the rush of his pathos, to the elasticity and keen sparkle of his wit, without forgetting, as our eyes light on the seething, flashing cascades of his prose, that there is a deep, calm, wide ocean, called Goethe.

IX

BÖRNE

It is in the first volumes of the *Letters from Paris* that Börne reaches his high-water mark as an author. He was not capable of writing books, not even of writing essays and dissertations ; for his explosions of emotion or thought there was no form so suitable as that of a letter. And these are real letters, not newspaper-articles, nor even newspaper correspondence, but letters written to a friend, without thought of publication until that friend took the initiative, and asked Börne's permission to make an experimental selection of passages which might be of interest to the general public.

The friend in question was Frau Jeannette Wohl, a lady who plays an important part in Börne's life, though perhaps not so important a part as he plays in hers. For upwards of twenty years, from 1816, when he made her acquaintance, till his death in 1837, he gave her his entire confidence, and rarely took any step without consulting her ; and to her, during the same period, his career as an author, his health, his circumstances generally, were of more importance than all else.

When they saw each other for the first time, he was thirty and she thirty-three. She had been married to a rich man, with whom she had lived unhappily. After nursing him through a long illness, she got a divorce from him, refusing to accept any share of his fortune or to retain his name. When Börne and she lived in the same town, he read aloud to her everything that he wrote ; when they were separated, she would at one time urge him to work, eager that he should win fame and independence ; at another, fearing that he was too diligent, and that his health, at all times precarious, might suffer, she would beg him not to be too conscientious in the fulfilment of his engagements to the publishers, but to allow himself sufficient leisure and re-creation.

Jealous of his honour, she underwent long periods of anxiety and irritation when it seemed to her that he was neglecting his duty to the public. Börne had taken payment in advance from the subscribers to *Die Wage* for the second volume of that periodical, and then, after bringing out only five numbers, made a lengthy pause, partly because he was tired of the work, and partly because, being in pecuniary difficulties, he was anxious to find more remunerative employment. Her letters, which he always looked for with almost feverish eagerness, at this time keep *Die Wage* before his eyes by every device which the ingenuity and perseverance of an anxious woman can suggest. She entreats and threatens, she scolds and teases, she sends him four long pages with nothing upon them except *Die Wage, Die Wage.*

But she is often quite as anxious to distract and amuse him, to prevent him from over-exerting himself and to keep up his spirits. When he is taken seriously ill at a distance from her, she grieves that she is not able to look after him, has once actually made up her mind to hazard her reputation by going to him ; she knows very well that if she does, people will no longer believe that what unites them is only friendship.

It was in reality a feeling midway between friendship and love, for which no name exists. After Jeannette's death there was found among her papers an ordinary *Gesindebüchlein der freien Stadt Frankfurt,*[1] on the cover of which Börne had written his name, with the usual particulars. On its first page stands :

Took service when ?	With whom ?	For how long ?	In what capacity ?	Left service when ?
15 Jan. 1818.	Frau Wohl.	For ever.	As friend.	On the day of his death.

There could be no more laconic expression of a volun-

[1] The "service-book" which German employés are required to keep.

tary lifelong devotion. And the last words were literally
fulfilled, for it was on Jeannette's face that the dying man's
last look rested, and to her that he spoke his last words :
" You have given me much happiness."

Jeannette Wohl's portrait, which Börne declared to be
a good one, shows us a woman with a longish face, regular,
pleasing features, a high forehead, an expressive, beautifully
formed mouth, and bright, kindly eyes ; the firm chin indicates energy. Her voice is said to have been remarkably
sweet. Hers was not a particularly original, and still less
was it a productive mind ; she was one of those women
who can merge their own individuality in that of the man
to whom they are devoted. To Börne, the author, her natural
feminine capacity for inspiring a man with confidence in
himself was invaluable ; she was as much offended by any
disparaging remark he made on the subject of his own
ability or deserts, as if it had been made by another. She
was comfort and consolation to him in human form. In
her he had a being on whom he could place absolute reli-
ance, to whom he could confide everything without the
slightest fear of ever being misunderstood, far less betrayed,
and to whom he could address all his literary efforts. She
was to him an epitome of the ideal public for whom he wrote.

In one of his confidential letters he writes that his feeling
for Jeannette is described in the following passage from *La
Nouvelle Héloïse :* " C'est cette union touchante d'une sensi-
bilité si vive et d'une inaltérable douceur ; c'est cette pitié
si tendre à tous les maux d'autrui ; c'est cet esprit juste et
ce goût exquis qui tirent leur pureté de celle de l'âme ; ce sont,
en un mot, les charmes des sentiments, bien plus que ceux
de la personne, que j'adore en vous." And we learn, from
a letter of Jeannette's written in 1833, after this friendship
had lasted seventeen years, that the attraction he exercised
was at least equal to that which he experienced. She
describes as a sort of *idée fixe*, or chronic ailment, the excitement that takes possession of her about the time when the
mail may be expected. The day she writes, she had been
obliged to give up her usual occupations and lie on the sofa,
and when at last the letter arrives, she weeps for joy.

She looks after his money matters, calculates the payments due to him, draws his police pension for him ; at one time, when he has a great longing to travel in Italy, but cannot do it for want of means, she takes a lottery ticket, in the hope of winning the necessary sum, and when she is disappointed in this, wishes to sell her piano, but finds she cannot raise the required amount in this way either.[1] And all this without the incentive of love, in the narrower sense of the word. Her friends believed her to be capable of doing even more for him. At the time that it first occurred to her that Börne ought to publish his letters to her, she expressed to a cousin the naïve doubt if it were possible to publish letters before the death of the person to whom they were addressed, to which the cousin replied that she had not the least doubt that Jeannette was quite ready to let herself be buried if it would do any good to Dr. Börne.

They often travelled together, and sometimes, it would seem, lived together ; but the nature of their relation to each other never altered. It is probable that at one time, in the first stage of their friendship, Börne tried to persuade Jeannette to marry him, but her fear lest the relation existing between them might lose its charm by being turned into an ordinary, everyday marriage, a fear which Börne himself afterwards shared, proved an insurmountable obstacle. Considering that they were both free to dispose of themselves as they would, it seems hardly possible that their relation could have remained what it was for all these years without the existence of some slight, it might be almost unconscious, physical antipathy on her side, or on both sides. An outward hindrance to their union undoubtedly existed in the difference of their creeds. Börne belonged to the Christian, Jeannette to the Jewish confession ; her orthodox mother was strongly opposed to her becoming a Christian, and in those days great difficulties were placed in the way of mixed marriages. But this was not the main difficulty. Jeannette herself writes that to marry Börne

[1] On this occasion Börne writes : " Love has affected the reason of many a human being, but I never heard of human kindness doing so. No one was capable of this but you. . . . It is well that you have never found the man of your heart—you cannot even stand wine mixed with water."

would require "more courage and more self-confidence" than she possesses. And in this instance we see the man whom we knew in his youth as the passionate lover, and who all his life long suffered from a jealous disposition, quickly rise to the height of pure devotion ; he constantly urges Jeannette, for her own sake, to marry a man worthy of her, and make a happy home.

In 1821, in answer to the words just quoted, Börne writes: "I swear to you by Almighty God that, ardent and often expressed as my desire to make you mine may have been, it has always been more of your happiness than of my own that I have thought. My love for you makes me happy ; what more could marriage give me, since it could not increase that love ? Though I did not confess it to you, I always dreaded that marriage might drag down our beautiful friendship to the level of everyday, sordid reality. But I thought, what I still think, that *you* would gain something by it, and this would indirectly have increased my happiness. So there is nothing to prevent you from marrying another man ; you and I should lose nothing by that."

Strange to say, the truth of this last, audacious assertion was put to the proof. At a somewhat advanced age, Jeannette actually fell in love with and married a man much younger than herself. It was their mutual admiration for Börne that brought the couple together, and in Jeannette's answer to the letter in which Straus asks her to marry him there is a long reference to Börne, so enlightening in its simple eloquence that it cannot be dispensed with in this estimate of his character as a man and as an author. She writes :

"The Doctor has no one in the world but me ; I am to him friend, sister, all that these words convey of kindliness, friendliness, sympathy. Can you grudge this to him, to whom life has given nothing else, and who has reconciled himself to his fate . . . is even contented with it. . . . I can think of no other possibility than that the Doctor should be free to come to us when, where, and for as long as he chooses ; for altogether, if he wishes. I can't say *you*, my

F

heart is too full ; canst *thou* think anything else possible ?
If so, then all is different from what I thought. I !—we !—
dream of deserting a man like the Doctor—why, he would be
a ruined, a lost man ! I would rather give up everything,
rather die, than have that upon my conscience ; I could not
do it, even if I would. . . . I am trembling all over, and as
pale as death from writing even these few words on the
subject. For nothing agitates me so deeply as the very
thought of such treason, of such infidelity to such fidelity.
As long as I live, till I draw my last breath, I shall feel for
Börne the love of a daughter for her father, of a sister for
her brother, of a friend for a friend. If you do not understand, cannot grasp the situation, do not know me well
enough—then all is over, all is night. I can write no more.
But no more is necessary. I am thankful this is over."[1]

Events proved that Straus thoroughly entered into
Jeannette's feelings, indeed shared them. He, too, became a faithful friend to Börne. For five months in the
summer of 1833 Börne lived with them in Switzerland.
They then removed, for his sake, to Paris, where they all
lived together from the end of 1833 till his death, spending
the summers at Auteuil. The one person who permitted
himself to make disparaging comment on this arrangement
was Heine, in that unfortunate passage in his book, *Ludwig
Börne*, which led to the duel in which he was wounded by
Straus. Heine afterwards, of his own free will, expunged
the passage. But in anger and grief at the harm done to
his reputation by this work on Börne, he was heard to call
Jeannette the baleful woman who, on his triumphal progress
as Germany's chosen poet, crossed his path, prophesying
evil, and caused him to start back and drop his laurel wreath
in the dirt.[2]

It is certain that Jeannette never forgave Heine his
unpardonable molestation ; yet no one could have been less
of a Megæra. What Börne once wrote to her, joking, as he

---

[1] All this information on the subject of Jeannette is to be found in Gottlieb
Schnapper-Arndt's article : *Jeannette Straus-Wohl und ihre Beziehungen su Börne.*
Westermanns Monatshefte, April 1887.

[2] Alfred Meissner : *Erinnerungen*, p. 79, &c.

often did, on the subject of her faulty orthography, was almost true, namely, that in the letter he had received that day there were more faults than she had herself, for there was one.

In her opinions we can follow the different steps of Börne's political development. After the Revolution of July she, too, is a radical democrat. In the expressive words of her biographer, Schnapper-Arndt : " She most frequently thinks with Börne, at times in opposition to him, never without him. But she does seem to be perfectly independent in her passionate sympathy with the revolt of the Polish nation, a feeling so strong that it leads her to heap reproaches on Börne for being capable at such a moment of writing about the Italian opera in Paris. The Polish scythemen, the liberty of Poland—nothing else is worthy to be mentioned along with this. It seems to her that every one must help ; she gives her own most cherished possessions to the cause ; and nothing can exceed her shame when Germany shows itself indifferent to it, nothing her joy when she can send Börne proofs of the fact that a storm of sympathy and enthusiasm is sweeping over the country."

X

BÖRNE

THE progress of the insurrection in Poland, which lasted from the winter of 1830 till the summer of 1831, was followed with lively sympathy by almost all the nations of Europe. All knew that the struggle in Poland was deciding whether absolutism or national liberty was to prevail in the Europe of the future. The movements of the combatants were eagerly noted; every victory of the Poles was hailed with popular rejoicing, every defeat was heard of with sorrow. Towards the close of the struggle, when it became evident that the Poles, unaided, could not triumph, numerous appeals were addressed by German subjects to their respective governments, urging them to assist Poland. The Germans then possessed the quality, which Bismarck afterwards laid to their charge as a fault—a fault of which he has cured them—of being almost more interested in the welfare of other nations than in their own, to the extent even of desiring that welfare when it could only be purchased by some surrender of power on the part of Germany.

When all was over with the Poles, the Germans tried to give proof of their sympathy by showing as much hospitality as possible to the Polish refugees on their wanderings through Central Europe to France. They everywhere met with a warm reception; a committee was appointed in almost every German town to collect money for them and help them on their journey. Jeannette Wohl's letters to Börne at this time contain many significant details. She tells that a number of Polish officers who came by water from Hanau to Frankfort-on-Main were escorted all the way by enthusiasts, that bands played and salutes were fired as they entered the town, and that they were carried shoulder high through the crowd. When bands of Poles march through the town, all heads are uncovered as they pass. The town defrays their expenses at the hotels. A wounded Polish officer, who dies at one of the hotels, is followed to his grave by thousands, including the city militia. A goldsmith sets a splinter of iron taken from the wound of another Polish officer in the shape of a little sword, and presents it to him.

With the fall of Poland the bulwark which protected Germany from the influence of the Russian autocracy was broken down. The defeat of the Poles was a defeat for the champions of liberty in every country. The shock was a violent one.

A man who lived at Bremerhafen at the time when the infernal machine devised by the wholesale murderer, Thomas, exploded, tells how, immediately after he had heard the report of the fearful explosion, a torn, bleeding hand flew in at his open window and fell upon the desk at which he sat writing. Something of the same kind happened to German authors when Warsaw capitulated. Shattered Poland's dissevered hand fell without warning upon their desks. Heine writes in 1831, in his introduction to Kahldorf's book on the aristocracy: "I feel while I am writing as if the blood shed at Warsaw were gushing from my paper, and as if the Berlin officers' and diplomatists' shouts of joy were ringing in my ears."

The three Powers that had divided Poland determined to take immediate advantage of the victory to overpower dismayed European Liberalism, and this in four countries at the same time—in Germany, where the Bundestag was to inaugurate, and Prussia and Austria to carry out, a still more energetic reaction ; in Italy, which was once more to be occupied by Austria ; in Portugal, where Don Miguel was to be supported against his brother ; and in the Netherlands, where the King of Holland was to be assisted in his struggle with rebellious Belgium.

Immediately after the suppression of the Polish revolt, a note was addressed by the Cabinet of St. Petersburg to the German governments, in which Russia advised them to keep the revolutionary tendencies in their respective countries in check, and offered them her assistance in doing so. The censorship at once became more severe, and many Liberal newspapers and periodicals were suppressed. The Chambers of the South German States protested, and the utterances of the Liberal press, in spite of all warnings and threats, became more violent and reckless from day to. day. The general belief had hitherto been that it was the desire of the sovereigns to meet the wishes of their people, but that they were held back by their advisers. Now this belief fell to the ground. The conviction became general that the unification of all the German countries in one constitutional, strongly democratic State was at hand. Politically short-sighted, and imbued with all manner of optimistic ideas, the general public were unable to believe that such a movement as that originated by the Revolution of July could exhaust itself without any political result. The champions of Liberalism had preached " progress " as a religion, and people had arrived at the belief that progress must inevitably be victorious, and that each attempt at reaction would actually work for good in the end.

Such was the state of public opinion at the time of the publication of the first volume of Börne's *Letters from Paris*, which gained him great popularity. They were promptly suppressed. (November 1831.) This suppression, and the abuse heaped on the author by his opponents, added to the sensation which the bold language of the book had created.

In these letters, Börne's style is only occasionally humorous, whereas in his earlier writings it invariably was so. We seldom find the quiet, resigned sort of humour distinguishing, for instance, his characteristic description of his capture by night and his imprisonment in Frankfort in 1820: " I was refused a boot-jack (*Stiefelknecht* = boot servant or slave), that the distressing symbol of servitude might not be always before my eyes. I was only allowed to use knife and fork in the presence of a warder, in case I should injure myself. Paper, pen, and ink were granted me only after repeated entreaties, and paper in restricted quantity ; they were afraid my health might suffer from my sitting still too much. Every evening a warder came with a lantern to examine the stove and see that it did not smoke, as smoke might be injurious to my fine eyes; he also examined the grating in front of the window, to make sure that thieves could not break in, &c., &c."

It is only at the commencement of his stay in Paris, while he is kept in a state of constant elation by the supposed attainment of great political results, that he still jests lightly and freely (as, for example, on the subject of the many Princes Henry of Reuss, Greiz, and Schleiz, who are now being punished by the revolution in Gera for all the agony the committing to memory of their respective numbers cost him at school); the jesting tone soon vanishes from his letters, and the striking, convincing similes are all that remains of his old style.

His chief feeling, when he thinks of his Fatherland, is shame. In the Days of July, Englishmen and Dutchmen, Spaniards and Italians, Poles and Greeks, helped to fight for the liberty of France, which means the liberty of all nations; but no Germans were there. With its administration of justice, its censorship, and its guilds, Germany will soon be the antiquarian museum of Europe. But more obnoxious to him than anything else is the German spirit of loyalty and humility. The Spaniards, the Italians, the Russians, and all the others are slaves; the people that speak the German tongue are lackeys. Slavery only makes men unhappy, it does not degrade them; servitude degrades. (January 25th 1831.) At an international dinner in Paris, when speeches were being made by Liberals of every nationality, shame for his country prevented him from getting up to speak on its behalf. He thought: These Poles, these Spaniards, who have spoken, represent their country. "But what do I represent? what achievements do I recall? I stand alone, I am a lackey, wearing, like all other Germans, the livery of Count Münch-Bellinghausen." (14th December 1831.)

Closely connected with this feeling of shame is an irritability, an inclination to be indignant with every one and everything, which gives a certain impression of weakness, of failing health. Everything, great and small, is "infuriating"

—from the long-suffering of the nations and their slowness to rise in revolt, to a rude letter from Spontini to the Berlin orchestra ; from the proposal to grant Louis Philippe a liberal civil-list, to the deficiencies of an encyclopædia.[1] As time goes on he actually seeks out provocations. We come upon such expressions as : " I am cheerful, for I have been angry ;" or " You cannot give me greater pleasure than by reporting cases of German stupidity to me."

But in the years immediately following the Revolution of July, shame and anger are drowned in a storm-tossed sea of hope. Börne feels as absolutely certain of the speedy approach of a universal conflagration, followed by the victory of liberty, as the first Christians felt of the immediate end of the world, followed by the day of judgment, with its decree of salvation for the elect, and damnation for the hard of heart. He is in a state of excitement which makes it impossible for him to be the chronicle-writer of his time ; he feels that it is his mission to be its prophet, in twelve long volumes, if need be.[2]

Alas, it is only the pessimistic prophets who, sooner or later, always prove to be right. And Börne was an optimistic prophet, an enthusiast, naïvely and incorrigibly given to believing in what he wished. Events in France have inspired him with the belief that the death-knell of the reaction has sounded. He seriously reproaches himself for being ashamed to kiss such and such a Frenchman's hand, "the hand which has burst our fetters, and given to us serfs the accolade of knighthood." (17th September 1830.) He knows that the end is at hand. On the occasion of Charles X.'s laying some foundation-stone, Börne remarks

---

[1] Stock expressions : "O, es ist zum Rasendwerden ! (it is maddening !) O, ich habe eine Wuth ! (I am in a transport of rage !)." On the subject of the encyclopædia : "Eine starke halbe Stunde musste ich das Schreiben unterbrechen, und meine Wuth war grenzenlos." (I had to stop writing for a good half hour, and was infuriated beyond all bounds.)

[2] "Was, wo, worauf, womit soll ich schreiben ? Der Boden zittert, es zittert der Tisch, das Pult, Hand und Herz zittern, und die Geschichte, vom Sturme bewegt, zittert selbst. . . . Prophet wollte ich sein zwölf Bände durch."

What, where, upon what, with what am I to write ? The ground, the table, the desk, hand and heart tremble, shaken by the hurricane, history itself trembles. . . . A prophet I would be, throughout twelve volumes.

that it is high time for kings to stop making themselves
ridiculous by laying the foundation-stones of buildings.   It
would be more suitable for them now to nail the last tile on
the roofs.   For the time is at hand when the royal cooks
will ask each other : " For whom shall we be preparing
dinner to-morrow ? "   (19th September 1830.)   A month
after this, being asked what he thinks likely to happen, he
expresses his firm conviction that the following spring will
see the whole of Europe in conflagration.   He pities the
diplomatists, positively feels sympathy for them.   When
the Polish insurrection breaks out, he does not believe,
taking the great strength of the Russians into consideration,
that it will be as easy for the Poles as for the Belgians to
attain their object, but is sure that they will succeed in
the end.   And like a refrain recurs the assertion that, one
after another, all the countries of Europe will emancipate
themselves, Germany alone remaining in its miserable condition.   And yet at times he foresees the salvation of
Germany.   When the cholera is raging in Moscow, he
understands its signification, sees the finger of God in it :
" This is once more the naked hand of God.   The Powers
are prevented from gathering together great armies, and if,
in spite of everything, they persist in doing so . . . I have
a presentiment—no, it is more than that, I *know* that the
cholera will do what as yet nothing else has had the power
to do, it will rouse the most procrastinating and timid nation
on the face of the earth to show courage."   (3rd November
1830.)   His confidence in the ultimate success of the Poles
increased, supporting itself on the theory that those always
win who have no choice but victory or death.   At the close
of the year 1830 he is certain that the ruling sovereigns are
doomed ; his " modest " New Year's wish for his friend and
himself is, that 1831 may be a better year for them than
it will be for emperors and kings.   He will have to say
to his servant : " If an emperor comes, keep your eye upon
him, and don't leave him alone in my room."   And he ends
by assuring him that in 1831 a dozen of eggs will be of
more value than a dozen princes.   (26th December 1830.)

On the 8th of January 1831, he maintains that if only

the Poles can avoid a pitched battle, the Russians, "power-ful as they are, are lost." And he still takes it for granted that the French will take up arms in defence of Poland: France would be insane (*ganz von Sinnen*) if she did not take advantage of this unique opportunity to weaken the power of Russia. On the 11th of February he is perfectly positive that there will be war. He himself has never doubted it for a single day, and many who would not believe it before, have come round to his opinion. Out-bursts of rejoicing are frequent. The Poles have once more received help from above ; there is "tolerably certain" news of rebellion having broken out in several Russian provinces. On the 6th of March, when things are looking e.:tremely bad for Poland, he has another false piece of news to rejoice over. A Parisian commercial house has re-ceived intelligence that the Russian forces have been scattered, and also that the Lithuanians are in revolt behind them, "which will decide matters." He is jubilant. From this time onwards, tyrants will be threatened with the Poles, as naughty children are threatened with the chimney-sweep. Nicholas boasted that he would roll the Poles together like a ball of yarn ; the ball has turned into a bomb, which has blown him to pieces ! Börne actually has visions of Paris illuminated on the occasion. On the 18th of March, when it is no longer possible to believe in the truth of the favour-able news, he is already mounted on a new chimera. All is well ; for in France itself a great change is impending: "Matters here are in such a position, that I daily, nay hourly, expect a revolution. Things cannot continue as they are for four weeks longer. . . . "

It is undoubtedly a strong proof of Börne's honesty that he allowed Jeannette to publish his letters as they came from his pen, unedited, without any suppression or modifi-cation of prophetic passages to which facts speedily gave the lie. But their perusal does not increase our faith in him as a politician. The contradiction between what is prophesied and what happens is at times so marked as to be comical. On the 25th of December he is in despair because of Lafayette's indecision : Lafayette is

omnipotent, can bring about whatever he pleases, has only
to threaten to give up the command of the National Guard
to reduce the king, the ministers, and the Chambers to
immediate submission.   Next day, the 26th of December,
he announces shortly that Lafayette has been deposed from
his command, without so much as a dog barking.   Strange,
says the reader to himself, that such an eager politician
should never have felt it a necessity to study the science
of politics, in order to be able to form his conclusions with
some understanding of the subject—that he should have
been perfectly satisfied to produce ephemeral journalistic
effusions, of value to-day, to-morrow cast into the oven.

What constantly misleads Börne is that optimism of
his, which has been already alluded to, an optimism at
once naïve and fanatical, which perpetually discovers reasons
why the evil that happens is at the same time the best thing
that could happen.   In March 1831, he trembles for the
Poles, and declares that he is prepared for the worst.   "But,"
he continues, "such a victory would be more disastrous
for the Russians than all their defeats.   The arrogant
Nicholas would become presumptuous, and believe that
he could dispose of France as easily as of Poland."   What
a ground of comfort!   Börne goes on hoping for a revolution in Paris which shall shake all thrones.   But it does
not come.   He presently discovers that this quietness of
France is more dangerous for the crowned heads than
anything else could be.   On the 30th of November 1831,
he writes: "For forty years France has been the crater
of Europe.   When that crater ceases to shoot forth flames,
no throne in Europe will be safe for one night. . . . Nothing
could have been so disastrous for the monarchs as the fall
of Warsaw.   They have ruined a miracle, and therefore now
believe themselves capable of working miracles."   In other
words : A revolution in Paris is good, no revolution is still
better.   The victory of Poland would have been the ruin
of the monarchs ; the fall of Poland is more fatal for them
still.

At the bottom of all this is Börne's very remarkable,
implicit faith in God, which is but rarely disturbed by the

doubts of his ever active brain.   The formula to which
he almost always has recourse when he needs comfort
is, that he trusts in God.   Nicholas advances against the
Poles with an overwhelming force ; Börne " trusts in God."
It is, as a matter of fact, only the Polish nobility who have
risen in revolt, but Börne "trusts in the wisdom of God
and the stupidity of his so-called representatives."   He himself is, he declares, wiser than all the rest in France, as he
was wiser than the rest in Germany ; why ?   Because he
" believes in God and nature," while the others believe in
men and politics.

Yet at times his faith wavers.   We saw how at first he
rejoiced over the cholera, saw the finger of God in it, felt
that it would drive even the Germans to revolution.   Only
two months later (19th January 1831) he describes its actual
effect, the manner in which it is paralysing the nations and
aiding in the demolition of such liberty as still exists.   At
first he wrote : " What nothing else has been able to do, the
cholera will do ; " now it is the exact opposite : " What no
Emperor of Russia, no devil could prevent, the cholera
prevents."   And he who saw in that plague " God's naked
hand," now exclaims : " And the priests would have us
believe that this is a judgment of God ! "   Nine months later
(25th November) he gets out of the difficulty with a witty,
thoughtless joke : " It is not often that God sends a heavenly
commission of justice down to earth to investigate into the
stewardship of his representatives, and so far, when such a
thing has happened, it has not improved matters.   The
heavenly emissaries are out of their element on earth ; they
make mistakes, they even allow themselves to be bribed.
We saw this lately, in the case of the Asiatic cholera, which
punished the oppressed in place of the oppressors.   God
only helps those who help themselves." [1]

Once only, when the fall of Poland is evidently at hand
(5th March 1831), we feel that Börne's faith in his system
is seriously shaken.   When the Russians are getting the
upper hand, he, as usual, makes free use of his favourite
words—God, the devil, &c.   He comes to the conclusion

[1] *Börne*, iii. 75, 86, 172 ; 43, 99, 267.

that "not even the wisdom of God, nothing but the stupidity
of the devil can save Poland now." And then he interrupts
himself with a question : "But is there a God at all ? My
heart does not doubt it yet, but one's brain feels bewildered
enough at times. And even if he does exist, of what use
is an eternal God to mortal man ? Were he mortal like
us . . . he would take account of time and life, would not
delay justice so long, would not wait to pay to future generations that which was their forefathers' due. Liberty can and
will triumph, sooner or later ; but why not now ? It may
triumph the very day after the fall of Poland ; and that
would be enough to break one's heart. . . . Can there be a
God ? Is this justice ? We loathe cannibals, stupid savages,
who only eat the flesh of their enemies. But we are reconciled to a far worse cannibalism—to the torturing,
slaughtering, hewing asunder of the present, body and soul,
with its joys and its happiness, its wishes and its hopes, to
satisfy the appetite of the future." [1]

A few days later, however, he returns to his accustomed
faith in God and to that optimism over which no disappoint-
ments can prevail.

Here and there in these letters we come upon sheer
political twaddle, such as the fantasies on the consequences
of the revolt in Hanover, and here and there on proofs
of a positively foolish credulity, as, for example, when
Börne allows himself to be persuaded that it is Metternich
who has instigated the disturbances in South Germany in
order that he may take possession of Bavaria while the
troops are occupied ; and again, that it is Louis Philippe's
secret intention to reinstate the dynasty of Charles X. on the
throne. [2]

But frequently too we come upon utterances that show
real political sagacity, a natural capacity for grasping a
situation, and an unusual gift of prevision.

On the 9th of November 1830, only four months after
the Revolution, Börne already perceives that all that has
happened amounts to no more than this, that the industrial
magnates, those who understand nothing but "fear and

---

[1] *Börne*, iii. 159, 160.   [2] Ibid., 98, 39, 270.

money," have come into power. And he is quite certain that, since this Revolution has not attained its object, those in power refusing to see anything in it but a change of dynasty, a new revolution is unavoidable, "and may be expected without fail." A week later, with correct appreciation of the facts, and logical deduction, he explains how events will follow on one another : As these merchants and manufacturers, who for fifteen years have been declaiming against aristocracy, have hardly got into power before they endeavour to form a new aristocracy, of monied men, of adventurers, not based like the old on a principle, but upon privileges conferred by the possession of property ; the French people, with their passion for equality, will, the next time they make a revolution, attack that which is now the foundation of privilege, namely, property ; and this process will be accompanied by such horrors as no previous revolution has witnessed. Börne, we observe, has a prevision of socialism as a power ; he prophesies the Commune. A year later (1st December 1831) he feels so certain how things will go that he writes : " I so plainly foresee the great war between the poor and the rich that I feel as if we were in the middle of it now ; " and at this period, in spite of his strong moral bias, he has come to the conclusion that the first thing to be aimed at is the support of right by might. If this is not practicable, then all that can be done is to touch men's hearts, to gain them for the good cause by working upon their feelings, and to pursue tyranny with ridicule, hate, and contempt. It is of no use whatever to be simply honest, to have the right on one's side. No ; " their honesty is their bane. They imagine that the main thing is to be, and to prove that they are, right. They talk of liberty as a barrister would talk of some piece of property. As if it were reasons that were wanted here ! " (1st February 1831.)

The man who shows himself to us in these letters, is, after all, a political enthusiast, a lover of liberty, rather than a statesman. He not only loves the common people but, like Rousseau, he has a true admiration for those who have not been " spoiled " by wealth or education ; and this admiration

goes hand in hand with a steadily increasing hatred of
all the legitimate sovereigns and princes of Europe, which,
when Börne casts all moderation from him along with his
illusions, turns into veritable nihilism. "To think that ten
yards of hempen cord would suffice to give the world peace,
happiness, and quiet." [1] The peoples—the sovereigns,—the
peoples—the sovereigns ; it was between these poles that the
pendulum of Börne's political thought incessantly swung ;
they were the poles of the political thought of the time.
And it was natural enough that he should stop short at this
antithesis, because he was essentially a democrat, such a
confirmed democrat that, as he himself plainly tells us, he
took no interest whatever in the study of the individual
human being. It was as much of a nuisance to him to
have to inquire into the peculiarities distinguishing one
human being from another, as it was to have to decipher
extremely minute handwriting. He preferred to occupy
himself with humanity in the mass and with books.
(3rd November 1830.) It is no wonder that we miss in
him the delicate psychological insight which we look for
in a great writer. To compensate for this deficiency we
have the sympathy with whole nations, with whole classes,
with a wide circle of readers, which enables an author to
electrify a public, and ensures popularity during his lifetime even to a peculiarly audacious writer occupying a
peculiarly precarious position.

Not that Börne is unjust or prejudiced in his judgment
of individuals. On the contrary, he shows the calm bene-
volence of superior intelligence ; though he also undoubtedly
at times evinces a real middle-class antipathy to what is
over-aristocratic, and corresponding indulgence towards what
is commonplace. When De Musset appears, he is at once
struck by a kinship with Heine which surprises him in a
Frenchman. He promptly recognises, even over-estimates
Berlioz's genius, and every one knows how neglected and
misunderstood Berlioz was. Prince Pückler he criticises
appreciatively, without any warmth, but with a proper discernment of his merits ; only he cannot understand how it

---

[1] "Und mit Zehn Ellen Hanf wäre der Welt Friede, Glück, und Ruhe zu geben."

was possible for any one to believe that Pückler's bright, but essentially unpoetical letters, could have been written by Heine. As regards Heine himself, it is for long only his worship of Napoleon that is distinctly antipathetic to Börne, who appreciates, nay admires him in every other respect.

There is something suggestive in Börne's sincere admiration for Paul de Kock, in the warm appreciation with which he mentions him, and the zest with which he perseveringly reads eight volumes of his novels on end. It is their naïve and faithful representation of the life of the Parisian *petit bourgeois* that seems to Börne so admirable. He goes the length, though half in jest, of praising De Kock's philosophy of life, and on this hardly suitable occasion mounts his old hobby, and writes: "Though he does not, like Goethe in *Wilhelm Meister*, serve up didactic letters with truffles, he gives us good strong philosophy dressed in bourgeois fashion." (3rd March 1831.) Paul de Kock exalted at the expense of Goethe!

This sort of criticism says little for Börne's æsthetic sense. Of his political sagacity convincing proof is given by his pronouncements on Talleyrand. In 1830 he at once feels quite confident that Talleyrand will serve France well in London, and does not allow his confidence to be shaken by the Parisians' hatred of that diplomatist. He sees the absurdity of the loud complaint of the Liberal newspapers that Talleyrand, as one of the framers of the Peace of Vienna, is certain to support the Holy Alliance. He comprehends that neither the Holy Alliance nor anything else is holy to Talleyrand. And long afterwards he again refers to the unreasonableness of the accusation brought against that sagacious diplomatist of having served and betrayed every government in turn, acutely remarking that he did not betray governments, he only deserted them, and that not until they were dead. What Börne reads in Talleyrand's hard face is necessity, cast as it were in bronze.

But the chief cause of the leniency of Börne's judgments is to be sought, not in his intellect, but in his heart, in the tenderness of his nature, in the strong bias towards kindly interpretation, which is not contradicted by his many violent, inconsiderate utterances ; for these themselves, closely examined, prove to be but expressions of his love to his kind. He was a loving-hearted man, and in so far a Christian by nature, by instinct. This is the explanation of his conversion to Christianity. The reproach of hypocrisy in his case is a foolish one; his conception of Christianity may not have been profound, but he acted from honest, independent conviction. He became a Christian because he was a democrat and a humanitarian. To him Christianity was not simply a continuation and supplement of Judaism, it was rather the religion of humanity, and more especially " the religion of all poor devils." Every man who loved his kind was in Börne's eyes a Christian. Christianity was moreover to him the religion of liberty, especially in its Catholic form ; for it was as Catholicism that it had destroyed the world-empire of the Romans. In the ardent love of liberty of these Poles with whom he has so much sympathy, he sees a proof of the liberalising power of Catholicism.[1]

Börne does not personally believe in the dogmas of Christianity, or consider that faith is its essence ; yet any attack on these dogmas is most repugnant to him. He sneers at Saint-Simonism because of its antagonism to the Christian religion, and he considers Strauss's *Life of Jesus* to be not only a useless, but a mischievous book. All this makes it easy to understand how it was possible for him, in the last years of his life, to be completely carried away by a democratic Catholic like Lamennais, whose *Paroles d'un Croyant*, an attempt to blend Liberalism with religion, he translated and overrated. Religious Radicalism, as here expressed, was the magic formula to which the free and the locked-up powers of his own soul responded.

In the course of the first volumes of the *Letters from Paris*, Börne, following the general trend of Oppositionist feeling

---

[1] " Das einzige Volk im Norden, das seit dreihundert Jahren nie aufgehört sich für die Freiheit zu erheben, ist das polnische, und es blieb katholisch."

The one nation of the North that for three hundred years has not ceased to make a stand for liberty, is Poland, and Poland remained Catholic.

in Germany, progressed from enthusiasm for constitutionalism to hope of revolution. In April 1832, not six months after their publication, one of the leaders of the Opposition, Dr Siebenpfeiffer, issued a general invitation to all the different German nationalities to attend a great national festival, to be held at the castle of Hambach, near Neustadt on the Haardt, on the 27th of May, the anniversary of the concession of the Bavarian constitution. It was to be a festival of brotherhood for all whose desire and aim was the regeneration of Germany. This festival, however, seemed so suspicious to the government of Rhenish Bavaria, that it was forbidden ; strangers were prohibited from visiting Neustadt or its environs from the 26th to the 28th of May, and any assemblage of more than five persons in the streets or other public places was forbidden. These prohibitions excited such general discontent that the authorities were obliged to withdraw them.

People streamed to the festival from every point of the compass. Almost every German country sent representatives—the majority, of course, being inhabitants of the Palatinate itself. Even Frenchmen were there in large numbers, and Poles naturally were not lacking. The assembly numbered about thirty thousand in all.

Börne, who came from Paris, was the most fêted guest. His journey to Neustadt was a sort of triumphal procession. He was cheered everywhere. Torchlight processions and serenades were the order of the day.

He writes from Freiburg: " You have no idea what an impression my *Letters from Paris* have made in Germany. I never expected anything like it myself. Meyer, Wurm, and others had given out, had printed, that I could never again show myself in Germany, because I should be turned out of all respectable society. Nice prophets they are! I have done nothing but receive homage ever since I arrived. My room is never empty. I often have not chairs enough for my visitors. At the Hambach festival all present desired to make my acquaintance. It was so fatiguing that it has made me ill. When I made my appearance on the street in Neustadt, shouts were heard

from the restaurants and from the passing carriages of:
' Hurrah for Börne! hurrah for the author of the *Letters from
Paris!*' The Heidelberg students serenaded me. All the
patriots, Wirth and the rest, declared that the credit of the
patriotic movement in Germany was due to me; I was
first; the others all came after. Many, moved to tears, and
unable to speak for emotion, embraced me warmly. It has
been the same thing here in Freiburg. The students came
to my house in the evening, serenaded me, and shouted:
' Hurrah for the champion of German liberty!' . . . What
will my critics say to this, those critics who called me a bad
patriot? Public opinion does not allow itself to be misled."
Absurdly enough, with all this enthusiasm, his watch was
stolen at the Hambach festival.

On the morning of the 27th of May, the enormous
procession made its way from Neustadt to the ruins of the
castle of Hambach. Every one wore black, red, and gold
colours, and black, red, and gold flags were carried in
front of the procession, the ranks of which were swelled
by a great number of women, wearing black, red, and gold
belts. Siebenpfeiffer and the Bavarian Liberal journalist,
Wirth, were the principal speakers. They proclaimed the
sovereignty of the people to be the foundation on which
every state must rest, and declared that Germany would
ere long be a republic. All the speeches made were
violent, and all described the degradation of Germany as
the work of her sovereigns, in combination with the aristocrats. Wirth proposed the toast (for which he had afterwards to do penance by a long imprisonment) of "The
united free states of Germany," and "federated republican
Europe," and shouted as he waved the sword of honour
that had been presented to him: "Accursed, three times
accursed be the rulers of Germany!" These words
were re-echoed by part of the assembly; there were
shouts of: "Down with kings and princes! To arms!
To arms!"

The participators in the Hambach festival had, however, no immediate, practical aim in view. Supposing the
moment to have been favourable — a tolerably doubtful

supposition—they allowed it to pass without taking advantage of it.

Heine writes humorously and bitterly: "I dare hardly tell the story, it seems so incredible, yet I have it from a reliable source, from a man who is an honest and truthful republican, and was himself a member of the committtee at Hambach which deliberated on the impending revolution. This man told me in confidence that, when it came to the question of competence, to a dispute as to whether the patriots then assembled at Hambach were really competent to begin a revolution in the name of the whole of Germany, those who advised immediate action were outvoted, and the conclusion arrived at was that they were incompetent." Heine calls this the best story he has ever heard, good enough to make him forget all the troubles of this vale of tears, and even to cheer him after death in the dusky tedium of the realm of shades. Then he speaks words of comfort to kings and princes, tells them how it is quite unnecessary that they should imprison any more worthy citizens ; they may sleep in peace ; they are in no danger ; the German revolution is still far off ; the question of competence is not yet decided.[1]

For many years after he made Heine's literary and personal acquaintance, Börne's feeling towards that author was a friendly one ; he spoke of him with affection, gave him his full due as a poet, and more especially appreciated him as a great power in the service of universal emancipation. But their natures were too unlike to permit of his judgment being quite unprejudiced. From 1831 onwards we come upon spiteful references to Heine in the Letters. Although Börne was devoid of petty vanity, the frequent comparisons made between Heine and himself rankled in his mind, especially as, in the matter of ability and gifts, they were often to his disadvantage. And Heine's *Französische Zustände* ("The Situation in France") offended and wounded him ; its perusal roused in him a feeling of ill-humour to which he gave vent (in the last volume of the *Letters from Paris*) in cutting satire, which

[1] Heine: *Sämmtliche Werke*, xii. 153.

struck Heine as it were from above, and, in the eyes of many readers, stamped him with the brand of political untrustworthiness.

It was in reality the deep-seated antagonism between the natures of the two fellow-combatants that found vent on this occasion. Börne did not understand the real nature of the difference between himself and Heine. To him it seemed to be the difference between manly earnestness and boyish frivolity, or, taken in its highest aspect, between devotion to truth and devotion to form, to art. With accurate perception he detected and exposed some of the small puerilities and snobberies of which Heine, when dazzled by the tinsel of life, could at a time be guilty, and also some of his unjust mockeries of ideal endeavour clothed in clumsy or naïvely popular form. Börne detested the Rothschilds, by whom Heine was impressed and fascinated. Börne, who felt out of his element in drawing-rooms, was quite at home among democratic artisans, and in gatherings of German emigrants, no matter how wild the schemes they planned, or how unpractical the undertakings for which they collected money ; Heine, on the contrary, was annoyed by the constant solicitations to support this or that democratic undertaking, was quite unsuited to be a member of the democratic fraternity, preferred, in spite of his revolutionary leanings, to keep himself to himself, and had no intention whatever of being on terms of hail fellow well met with any chance band of emigrant fellow-countrymen.

In a letter dated the 25th of February 1833, Börne jeers at Heine for various things, amongst others for writing of the inhuman policy pursued by Austria for the last three hundred years as "sublime perseverance" ; for calling King Louis of Bavaria, whom he afterwards so unmercifully satirised, "one of the noblest and most intellectual monarchs that ever sat upon a throne"; and for declaring it to be "courageous and admirable" of the Messrs. Rothschild to remain in Paris during the cholera, while he, at the same time, casts ridicule on the unpaid exertions of the German patriots. On these points, and others, Börne is right, but nevertheless he shows no delicate discernment or profound comprehension of Heine's real character.

In the case of Heine, as in the case of Goethe, he stood face to face with a genius he was unable to judge impartially, though he by no means wronged his restless contemporary to the same extent or in the same manner as he did his great predecessor.

XI

HEINE

FOR Heinrich Heine also, as already observed, the present moment in the development of the new German Empire is an unfavourable one. He is reproached with so much, that it is difficult to summarise. First there is his infatuation for France, and his supposed or real frivolity; then his un-German extraction and wit, his sentimentality, his foppery, his wantonness; and lastly, the defiant manner in which he parades his irreligion. New Germany is indifferent in religious matters, but tacitly so, and in the matter of morals it is thoroughly disciplined. In the Germany of to-day the highest virtues, truthfulness, independence, high spirit, and sensitiveness, are of much less account than dutifulness, correctness, social discipline, military smartness —*Schneidigkeit*, as it is called. In Heine's time the opposite was the case. No value was put on discipline. Piety counted for more than religion, humanity for more than patriotism. The best men of those days did not regard patriotism as an unqualified virtue; nor did they consider that justice ceased to be a virtue when shown to another nation.

To an abstract Radical bent of mind there was added in Heine's case the hatred of Prussia, whose future he did not foresee, whose strength he did not realise—that strength of which Carlyle gives us the best idea in his delineation of the father of Frederick the Great, a strength which lay in the ability, by means of sober severity, to conquer chaos, crush all foolish opposition, and rule. Heine's was no undefined dislike, it was the Rhinelander's mortal enmity to Prussia. Read his lines to the Prussian eagle:

> " Du hässlicher Vogel ! wirst du einst,
> Mir in die Hände fallen,
> So rupfe ich dir die Federn aus
> Und haue dir ab die Krallen.

Du sollst mir dann in luft'ger Höh'
Auf einer Stange sitzen
Und ich rufe zum lustigen Schiessen herbei
Die *rheinischen* Bogenschützen."[1]

At the Congress of Vienna, after repeatedly refusing, Prussia at last consented to take over the Rhine Provinces. Instead of the rounding off of her frontier in the east for which she had hoped, she thus acquired territory at a distance, and came to rule over a race of Germans totally unlike the Old-Prussians. This Rhine Province was the region where, in days gone by, the line of separation between Kelts and Germans lay. Most of it had been included in the Roman military province. At a later period the land came under priestly rule, which accounts for the fact that it was in no way influenced in the eighteenth century by the spirit of Frederick the Great. Old, decaying clericalism came here into direct contact with the French Revolution, and the propagators of the revolutionary ideas were joyfully welcomed.

The Old-Prussian's feeling towards the Rhinelanders was the distrust of antipathy, a feeling the Rhinelanders returned with interest. At the Rhine the Prussians were, and continued to be, strangers, unwelcome strangers. When he spoke of a son serving in the army, the Rhinelander said: "He is with the Prussians." The government official transferred from Berlin to Cologne or Düsseldorf put on airs, and disparaged everything, and the Rhinelander long regarded a transfer to one of the old Prussian provinces as a sort of exile to Siberia. Complaints were heard everywhere of Prussia's inability to gain the affections of the peoples she had conquered.[2]

Heinrich Heine was born near the close of the century at Düsseldorf, then capital of the duchy of Jülich-Cleve-Berg. For six years the town was garrisoned by French revolutionary troops. They took their departure in 1801, and Max Joseph of Pfalz-Zweibrücken became Grand Duke; but

---

[1] If I ever get hold of thee, thou ugly bird, I will pluck out thy feathers and cut off thy claws, perch thee high in air on a pole, and call the archers of the Rhineland to the merry shooting-match.

[2] K. Mendelssohn-Bartholdy: *Preussen und Frankreich zur Zeit der Julirevolution*, p. 25, &c.

HEINRICH HEINE

in 1806 he was made King of Bavaria, and Joachim Murat was installed as Grand Duke in his stead. Only two years later Murat had to make way for the eldest son of the King of Holland, or, in reality, as the boy was not of age, for Napoleon, as his guardian. The country was now governed exactly according to the French pattern ; serfdom, feudal law, and statute-labour were abolished, and complete religious liberty was proclaimed. This last innovation led to Napoleon's being revered by the Jewish population of the Rhine Provinces as their saviour from the oppression of a thousand years.

There can be no doubt that the contact with the audacious, victorious Frenchmen of that day powerfully influenced Heine's mental development. His respect for traditional authority was early undermined. His natural wit was developed in the direction of what the French call *esprit*. The germs of his enthusiastic admiration for Napoleon were generated. That enthusiasm seems to us to-day to be an isolated phenomenon in the German literature of the century ; in reality it was very far from being so.

Let us go back to Wieland, and we shall find that he held Napoleon in the same high estimation, even before such an opinion had been justified by the events of history. In 1798 he declares that France stands in need of a dictator, and that no one is fit for the post except General Bonaparte, then in Egypt. In 1800 he prophesies that Bonaparte will and must make himself king, and defends him against the attacks of the English newspapers. Napoleon, having been told of these prophecies, had a lengthy interview with Wieland at Erfurt in 1808.

None of the great Germans at the end of the eighteenth and beginning of the nineteenth century knew what national enmity meant. It was without a spark of any such feeling that Goethe, in the capacity of spectator, made the campaign of 1793 in France. Schiller valued his certificate of French citizenship, and believed that it might come to be of use to his children. Knebel, Goethe's friend, wished that he dared sing Napoleon's victories. Goethe himself looked on with complacency while Napoleon shattered the kingdom of

Frederick the Great into fragments; it is evident that he must have regarded that kingdom of Prussia as a passing phenomenon in the history of Germany. He had witnessed Napoleon's rise and victorious career, and had seen him suppress that anarchy which was so hateful to himself, the aristocrat and evolutionist. At last he made his personal acquaintance, saw him surrounded by his marshals, in an atmosphere of brightness, amiability, geniality, general irresistibility. The personal impression made upon him by Napoleon was such as to increase his previous admiration for him. Hence it was that even after the Russian campaign, even during the rehabilitation of Germany, Goethe continued to say: " It is all of no use; the man is too strong for them." It was not till all was over that he made a sort of compulsory amends by writing a play for the fête on the occasion of the peace.

Goethe's valuation of Napoleon has been the subject of much discussion ; less well known is the impression which the great Frenchman made on Hegel, who, as Heine's teacher and chosen philosopher, influenced him quite as much as Goethe. Hegel was born a subject of the small, despotically-ruled State of Würtemberg. He longed for a fatherland, but had never known what it was to have one, and in the beginning of the century he was so embittered by the situation in Germany, and roused to such anger and scorn by the political stupidity of his countrymen, that he, like Goethe, welcomed Napoleon with the unqualified enthusiasm of a cosmopolitan. He had spent his youth dreaming of a possible reconciliation of the real with the ideal, but had never come into contact with a real living power until Napoleon crossed his path and aroused his enthusiasm. It was said of Goethe that he took advantage of the distraction caused by the roar of the cannon at Jena to marry Christiane Vulpius without rousing remark; of Hegel it was said that he finished his work *Die Phænomenologie des Geistes* (" Philosophy of Mind ") in Jena itself, while the battle was raging. It is a fact that it was exactly at this time that he despatched the last pages of the work to his publisher ; and there is a very striking contrast between his calm indifference to the ruin of Prussia and his keen anxiety lest any of the precious packets of manuscript should be lost in transit at that unsettled time. A letter to his publisher, which accompanied one of the packets, bears the date of the battle.

In the work, to which the finishing touches were put under such circumstances, Hegel expounded his theory of the development of the human mind with a curious mixture of historical and psychological argument. He maintained that humanity had now reached its goal, that such individual mortals as had attained to the highest degree of understanding, now possessed the insight of gods, that their lives, lives of far-reaching influence, were now simply the harmonious unfolding of an existence such as the Greeks imagined that of their gods to be, absolutely contented, absolutely reconciled. While Hegel was writing his concluding words, which are to the effect that history is but a play of the spirit that is conscious of itself as spirit, Napoleon drew rein at the gates of Jena.

And Hegel saw him, and seeing him, rejoiced. " I have seen the emperor, that soul of the world," he writes from Jena. " It truly gives one a strange feeling to see one such single individual who, concentrated on a single point, sitting on his horse here in Jena, influences and rules the world. As far as the Prussians are concerned, nothing better could have been prognosticated—but only such a man could have made such way between Thursday and Monday; it is impossible to refuse him admiration." And it is not only the emperor Hegel admires, but the whole French people. Three months later he writes that in the history of the day he sees convincing proof that culture overcomes barbarism, that intellect overcomes unintellectuality. And he even adds : " I have long wished the French army success, now all do so; nor can it fail to be successful, considering the enormous difference between its leaders and soldiers and those of the enemy." [1]

If Heine had ever imagined that his enthusiasm for Napoleon required any apology, he might have found one in the fact that he was but following in the footsteps of the man

[1] Haym : *Hegel und seine Zeit.*

whom he invariably spoke of with reverence as "the great Hegel, the greatest philosopher Germany has produced since Leibnitz," the man of whom he makes the very questionable assertion that he quite unquestionably "towers high above Kant," and whom he criticises with such lenient and gentle disparagement as the following utterance conveys : " Hegel allowed himself to be crowned in Berlin, and alas, to be anointed too."

Not only Heine's great models and teachers, but contemporaries like Varnhagen von Ense, who had actually shed his blood in the war against Napoleon, shared his enthusiasm, and were equally free from patriotic enmity to France. Of the Dane Baggesen, who, half German by nature, was fain to be more German than the Germans, Varnhagen writes : " His hatred of Napoleon and the French is peculiarly offensive; it is an aversion which amounts to loathing, and yet it is groundless, for all that is good in us Germans, all that we are proudest of in ourselves, he holds in horror and would fain suppress with the help of Kant, Jacobi, Voss, and Klopstock." Kant is evidently included in this list on account of the very un-German "categorical imperative," the others on account of the extreme narrowness of their patriotism.

The cult of Napoleon is thus, we see, to be traced in the words and works of the men who had the greatest influence on Heine's development and on that of young Germany in general.

It inspired Heine's muse several years before it became epidemic in France, and Heine rises to an equal height of enthusiasm with Beyle and Hugo. It is not too much to say that the poetic expression of this enthusiasm in his youthful poem *The Two Grenadiers* (which he probably wrote at the age of eighteen, though he himself claims to have written it at sixteen) surpasses anything of the same nature that exists in French. Not even Béranger's *Souvenirs du Peuple* is so simply grand, although it, better than any other poem, has given tangible and touching expression to the French popular Napoleonic legend. In Heine's *Grenadiers* the rhythm of each line answers exactly to its mood and matter—the mournful iambics : *Der Andre sprach : das Lied ist aus ;* the fiery anapæsts : *Dann reitet mein Kaiser wohl über mein Grab.* The grenadier's impossible request to his comrade to carry his corpse to France passes almost unnoticed. The wildness of the principal strophe : *Was schert mich Weib, was schert mich Kind,* the grenadier's protest against the supposition that he is tied by the wife and child he has left at home, contrasts forcibly with the sentimentality of the Romantic style. It is only ostensibly that this poem glorifies fidelity to Napoleon personally ; what it really glorifies is loving fidelity to the great leader, unbounded enthusiasm for the great personality.

The gift of describing by means of introducing characters into lyric poetry was common to both Béranger and Heine. But Béranger was a song-writer, Heine a genius. *The Two Grenadiers* begins, as Heine almost always begins, quietly, smoothly. Nothing could be more unlike this than Victor Hugo's lyric attack : *Lui! toujours lui!* Heine does not produce his effect by direct representation, but by delineation of the less important, of the small things in which the great are reflected, and which provide a standard to gauge them by ; then at last, following on and issuing from the simple dialogue, comes the burst of visionary enthusiasm.

That the object of this worship was hardly worthy of it, does not make the feeling itself less admirable. It is a feeling of exactly the same kind that Heine describes in the *Reisebilder,* when he tells how, as a child, he saw Napoleon riding through the ducal garden in Düsseldorf. The chapter begins : "But what were my feelings when I saw himself, saw him with my own highly-favoured eyes, himself, Hosannah ! the Emperor !" Note the *Hosannah !* In the moment of ecstasy, the recollections of childhood bring the Old Testament cry of salutation and rejoicing to his lips. And what did the child think on the occasion ? He remembered that it was forbidden, under a penalty of five thalers, to ride through the avenue. And, lo and behold ! there was the emperor, with all his officers, riding straight through—the shuddering trees bent forward as he passed. . . .

As a political poet, Heine is considered to be revolutionary, and so he was. But his political animosity is exclusively aroused by medieval conditions, medieval beliefs. He is anti-clerical in good earnest, but not democratic in good earnest. His longest political poem, *Deutschland, ein Wintermärchen*, ("Germany, a Winter's Tale"), gives abundant evidence of this. It rises to real passion only where the poet's invisible companion, the lictor with the terrible axe, breaks up the skeletons of the Three Kings in the Cathedral of Cologne, "the miserable skeletons of superstition." But it is in this great poem, Heine's most important work, that we have the clearest expression of the political feelings and principles which animated him, the element, new to German poetry, of warlike challenge and hand-to-hand struggle. Nothing of the kind is to be found in Goethe. In the end, indeed, Goethe was persuaded of "the absolute pitiableness of the time," but he feared that the overthrow of existing authorities would only make things worse. Not even in Schiller can we find any direct reference to the politics of the day. His political feeling finds a vent in dramas whose theme is liberty. But in Heine, from 1830 onwards, we have always this direct expression of the faith that was in him. His soul was in politics. And in politics he was honest, even in cases where his honesty was misunderstood.

Turn to that passage in the *Reisebilder* which is most frequently cited as an expression of his boastfulness and affectation, the passage following on the description of his visit to the battlefield of Marengo : " 'This will be a fine day,' called my travelling companion.—Yes, it will be a fine day, silently echoed my heart, uplifted in prayer, trembling with sadness and joyfulness. Yes, it will be a fine day, and the sun of liberty will gladden the earth. A new generation will spring up and flourish, begotten in free embrace, not in a prison bed, under the control of clerical warders ; and this free birth will generate free thoughts and feelings, of which we born serfs have not even a presentiment . . ." then at the end these words : " I know not if I deserve that a laurel wreath should one day be laid on my coffin. Poetry, dearly as I have loved it, has always been to me but a divine plaything, or a weapon consecrated to divine purposes. . . . But lay on my coffin a *sword*, for I was a brave soldier in the Liberation War of humanity."

This political warfare of Heine's is spoken of with the utmost contempt by German historians of literature, historians proper, and literary critics; not only by Menzel, but by such men as Goedeke, Treitschke, Grisebach (Heine's imitator and denouncer), and Hehn, whose perception in other cases is so remarkably acute. Even Scherer is cold and depreciatory. When the Italian poet Carducci some years ago celebrated Heine in an ode as a hero in the struggle of liberty, even Karl Hillebrand, the best literary critic in Germany, who had at one time been Heine's secretary, and had always spoken of him with reverence and admiration, made a sort of protest, declaring that Heine himself had never taken the thing so seriously. This disfavour and distrust is not surprising. The frivolity in Heine's character led in his youth to repellent political vacillation. In 1827, in the hope of being appointed to a professorship at Munich, he was ready to disown his previous principles to please King Louis, but gained nothing by it. He offered at the same time to defend the wretched Duke of Brunswick, the diamond-Duke, in return for a Brunswick order ; but in this case also he was disappointed. It was not till 1830 that he began to show political strength of character.

We must also remember that in Heine's writings there is an absence of all "pathetic gesture." He was too proud to employ it. Germans cannot understand this. But grievous wrong is done him. The pathos was in his soul. His whole soul is in the little poem *Enfant Perdu*, with which one of the divisions of *Romancero* concludes, and which he wrote when he was no longer young. He really was what he here calls himself, an advanced and forgotten outpost, left to be shot down. And when, in his posthumous prose hymn, he cries : "I am the sword, I am flame," it is but the truth. The light of his flame, the sparks of his sword-blows, still shine bright. Many still warm themselves at his fire.

As already mentioned, Börne, in his *Letters from Paris,*
calls Heine an inconsistent, vacillating, characterless politician.   He does not so much reproach him with overrating himself personally as with overrating the influence of the individual human being.   For it is Börne's
opinion that the individual is no longer of much importance.   Even a Voltaire or a Rousseau would not be a
powerful influence nowadays.   Individuals are now merely
the heralds of the people.   This Heine forgets.   Then, in
his desire to please the democrats, he declares that the
Jesuitic-aristocratic party in Germany malign him because
he makes a bold stand against absolutism ; but almost at
the same time, in order to curry favour with the aristocrats,
says that he has made a stand against Jacobinism, and that
he is, and always will be, a good monarchist.

Börne does not always understand a joke.   Heine gives
a droll account of a Paris millinery establishment which
he frequented the summer before he writes, where he, as a
royalist, was one against sixteen, the eight young shop-girls
and their eight lovers being all violently aggressive republicans.   Elsewhere he writes : "God knows I am no Republican.   I know that when the Republicans are victorious,
they will cut off my head . . . a piece of foolishness for
which I am quite ready to forgive them."   Börne adds :
"Not I. . A lunatic asylum would be the proper place for
Republicans that were such fools as to suppose that it was
necessary to get rid of Heine in order to attain their
aims."

In spite of their jesting tone, there is something in these
and similar utterances of Heine's which puzzles the reader.
Intermittent outbursts of violent Radicalism, everywhere an
undertone of the most pronounced revolutionary feeling—
and these constantly recurring assurances that he is not a
Jacobin, not even a Republican.

An explanation is required, an explanation which no one
has yet offered.

For to say that Heine was characterless, characterless
to such a degree, that in the most serious matters, and with
the eyes of two great nations upon him, he perpetually con-

tradicted himself, is no explanation at all. The vagueness, the contradiction must lie in his principles.

Remember his faithful, boundless devotion to Napoleon, which once more and for the last time finds expression in the *Winter's Tale*, in the dirge of the dead emperor, brought in his coffin from St. Helena to Paris:

> " Die elysäischen Felder entlang,
> Durch des Triumphes Bogen,
> Wohl durch den Nebel, wohl über den Schnee
> Kam langsam der Zug gezogen. . . ." [1]

And then think of the scene (from the *Reisebilder*) on the battlefield of Marengo. The Russian asks Heine: " Are you a good Russian ? " And Heine answers : " Yes, I am a good Russian." For, he goes on to explain, the incessant change of war-cries and of representatives in the great struggle has now led to this—that the most enthusiastic friends of the Revolution look for the salvation of the world from the domination of Russia, look upon the Emperor Nicholas as the standard-bearer of liberty in Europe. The Russian government is permeated with Liberal ideas, its absolutism is simply a dictatorship, which gives it the power to put these ideas into practice, &c., &c.

The mistake is colossal in its simplicity. But for our present purpose this is of no consequence. What interests us is the fact that Russian absolutism, thus understood by Heine, received from him the same measure of approval and sympathy as he had formerly bestowed on the rule of Napoleon. Give this due consideration. Heine, the most advanced representative of Radicalism among the poets of his time, declares the Emperor Nicholas, the most tyrannical autocrat of his time, to be the standard-bearer of liberty ! Can this be the same man who took a childish pleasure in invariably associating in his mind the thought of royal or imperial rank with the thought of the guillotine ? Remember his words to Barbarossa : " Du wirst hier an ein Brett geschnallt—das senkt sich, &c., &c." (They fasten you to a plank—it is lowered, &c.), and the concluding

---

[1] Through the mist, over the snow, came the solemn, slow procession ; it passed beneath the triumphal arch, it traversed the Elysian fields. . . .

H

apostrophe to the venerable old emperor : " Die Repub-
likaner lachen uns aus—sehn sie an unserer Spitze—so
ein Gespenst mit Scepter und Kron. . . ." (The Republicans will laugh us to scorn, if they see us led by an old
spectre like you, with sceptre and crown). We see that he
sets some value on the opinion of the Republicans, sees
things to a certain extent from their standpoint.

Or again, think of that extraordinarily witty poem
" 1649—1793—? " which first treats of the short and
sharp justice meted out to kings in the English and French
Revolutions, and then prophesies the impending German
revolution, but declares that :

> " Der Deutsche wird die Majestät
> Behandeln stets mit Pietät.
> In einer sechsspännigen Hofkarosse,
> Schwarz panaschirt und beflort die Rosse—
> Hoch auf dem Bock mit der Trauerpeitsche
> Der weinende Kutscher—so wird der deutsche
> Monarch einst nach dem Richtplatz kutschirt,
> Und unterthänigst guillotinirt.' [1]

If this is not simply playing with words and with feelings,
there must be an explanation of it, a key to it which Heine
himself did not possess. For that there is self-contradiction
in such words is undeniable.

The explanation is that Heine was at one and the same
time a passionate lover of liberty and an out-and-out
aristocrat. He had the freedom-loving nature's thirst for
liberty, pined and languished for it, and loved it with his
whole soul ; but he had also the great nature's admiration
for human greatness, and the refined nature's nervous horror
of the rule of mediocrity.

In other words, there was not a drop of conservative
blood in Heinrich Heine's heart. His blood was revolutionary. But neither was there a drop of democratic blood
in his heart. His blood was aristocratic, his desire was to
see genius acknowledged as leader and ruler.

---

[1] The German will ever treat royalty with respect. 'Tis in a carriage of state,
drawn by six horses with sable plumes and trappings—on the box a weeping coach
man with crape-bound whip—that the German monarch will be driven to the place
of execution, and there most submissively guillotined.

When, in his historical retrospects or previsions, he sees
a worthless king or emperor guillotined, he applauds. But
he would give to Cæsar that which is Cæsar's. *Apodote ta
Kaisaros Kaisari* is the saying of Jesus which is most deeply
engraved on his mind. He does not dread a condition of
liberty, to which any liberty we have yet known on earth
is child's play ; but he does not believe that liberty would
result from the realisation of the Philistine ideals of the
average mind. All mediocrity, Liberal and Republican
mediocrity included, he abhors, as inimical to great individuality, to great liberty.

Hence his distrust of the North American Republic, his
want of enthusiasm for its liberty :

> " Manchmal kommt mir in den Sinn
> Nach Amerika zu segeln,
> Nach dem grossen Freiheitsstall,
> Der bewohnt von Gleichheitsflegeln. . . ."[1]

If Heine adores the *Marseillaise*, it is because the *Marseillaise* is to him the symbol of the great revolt. If he
worships Napoleon, it is because Napoleon is the over-
thrower of kings and of the old order of the world ; and
if, in Napoleon's case, he overlooks all that is inimical
to liberty, it is because Napoleon is in his eyes the
representative of the people, free from any suspicion of
democratic mediocrity.

It is only at a rare time, when he is despondent, when
he is not himself, but is making use of a borrowed formula,
that Heine commits himself to the foolish, plebeian assertion
that the power of the great personality is a thing of the
past—a theory which is in reality nothing but the classic
expression of middle-class envy. In his heart of hearts
Heine is so convinced of the contrary that he can go to
the mad extreme of imagining Nicholas, the obdurate representative of the principle of coercion, to be the chief
champion of liberty in Europe. But Nicholas was at least
a personality, a power. And Heine was genius enough to
feel that in the last instance personalities and powers are

---

[1] At times the fancy takes me to set sail for America, that great liberty-stable,
where the equality-bumpkins congregate. . . .

the only things that count. Numbers do not, neither do monarchs, not even in quantities. Hence Heine's standing joke on the subject of the three dozen German monarchs.

What Heine dreaded was perhaps in the first place a life without beauty. Fourier's Phalanstery, the great home of labour, where everything, down to the beer, is equally distributed, where there is no room for any superfluity, not even for the superfluity which is known by the name of art, seemed to him to be inevitable in the future, but did not satisfy him.

But still more repugnant to him was a life without all greatness, with equality in mediocrity as its religion, and hatred to genius, to inquiring minds, to those who openly discard Nazarene asceticism, as its only real morality. And equally repugnant to him was society as he knew it, dominated by an unintellectual clergy and an unrefined aristocracy, and society as he foresaw it, composed of emancipated slave souls, who had only exchanged the servility which was their instinct for free indulgence in the envy which lay at the root of all their morality.

He certainly took part with those who rose in revolution against Louis XVI., that worthy locksmith who became a king. But he as certainly took part with Cæsar against Brutus, that dunce of a usurer, who could do nothing but stick a knife into a great man.

Heine imagined himself to be a monarchist ; he called himself so from sincere conviction, because he was a Cæsarian, and had not the word to express it. He imagined himself to be a democrat, and called himself so ; because he was born a plebeian, hated all unjust privileges of birth, and felt himself in eternal opposition to the squirearchy and the clergy. But in his inmost soul he was consistent. The apparent contradiction in his political sympathies and tendencies arose from the fact that he loved greatness and beauty as truly as he loved liberty, and that he was not prepared to sacrifice the highest development of humanity on the altar of unreal equality and real mediocrity.

XII

HEINE

It seems most probable that Heinrich Heine was born on the 13th of December 1797. His father, Samson Heine of Hanover, as a young man took part in a campaign in Flanders and Brabant, in the capacity of quartermaster (with the rank of an officer) to the Duke of Cumberland, but after his marriage with Peira (Betty) von Geldern, settled down as a merchant in Düsseldorf. He was a handsome, placid, grave man, without much ability, even as a merchant. He had no taste for art or poetry, but he had a childish love of a fine uniform, and aristocratic tastes for gambling, actresses, dogs, and horses. He is said to have taken twelve horses with him when he removed to Düsseldorf. The poet's mother was a woman of keen intelligence and deep feeling, and was very musical. She had received a good education, spoke French and English as fluently as German, was a disciple of Rousseau, whose *Émile* she had studied, and an admirer of Goethe. She early rebelled against prejudice and conventionality, and differed from her husband, who reverenced Napoleon, in being an ardent patriot. Education was her hobby, and she taught her children with great care and patience. Both parents were free-thinkers in the matter of religion—the father indifferent, the mother a deist ; but they brought up their children in the observance of the old Jewish ritual.

After a short time at a Jewish school for young children, where, it may be, the foundation was laid for that knowledge of the Bible which is so conspicuous in his writings, Heinrich was placed in an educational establishment carried on in an old Franciscan monastery by French ecclesiastics, principally Jesuits, who were at the same time educated men of the world. He had had a happy childhood in his home, and at school, too, he found friends and protectors, who took his part when his religion or his mocking tongue threatened to get him into trouble.

The earliest noticeable peculiarity in the future poet was a nervousness, which steadily grew upon him, and which showed itself in the disagreeable and even painful effect produced in him by any kind of noise. Piano-playing and loud talk, at times even his sister's sweet, melodious voice, affected him as screaming affects ordinary nerves. And his sense of smell was as acute as his hearing. From a child he, like Goethe, loathed tobacco smoke. He had no taste for music, and never learned to dance. At fifteen he began to write good verse.

The Rhineland, with its joyousness, but also with its superstition, tradition, and legend ; the Catholic worship of these parts, with its medieval buildings and ceremonies and pilgrimages, over which the Romantic poetry of the day cast a transfiguring halo; the impressions produced by Jewish descent, by the poetry of the Bible, and by the craving for liberty, and the self-contempt engendered in the Jews by oppression ; the enthusiasm for the French and for Napoleon, and afterwards, following quickly upon this, the patriotic awakening of Germany, which led all the pupils in the highest class of the school, Heine among them, to attempt (most of them in vain) to enlist as volunteers in the War of Liberation—all these outward conditions and psychological experiences formed and set their imprint on the boy's mind. The great humorists, such as Cervantes and Swift, were his chosen reading; *Don Quixote* and *Gulliver's Travels* his favourite books.

In his sixteenth year he had a first romantic attachment to a girl of his own age, Josepha by name, the daughter of an executioner, who lived with her aunt, the widow of another executioner, a woman avoided and feared by all. Heine has told us that the young girl was strangely pale, that her movements were rhythmic and dignified, that she had finely cut features, large, dark eyes, and blood-red hair. She knew and taught him many ballads, was, he himself tells us, the first to awaken his taste for popular poetry, and altogether, what with her radiant beauty and the atmosphere of weirdness and horror that surrounded her, exercised no small influence on the budding poet. In Heine's first poems we observe a tendency towards thoughts of death and the grave, which seems to have been one resultof the tender attachment of the two children. In No. 6 of the *Dream Pictures*, the eternal damnation which is the price that must be paid for the possession of the beautiful woman who appears in the dream, seems to symbolise the dishonour which clung to the executioner's whole race, and acted like a curse on all who dared to connect themselves with it.

After 1816, Josepha's image is supplanted in Heine's soul by that of another young girl. His parents, on whom the brilliant career of the Rothschilds had made a great impression, destined their Harry (as he was originally called) to be a merchant. They sent him first to a commercial school in Düsseldorf, then for a few months to a banker in Frankfort, and finally placed him in an office in Hamburg, where his uncle, the well-known Salomon Heine, had risen to be a great man in the commercial world. In 1818, with the help of this rich uncle, on whom he remained practically dependent for the rest of his life, Heine began business for himself, as a commission agent for English drapery goods. Few were surprised when, in the following spring, the firm of "Harry Heine & Co." stopped payment. But in his uncle's house Heine had found not only the crusty benefactor who, generous to his nephew as he was, never understood him and was always irritated by him, but also, in that benefactor's third daughter Amalie, the woman who was to be the fate of his youth, and whom he has extolled and execrated under various names—Maria, Zuleima, in correspondence Molly. He is never tired of celebrating her charms ; she shines in beauty resplendent as that of the goddess who emerged from the sea foam ; her eyes, lips, and cheeks are those of the Madonna in the Cathedral of Cologne ; her eyes are violets, her hands lilies, &c., &c. But it does not appear that she ever loved him. He hoped in time to win her affections, and it is possible that he may now and again have received tokens of her favour ;

from his poems we are led to understand that her marriage
to a landed proprietor from Königsberg, in the year 1821,
stunned him at the time, and was afterwards regarded by
him as unpardonable treachery.

Heine had shown how little fitted he was for the career
of a merchant, and had moreover acquired a thorough
distaste for it ; fresh help from his uncle now enabled him
to prepare himself for one of the learned professions.   In
1819, soon after the Jewish Reform secession, he left
Hamburg, and travelled by Düsseldorf to Bonn, there to
study law and work for the degree which his uncle required
that he should take.

The University of Bonn, which was closed for several years
during the French rule, had lately been reopened, and had
a staff of excellent professors.   But it was just at this time
that, in consequence of the Resolutions of Karlsbad, the
prosecution of the students' unions (Burschenschaften) and
of all national movements among the students began ; and
almost immediately after his arrival at the university, Heine,
having taken part in a fête on the anniversary of the
battle of Leipzig, was summoned before a magistrate and
involved in a petty and futile political law-suit, which could
not fail to arouse in him a keen personal detestation of the
new reaction.   The certificate he received at the matricula-
tion examination in 1819 was to the effect that he knew
no Greek, had only a slight and unpractical knowledge of
Latin, and was not qualified to enter for examination in
mathematics at all ; but that he was "not entirely wanting in knowledge of history" and that "his German work,
though strange in style, showed praiseworthy effort."

The young student, in the velvet coat and frilled shirt,
with lace falling over his white, beautifully shaped hands,
aimed at careless elegance in dress and deportment.   He
was of middle height ; his light-brown hair, which he wore
rather long, framed a beardless, regular-featured face.   The
nose was almost Grecian, the eyes were blue, the mouth
was large and expressive, and the lips were often parted
in that cold, scornful smile so frequently referred to in his
poems.

He attended lectures on the history of the German
language, on the *Germania* of Tacitus, on the *Niebelungenlied*, and other historical and literary subjects ; dividing
his time between these and the law course, lectures on
Roman law, German law, &c. A professor who had an
undoubted influence upon the young poet was A. W. Schlegel,
the leader of the Romantic school. To him Heine showed
his verses. *Almansor* was written about this time.

Towards the end of 1820 Heine left Bonn for Göttingen,
with the good intention of applying himself diligently to
the study of law at the university there. But, as he tells
us very plainly in the *Harzreise*, the place was distasteful to him, and in the course of a few months, moreover,
on account of some trifling quarrel with another student,
he was rusticated. This led to his going to Berlin in 1821.
There, in Varnhagen's house, the intellectual centre of the
day, where Rahel gathered around her the aristocracy of
culture, talent, and birth, he soon made acquaintance with
the élite of the best society of the capital. At night, in
Lutter and Wegener's restaurant in the Behrenstrasse (still
in existence), he met the leading lights and genial Bohemians
of the day, among them men like E. T. W. Hoffmann and
Grabbe.   And here, after several fruitless attempts, he
succeeded in finding a publisher, who was willing to take
the risk of bringing out his first collection of poems and
to give him forty copies of the book by way of payment.
It appeared in December, 1821, made his name known,
almost famous, and at once called forth both imitations
and parodies.

At the university Heine attended the lectures of the first
scholars of the day—Hegel, to whom he was ardently devoted ; Bopp, the great authority on Sanscrit ; Wolf, the
classical philologist ; and Eduard Gans, the great lawyer. He
entered with youthful zeal into the schemes of a circle of
men whose object it was to bring about a reform of Judaism,
and who were attempting to initiate the Jews into the ideas
of European culture. With an equal amount of youthful
bitterness, he attacked in *Almansor*, in foreign garb, the
renegade Jews who deserted the common cause ; and also,

though indirectly, Christianity, which he regarded as a hostile
power. *Almansor* was published, along with Heine's other
youthful work, *William Ratcliff*, in 1823 ; it was acted, but
had no success, because of the race hatred felt for its
author.[1]

The life Heine led in Berlin was not compatible with
any proper progress in his studies. It was but a continuation of the dissipated life to which he had accustomed
himself in Hamburg. In 1823 he determined to turn over
a new leaf, and consequently left Berlin, went first to his
parents at Lüneburg, thence to Hamburg, and from Hamburg
returned to Göttingen, where in 1825 he took his degree of
Doctor of Law. Immediately after this he was baptized.
He did not change his religion from conviction of the truth
of Christianity ; on the contrary, his antipathy to it was
strong, and he was thoroughly ashamed of the step which
he took simply with the aim of extricating himself from
the humiliating and galling position of dependence on his
uncle; income, office, or profession being attainable on no
other condition. His frame of mind at this time is depicted in that overrated fragment, *Der Rabbi von Bacharach*,
which, in spite of some spirited and artistic passages, really
proves that Heine was incapable of writing a historical
novel. At the end of this work, the author, in the disguise of a fictitious character, confesses the shame he felt
at going over to a religion which to him was the enemy's
camp.

In the correspondence between Varnhagen and Rahel,
we find occasional allusions to Heine, which give us a
good idea of him as he was in those days. Curiously
enough, the first time Varnhagen mentions "our little Heine,"
he quotes an exhortation of Rahel's to the young man,
which is very remarkable, because it shows with what acute
perception she had at once discovered the very author with
whom he had, indeed, something in common, but whom it
would have been fatal to him, both personally and in a literary
sense, to resemble. The exhortation is : " You must not
become a Brentano. I cannot stand that ! " At another

---

[1] G. Karpeles : *Biographie Heinrich Heine's*, 1885.

time she writes jestingly : "Heine must and shall be real, even if he has to be thrashed into it.

'Be real, O man !'"

And Varnhagen, too, understood him well. How acute is the following remark in a letter to Rahel, written six years later : "And now, in addition to all the other wise and clever people who entertain you, you have Heine with you, the original, the far-travelled, the fresh Heine ! Fresh in this case does not necessarily mean fresh from the sea ; for salt herring, too, and that because they *are* salted, may be called fresh." The same idea recurs in an observation he makes on Heine at the age of thirty : "I hope you will see him often, and that he will try to benefit by his intercourse with you. He requires to be preserved in a good spiritual atmosphere, for there is something about him that spoils easily."[1]

Rahel and Varnhagen were the first to proclaim Heine's talent. The earliest laudatory notice of his poems was written by his fashionable diplomatic patron. Yet it is plain that they detected and deplored the weaknesses in his character, which might become dangerous, even fatal, to his great poetic gifts.

---

[1] *Briefwechsel zwischen Varnhagen und Rahel*, vi. 48, 56, 316, 344. Other interesting utterances of Rahel's on the subject of Heine are as follows : "I hardly see Heine ; he is entirely taken up with himself, says he must work hard, is almost surprised that such a real thing as his father's death, his mother's grief, should affect him. . . . He looks healthier, hardly complains now at all ; but slight grimaces that used to be only occasional with him, have grown to be habitual, and are not becoming ; for instance a twitching of the mouth in speaking, which I used to think rather fascinating, though it was no good sign." "I was intending to write about Heine. The conclusion I have come to is, that his talent is very great, but that unless it matures, it will lose all substance, will degenerate into hollow mannerism." Varnhagen answers : "The one hope for Heine is that he should gain the foothold of truth ; once firmly established on that, he may let his talent sally forth to seek prey and disport itself where it will" (vi. 347, 356, 365).

XIII

HEINE

THE most popular of Heine's books in our day, that with which his name is most inseparably connected, the *Buch der Lieder* of 1827, consists of groups of poems belonging to different years and periods.

The first group, *Junge Leiden* (1817-1821), is, as such, the weakest. It is divided into four parts : Dream Pictures, Songs, Romances, Sonnets. The subjects treated are : early recollections of Düsseldorf and of a happy childhood there, his love to his mother, Napoleon worship, much Catholic Rhineland romance, churchyard dances of death with rattle of bones, and all sorts of visions. We have the jesting tone—jocose complaints of the embarrassments resulting from the all too speedy disappearance of the ducats ; and the bitter tone, produced by the poet's resentment of the humiliations to which he, as an unsuccessful and defaulting young merchant, was subjected by the wealthy citizens of Hamburg. We have outbursts of affection for college friends, and of admiration for A. W. Schlegel, a man as distinguished in the literary world as at the university ; and also patriotic outbursts in the " Burschen" style, which Heine quickly tired of. We have passionate expression of the self-consciousness of genius, and we have love-griefs and plaints of various sorts—first love's aspirations (blended in E. T. W. Hoffmann's manner with churchyard horrors), and then exceedingly sentimental laments over unreturned love, and outbursts of wild, despairing accusation of the false one, who has given him his deathblow, and who drinks his blood and eats his heart at her wedding feast. In one single poem, *Die Fensterschau*, the mood suddenly changes into a sort of coarse jollity.

Of these youthful poems, which for the most part are

old-fashioned in form, the best are the famous epigrammatic quatrain beginning : "Anfangs wollt' ich fast verzagen" (I at first was near despairing), the earliest example of the condensation of Heine's style ; a few of the sonnets, which are much more passionate than the great majority of German sonnets ; and lastly, among the romances, *Belsazer*, probably inspired by Byron's *Hebrew Melodies*, and the inimitable ballad of the *Two Grenadiers*, already referred to.

The second group, which owes its odd title, *Lyric Intermezzo*, to the fact that it first appeared as a lyric interlude between the two bad tragedies, *Almansor* and *Ratcliff*, published in 1823, treats of the same subjects as the first, but in more uncommon forms and with freer artistic manipulation. Two critics, Ernst Elster and Wilhelm Bölsche (the former in the introduction to his edition of the original text of the *Buch der Lieder*, the latter in an independent work on Heine), have pointed out with much critical acumen that in this division we seldom have a direct expression of the poet's love troubles, but rather a sort of extract of them, which he gives us from memory. His imagination runs riot among the old sufferings, now and again actually playing with them ; hence we have an occasional unlucky expression ; the reader at times doubts the reality of the feeling, and becomes suspicious of the constant assurances of a killing grief, in despite of which life goes on and art is not neglected.

But it was only natural that Heine should fall back upon this one passion, even though it had received no new nourishment in the interval. He had felt none since which could compare with it in strength or in influence upon his inner life. It was, and it remained, the most important incident in his life. It seems as if any happiness it brought him had been most transient ; hence the first time he sang of his love he dwelt exclusively on its woes, on the absence of all return, on his forsakenness, on the treachery and cold cruelty of the beloved. Now that he was so far disenthralled, he related the whole real or imaginary history of the passion, from the day when it first awoke to life to the hour when he was as dead for her ; and imparted greater piquancy

and fulness to its life story by giving each of its separate
moments some background drawn from nature in one or
other of her many moods.   In the *Dream Pictures* night
reigned supreme.   Now we have the budding of the leaf, the
singing of the birds, and the starlight of May.

That the love supposed to be at first felt by the beloved
one for the poet is only a fiction, and does not really agree
with the facts of the case, Heine involuntarily discloses when
he paints tender scenes between them.   For in these the
lover never feels himself to be the possessor ; even when
he holds the object of his desire in his arms his only feeling
is longing :

> " Lehn deine Wang' an meine Wang',
>   Dann fliessen die Thränen zusammen !
> Und an mein Herz drück fest dein Herz,
>   Dann schlagen zusammen die Flammen !
>
> Und wenn in die grosse Flamme fliesst
>   Der Strom von unseren Thränen,
> Und wenn dich mein Arm gewaltig umschliesst—
>   *Sterb' ich vor Liebessehnen.*" [1]

This favoured lover, who, when the flames meet, dies of
longing, betrays himself to be in reality a thoroughly un-
satisfied lover.

Hence the best of the purely erotic poems are those
which express love's longing and those which depict its sad
decay.   Conspicuous amongst the poems of tender longing
is the charming Oriental song, *Auf Flügeln des Gesanges,
Herzliebchen, trag' ich dich fort*, which fascinates by its
exotic Indian landscape and by its delicate fervency of
feeling.   Heine longed for India as Goethe longed for Italy;
his spiritual home was on the banks of the Ganges, as

---

[1] Thy cheek incline, dear love to mine,
    Then our tears in one stream will meet, love !
Let thy heart be pressed till on mine it rest,
    Then the flames together will beat, love !

And when the stream of our tears shall light
    On that flame so fiercely burning,
And within my arms I clasp thee tight—
    I shall die with love's wild yearning.
                     (Translated by Sir Theodore Martin.)

Goethe's was on the banks of the Tiber. It is probable that Bopp's lectures first turned his thoughts in the direction of that Oriental dream-land ; but in picturing it he employs the purely imaginative, Romantic style, which he inherited, remodelled for himself, and used in painting the far-off and alluring.

How simply beautiful is such a verse as :

> " Dort wollen wir niedersinken
> Unter dem Palmenbaum,
> Und Lieb' und Ruhe trinken
> Und träumen seligen Traum."[1]

But a verse like :

> " Dort liegt ein rothblühender Garten
> Im stillen Mondenschein,
> Die Lotosblumen erwarten
> Ihr trautes Schwesterlein."[2]

beautiful as it is, caressing as it sounds, has something of the unnaturalness which often strikes the reader in Heine's painting of nature. The colouring is vivid, but not real ; local colours obtrude themselves to the detriment of the general tone. " Rothblühender," (red-blooming) is hardly the word that it would naturally occur to one to use in describing a garden seen by moonlight. In the lines : " Gegenüber am Fenster sassen *Rosengesichter* dämmernd und *mond*beglänzt " (At the opposite window glimmered rose-faces, bright in the moonlight glow), from the later poem *Abenddämmerung* (" Twilight "), we have the same sort of effect, produced at the same expense of naturalness. The declaration that the lotus flowers are expecting their dear sister sounds like an old-fashioned compliment in the midst of

---

[1] We'll lie there, in slumber sinking,
'Neath the palm tree by the stream,
Raptures and rest deep drinking,
Dreaming the happiest dream.

(C. G. LELAND.)

[2] There a red-blooming garden is lying
In the moonlight silent and clear ;
The lotus flowers are sighing
For their sister so gentle and dear.

(E. A. BOWRING.)

this gorgeous Ganges imagery.   We have much the same expression in the stanza :

> " Es flüstern und sprechen die Blumen
> Und schau'n mitleidig mich an :
> Sei unsrer Schwester nicht böse,
> Du trauriger, blasser Mann ! " [1]

This is a madrigal style which Heine leaves behind in his later work.

Another of the verses in this wonderfully emotional song of the Ganges has characteristics which point to Heine's derivation from the Romantic school, with its arbitrary interpretation of nature :

> " Die Veilchen kichern und kosen
> Und schau'n nach den Sternen empor." [2]

It is quite audacious enough to represent violets as caressing each other ; we are reminded of Hans Andersen's enchanted gardens ; to make them titter is certainly too much of a good thing.   Émile Zola affects this same style in his description of the Paradou garden.

The next song, which is conceived in the same spirit, the song of the lotus flower that fears the splendour of the sun, is a charming poem, despite its flower-innocence, marvellously, meltingly sensuous.   Sensual-spiritual desire is here intensified till it reaches the verge of hysteria ; for the poet, not content with making the lotus flower blossom and glow and shine and exhale fragrance and tremble, when her lover, the moon, awakes her with his rays, actually makes her weep.[3]

Next in real feeling to the poems of desire come those

---

[1] The flowers are whisper.ng and talking ;
   With pity my features they scan :
O, pray do not chide our sister,
   Thou sorrowful, pale-faced man !

[2] The violets titter, caressing,
   Peeping up as the planets appear.
                                        (C. G. LELAND.)

[3] *Cf.* W. Kirchbach : *Heine's Dichterwerkstatt*, in *Magazin für die Litteratur*, Jahrgang 57, Nr. 18, 19, 20.

that express the relinquishment, the cessation of the passion. The finest example is poem No. 59 in the *Intermezzo*, which in its first verse describes the falling of a star, the star of love, from heaven; in its second, the falling of the apple-blossoms from the tree; in its third, the sinking of a swan to its watery grave; then sums all up in the concluding verse:

> " Es ist so still und dunkel !
> Verweht ist Blatt und Blüth',
> Der Stern ist knisternd zerstoben,
> Verklungen das Schwanenlied." [1]

It is very characteristic of Heine that, as the poem stands, it does not produce the impression that he has really witnessed any one of the three natural scenes depicted; they are simply symbols, arbitrarily selected and combined.

Amongst this passionate verse he has interspersed poems of a totally different description, treating of far more trivial amours. Some of the most exceptionable of these he did not include in the *Buch der Lieder*, not even, for example, the very harmless :

> " Du sollst mich liebend umschliessen,
> Geliebtes, schönes Weib !
> Umschling mich mit Armen und Füssen
> Und mit dem geschmeidigen Leib !" [2]

But we have, among others, *Die Welt ist dumm, die Welt ist blind* (" The world is stupid, the world is blind "), with its description of burning kisses. There are also other epigrammatic verses of a serious, passionate character, such as

---

[1] The silence and the night fall,
The blossoms all have fled,
In sparks the star has vanished,
The swan and his song are dead.
(H. F.

[2] Come, twine in wild rapture round me,
Fair woman, beloved and warm,
Till thy feet and hands have bound me,
And I'm wreathed with thy supple form !
(LELAND.)

I

the well-known *Ich hab' dich geliebet und liebe dich noch*
("I have loved thee long, and I love thee now"); and,
finally, in the very famous *Ein Jüngling liebt ein Mädchen,
die hat einen Andern erwählt* ("A young man loves a maiden,
who another to him prefers"), with intentional triviality of
diction, and with an impersonality which is unusual with
him, Heine generalises the human fate which has made of
him an erotic poet.

To the collection of poems which form the second part
of the *Lyric Intermezzo*, the title *Heimkehr* ("The Home-
Coming") is given. They were written in 1823–1824 in
Hamburg and Cuxhaven, and the "home-coming" is the
poet's return to Hamburg, the scene of his love romance,
where the sight of all the familiar surroundings causes his
heart's wounds to bleed afresh. With this main theme is
associated another, new in German poetry—the sea, which
Heine now saw for the first time.

Mingled with the lamentations over his lost love, which
the sight of the environments of the old tragedy calls forth,
are records of new impressions. There is first a wild outbreak of the old passion ; he broods once more over all its
agonies; he is miserable in the streets, where he feels as if the
houses were falling on him, and still more miserable in the
rooms where she plighted her faith to him. What is new in
these songs of unhappy love is the hatred, always alike passionate and wild, that flames up over the grave of buried
happiness.

But on his travels the poet has met the family of his
beloved, and her younger sister resembles her, especially
when she laughs ; she has the same eyes, the eyes that have
made him so unhappy. In a letter dated August 23rd,
1823, he tells his best friend that " a new folly has been
engrafted on the old." Ernst Elster's careful study of
letters and poems has enabled him to show that about this
time Heine's first and very unfortunate passionate attachment to Amalie Heine was superseded by a passion for
Therese Heine, who was her sister's junior by eight years.
Eveline and Ottilie are the poetic names bestowed on
Therese. The new passion was a violent one, but in all

probability met with as little return as the first.   Hence the
well-known lines :

> " Wer zum ersten Male liebt,
>   Sei's auch glücklos, ist ein Gott ;
>   Aber wer zum zweiten Male
>   Glücklos liebt, der ist ein Narr.
>
>   Ich, ein solcher Narr, ich liebe
>   Wieder ohne Gegenliebe ;
>   Sonne, Mond und Sterne lachen,
>   Und ich lache mit—und sterbe." [1]

In the year 1828 Therese Heine was engaged and
married to a Dr. Adolf Halle.   Among Heine's posthumous
poems are bitterly satirical verses on the bridegroom and the
wedding.   He had the unchivalrous poet's habit of reveng-
ing himself by satire when he met with a rebuff.   But the
poems in *Heimkehr* which refer to Therese are not inspired
with the bitterness and hatred which Heine frequently displays in writing of her elder sister.   He praises Therese's
beauty, her lovely eyes, her purity ; she is like a flower ; he
prays to her as others pray to Paul and Peter and the
Madonna ; and he struggles against his feelings, dreads this
new passion.   Both pride and shyness forbid him to declare
it ; it would be better for her if she did not love him ; at times
he has himself tried to prevent the awakening of love in her
soul ; but, having been only too successful in the attempt,
the desire for her love once more asserts itself.   He is too
proud to speak of his passion and of his suffering, mockery
and jests are on his lips, while inwardly he is bleeding to
death ; but she does not understand him, does not see

---

[1] He who for the first time loves,
    Though unloved, is still a god ;
    But the man who loves a second
    And in vain, must be a fool.

    Such a fool am I, now loving
    Once again, without return ;
    Sun and moon and stars are smiling,
    And I smile with them—and perish.
                                    (LELAND.)

that his heart is trembling, is breaking. Hence these
lines :

> " O, dieser Mund ist viel zu stolz
> Und kann nur küssen und scherzen ;
> Er spräche vielleicht ein höhnisches Wort,
> Während ich sterbe vor Schmerzen." [1]

But this time the threat of dying is not intended to be
taken literally. For in another poem we find the sincere
assurance :

> " Glaub' nicht, dass ich mich erschiesse,
> Wie schlimm auch die Sachen steh'n !
> Das Alles, meine Süsse,
> Ist mir schon einmal gescheh'n." [2]

Undoubtedly, however, he felt deeply and suffered
greatly this time also. Strange as it sounds, cousin-love,
which is, as a rule, merely the initiation into the life of
passion, its first preliminary stage,[3] was the only serious, and
not perfectly transient passion known to young Heine.
And no feeling experienced later, in his mature manhood,
approached in intensity to this youthful twin-passion for two
sisters, the second of whom reminded him of the first.

Among the emotional poems which refer to this episode
in his psychic history, Heine introduced (exactly as he did

---

[1] Alas, this mouth is far too proud,
  'Twas made but for kissing and sighing ;
Perchance it may speak a scornful word,
  While I with sorrow am dying

                              (BOWRING.)

[2] Fear not that I shall languish,
  Or shoot myself : oh, no !
I've gone through all this anguish
  Already, long ago.

                              (LELAND.)

[3] Aux prés de l'enfance on cueille
Les petites amourettes
Qu'on jette au vent feuille à feuille,
Ainsi que des pâquerettes ;
On cueille dans ces prairies
Les voisines, les cousines,
Les amourettes fleuries
Et qui n'ont pas de racines.

                              (RICHEPIN.)

in the *Intermezzo*) verses relating to less serious love affairs, to college adventures, and even to quite low, venal, erotic pleasures. He omitted from the *Buch der Lieder* some of the most objectionable of these, which originally formed part of the *Heimkehr*, amongst others the amusing, though impudent:

> " Blamier mich nicht, mein schönes Kind,
> Und grüss mich nicht unter den Linden ;
> Wenn wir nachher zu Hause sind,
> Wird sich schon Alles finden." [1]

—and even such a merry wanton rhyme as :

> " Himmlisch war's, wenn ich bezwang
> Meine sündige Begier ;
> Aber wenn's mir nicht gelang,
> Hatt' ich doch ein gross Plaisir." [2]

What we are most struck by in the poems of this division is the author's double gift of song and painting. Along with the capacity for producing those outbursts of mixed passion, which sound like the unaffected heart-cry of modern humanity, he here reveals a special talent for painting, for producing figures by means of light and shade and colour, without outline.

There is the scene in the lonely parsonage, with the disunited, despairing family (*Der bleiche, herbstliche Halbmond*). The son is determined to be a highway robber, the daughter has made up her mind to sell herself to the Count. With all its vividness, however, this scene is not one of the best. There is too much old-fashioned Romanticism in the idea of the dead father in his black robes standing outside, knocking at the window. The next poem, *Das ist ein schlechtes Wetter*, is a most masterly production. We see the little old woman hobbling across the street with

[1] Don't compromise me, my pretty one,
  Don't bow to me in " Rotten Row " ;
At home together afterwards
  I'll make up for it, that you know.

[2] 'Twas heavenly joy to overcome
  Each sinful wish and thought ;
But when I couldn't, truth to tell,
  That, too, much pleasure brought.

her lantern late on the dark and stormy evening, to make purchases for her tall, beautiful daughter, who is lying in the arm-chair at home, blinking sleepily at the light, her golden locks falling over her sweet face—it is like an old Dutch painting.

Still finer is the group of eight poems which was the result of his stay at Cuxhaven. *Wir sassen am Fischerhause* is a little marvel of artistic ability—that talk with the girls, sitting outside the fisherman's hut, in which far-off India and Ultima Thule are described in a few words : " By the Ganges all is brightness and fragrance, giant trees blossom, and beautiful, tranquil men and women kneel to the lotus flowers. In Lapland the people are dirty and small ; their heads are flat and their mouths are wide ; they cower round the fire, roast fish, and screech and scream."

Then there are merry poems, treating of light characters like the girl whom he searches for through the whole town and finds in a fashionable hotel, and the girl in whose heart the blue hussars are quartered.

And lastly, there are single epigrammatic verses, which every one now knows by heart, but which, at the time they appeared, gave great offence and made enemies for their author. Especially noteworthy is the famous :

> " Selten habt ihr mich verstanden,
> Selten auch verstand ich euch,
> Nur wenn wir im Koth uns fanden,
> So verstanden wir uns gleich." [1]

It is incomprehensible that this verse should ever have been regarded as a confession of unclean instincts. It only applies to those who find their way straight to any exceptionable or indecent passage in a book, as the sow finds her way to the mire, and stops there. That it never occurred to Heine that he was making any admission of having desired to appeal to his reader's sensual instincts or cynic

---

[1] Little by thee comprehended,
    Little knew I thee, good brother ;
   When we in the mud descended
    Soon we understood each other.
                              (LELAND.)

tendencies is best proved by the poem which immediately follows on the lines in question, the one beginning:

> " Doch die Kastraten klagten,
>   Als ich meine Stimm' erhob ;
>   Sie klagten und sie sagten :
>   Ich sänge viel zu grob." [1]

He could not have declared more unmistakably that, where he is straightforward, plain-spoken, or cynical, it is only the result of his modern tendency to realistic truthfulness, of his antipathy to romantic embellishment, and of his instinctive inclination to face the bitter truth of life.

And there is quite as little justification for the general complaint of what Julian Schmidt has called the low-mindedness of Heine's sudden leaps from the sublime to the sordid. We have a typical instance of these sudden changes of style and mood in the poem *Frieden* (" Peace "), one of the group of North Sea poems, in which Heine, during a calm at sea, beholds the giant form of Jesus, the Prince of Peace, striding over sea and land. He is clothed in white ; his head touches the clouds ; the heart in his breast is the sun, the red, flaming sun, and this sun–heart sheds its illuminating, warming rays over land and sea. Then there is a sudden revulsion of mood. Heine calls to mind a miserable, canting fellow in Berlin, weak in mind and body, strong in faith—what would not *he* give to be able to hit upon such pious imagery, by means of which he might ingratiate himself with those in power and perhaps attain to the position of court-councillor in the pious town on the Spree—what dreams he would have of a hundred thalers rise in salary !

Heine most undoubtedly spoiled the effect of his beautiful vision. He broke up his poem, shattered its melody with grotesque discords ; but yet it is easy to understand that in the case of a poet with his experience of modern life, the second vision was a perfectly natural sequel to the first ;

---

[1] How the eunuchs were complaining
   At the roughness of my song !
   Complaining and explaining
   That my voice was much too strong.
                                        (LELAND.)

and in any case it is unjustifiable to speak of this connection
of ideas, this "idea-leap," as a symptom of low-mindedness.
In this connection Wilhelm Bölsche makes the true and
pertinent observation that no one has accused Goethe of
low-mindedness because he allows the gibes of Mephistopheles to follow directly upon Faust's confession of faith
to Gretchen (*Heinrich Heine*, p. 106). And yet the only
difference is that in *Faust* the pathos and the ribaldry are
put into the mouths of two people, whereas in the lyric
poem the poet makes himself directly responsible for
both.

Almost at the end of this collection (*Heimkehr*), we come
upon a couple of poems which are distinguished by depth
of feeling and perfection of form. The particular arrangement of their rhymes would distinguish them from the
majority of the small poems, if nothing else did, as it is
one we seldom meet with in Heine. The first, *Dämmernd
liegt der Sommerabend* ("Summer eve with day is striving"),
which describes the beautiful elf-maiden bathing in the river
by moonlight, has the diaphanous haze of a Corot landscape. The rhythmic treatment of the second gives it a
unique place in the collection. It is the pathetic, fantastic:

> " Der Tod, das ist die kühle Nacht,
>   Das Leben ist der schwüle Tag.
>   Es dunkelt schon, mich schläfert,
>   Der Tag hat mich müd gemacht.
>
> Über mein Bett erhebt sich ein Baum,
>   Drin singt die junge Nachtigall ;
>   Sie singt von lauter Liebe,
>   Ich hör' es sogar im Traum." [1]

---

[1] Death is a cool and pleasant night,
    Life is a sultry day.
    'Tis growing dark—I'm weary,
    For day has tired me with his light.

Over my bed a fair tree gleams,
    And in it sits a nightingale :
    She sings of naught save love,
    I hear it even in dreams.

(LELAND.)

The next division of the *Buch der Lieder, Aus der Harz-reise* (1824), contains the delightful mountain-rhymes conceived in the course of a walking tour which Heine took by way of refreshment after his law studies in Göttingen.   Here we have charming pictures of mountain scenery and peasant life, and a tone of witty, bold self-laudation, kept up with irresistible audacity.   The beautiful and witty poem about the knight of the Holy Spirit was doubtless suggested by the catechising scene in *Faust*, but has an originality of its own which has made it popular all the world over.

The *Buch der Lieder* closes with the North Sea poems (*Die Nordsee*, 1825–1826), inspired by two visits to Norderney, and written in forcible, irregular rhythm.   In them we observe first and foremost a particular understanding of nature which is a new gain for German poetry.

As far as nature was concerned, Goethe seemed to have exhausted everything.   His love for every living thing, his feeling of kinship with animals and plants, his persuasion that the human being is one with all other beings, his intuition of the unity that underlies perpetual change of form——this gift of resolving all nature into feeling was his earliest characteristic.   It was soon superseded, or rather supplemented, by his capacity for observing and reproducing natural scenes without any ascription of his own feelings to them.   He studies nature, becomes an observer and investigator, and finally, thanks to the steadily increasing profundity of his observation, in combination with his genial intuition, an epoch-making discoverer in two great domains of natural science.   We see him pass through all the phases of a great mind in its relation to nature——the emotional, the religious-pantheistic, the poetic-scientific——and see him in the end lay such exclusive stress upon material impressions that he thrusts all that is psychical from him as merely disturbing.   His views become more and more positive and realistic.   In his essay on granite he writes: "I do not fear the reproach of its being a spirit of contradiction that has led me from the observation and delineation of the human heart, that youngest, most multiform, most mobile, most changeable part of creation, that which it is easiest to unsettle and to shake, to the observation of nature's oldest, firmest, deepest, most immovable son "[1] —namely, granite.

In what domain was it still possible for a German poet to display fresh, original understanding of nature ? From the human heart to granite Goethe had embraced them all.

There was one left. Goethe had never sung the sea. He saw it for the first time when he was nearly forty, in Venice, from the Lido. " I heard a loud noise," he writes ; " it was the sea, and I soon saw it, rolling high waves up the beach, as it drew back. It was midday and ebb-tide. At last, then, I have seen the sea also with my own eyes." A little further on we come upon the short sentence : " Yes, the sea is a wonderful sight." In the Fifth Act of the Second Part of *Faust*, where the sea and navigation are touched on, it is less the sea itself that is in question than the rescuing of land from it and the making of canals. This was all that Goethe had written about the sea.

In Heine's North Sea poems we hear, for the first time in German poetry, the roar of the ocean, with all its freshness and in all its might. Here for the first time we have shells in the sand beneath our feet, and sea-gulls in the air above us. The sea is painted in storm and calm, from the shore and from the ship, by day and by night, with the peace that at times lies over it, and with the madness of the hurricane ; we have the sweet day-dreams to which it gives rise, and also the sea-sickness ; there arise from its depths and there hover over its expanse a whole company of mythic figures, old and new, old that have been metamorphosed into new, a world of gods and goddesses, Tritons and Oceanides, at times pathetic, more frequently burlesque. And yet there is comparatively little description ; it is the poet's own memories, griefs, and hopes that fill these poems. And it is his intense longing to be able to breathe freely that breaks forth in the famous cry with which the ten thousand Greeks, after their long and terrible march, hailed the

---

[1] Goethe : *Werke*, xxxiii. 164.

element that spoke to them of home: "Thalatta! Thalatta!—
I salute thee, O eternal sea!"

Amongst these poems are some of Heine's most beautiful and unforgettable. First there is the humorously frivolous idyll *Die Nacht am Strande* ("Night by the Seashore"); the poet's visit to the pretty fisherman's daughter, with the masterly description of her appearance, as she sits bending over the fire:

> "Dass die flackernd rothen Lichter
> Zauberlieblich wiederstrahlen
> Auf das glühende Antlitz,
> Auf die zarte, weisse Schulter,
> Die rührend hervorlauscht
> Aus dem groben, grauen Hemde,
> Und auf die kleine, sorgsame Hand,
> Die das Unterröckchen fester bindet
> Um die feine Hüfte."[1]

Then we come on a poem which is unique in its lyric vigour, *Erklärung* ("Declaration"), to that Agnes whose name the poet would fain write on the dark vault of heaven with the highest fir of Norway, dipped in the crater of Etna. And there is also the little, reflective poem *Fragen* ("Questions"), admirable in its pregnant brevity, which gives us an idea of the mood in which Heine conceived the foolhardy idea of writing a "Faust," after Goethe, a plan which he actually did not hesitate to mention to Goethe himself, when he visited him in Weimar. In some of these North Sea poems, and that even when he is belittling and sneering at himself, there is a repellent tone of self-satisfaction. Amongst those which are quite free from it, must be

---

[1] Till the flashing, ruddy flame-rays
Shine again in magic lustre
On her glowing countenance,
On the soft and snow-white shoulder
Which so touchingly peers out
From its coarse grey linen covering,
And on the busy little hand
Which is fastening the garment
That conceals her slender limbs.
(Adapted from LELAND.)

mentioned that masterly piece of pure humour, *Im Hafen*
("In Harbour"), the immortal fantasy of the Town Cellar
of Bremen, in which Heine, whose sobriety was almost
equivalent to total abstinence, gives us a most irresistible
picture of a clever man's merry carouse.

XIV

HEINE

IT is impossible for a northerner of mature years and fairly sound artistic training to study Heinrich Heine's poems without feeling his taste offended by figures and expressions which in Heine's case early became lifeless mannerisms. The Romance nations do not feel this. One actually hears competent critics of Romance nationality compare Heine's lyrics with Goethe's, and give the preference to Heine's as more plastic and more spiritual. To Romance readers Goethe is, as a rule, wanting in transparency ; the French say of Heine : *On y voit mieux*. They do not feel that in Goethe's case words always represent things ; whereas in Heine's case, expressions are often set pieces, which are inserted to produce a certain poetical effect, but which have no vision, no actuality behind them. Few poets have made such abuse of lily-hands, rose-cheeks, and violet-eyes, these monstrous colour-blotches, in describing female beauty, or of the various attributes of spring—flowers that exhale fragrance, nightingales that sing both day and night—in proclaiming the praises of the lovely month of May. The nightingale in particular becomes under his treatment a purely heraldic bird in the coat-of-arms of love.

In Goethe's case all the words are images, and this is the reason why he requires to employ so little imagery. In Heine's the words are constantly allegories, devoid of perspicuity and of that inward connection which is the logic of poetry. Take as an instance : " Aus meinen Thränen spriessen — vie' blühende Blumen hervor," [1] where by flowers poems are meant ; or : " Sprüh'n einmal vert

---

[1] Up from my tears are growing
Fair flowers in many vales.

(LELAND.)

dächt'ge Funken—aus den Rosen, sorge nie—diese Welt glaubt nicht an Flammen—und sie nimmt's für Poesie,"[1] where we are presented with a skein of images more entangled than those of the notorious old Scandinavian transcriptions of the decadent period in Skaldic poetry—sparks struck out of roses ; sparks, which the everyday world will not accept as fire ; rose sparks, which are called poetry !

What one objects to most in these poems with their allegorical rhetoric is the combination of sentimentality and materialism. Sighs and tears are talked of as if sighs were very loud breaths and tears very tangible substances. We have, for instance : "Und meine Seufzer werden—ein Nachtigallenchor" (And from my sighs go flying, A choir of nightingales), still further materialised by the addition of : " Und vor deinem Fenster soll singen—das Lied der Nachtigall" (And the nightingales at thy window, Shall sing all the summer hours). A still more striking instance is to be found in the typical poem of the lonely tear :

> " Was will die einsame Thräne ?
> Sie trübt mir ja den Blick,
> Sie blieb aus alten Zeiten
> In meinem Auge zurück."[2]

We are initiated into this particular tear's family history and present lonely situation ; it had many bright sisters, who now are no more, so that it is left solitary in its eyecorner. It is addressed much as one would address any good old comrade, told to go its way, now that all the others have gone :

> " Du alte, einsame Thräne,
> Zerfliesse jetzunder auch ! "[3]

---

[1] If suspicious sparks should issue
From the roses—fearless be !
This dull world in flames believes not,
But believes them poetry.
                                (BOWRING.)

[2] What means this lonely tear-drop
 · Which dims mine eye to-day?
It is the last now left me
Where once so many lay.

[3] Thou tear-drop old and lonely,
Do thou, too, pass away !

The sentimentality is so crude that no parody could be more comic than this mournful apostrophe, which the arch-scoffer wrote in all good faith.

Every defect in the artist as a man, comes out in his art. It is always a want of simplicity, of genuine feeling, that produces the sentimental or ostentatious or clap-trap expression. Heine's shortcomings in this way are strongly felt when we compare certain outbursts of his with Goethe's expression of similar feelings.

Take, for example, the poem in which Heine describes himself as the ill-fated Atlas ; condemned to bear the whole world of suffering :

> " Du stolzes Herz, du hast es ja gewollt,
> Du wolltest glücklich sein, unendlich glücklich,
> Oder unendlich elend, stolzes Herz !
> Und jetzo bist du elend." [1]

These are lines one does not forget. But the exclamation of the first line, which expresses a perilous extreme of self-reliance, becomes self-complacency when Heine's stanza is placed alongside of Goethe's simple and grand

> " Alles geben die Götter, die Unendlichen,
> Ihren Lieblingen ganz :
> Alle Freuden, die unendlichen,
> Alle Schmerzen, die unendlichen,
> Ganz." [2]

It would be most unreasonable to blame Heine because he employs other and more violent methods than Goethe does—to say, for instance, of a poem like *Ein Jüngling liebt ein Mädchen* (" A young man loves a maiden "), that Goethe would have shrunk from the grotesqueness of the bitter, desperate ending : " Und wem sie just passieret, Dem bricht das Herz entzwei " (And he to whom it happens, It breaks his heart in two). It would have been abhorrent to him

---

[1] Proud heart, 'twas thine own choice,
Thou chosest to be happy, infinitely happy,
Or infinitely miserable, proud heart !
And now thou art miserable.

[2] What the eternal Gods give to their favourites, they give without alloy—infinite joy, infinite sorrow—without alloy.

for much the same reason that it would have been abhorrent to an old Greek. What is simply new, simply *modern* in the feeling, is justifiable. Even the grotesqueness is in this case artistically led up to.

But at times the grotesque grimace is all that is left of the modern element. Take that famous poem: *Mein Herz, mein Herz ist traurig* (" My heart, my heart is heavy "). It contains an admirable description of a wide landscape, viewed from the height of the old bastion. We see the blue town moat, with a boy fishing from a boat, and away on the other side of the moat, small and clear, we see summer-houses and gardens, men and oxen, meadows and woods, girls bleaching clothes, a turning mill-wheel sending out diamond dust, and at the foot of the old grey tower a sentry-box, with the sentry walking up and down, his gun flashing in the sunlight. H. C. Andersen, writing of this poem, remarks, " And the end is so *affecting*: ' Ich wollt', er schösse mich todt' " (I wish he would shoot me dead). Affecting ? No. Startling ; for nothing has prepared us for it. The ejaculation is possibly not entirely insincere ; but it is so nervous that it is practically meaningless ; it is in so far untruthful, that these big words only express a momentary mood, not a serious, determined desire.

Goethe has expressed, if not longing for death, at least reconciliation to the idea of death, in the famous, immortal lines :

" Ueber allen Gipfeln
Ist Ruh.
In allen Wipfeln
Spürest du
Kaum einen Hauch.
Die Vögelein schweigen im Walde.
Warte nur, balde
Ruhest du auch." [1]

---

[1] O'er all the hill tops
Is quiet now,
In all the tree tops
Hearest thou
Hardly a breath ;
The birds are asleep in the trees.
Wait ; soon like these
Thou too shalt rest.

(LONGFELLOW.)

It is unnecessary to direct attention to the contrast between the two poet-natures which is revealed by a comparison of this melody in words with Heine's discord; but note, from the purely artistic point of view, how marvellously in keeping all the different parts of the little poem are. It is one breath from the first word to the last: The calm of evening over the forest and in the human soul, the cessation of all desire, the resolution of all discords, the heart, great and tender, feeling itself one with all nature.

Alongside of this perfection, the defects of Heine's lyric effect-style, in its occasional inartistic application, show up only too glaringly. It is akin, in its weaknesses, to the allegorising, fantastic style of the German Romanticists, from whom Heine, the poet, is lineally descended. And yet he is as far from being a genuine Romanticist as he is from being what some consider him, a genuine modern realist.

He calls his *Atta Troll* the last free forest ditty of Romance. Others have, in unfriendly criticism, called his poetry the decomposition process of Romance. "I wrote *Atta Troll*," he says, "for my own amusement, in the whimsical dream-style that prevailed in that Romantic school in which I passed the pleasantest years of my youth, and ended up by thrashing the schoolmaster." But in this case the Romanticism is really only the rich, glittering garment, in which the modern spirit masques, and which it finally throws off. None of the elements of Romance are wanting—animals talk, bears exchange ideas, we listen to a pug-dog's confidences, and we are conducted into a legendary region, the valley of Roncesvalles. Not even the blue flower is wanting:

> "Ronceval, du edles Thal,
> Wenn ich deinen Namen höre,
> Bebt und duftet mir im Herzen
> Die verscholl'ne blaue Blume."[1]

The dream-world reveals itself to us; great spirit eyes look into ours. The poet, with his guide, goes hunting in the

[1] Ronceval, thou noble valley!
Whensoe'er I hear thy name,
That blue flower so long departed
O'er my spirit sheds its fragrance.

(BOWRING.)

K

Pyrenees. This guide has an old mother, who is reputed to be a witch. We are introduced into the witch's hovel, with the stuffed birds, the ghost-like vultures, and at night bears and ghosts perform a burlesque and weird dance.

The spirit as well as the style of this poem is Romantic to a certain point; there are declamations against the clumsy, didactic poetry of the day, against utilitarianism as applied to poetry, and there is literary satire (of Freiligrath, Karl Mayer, Gustav Pfizer) in the style favoured by the Romanticists.

And yet there is sedulous realism in the representation of localities and circumstances. Strictly speaking, the poem is simply an account of a stay which Heine and a young French lady friend make at Cauterets in the Pyrenees, where they see a bear dance in the market-place. The bear escapes from his master, takes flight to the mountains, where he is hunted down, shot, and flayed by Laskaro, the guide. The poet's Juliette gets the skin to lay on the floor by her bed; and Heine gives us the superfluous information that many a night he himself has stood bare-footed on this same skin.

So the tale is realistic enough. The details of the journey too are faithfully reproduced. We get the impression that Heine's description of the little mountain town up to which he clambered, and where the children danced in a circle to the accompaniment of their own singing, exactly corresponds with what he saw and heard. Even the refrain of the song: *Girofflino, Girofflette,* is doubtless the real one.

Nevertheless the finest, most powerful parts of this poem are not in the least realistic. They are visions. And the finest vision is that in which by night from the window of the cottage the poet watches the whole Wild Hunt tear three times round the horizon. He never did finer figure-painting than the passage in which we follow the shining figures across the darkness of the night sky—Diana, the fairy Abunde, and the beautiful Herodias, in wild wantonness playing at ball with the Baptist's bloody head.

A parallel may be drawn between Heine's art and that of Rembrandt. There is nothing academic about either of them; both bear the distinct stamp of modernity. But

when we call Heine a great realistic poet, we make an
assertion of the same qualified truth as when we call Rembrandt the great colourist. Rembrandt cannot be said to
be one of the greatest colour-realists, for the reason that
several painters surpass him in the power of reproducing
local colour and its exact value, and of showing the actual
form and colour of an object seen in half darkness. It is
not colour, but light, that is the main thing with Rembrandt.[1] To him light is life ; the battle of life is the battle
of light, and the tragedy of life is the tragedy of light,
struggling and dying in damp and darkness. To indicate
in what his real greatness as a painter lies, he ought rather
to be called a luminist (an expression of Fromentin's) than
a colourist, if by luminist we understand an artist whose
specialty is the apprehension and treatment of light. He
sometimes sacrifices drawing, even painting, in his eagerness to produce some effect of light. Think, for example,
of the badly painted corpse in the *Lesson in Anatomy*.
But it is exactly what makes him less successful than the
realists in tasks requiring absolute truthfulness—the painting of hands, the exact reproduction of stuffs—that makes
him so great when he causes light to express what it alone
indicates to him, the inner life, the world of waking visions.

Something similar to this is the case with Heine. How
few real figures this great poet has bequeathed to us ! Those
who would measure his deserts by what he has done in this
way find themselves obliged to fall back upon that crude,
grotesque sketch of an old Jew servant, Hyacinth, as his
best character.

No, if Heine is to be judged by his pictures of real life,
many an inferior poet surpasses him.

But think of his visions, of the world of waking dreams
in his poems and in his prose ! As a rule he starts closer to
earth than other poets, but presently, above the darkness of
earth a gleaming vision appears—and disappears.

This is felt even in such small poems as the one already
referred to as containing the talk in the fisherman's cottage
about the Ganges and Lapland.

[1] *Cf.* Fromentin : *Les maîtres d'autrefois.*

Think too of the way in which Heine calls up the image of Napoleon before his readers. In the *Two Grenadiers* it has the effect of a vision. The words, " Dann reitet mein Kaiser wohl über mein Grab " ('Tis my Emperor riding, right over my grave), are like a revelation in the darkness of night, illuminated by the glitter of swords. In the equally admirable description in the *Reisebilder*, the vision is conjured up in the form of a recollection of childhood.

Or remember how Heine brings the image of Jesus before us. In the poem *Frieden* (" Peace ") he sees him, robed in glittering white, striding over the waves. In *Deutschland, ein Wintermärchen* (" Germany, a Winter's Tale "), he paints a grey, winter morning on the Paderborn heath ; when the mist rises, he sees by the side of the road, in the dawning light, a wooden crucifix with the image of the great enthusiast, who desired to save mankind, and now hangs there " as a warning to others."

> " Sie haben dir übel mitgespielt,
> Die Herren vom hohen Rathe." [1]

The heart-felt sadness, the bitter humour, that find expression in familiar, disparaging comment, heighten the impression of human grandeur, of solemn horror, much as this same impression is intensified when Hamlet, hearing his father's ghost under ground, calls : " Well said, old mole ! Canst work i' the earth so fast ? " In the flash of Heine's wit the reader sees Jesus, not now as the Prince of Peace, but as the man who scourged the desecrators of the Temple and sent fire upon earth.

The Winter's Tale is, taken as a whole, a characteristic example of Heine's artistic procedure. All the twenty-seven divisions of the long poem are constructed on the same plan. They begin close to earth, materially, with reminiscences of travel, vulgar realistic impressions ; then the writer, without warning, by unnoticeable transitions, rises to the height of passion, to powerful pathos, wild

---

[1] A sorry trick they played thee indeed,
The lords of the council stately.

(BOWRING.)

contempt, glowing admiration, destructive or constructive enthusiasm, divine madness that, as it were, rolls thunderbolt on thunderbolt; and then all sinks back once more into the grey dulness of everyday events and situations.

Heine arrives at Cologne, sups on an omelet and ham, drinks a bottle of Rhenish wine, and then saunters out into the streets. He calls the town's past days to mind : here the priests had free play, here men and books were burned at the stake ; here stupidity and malice wantoned like dogs on the open street. Suddenly in the moonlight the Cathedral, the great spiritual Bastille, appears to his sight and arouses his wrath. As he saunters along, he catches sight of a figure behind him which it seems to him he ought to know. And now we glide into a perfectly new world, the world of vision. The figure follows him as if it were his shadow, stopping when he stops. He has often noticed it beside him before, when he sat late at night at his desk. Under its cloak it holds, and always has held, something that glitters strangely and that resembles an axe, an executioner's axe. This figure is the poet's lictor, who follows his master, instead of preceding him as the Roman lictor did.

In the succeeding divisions Barbarossa reveals himself in the same visionary style, coming and going twice.

Heine is an epoch-maker, not only in German lyric poetry, but in poetry in general. He introduced a new style, the combination of sentiment and humour in lyric poetry, and a new idea, the introduction of prose into poetry, either by way of foil or by way of parody. His position as epoch-maker is due to his historic position, to his having lived at the period when Romantic perversion of reality was giving way to pessimistic realism ; this explains the fusion of the two elements which we find in his writings.

Hence, too, it comes that the most characteristic domain in the province of his art is the domain of chiaroscuro, a chiaroscuro akin to Rembrandt's.

To make the central objects stand out from the shadow or half-darkness in which they are concealed ; to make light, natural light, produce a ghostly, supernatural effect by conjuring it forth from a sea of dark shadow-waves, bringing it flickering or flaring out of half-darkness ; to make darkness penetrable, half-darkness transparent—this is Rembrandt's art.

Heine's, which is closely related, consists in gradually, imperceptibly, conjuring forth out of the world of reality, and back into it again, a perfectly modern, fantastic dream-world.

At times the vision is in a full blaze of light, and the reality hidden in black darkness ; but presently the vision fades, and the reality gradually emerges into the light.

XV

HEINE AND GOETHE

IT has already been mentioned that Heine, when a student in Bonn, conceived an enthusiastic admiration for the founder of the Romantic school. A. W. Schlegel's personality was as attractive to him as his teaching. In Schlegel, Heine admired the man who had guided German poetry from artificiality to truth. He was dazzled, too, by the fashionable professor's aristocratic bearing, his knowledge of the world, his acquaintance with the good society and famous people of the day.

He was also touched by the kindly interest which Schlegel showed in himself and his first literary efforts. It was to Schlegel that he was indebted for his early initiation into the secrets of metrical art, and for something more valuable still, confidence in his own powers and his future.

In Heine's first prose article, that on Romanticism, written in 1820, he expresses his gratitude and makes his Romantic confession of faith in the same breath. He protests against the idea of Romanticism being " a mixture of Spanish enamel, Scotch mists, and Italian jingle " ; no, Romantic poetry ought not to be obscure and vague ; its images may be as plastic in contour as those of classic poetry. " Hence it is," he writes, " that our two greatest Romanticists, Goethe and A. W. Schlegel, are at the same time our greatest plastic artists." And he names Goethe's *Faust* and Schlegel's *Rome* in the same breath, as models of plastic outline, concluding pathetically : " O, that those who love to call themselves Schlegelians would lay this to heart !" This passage should be noted by those whose only knowledge of Heine's connection with Schlegel is derived from the low attack on the latter's private life in *Die Romantische Schule*. It was to A. W. Schlegel, moreover, that Heine addressed his three first sonnets. In the earliest he thanks him for his personal kindness, and declares his own great indebtedness to him ; in the second he extols him for the service which he has rendered to German poetry by banishing that caricature in hoop and patches which in his day figured as the Muse ; in the third he praises him for his introduction of English, Spanish, early German, Italian, and Indian poetry into modern German literature. The tone is enthusiastic :

> " Der schlimmste Wurm : des Zweifels Dolchgedanken,
> Das schlimmste Gift : an eigner Kraft verzagen,
> Das wollt' mir fast des Lebens Mark zernagen ;
> Ich war ein Reis, dem seine Stützen sanken.
>
> Da mochtest du das arme Reis beklagen,
> An deinem güt'gen Wort lässt du es ranken,
> Und dir, mein hoher Meister, soll ich's danken,
> Wird einst das schwache Reislein Blüthen tragen," &c.[1]

It is under this first Romantic influence that Heine writes his earliest, purely Romantic poems in archaistic style, verses like :

> " Die du bist so schön und rein,
> Wunnevolles Magedein,
> Deinem Dienste ganz allein
> Möcht' ich wohl mein Leben weihn.
>
> Deine süssen Aeugelein
> Glänzen mild wie Mondenschein,
> Helle Rosenlichter streun
> Deine rothen Wängelein."

This reminds us forcibly of Tieck's earliest verses, those introduced into his tales. In the one little poem from which these stanzas are taken, we come upon Wunne, Magedein, Aeugelein, Wängelein, Mündchen, weiland, a whole string of diminutives and archaisms.

---

[1] The most dangerous worm—doubt, with its dagger tooth ; the most deadly poison —distrust of one's own powers, were eating away my life ; I was a sapling bereft of its supports.

Thou hadst pity on the poor sapling, thou gavest it the support of encouraging words ; if ever the weak sapling blossoms, thine, great master, be the praise.

Heine's next model was a genial, true poet, who died in 1827, at the early age of thirty-one—Wilhelm Müller, the author of the *Müllerlieder*, particularly well known from Schubert's musical setting, and of the *Griechenlieder*, which were equally admired in their day. A son of Wilhelm Müller's is the well-known German-English philologist, Max Müller, whose novel, *Deutsche Liebe*, the story of the tender love of a young German savant for a sickly, bed-ridden princess, is said to be based on events in his father's life.

On the 7th of June 1826, Heine writes to Müller: "I am magnanimous enough to confess frankly that the resemblance of my little Intermezzo metre [the one most frequently employed by Heine] to your usual metre is not purely accidental ; the secret of its cadence was in all probability learned from your verses." He goes on to explain that he had early felt the influence of the German popular ballad and song, and that at Bonn, Schlegel had initiated him into the art of verses ; "but," he adds, "it is in your verse that I seem for the first time to have found the clear ring, the true simplicity, which I have always aimed at. How clear, how simple your poems are, and they are one and all popular poems. In mine only the form is popular ; the ideas are those of conventional society."

It was from Müller that Heine first learned how to evolve new popular forms out of the old. To behold as it were with our own eyes the birth and growth of Heine's style, we only need to set certain of his verses alongside of Müller's.

Müller writes :

> "Wir sassen so traulich beisammen
> Im kühlen Erlendach,
> Wir schauten so traulich zusammen
> Hinab in den rieselnden Bach."

And Heine :

> "Wir sassen am Fischerhause
> Und schauten nach der See,
> Die Abendnebel kamen
> Und stiegen in die Höh'."

How closely this last stanza resembles such a stanza of Müller's as:

> "Die Abendnebel sinken
> Hernieder kalt und schwer,
> Und Todesengel schweben
> In ihren Dampf umher." [1]

These are the introductory lines of a long, beautiful poem called *Hirtenbiwouak in der römischen Campagna*, the most important part of which is the shepherd's song of longing for his sweetheart. How much Heine must have learned from such a verse as that which describes the young girl:

> "Darunter sitzt ein Mädchen,
> Die Spindel in der Hand,
> Und spinnt und sinnt und schauet
> Herab in's eb'ne Land."

We do not find Wilhelm Müller marring the impression of his idyll by any sudden revulsion of mood; there is nothing of the devil in him; the gentle andante is maintained to the end of the piece. But it is not in this that the principal difference between his style and Heine's lies; for Heine at times retains his tranquil mood throughout a whole poem. The essential difference is the extraordinary condensation of Heine's style, as compared with Müller's. He gives in one verse, at most two, what the other requires ten to express.

The novelty in his lyric style is its unparalleled condensation. The poems are all epitomes. They present us with a spiced, fragrant essence of passion, experience, bitterness, mockery, wit, emotion, and fancy; an essence of poetry and prose in combination. Psychologists talk of a condensation of thought; [2] in comparison with the pupil's thought, the master's is condensed. In the history of all mechanism, increasing condensation is to be observed. Once there were only church clocks; now people carry clocks in their pockets. That is to say, the mechanism which once required for its wheels and springs the space provided by a church clock, now finds room enough in

---

[1] Wilhelm Müller: *Gedichte*, i. p. 26; "Thränenregen," p. 194; "Dasselbe noch einmal."

[2] Lazarus: *Das Leben der Seele*, 2nd edition, p. 229.

a watch. In like manner, many an old tragedy does not contain more thoughts or more feeling than a Heine poem of two or three verses.

Heine's short stanza has, then, two advantages over Wilhelm Müller's—more passion, and much greater condensation of style.

In his favourite short iambic metre, Heine is influenced by Wilhelm Müller, in his trochees he resembles another Romantic, far more Romantic poet, Clemens Brentano. In Heine's *Romancero* there are some curious correspondences with Brentano's *Romanzen vom Rosenkranze* (" Romances of the Rosary "). These latter were written before *Romancero*, but as they were not published till 1853, Heine cannot possibly have been influenced by them.

In the second of the *Rosary Romances* we read of the hero, Cosmo, that :

> " Aus dem Wasserspiegel mahnt
> Ihn des Alters ernste Bote :
> Du wirst bald die Schuld bezahlen,
> Spricht des Hauptes Silberlocke." [1]

In Heine's posthumous poem *Bimini,* one of the divisions begins :

> " Einsam auf dem Strand von Cuba,
> Vor dem stillen Wasserspiegel,
> Steht ein Mensch und er betrachtet
> In der Flut sein Konterfei.
>
> Eben nicht mit sonderlichem
> Wohlgefallen scheint der Greis
> In dem Wasser zu betrachten
> Sein bekümmert Spiegelbildniss." [2]

Metre, situation, idea are identical in the two passages.

---

[1] The solemn messengers of age, the white locks of the man who gazes at him from the water-mirror, cry : Soon thou must pay thy debt.

[2] On the shore of Cuba's island
Stands an old man solitary,
Gazing at his own reflection
In the tranquil water-mirror.

Not with any special pleasure
Does the sad and aged man
See beneath him in the water
His own image, sorrowful.

There is also a certain resemblance between the tale of a mystery-book in the Ninth Romance of the Rosary and the story of the beautiful casket in Heine's poem of *Jehuda ben Halevy*.[1] Only that Brentano's story of the passing of the mystery-book from hand to hand, through many ages, merely opens up to us a Romantic wonder-world, whereas Heine's tale of the wanderings of the casket is at the same time a jest at the vicissitudes of life : the pearls first belong to Smerdis, who gives them to Atossa, then to the great Alexander, who gives them to Thais, then in course of time to Cleopatra, to a Moorish sultan, to the regalia of Castille, and to the Baroness Solomon Rothschild, in a compliment to whom the life-history of the casket terminates.

It is quite certain that Heine is indebted to Clemens Brentano for the subject of what in Germany is the best known and most sung of all his songs, the song of *Lorelei*, " Ich weiss nicht was soll es bedeuten."

As far back as 1802 Brentano had published, in his *Godwi*, a ballad entitled " Lorelei." It is not the story of a siren, but of a young girl of Bacharach on the Rhine, who was so beautiful that all men fell in love with her. She was accused of witchcraft. But the bishop, who ought to have condemned her to be burned, fell in love with her himself. · She desires to die, for the one man she loves will have nothing to say to her and has gone away ; so, on her way to the convent to which the bishop is sending her, she climbs a high cliff, Lurelei (Ley means slate-rock), and in despairing longing for her beloved, throws herself into the Rhine.

This ballad suggested to a writer called Nikolaus Vogt the fabrication of a Rhine legend, which he published in 1811, passing it off as an old one. In it Lorelei, on her way to the convent, sees the man of her heart sail past her on the Rhine, and throws herself from the cliff in grief at having failed to win him. Three of her adorers follow her to a watery grave. Hence a rock in that neighbourhood

[1] *Cf.* Eduard Grisebach : *Die deutsche Litteratur*, p. 254, &c. ; where, however, a definite influence is insisted on, regardless of Heine's priority.

is known by the name of the Dreiritterstein (Rock of the
Three Knights). The last incident was perhaps suggested
by the ending of Brentano's poem:

> " Wer hat dies' Lied gesungen?
> Ein Schiffer auf dem Rhein.
> Und immer hat geklungen
> Vom hohen Felsenstein :
>   Lore Lay !
>   Lore Lay !
>   Lore Lay !
> Als wären es unser Drei."[1]

From this fabricated legend a certain Count Loeben, in
1821, took the theme for a poem, *Lorelei*,[2] in which the
young girl who drowns herself is transformed into a mer-
maid, whose singing lures into the depths those who are
sailing past:

> " Da wo der Mondschein blitzet
> Um's hohe Felsgestein,
> Das Zauberfräulein sitzet
> Und schauet auf den Rhein.
>
> Es schauet herüber, hinüber,
> Es schauet hinab, hinauf,
> Die Schifflein ziehen vorüber,
> Lieb' Knabe, sieh nicht auf !
>
> Sie singt dir hold am Ohre,
> Sie blickt dich thöricht an,
> Sie ist die schöne Lore,
> Sie hat dir's angethan," &c.[3]

Now take Heine's world-famed poem, first a students'
song, then a popular song, melting and thrilling with the
tender harmony of melody and words. The direct imitation is unmistakable. The theme is the same, the metre is

---

[1] Who was it sang this song? A boatman on the Rhine. And still we heard
the cry, from the high cliff o'erhead : " Lore Lay ! Lore Lay ! Lore Lay !" Me-
seemed that we were three.

[2] A. Strodtmann : H. Heine's *Leben und Werke*, 2nd edition, i. 696.

[3] Where the moonlight glitters on the lofty cliff, there the magic-maiden sits, and
gazes on the Rhine. She looks across the stream, looks up the stream and down ;
softly the boats glide past—look not on her, O youth ! She sings so sweetly in your
ear, she looks at you bewitchingly ; she is the lovely Lore, and in her spells you're
caught.

the same, even some of the rhymes are the same : "blitzet—
sitzet ; " instead of " an—gethan, Kahn—gethan." But what
a difference ! Feeling has been added. First the personal
starting - point, the inexplicable melancholy of the nar-
rator and his inability to banish the old legend from his
thoughts, then the instantaneous, clear, definite picture of
the landscape :

> " Die Luft ist kühl, und es dunkelt,
> Und ruhig fliesst der Rhein,
> Der Gipfel des Berges funkelt
> Im Abendsonnenschein.
>
> Die schönste Jungfrau sitzet
> Dort oben wunderbar,
> Ihr gold'nes Geschmeide blitzet,
> Sie kämmt ihr goldenes Haar." [1]

And something more has been added — that element of
dæmonic passion which the earlier manipulators of the theme
were unable to communicate to it. Heine here represents
an elemental luring power, akin to that delineated with simpler
means and more powerful effect by Goethe in *Der Fischer*.
But Goethe, in conformity with his nature, describes a
tranquil, enchanting ensnarement ; Heine, in conformity
with his, an instantaneous, irresistible, maddening bewitch-
ment.

A still more profound insight into Heine's art, in the
making, and into the manner in which his fancy deals with
a theme, is perhaps to be gained by observing how he makes
use of a subject which offers itself to him in prose.

In Henri Beyle's book, *De l'amour*, he evidently found
the three following anecdotes, translated from the Arabic.
1. Sahid ben Agba one day asked an Arab: "Of what

---

[1] The cool air darkens, and listen,
> How softly flows the Rhine !
> The mountain peaks still glisten
> Where the evening sunbeams shine.
>
> The fairest maid sits dreaming
> In radiant beauty there.
> Her gold and her jewels are gleaming,
> She combeth her golden hair.

(E. LAZARUS.)

tribe art thou?" "Of that tribe," answered the Arabian, "in which men die when they love." "Then thou art of the tribe of Asra?" "Yea, verily, by the Lord of Kaaba!" "Whence comes it that ye love thus?" "Our women are beautiful, and our young men chaste." 2. A man once asked Arua ben Hezam of the tribe of Asra: "Is it true that ye love with a tenderness surpassing that of all other men?" "It is true," answered Arua. "Thirty young men of my tribe have I seen carried off by death, whose only sickness was that of love." 3. An Arab of the tribe Beni-Fazarat said one day to an Arab of the tribe Beni-Asra: "Ye think that to die of love is a sweet and noble death; whereas it is nought but weakness and foolishness." "Thou would'st not speak so," answered the other, "had'st thou seen the great dark, long-lashed eyes of our veiled women, seen their teeth gleam between their brown lips when they smile."

Here we have the origin of Heine's famous *Der Asra*: "Täglich ging die wunderschöne." He first paints the place for us—the garden with the fountain whose white waters flash; then he shows us the slave, standing there every day when the sultan's daughter comes to walk, paler every day; then he tells how the princess one evening closely questions the slave: "I would know thy name, thy race, thy family . . .":

> "Und der Sklave sprach: 'ich heisse
> Mohamet, ich bin aus Yemen
> Und mein Stamm sind jene Asra,
> Welche sterben, wenn sie lieben.'"[1]

Heine, as we see, has disdained all explanations. We enjoy the marvellous conciseness of these monumental words, this power as it were of hewing out the speech in stone. But, what, on closer investigation, is the spiritual substance of the poem? Not much more than a laconic combination of the words love and death. It is the same

---

[1] Spake the youthful slave, "My name is
Mahomet, I come from Yemen;
And by birth I am an Asra,
One who dieth when he loves."

(E. LAZARUS.)

combination that is to be found in all Heine's youthful poems, in the shape of love and suffering, love and poison, love and suicide—in Alfred de Musset, too, there is the same stereotyped coupling of *l'amour* and *la mort*.

Here, as in general with Heine, the expression is epigrammatic, therefore quite simple.

We have now sufficient material before us to give us a certain insight into the formation of Heine's poetic style. It will be interesting to study it finished and fully developed.

We may start from the last-mentioned poem with its epigrammatic point. It is characteristic of Heine that neither here nor elsewhere does he deeply concern himself with the true inwardness of a feeling ; he only, as a rule, points and sharpens the expression of it. This is the case even with the feeling of love, which he has treated more frequently than any other. And it is characteristic of his want of the power to put himself in another's place, that it has only been possible for him to give expression to masculine love ; he has never put a passionate utterance of feeling into the mouth of a woman.

Nothing would have been more impossible for Heine than to write such a poem as Goethe's famous :

> " Freudvoll und leidvoll,
> Gedankenvoll sein,
> Langen und bangen
> In schwebender Pein,
> Himmelhoch jauchzend,
> Zum Tode betrübt,
> Glücklich allein
> Ist die Seele die liebt." [1]

---

[1] Gladness
And sadness
And pensiveness blending ;
Yearning
And burning
In torment ne'er ending ;
Sad unto death,
Proudly soaring above,
Happy alone
Is the soul that doth love.
(BOWRING.)

For this is the living delineation of a woman's heart, this is the very inner life of love, its pulsation, its oscillation between bliss and woe. The epigrammatic quality of Heine's style alone would make such an unfolding of the emotional life impossible. And there is the same concentration when he narrates an event. It is a condensation without parallel in poetry; he produces his effect by making the briefest possible statement or suggestion. As an example of this take the lines:

> " Es war ein alter König,
> Sein Herz war schwer, sein Haupt war grau ;
> Der arme, alte König
> Er nahm eine junge Frau.
>
> Es war ein schöner Page,
> Blond war sein Haupt, leicht war sein Sinn,
> Er trug die seid'ne Schleppe
> Der jungen Königin." [1]

Observe the telling effect of the inversion : " Blond war sein Haupt ; " it is as if the verse began to rejoice and dance Then comes the end :

> " Kennst du das alte Liedchen?
> Es klingt so süss, es klingt so trüb ;
> Sie mussten beide sterben,
> Sie hatten sich viel zu lieb." [2]

This is admirable. But we are not told the story; we only suspect it as we suspect the story of the slave and the sultan's daughter. And here again love is coupled with death.

---

[1] There was an aged monarch,
His heart was sad, his head was grey ;
This foolish, fond old monarch
A young wife took one day.

There was a handsome page, too,
Fair was his hair and light his mien ;
The silken train he carried
Of the beautiful young queen.
(BOWRING.)

[2] Dost know the ancient ballad ?
It sounds so sweet, it sounds so sad :
Both of them had to perish
Too much love to each other they had.

L

A certain emptiness in Heine's conception of love strikes us here again. This love has no real substance, no spiritual significance. It was not till shortly before he lay down upon his death-bed that Heine began to describe a love that has real inward substance. The love of the *Buch der Lieder* is for the most part wrath excited by coldness or faithlessness, an unfruitful thing, that awakens no sympathy. The later of the love-poems are frequently sensual or frivolous, and the more exaggerated the expression, the less are we affected by the value of the feeling :

> " Mein Herz ist wie die Sonne,
> So flammend anzuseh'n.
> Und in ein Meer von Liebe
> Versinkt es gross und schön." [1]

There is too much self-observation and too much boastfulness in this youthful rodomontade. And it is the same with :

> " Ich hab' dich geliebet und liebe dich noch,
> Und fiele die Welt zusammen,
> Aus ihren Trümmern stiegen doch
> Hervor meiner Liebe Flammen." [2]

Admitting that this is probably so expressed for the sake of artistic effect, we must also admit that the style is a good, perfectly modern style. We can see it all with the mind's eye. The heart sinks like the sun into a sea. From the ruins of the world rise the flames of love. And still more powerful and much more picturesque is the scene in which the name of Agnes is written on the vault of heaven. What is wanting is substance in the feeling. Think, for

---

[1] My heart is like the sun, dear,
　Yon kindled flame above ;
　And sinks in large-orbed beauty
　Within a sea of love.
　　　　　(E. LAZARUS.)

[2] I have loved thee long, and I love thee now
　And, though the world should perish,
　O'er its dying embers still would glow
　The flames of the love I cherish.
　　　　　(LELAND.)

the sake of comparison, of those profoundly human lines of Goethe's:

> " Kanntest jeden Zug in meinem Wesen,
> Spähtest, wo die reinste Nerve klingt,
> Konntest mich mit einem Blicke lesen,
> Den so schwer ein sterblich Aug' durchdringt."[1]

—or of the following, which complete the impression:

> " Tropftest Mässigung dem heissen Blute,
> Richtetest den wilden, wirren Lauf,
> Und in deinen Engelsarmen ruhte
> Die zerstörte Brust sich wieder auf."[2]

This is the expression of the healthiest, fullest, mutual sympathy, of love's gratitude, of perfect understanding. For such feeling Heine did not find expression until, with the shadow of death upon him, he loved *la Mouche*, the guardian angel of his death-bed. Until then it is never the healthy, tranquillising, happy element in love that he concerns himself with. It is in another domain that he is master. The modern poet, he reproduces passionate desire with a Correggio-like blending of colours and tones that is more effective than Goethe's antique limpidity. With Goethe desire is Greek or Italian. Think, for instance, of the poem of the orange:

> " Ich trete zu dem Baume
> Und sage: Pomeranze!
> Du reife Pomeranze;
> Du süsse Pomeranze!
> Ich schüttle, fühl', ich schüttle,
> O fall in meinen Schoos!"[3]

---

[1] Thou knewest every impulse of my nature, thine eye detected where the nerve thrilled keenest, thou couldst read me at a glance, me, so impenetrable to mortal eye.

[2] The hot blood by thee was tempered, the wild, aimless course by thee directed; and in thine angel arms the torn breast found rest and healing

> [3] I take my stand beneath the tree,
> And cry: O orange!
> O orange ripe!
> O orange sweet!
> Feel, feel how I shake thy tree!
> O fall into my lap!

Then compare the feeling, the glow, the fragrance, the exuberance of such a poem of desire as Heine's wonderful : *Die Lotosblume ängstigt sich vor der Sonne Pracht* ("The lotus-flower is fearful of the sun's resplendent beam").

It is very characteristic of the two poets that (as has already been noted), whenever the representation of love-longing glides into a delineation of foreign lands, Goethe prefers to paint Italy, Heine Hindostan. In Mignon's song of longing, without a superlative or a diminutive, with a power like that of a God, Goethe summons before our eyes the picture of the classic land where the citrons bloom. There is a power in it all, a force in each distinguishing trait, that Heine does not attain to. But compare this with the bewitching sweetness of Heine's *Auf Flügeln des Gesanges* ("Oh, I would bear thee, my love, my bride, afar on the wings of song"), the dreamy longing, the charm and the mystery of the perspective that opens out to us :

> " Es hüpfen herbei und lauschen
> Die frommen, klugen Gazelln,
> Und in der Ferne rauschen
> Des heiligen Stromes Welln."[1]

This is an immortal stanza. Goethe, even when he gives the reins to longing, is always, like his own goldsmith of Ephesus, the great, wise heathen, who makes images of the gods ; in Heine's visionary brain there was that particle of divine frenzy without which it had been impossible for the Düsseldorf merchant's son to understand and reproduce the fatalistic, self-effacing dreaminess of ancient India.

Heine's peculiarities of style stand out even more sharply against the background of Goethe's, when we compare the way in which the two give expression to what is not exactly desire, but the pure longing of love.

Think of the following lines, which Goethe puts into Mignon's mouth :

---

[1] Gazelles come bounding from the brake,
  And pause, and look shyly round ;
And the waves of the sacred river make
  A far-off slumb'rous sound.
                    (Sir THEODORE MARTIN.)

" Nur wer die Sehnsucht kennt, weiss was ich leide,
    Allein und abgetrennt von aller Freude,
    Seh' ich an's Firmament nach jener Seite.
    Ach, der mich liebt und kennt, ist in der Weite.—
    Es schwindelt mir, es brennt mein Eingeweide.
    Nur wer die Sehnsucht kennt, weiss was ich leide." [1]

This is the master in the fulness of his power.   Much
art has been expended in the representation of the wearing
monotony of longing—the five doubly rhyming lines, the
languishing metre—interrupted by the audacious, realistic
expression : " Es schwindelt mir, es brennt mein Einge-
weide."

Now compare with this, one of Heine's most perfect
expressions of pure love-longing, and we shall see what the
plastic fancy and the perfected laconicism of style which we
traced in course of development have succeeded in producing for time and eternity :

" Ein Fichtenbaum steht einsam
    Im Norden auf kahler Höh'.
    Ihn schläfert : mit weisser Decke
    Umhüllen ihn Eis und Schnee.

Er träumt von einer Palme,
    Die fern im Morgenland
    Einsam und schweigend trauert
    Auf brennender Felsenwand." [2]

---

[1] My grief no mortals know, except the yearning !
    Alone, a prey to woe, all pleasure spurning,
    Up towards the sky I throw a gaze discerning.
    He who my love doth know seems ne'er returning ;
    With strange and fiery glow *my heart is burning.**
    My grief no mortals know, except the yearning.
                                            (BOWRING.)

[2] A pine-tree stands alone on
    A bare bleak northern height ;
    The ice and snow they swathe it
    As it sleeps there, all in white.

'Tis dreaming of a palm-tree,
    In a far-off Eastern land,
    That mourns, alone and silent,
    On a ledge of burning sand.
                            (Sir THEODORE MARTIN.)

* In the original, *my bowels are burning.*

This is hardly rhymed. The only real rhyme is the very commonplace *Land* and *Wand*. The pine dreams in the snow, the palm grieves dumbly in the burning heat—that is all. It is not seen, it is fancied or invented, hence it cannot be painted (though I did once see a painting of it in a German exhibition, an idiotically absurd, double picture) ; but it is, nevertheless, an unforgettable, an immortal poem. And the reason is that the symbol is so marvellously effective in its simplicity—these two clear outlines instinct with feeling, which express the impossibility of overcoming the obstacle which prevents the union of two who really belong to each other.

If Goethe's strength lies in the expression of healthy feelings, comparatively simple and uncomplicated, Heine's lies in the expression of complex modern feeling, of feelings whose unsound state is the result of painful experiences. Goethe could never have written the following lines, with their jarring contrasts and enigmatical meaning :

> " Wenn ich in deine Augen seh'
> So schwindet all mein Leid und Weh :
>
> . . . .
>
> Doch wenn du sprichst : ich liebe dich !
> So muss ich weinen bitterlich." [1]

Why must he weep ? I have heard the naïve answer : Because she is lying. Alas ! it is not such a simple matter as that. He has heard these words from other lips, lips which have now ceased to utter words of love ; he knows how long such a passion as a rule lasts, and the sound of her voice startles him out of his forgetfulness—he doubts the durability of her feeling or the durability of his own.

It is very interesting to note the way in which Heine had wrestled with these words. Originally the last line

---

[1] Whene'er I look into thine eyes,
Then every fear that haunts me flies :

. . . . .

But when thou sayest : " I love thee ; "
Then must I weep, and bitterly.

(Sir THEODORE MARTIN.)

was : " Dann wein' ich still und bitterlich." Then the word
" bitterlich " was altered to " freudiglich," which changed
the original tenor of the poem, and finally the line received
its present form.[1]

Heine was not happy enough and not great enough to
attain to reconciliation with existence. It was not possible,
apart from all else, that the man who was so long an exile,
so long sick to death, should look upon life with the same
eyes as the man who was thoroughly sound and healthy, in
affluent circumstances, honoured by the great majority, the
friend of his sovereign. Hence the expressions of revolt,
of bitterness, and of cynicism so frequently to be found
in Heine are exceedingly rare in Goethe. Goethe, as a
rule, puts them into the mouth of his Mephistopheles.
Heine, who was destitute of the dramatic faculty, is himself responsible for every outburst, because he always
speaks in his own name. Goethe's bitterest utterances,
moreover, are not contained in his works. It is only in
the Paralipomena to *Faust*, for instance, that we find this
passage :

> " Nach kurzem Lärm legt Fama sich zur Ruh,
>   Vergessen wird der Held so wie der Lotterbube,
>   Der grösste König schliesst die Augen zu,
>   Und jeder Hund bepisst gleich seine Grube." [2]

Heine dwells upon the ideas which Goethe only calls
up to banish again. Goethe, too, can be blasphemous. He
wrote that poem which is so frequently quoted, so seldom
understood : *Wer nie sein Brod mit Thränen ass* (" He that
with tears did never eat his bread "). It is a bitter, passionate appeal against the ordering of the world. But its
bitterness is a bitterness that is choked with tears, not the
wild and desperate bitterness of Heine's splendid *Fragen*

---

[1] H. Hüffer : *Aus dem Leben Heinrich Heines*, p. 153.

[2] Fame's short-liv'd turmoil o'er, she sleeps,
    Hero and waif, oblivion's their doom ;
    The greatest king, life o'er, his eyes doth close,
    And straightway every dog defiles his tomb.
                                    (J. B.)

("Questions"), or the poem *Lass die heiligen Parabeln* ("Holy parable discarding"), in which occur the lines:

> "Warum schleppt sich blutend, elend,
>   Unter Kreuzlast der Gerechte,
> Während glücklich als ein Sieger
>   Trabt auf hohem Ross der Schlechte?
>
> Also fragen wir beständig,
>   Bis man uns mit einer Handvoll
> Erde endlich stopft die Mäuler,
>   Aber ist das eine Antwort?" [1]

The expression is here, as usual with Heine, on a lower plane, more terrestrial, more boldly outspoken, yet by no means unworthy of the subject.

Outbursts of satiety and weariness of life are not infrequent with him. We do not need to search long among his poems to find expressions of the mood of having done for good and all with principle, with endeavour. Nothing of this kind is to be found in Goethe. His *Vanitas vanitatum,* the song *Ich hab' meine Sache auf Nichts gestellt* ("My trust in nothing now is placed") has, very significantly, become a convivial drinking song. In other words, there is no real, bitter earnest about Goethe's desperation; therefore it soon changes into jovial recklessness. Goethe has not Heine's overpowering feeling of the misery of life, and in so far he is really less Christian.

If it is instructive to compare the two poets' lyric expression of fatalistic indifference, it is equally so to compare their expression of the feeling of aspiration, of manly resolve. In this case we may take the song *Feiger Gedanken* ("Cowardly Thoughts") from *Claudine von Villa Bella,* as characteristic of

---

[1] Wherefore bends the Just One, bleeding
   'Neath the cross's weight laborious,
 While upon his steed the Wicked
   Rides all-proudly and victorious?

 Thus are we for ever asking,
   Till at length our mouths securely
 With a clod of earth are fastened—
   That is not an answer, surely?
                                (BOWRING).

Goethe ; it might serve as a motto for his conduct throughout life. One can hardly imagine a more vigorous expression of manly determination than that of the lines :
" Allen Gewalten zum Trutz sich erhalten," &c. (A bold
front shown, to powers of earth and heaven).

Compare with this Heine's poem, *An die Jungen* (" To
the Young "). The impetuous rush of the rhythm and the
picturesque quadruple rhyme would alone suffice to make
this a splendid, fascinating composition. The first verse,
with its allusion to the golden apples which Hippomenes
dropped in front of Atalanta, is a whole poem in itself :

> " Lass dich nicht kirren, lass dich nicht wirren
>   Durch goldne Aepfel in deinem Lauf.
> Die Schwerter klirren, die Pfeile schwirren,
>   Doch halten sie nicht den Helden auf." [1]

From the picture and example of the hero, who will not
be stopped in his career, we pass to that of Alexander.
What is wanted is determination and boldness :

> " Ein kühnes Beginnen ist halbes Gewinnen,
>   Ein Alexander erbeutet die Welt,
> Kein langes Besinnen ! Die Königinnen
>   Erwarten schon kniend den Sieger im Zelt.
>
> Wir wagen und werben ! besteigen als Erben
>   Des alten Darius' Bett und Thron.
> O süsses Verderben ! o blühender Sterben !
>   Berauschter Triumphtod zu Babylon ! " [2]

---

[1] Heed not the confusion, resist the illusion
    Of golden apples that lie in thy way !
  The swords are clashing, the arrows are flashing,
    But they cannot long the hero delay.
                                        (BOWRING.)

[2] A daring beginning is half way to winning,
  ' An Alexander once conquered the earth !
  Restrain each soft feeling ! the queens are all kneeling
    In the tent, to reward thy victorious worth.

  Surmounting each burden, we win as our guerdon
    The bed of Darius of old, and his crown ;
  O deadly seduction ! O blissful destruction !
    To die drunk with triumph in Babylon town.
                                        (BOWRING.)

Upon victory follows the homage of the queens, then sweet perdition, seductive ruin, death in the intoxication of triumph—what Sardanapalian sentiment in this appeal to youth, this exhortation to relentless determination! The fight here is for honour, and for women as the spoil of battle, not that struggle for the combatant's own individual freedom, of which Goethe writes so simply :

> " Nimmer sich beugen,
> Kräftig sich zeigen,
> Rufet die Arme
> Der Götter herbei." [1]

Goethe's feeling is purer and fuller, the music of his language is simpler ; with Heine the melody is, as it were, gorgeously orchestrated. In Goethe's case there is nothing for the eye, not a single picture. It is characteristic that his idea is the grander, Heine's the more modern, more complex, just as Heine's metrical expression is more sensuously insinuating, produced by an art which devotes more attention to detail.

Now take a picturesque, descriptive subject—the Three Kings of the East, as they are called to mind at the Feast of the Epiphany. It is treated in a broad, lively, popular, genuinely naïve manner in Goethe's *Epiphanias:* " Die heil'gen drei König' mit ihrem Stern " (The Three Kings of the East with their Star). The three kings, the white, the brown, and the black, are described as they appeared when they went about, dressed up, from house to house in the country ; and the poem ends :

> " Die heil'gen drei König' sind wohlgesinnt,
> Sie suchen die Mutter und das Kind,
> Der Joseph fromm sitzt auch dabei,
> Der Ochs und Esel liegen auf Streu." [2]

---

[1] Nevermore yield thee !
Show life has steeled thee !
Thus call the arms of
The Gods to thine aid.

[2] The Three Kings of the East with reverence lowly
Seek out the babe and mother holy,
Good Joseph's there too, and close by
The ox and ass on the litter lie.

Heine does not view the legend in a more religious light than Goethe, but he settles his features into a more serious expression, speaks more concisely, draws with a sharper outline, obtains a totally different effect. Goethe rouses and cheers his readers by his broad and merry artlessness; Heine's words bore their way into men's minds and leave their sting there. He seems to aim at producing the same effect as that of an old Florentine painting .

> " Die heil'gen drei König' aus Morgenland,
>   Sie frugen in jedem Städtchen :
> Wo geht der Weg nach Bethlehem,
>   Ihr lieben Buben und Mädchen ?
>
> Die Jungen und Alten, sie wussten es nicht,
>   Die Könige zogen weiter,
> Sie folgten einem goldenen Stern,
>   Der leuchtete lieblich und heiter.
>
> Der Stern blieb steh'n über Josephs Haus,
>   Da sind sie hineingegangen,
> Das Oechslein brüllte, das Kindlein schrie,
>   Die heil'gen drei Könige sangen." [1]

There is a certain amount of waggery in this. What a a concert ! But also, what painting ! The fewest words possible—not a stroke, not a touch too much, and the most telling, prompt effect.

Let us now, in conclusion, think of one of those abstract figures which occur in all lyric poetry—more or less carefully wrought-out personifications of an idea such as peace, happiness, unhappiness—and in this domain also compare Heine

[1] The three holy kings from the Eastern land
        Inquired in every city :
    Where is the road to Bethlehem,
        Ye boys and maidens pretty ?

The young and the old, they could not tell,
        The kings went onward discreetly ;
    They follow'd the track of a golden star,
        That sparkled brightly and sweetly.

The star stood still over Joseph's house
        And they entered the dwelling lowly,
    The oxen bellowed, the infant cried,
        While sang the three kings holy.
                                        (BOWRING.)

with Goethe. Here again it will be observed that Goethe has the fuller note, Heine the firmer outline.

Goethe wrote these lines to peace :

> " Der du von dem Himmel bist,
>   Alles Leid und Schmerzen stillest,
>   Den, der doppelt elend ist,
>   Doppelt mit Erquickung füllest,
>   Ach, ich bin des Treibens müde !
>   Was soll all der Schmerz, die Lust ?
>   Süsser Friede !
>   Komm, ach komm in meine Brust ! " [1]

There is no picture here, no real personification. There is a crescendo movement through the first six lines, which culminates in the outburst : " Süsser Friede ! "——though we could not feel quite certain that this outburst was coming.

Now take Heine's personifications of fortune and misfortune, as contained in the following verses :

> " Das Glück ist eine leichte Dirne
>   Und weilt nicht gern am selben Ort,
>   Sie streicht das Haar dir von der Stirne
>   Und küsst dich rasch und flattert fort.
>
> Frau Unglück hat im Gegentheile
>   Dich liebefest an's Herz gedrückt,
>   Sie sagt, sie habe keine Eile,
>   Setzt sich zu dir an's Bett und strickt."

---

[1] Child of heaven, that soothing calm
      On every pain and sorrow pourest,
   And a doubly healing balm
      Find'st for him whose need is sorest,
   Oh, I am of life aweary !
      What availeth its unrest—
   Pain that findeth no release,
      Joy that at the best is dreary ?
          Gentle peace,
   Come, oh come unto my breast ! (Sir THEODORE MARTIN.)

[2] Oh, Joy, she is a lichtsome hizzy,
      She winna bide wi' ye ava' ;
   She strokes your broo an' maks ye dizzy
      Wi' ae fond kiss, then flits awa'.

   Dame Sorrow is a canty kimmer,
      A fond embrace ye'll hae frae her ;
   She vows she's naewise thrang, the limmer,
      Knits by your bed an' winna stir. (W. A.)

Seldom have two ideas been transformed into two living forms with so few strokes ; and there is nothing much finer in all modern myth-creation than the last two lines, between which are to be read the record of profound and terrible experience.

Heine, as we have seen, makes his earliest appearance in the Romantic school, and learns his trade from A. W. Schlegel, who imparts to him his own correct taste. In the earliest period of his development he is addicted to Romantic ghost stories and Romantic archaisms. Then, in the matter of metre, he begins to study and imitate Wilhelm Müller ; in his most famous poem he borrows from Clemens Brentano. He soon forms his own style, the distinguishing feature of which is extreme condensation of thought, feeling, and imagery. Heine makes everything present and living, introduces even into tranquil themes a nervous, at times dæmonic, passion, not infrequently exaggerates until he becomes grotesque, occasionally exchanges the light of day for the glaring brightness of electric light—a kind of unnaturalness which is nevertheless to be found in nature. His most effective poetic quality is pregnant brevity.

By reason of the blend of wit and imagination in his nature, he is inclined to produce his effects by contrasts, to seek for striking disharmonies and incongruities ; he has a special fancy for the effect produced by letting a commonplace, vulgar reality imperceptibly make way for a poetic vision, or allowing such a vision to fade and evaporate and give place to all too familiar reality.

His style is essentially modern—everything graphic, everything perspicuous. What is it that constitutes a great writer ? The possession of the power to call forth mental visions or moods, visions by means of moods or moods by means of visions. It was especially the latter faculty that Heine cultivated in himself ; he never fails in the matter of clear outline and picturesque effect.

At his zenith he can no longer be compared with his teachers and contemporaries. To gauge the power and versatility of his style it was necessary to compare it with the greatest style of the age—with Goethe's. In the process he often, as we have seen, comes far short, but it not so very seldom happens that he establishes his right to almost equal admiration. It is, however, enough for him that it is possible, and now and again necessary, to compare him with Goethe.

A style is the expression of a personality and a weapon in the warfare of literature. Goethe's style, with all its greatness, is not sufficiently complex to grapple with modern ideas. But Heine's, that weapon which in its best days was as finely tempered as those old Spanish blades which could be bent like osiers, but which no armour could snap, was better suited than any other to cope with modern life in its hardness and ugliness, its charm, its restlessness, and its wealth of glaring contrasts. It also possessed in the highest degree the power of working upon the nerves of modern readers, who have more inclination for spiced dishes and heating beverages than for plain food and pure wine.

XVI

HEINE

THERE can be little doubt that nothing has been more injurious to Heine's general reputation than his indiscreet loquacity on sexual subjects. Whole groups of his poems are in ill repute on this account; those, for instance, which compose the collection *Verschiedene* (Various), most of which have been unjustly condemned, although there are certainly some which are anything but sublime in their theme or refined in their treatment of it. In *Der Gott und die Bajadere* ("The God and the Bayadere") Goethe had shown how even a very equivocal subject can be ennobled by sublimity of style. And even when, as in the Venetian epigrams, he treats of Bayaderes who are certainly not purified by love, and dwells upon the poet's relations with them, the antique metre in itself produces the effect of distance, and we are not offended by any objectionable word. These few epigrams, too, lie almost buried in the mass of Goethe's writings. Moreover, in reading them, we feel that he is the man whom nature created in order that she might learn from him what she is like in her entirety.

With Heine, communicativeness on the subject of his relations with the other sex occupies too important a place, and is not always in good taste. It gains him ten readers for one whom it alienates, but it sometimes happens that the one thus lost was worth more than the ten gained.

And yet this frankness is, in a manner, his strength. It need not have been so personal, but it is quite indispensable in one who desires to compass not only the tragic, but also the comic hemisphere. And in this quality, and in his many shameless personal attacks, he resembles the greatest comic poet of all times.

Towards the end of his *Winter's Tale*, immediately after

the wanton passage in which he smells out the future of
Germany by putting his head down the opening of Charle-
magne's night-throne, he declares that the noblest of the
Graces have tuned the strings of his lyre, and that this lyre
is the same which was sounded in days gone by, by his
father, "the late Aristophanes, the favourite of the Muses."
He adds that in his last chapter he has attempted to imitate
The Birds, "the best of father's dramas."

He thus, we observe, prided himself on artistic descent
from the greatest comic poet of ancient Greece.

For a moment we are taken aback.   Other German
poets, such as Platen and Prutz, have imitated the form of
the Aristophanic comedy, its trimeters, choruses, parabases,
the whole of that irregular and yet regular form of art built
up by the Greek comic school; but Heine never even made
an attempt to master this poetical form, or any other.   It
is characteristic of him that, persevering and conscientious
as he was in ensuring the telling precision of the single
metrical or prose expression (I never saw a manuscript with
so many corrections as that of his *Atta Troll*, in the Royal
Library of Berlin), it was impossible for him to submit to
the artistic restriction of any of the great poetic forms.   It
tallies with this, that in his longer works the plan of the
whole is quite vague, but every single line has been gone
through again and again.

There is probably no exaggeration in saying that he
never, in his capacity as an artist, set himself a task and
carried it out.

Once only he attempted to write a long, connected prose
work, a romance or novel.   Whether, as some maintain, the
greater part of the manuscript was destroyed by a fire, or
whether, as I for one believe, the work was never completed,
the fact remains that all we have of it is a fragment.   And
even this fragment, *Der Rabbi von Bacharach*, is, when carefully examined, nothing but a very much antedated transcription of Heine's own private experiences.

Nor did he ever attempt a severely connected metrical
composition.   His only long poems, *Atta Troll* and *Deutschland, ein Wintermärchen* ("Germany, a Winter's Tale"), are

irregular, whimsical fantasies, soap-bubbles rocked upon cobweb tissue of the brain, only connected by a uniformity of tone and design.

The idea of translating or adapting Aristophanes would never have occurred to Heine. He was not like Goethe, who, in spite of his enormous original productivity, condescended to translate and adapt for his countrymen (Diderot, Benvenuto Cellini, Voltaire). When Goethe made acquaintance with Aristophanes, he was enchanted with him, and it is Goethe, not Heine, who undertakes to transplant *The Birds* on to German soil ; but it is characteristic that in his hands the play undergoes a metamorphosis, is transformed from a political into a literary satire. In Goethe's play the two discontented politicians have become literary adventurers ; in the owl (as proved by a letter from Jacobi to Heine) he satirises Klopstock, in the parrot, young Cramer. It was in the epilogue to this adaptation that Goethe bestowed on Aristophanes the immortal appellation, " der ungezogene Liebling der Grazien " (the froward favourite of the Graces), which suits Heine so well.

Heine was too lazy ever to have studied, translated, adapted, or imitated an ancient classic poet, but, supposing him to have done so, he would never, like Goethe or Platen, have made pure literary comedies of the Aristophanic plays ; it was the grand political satire that attracted him.

It is probable that Heine is the wittiest man that ever lived, or at least the wittiest man of modern times. Voltaire is, undoubtedly, looked upon as a sort of personification of wit ; but his wit is sensible and dry, not poetic and imaginative like Heine's.

Platen, the proud and stiff, acted unwisely when he wrote the work in which he satirises Heine, *Der romantische Oedipus,* in the outward form and style of the Aristophanic comedy, for he had nothing in common with Aristophanes but fine versification and coarse language. Heine, on the contrary, had all the chief qualities of Aristophanes combined—wit, wanton wildness, imagination, lyric sweetness, shamelessness, and grace. Without grace and wit, shamelessness is undoubtedly a base and repellent quality. But in this combination with noble qualities it is uncommon. The Aristophanic poet must not, cannot have the pride which shrinks from amusing the coarse minded, who only understand a man when they meet him in the mire. He dares not shrink from debasing himself to a certain point, in order to gain a wider field of vantage.

It is useless for an author to attempt, as Platen did, to impress his readers before all else with the idea of his high-mindedness, and to inspire them with respect for his person; it is useless for him to proclaim that he intends "to crush his antagonists with genuine wit." It is not possible to appear at one and the same time in the character of a refined gentleman and an Aristophanic poet. A man is a failure in the latter rôle if he sets more value on the esteem of others than on the triumph of art. The compensation in the case of the true Aristophanic poet is, that his poetry has a compass unattainable by the dignified poets (a Schiller or a Hugo); it reflects the whole of human life, from its highest functions to its lowest.

Though there are so few formal points of contact between Heine's lyric-satiric poems and the great fantastic comedies of Aristophanes, it is nevertheless probable that since the days of ancient Greece there has been no wit so nearly akin to the wit of Aristophanes as Heinrich Heine's.

This assertion is not based upon any misconception of the extraordinary dissimilarity in the character of their life-work. The Aristophanic comedy with its grand and exact technical structure is the expression of the artistic culture of a whole nation, a monument that commemorates the religious festivals of which it was the outcome. Aristophanes built upon a foundation laid, a substructure prepared, by a whole line of distinguished predecessors, whose style was similar, whose talent was akin to his, and to whose labours he succeeded, in much the same manner as Shakespeare did to the work of his predecessors; hence the Aristophanic comedy as a form of art is to a much greater extent a collective production than Heine's stanza is. Quite apart from our knowledge of the fact that Eupolis and Kratinos accused Aristophanes of making inadmissible use of the ideas of his predecessors, we can see for ourselves, from one of his own comedies, *The Knights*, that plays with titles like the Birds, the Wasps, the Frogs had already been produced by the comic poet Magnes ; the chorus disguised as reptiles, insects, birds, was thus not a thing invented by Aristophanes, it was an inheritance. It is only because we are not acquainted with the Greek poet's predecessors that his life's work appears to us to be a purely individual pro-duction, the type of grand fantastic comedy, in comparison with whose exuberance of life almost all modern comedy seems spiritless and weak.

His world is the topsy-turvy world. When, in the *Peace*, Trygaios saddles a stinking carrion-beetle and on it, as his Pegasus, mounts through the clouds to the dwellings of the Gods, or when he drags Peace up by a fathom-long rope from the deep well into which she has been thrown by War, these proceedings are represented as if there were nothing in the least unusual or impossible about them ; no explanation is offered ; and we are compelled to believe in them. When, in *The Birds*, we hear two silly fellows, who are posing as philosophers, disclose their crazy plans for building a city in the clouds, it all sounds very mad, and when we see the Birds receive these men with reverence, we do not conceive any higher opinion of their intelligence, we are only struck by the comicality of the birds being so stupid as to put their trust in them. But when we hear that the city is actually built, that fortune has attended the enterprise and that it has been crowned with success, we feel that the world set before us here is not our own every-day world, but one with whose laws things are compatible which are contrary to the laws of ours.

This new world is purely fantastic, in so far as it is antagonistic to the laws of probability and of nature. It is a world in which madness triumphs, and the poet pre-tends that this is as it should be. Not till the spectator begins to wonder *where* this topsy-turvy world can be, *where* such things happen, *where* political effrontery on such a gigantic scale, far from being confounded and put to shame, wins confidence and is rewarded——not till then is he led back to reality, to the recognition in this world of his own world, his own home, Athens.

Three of the Aristophanic comedies in our possession, *The Birds, The Frogs,* and *Peace,* do not pass, or pass only in part, on earth ; they are meteoric or underground dramas. And it is in these only that Gods are represented, and then merely that they may be rated, ridiculed, or beaten. In the world of reality they do not reveal themselves ; for it is only in the world of fancy that they are believed in.

Heine, the modern poet, dares not ask his readers to follow him into the same sort of supernatural world ; and yet he cannot dispense with the supernatural ; hence that constantly recurring use and abuse of dreams, for which hardly any parallel is to be found among other modern poets. Within the frame-work, as it were, of the dream, he dares to be extraordinary, to be Aristophanic.

As has been already remarked, he resembles Aristophanes in the depth of his shamelessness and in the height of his lyric flight.

Allusions to difficulties of digestion and the like, play a less important part in Heine's writings than in those of Aristophanes, who, however, we must remember, himself declared that he despised this kind of comicality. According to him its only recommendation was that it provoked the laughter of the least cultured part of the public. But such things are frequently referred to by Heine too, at times in the plainest of terms (notably in his attack on Platen), and with him, almost as often as with Aristophanes, we have to be on our guard against certain noisome insects.

Heine of course cannot allow himself the same freedom of speech in sexual matters as the old Greek did, but to make up for this, he never hesitates to make an allusion that will atone for any want of outspokenness. And now and then there is almost no circumlocution ; what as a general rule is indicated by a smile or a grimace is shouted to all and sundry with a loud guffaw, as, for instance, at the conclusion of *Deutschland,* and in such poems as *Der Ungläubige* (" The Unbeliever ").

And yet again, as with Aristophanes, so with Heine ;

from this constant insistence upon that in man which reminds us of his dwelling-place during the earliest stages of
his development, he rises to the purest, most delicate lyric
utterance. He, who so thoroughly comprehends the material origin of all living things, in one of his poems derives
them all from the song of the nightingale:

> " Im Anfang war die Nachtigall
> Und sang ihr Lied : Zükükt ! Zükükt ! " [1]

We cannot but be reminded of the beautiful lines in *The
Birds*:

> " Gentlest and dearest, thou dost sing
> Consorting still with mine thy lay,
> Lov'd partner of my wild-wood way,
> Thou'rt come, thou'rt come ; all hail ! all hail !
> I see thee now, sweet nightingale."
>
> (CARY.)

Heine, like Aristophanes, makes merry at the expense
of the Gods. His satire is naturally more cautious than the
old Greek's ; the modern world does not stand jesting on
this subject as well as the ancient world did. In the works
of Heine, who wrote under the censorship of the police and
of modern society, we have no counterpart to the scene in
The Frogs, where Dionysus, the god of comedy, who has
shown himself both boastful and cowardly, gets one thrashing after another, and at last appeals to his own priest, who
occupied a place of honour among the spectators, to help
him in his extremity. And yet there is not very much,
from playful banter to broad jocularity and the most biting
sarcasm, that Heine does not allow himself. Hyacinth's
valuation of the various religions (in the *Reisebilder*) is well
known. He will have nothing to say to Catholicism, which,
with its pealing of bells, its incense fumes, and its " Melan-
cholik," is no religion for a citizen of Hamburg ; he tests
Protestantism by buying lottery tickets with the numbers
which he finds on the hymn-board in a Lutheran church ;
and he disposes of Judaism in the well-known words : " It

---

[1] In the beginning was the nightingale,
Who sang her song: Zükükt ! Zükükt !

is not a religion at all, but a misfortune." In the amusing and audacious verses entitled *Disputation*, a rabbi and a Capucin monk defend their respective dogmas ; each, in offensive terms, boasts of the happiness conferred by his doctrine ; the royal bride who is to decide the dispute declares herself incapable of doing so, as the only thing she has noted is that they both stink. In a passage in his book on Börne, Heine's mockery of religion becomes almost dramatic. He tells how, when he was living on the island .of Helgoland, he was often drawn into arguments with a Prussian Councillor of Justice on the subject of the Trinity. During one of these discussions, the thinness of the flooring permitted them to hear distinctly what was being said in the room below, where a phlegmatic Dutch-man was instructing their hostess how to distinguish between cod, haberdine, and stock-fish—which are in reality one and the same fish, but with three names, denoting three different degrees of saltness.

As far as earthly potentates are concerned, Heine's comic assaults are not less audacious, not less fantastic than those of Aristophanes. Aristophanes showed courage in his attacks on Kleon and Theramenes ; he occasionally chanced to de-fend the good cause ; but as a rule it was the bad cause he upheld, for he made himself the spokesman of an indefen-sible conservatism, and of unjust personal animosities. Heine was less frequently unjust or mean, and he was never con-servative. But he recalls Aristophanes to us by his aristo-cratic propensities, by the grim character of his personal attacks (those on Meyerbeer, for instance), and also by the form of these attacks, for example the amusing way in which he turns to account well-known, pathetic passages from other poets.

He made witty attacks on Frederick William IV., in *Deutschland*, where Hammonia warns Heine himself against "the king of Thule," and in the poem *Der neue Alexander ;* and he wrote a whole series of satirical poems on King Ludwig of Bavaria and his doings. This latter king, whom Heine in past days had extolled, was flattered as a Mæcenas by a whole band of contemporary artists and poets. In the

Lobgesänge auf König Lüdewig, Heine falls foul of all his weaknesses, his gallery of beauty in the Munich palace, his bad verses, his annoyance when several of the famous men of science and artists whom he patronised allowed themselves to be persuaded to leave Bavaria and settle in Prussia. On the subject of the gallery of beauty we have:

> " Er liebt die Kunst, und die schönsten Frau'n,
> Die lässt er porträtiren,
> Er geht in diesem gemalten Serail
> Als Kunst-Eunuch spazieren." [1]

When writing of the migration to Prussia of the various men of note, Heine seizes the opportunity to give a side-hit at his old scape-goat, Massmann :

> " Der Schelling und der Cornelius,
> Sie mögen von dannen wandern,
> Dem einen erlosch im Kopf die Vernunft,
> Die Phantasie dem Andern.
>
> Doch dass man aus meiner Krone stahl
> Die beste Perle, dass man
> Mir meinen Turnkunstmeister geraubt,
> Das Menschenjuwel, den Massmann,
>
> Das hat mich gebeugt, das hat mich geknickt,
> Das hat mir die Seele zerschmettert,
> Mir fehlt jetzt der Mann, der in seiner Kunst
> Den höchsten Pfahl erklettert. . . ." [2]

---

[1] In love with art, he collects fair dames
In counterfeit presentment,
And in this painted harem finds,
Art-eunuch-like, contentment.

[2] That Schelling should go, and Cornelius too,
Without a tear I can see—
The one has lost his reasoning power,
The other all his fancy.

But to steal from my crown its brightest gem,
Its pearl of price, was cruel ;
My master-gymnast they've filched away,
Massmann, mankind's chief jewel.

This crime has bent and broken me,
'Tis soul-destroying, cynical—
I have lost the man who had clambered up
To his art's supremest pinnacle.

Of King Ludwig's essays in poetry he writes

> " Herr Ludwig ist ein grosser Poet,
> Und singt er, so stürzt Apollo
> Vor ihm auf die Knie und bittet und fleht :
> Halt ein ! ich werde sonst toll, o ! " [1]

Still wittier is the parody of King Ludwig's poetical style, in the inscription above the resting-place of Atta Troll in the Bavarian *Walhalla :*

> " Atta Troll, Tendenzbär, sittlich—
> Religiös ; als Gatte brünstig ;
> Durch Verführtsein von dem Zeitgeist
> Waldursprünglich Sansculotte ;
>
> Sehr schlecht tanzend, doch Gesinnung
> Tragend in der zott'gen Hochbrust
> Manchmal auch gestunken habend ;
> Kein Talent, doch ein Charakter ! " [2]

The harshness and the strained participial construction both remind us of the style of the royal effusions which any visitor to Munich may study for himself below the frescoes on the walls of the arcades.

This is merely personal satire of crowned heads ; but Heine's satire, like that of Aristophanes, is frequently directed against existing political, social, and literary conditions, and it is then that he is obliged to call the dream to his aid. With its help he descends into the depth of the earth, or mounts to a fantastic world above the clouds.

[1] King Ludwig is a poet great ;
When he sings, the mighty Apollo
Falls on his knees and begs and prays :
O stop ! or my death will follow !

[2] Atta Troll, a bear of impulse ;
Devotee ; a loving husband ;
Full of sans-culottic notions,
Thanks to the prevailing fashion.

Wretched dancer ; strong opinions
Bearing in his shaggy bosom ;
Often stinking very badly ;
Talentless, a character !

(BOWRING.)

This, as already mentioned, happens more especially in *Deutschland*. Observe with what care and skill Heine prepares for the fantastic description of Barbarossa's subterranean dwelling-place in the Kyffhäuser. First he introduces the refrain of an old legendary ballad : " Sonne, du klagende Flamme ! " (Sun, thou accusing flame !) with a sketch of the legend which tells how the sun acted as the accuser of the murderer of a young maiden ; then he describes the good old nurse who sang this ballad and told many an entrancing tale—the tale of the princess disguised as a goose-herd, the tale of the emperor who lived deep down in the earth below the mountain ; this second he relates at length—and presently all else is forgotten ; we see Barbarossa with his mail-clad followers, we hear him call them to horse, to arms, to battle, to avenge the wrong which the murderers have done to the golden-haired Germania. Then we return to the mood of the nursery ballad, and to its refrain : " Sonne ! du klagende Flamme ! " now chanted with enthusiasm and rejoicing. There is an Aristophanic *verve* in this poetic description of the old arsenal, the empty suits of armour, the faded flags, the sleeping soldiers, and then the sudden revulsion, the appeal to awakening power, the supplication that the Middle Ages may return again, as being infinitely preterable to the sanctimonious Prussia of the day, with her mixture of Gothic folly and modern falsehood. The two following cantos, which contain a further description of the interior of the mountain, and conversations with Barbarossa, take the form of an account of a dream which the poet had while travelling at night in the stage-coach.

The anti-Prussian rhapsody in the inn at Minden is prepared for in the same manner. Heine wants to summon forth the Prussian eagle, and to pluck him and shoot him. If Aristophanes had had the same designs, he would have introduced the eagle without more ado. Heine goes to work in his roundabout way. In the act of falling asleep he dreams that the red bed-curtain tassel above his head turns into an eagle with feathers and claws, which threatens to tear the liver out of his breast, and which he taunts with bitter hatred.

In a few single instances Heine's artistic procedure is bolder, more like that of the great Greek. One of these is the splendid harangue to the wolves at night in the Teutoburgerwald. At midnight the traveller hears them howling round his carriage, which has lost a wheel. He comes out and makes a speech to the savage brutes :

> " Mitwölfe, ich bin glücklich, heut'
> In eurer Mitte zu weilen,
> Wo so viel' edle Gemüther mir
> Mit Liebe entgegen heulen." [1]

And the speech is a humorous imitation of those which great men are in the habit of making on such occasions : This is an hour which to him will be ever memorable. They lie who say that he has joined the dogs ; the idea of becoming court-councillor to the lambs has never even occurred to him. From time to time he has dressed himself in a sheepskin, but only for the sake of the warmth ; he is and always will be a wolf.

In the scene between the poet and the strapping woman with the mural crown who represents Hamburg, we have, as Heine himself informs us, a direct imitation of the wedding of Peithetaerus and Basileia in *The Birds*. It is wanton and boyishly frolicsome ; its licentiousness is really more offensive than that of similar passages in Aristophanes, who never appears in his own plays except in defence of himself as a poet. Heine does not go the same length as Aristophanes, but he is more personal.

In *Atta Troll* the parallel between the two poets is still more obvious. Here Heine's imagination has freer play, because the hero is not a man, but a bear. There is fine fancy in the passage where the bear, after his flight, is described dancing for his cubs in the moonlight. There is inimitable humour in his declamation against the rights of man, and in his boast of the more ancient rights of bears,

---

[1] Brother wolves ! it gives me great pleasure to-day
   To tarry awhile midst your growling,
 Where so many noble spirits have met,
   Around me lovingly howling.
                              (BOWRING.)

which recalls the charming parabasis in *The Birds*, in which
it is established that the bird world is the oldest : Everything
proceeds from the original egg, the egg of Night, Love first
of all, and the birds are children of Love. Atta Troll's
pride in the animal world is most amusing, especially so
because Heine manages to insinuate into the bear's utterances sarcastic hits at persons whom he himself wishes
to depreciate—Freiligrath, for instance, whose popular but
foolish poem, *Löwenritt*, and infelicitous *Mohrenkönig* had
roused his mirthful derision :

> " Giebt es nicht gelehrte Hunde ?
> Und auch Pferde, welche rechnen ?
>
> . . . .
>
> Schreiben Esel nicht Kritiken ?
> Spielen Affen nicht Komödie ?
>
> . . . .
>
> Singen nicht die Nachtigallen ?
> Ist der Freiligrath kein Dichter ?
> Wer besäng' den Löwen besser ?
> Als sein Landsmann, das Kamel ? "[1]

A good deal of what the bear says, sounds like satire on
foolish communistic democracy. He holds forth volubly
against property—bears are born without pockets, but men
have pockets and stuff them ; and discourses eagerly on
equality :

> " Strenge Gleichheit ! Jeder Esel
> Sei befugt zum höchsten Staatsamt,
> Und der Löwe soll dagegen
> Mit dem Sack zur Mühle traben."[2]

---

[1] Are there not such things as learnèd
Dogs, and horses too, who reckon ?

. . . .

Write not asses criticisms?
Are not apes all good comedians?

. . . .

Are not nightingales good singers?
And is Freiligrath no poet?
Who can sing of lions better
Than their countryman, the camel ? * (Bowring.)

[2] Strict equality ! Each donkey
Be entitled to high office ;
On the other hand, the lion
Carry to the mill the sack. (Bowring.)

* In German slang equivalent to " blockhead."

But on the whole it is harmless, stingless satire, fantastical banter alike of the clerical party and communists, misanthropes and revolutionists, cosmopolitans and patriots—for the bear speaks like them all in turn. A very wonderful passage is Atta Troll's sermon against atheism and its development from his deism, the passage beginning :

> " Hüte dich vor Menschendenkart,
> Sie verdirbt dir Leib und Seele ;
> Unter allen Menschen giebt es
> Keinen ordentlichen Menschen."[1]

There is a gay profundity in the warning against Feuerbach and Bauer, and there is wit, as brilliant as Voltaire's, but richer, and warmer, in the description of the creative deity :

> " Droben in dem Sternenzelte,
> Auf dem gold'nen Herrscherstuhle,
> Weltregierend, majestätisch,
> Sitzt ein kolossaler Eisbär," &c. [2]

What humour there is in the description of the bear-saints who dance before his throne !

The bear gives us something of the phraseology of all the different parties in turn, but it is the bigoted Teuton that he chiefly favours ; it is he who is most severely satirised. The sleek bear-damsels remind us of a German pastor's daughters ; the youngest cub turns somersaults exactly like Massmann, and is, like him, the product of home education, has never been able to learn Greek or Latin, or any language but his mother-tongue.

By strange, fantastic detours Heine invariably brings his reader back to the realities of his native land.

---

[1] Guard against man's ways of thinking,
They destroy both soul and body ;
'Mongst all men there's no such thing as
Any good and decent man.

[2] In yon starry bright pavilion,
On the golden seat of power,
World-directing and majestic,
Sits a mighty polar-bear.
(BOWRING.)

Aristophanic, in this respect, is the passage in which, when it rains, the cry is heard : " Six-and-thirty kings for an umbrella ! " and again, when shelter is reached : " Six-and-thirty kings for a warm dressing-gown ! "

And absolutely Aristophanic is the suppressed passage, in which the bird Hut-Hut tells how Solomon and Balkis ask each other riddles in the realm of shades, riddles like :

> " Wer ist wohl der grösste Lump
> Unter allen deutschen Lumpen ;
> Die in allen sechs und dreissig·
> Deutschen Bundesstaaten leben ? " [1]

Balkis, to whom the question is put, sends secret messengers to make inquiry in every country and state in Germany, but each time she informs Solomon of the discovery of a specially contemptible wretch, he answers :

> " Kind ! es giebt noch einen grösser'n ! "
> (Child ! there is a worse one still !)

And it is explained to us as a peculiarity of Germany, that as often as we imagine we have discovered her most despicable character, one still more despicable makes his appearance. There is no progress so certain as the progress in general contemptibility. It was only yesterday that X. appeared to be the sorriest knave, to-day he is not to be named in comparison with N. N. Heine must have felt that he had plentiful stores of invention to draw upon, else he would hardly, in his final revision of the poem, have rejected this means of satirising his opponents, one by one, in the most amusing manner.

In purely literary satire, too, Heine's methods have a distinct resemblance to those of Aristophanes. An example of this is the hit in *Atta Troll* at the Swabian school of poets —the cat in the witch's cottage, which is a bewitched Swabian poet, who will turn into a man again when a pure

---

[1] Who, think you, is the paltriest wight
Amongst the crowd of worthless fellows
In all the different States of Germany,
Which are in number six-and-thirty ?

maiden can read Gustav Pfizer's poems on New Year's eve without falling asleep. Another example is the satire in the same poem on the following rather ridiculous lines of Freiligrath's *Der Mohrenfürst* (The Moorish Prince) with their far-fetched simile:

> " Aus dem schimmernd weissen Zelte hervor
> Tritt der schlachtgerüstete fürstliche Mohr;
> So tritt aus schimmernder Wolken Thor
> Der Mond, der verfinsterte, dunkle, hervor."[1]

It is a poem about a negro king, who is taken prisoner, brought to Europe, and made to play the drum outside a circus; while doing so he thinks of his former greatness, and beats his drum to pieces. The idea of the black man at the opening of the tent resembling the moon appearing through the clouds is undoubtedly comical.

In *Atta Troll* the red tongue hangs out of the bear's black jaws as the moon shows herself through white clouds. And towards the end of the poem Heine tells us how, in the Jardin des Plantes, he makes acquaintance with a negro caretaker, who confides to him that he is Freiligrath's negro king, that he has married a white Alsatian cook, whose feet remind him of the feet of the elephants in his native land, and whose French sounds to him like the negro tongue. She feeds him so well that he has developed a little round black stomach, which shows itself through the opening of his shirt like a black moon, appearing from behind white clouds.

And there is something especially Aristophanic in the recklessly brutal satire upon Platen in the second part of the *Reisebilder*. Certain amusing artifices in their literary warfare are common to the Greek and the German comic poet. In *The Frogs*, in the contest between Æschylus and Euripides (a poet whom Aristophanes hates), Æschylus tacks a refrain, equivalent to " spoiled his verse," to everything that Euripides recites. In the *Reisebilder* Heine revenges himself by making Hyacinth alternately tack the words *von vorn*

---

[1] From the glistening white tent the royal Moor issues forth, armed for the fray; even as the moon, gloomy and dark, issues from the glistening gate-way of the clouds.

(from the front) and *von hinten* (from behind) to the end of Platen's lines, thereby maliciously perverting their meaning.

The Aristophanic comedy resembles the majestic frescoes that cover the interior of some great dome ; to compare Heine's comic writings with those of Aristophanes, is to compare pictures carefully painted on the easel with such frescoes. In the Greek comedies there is the light and space of the Sistine Chapel ; in them, as in the frescoes of Michael Angelo, everything is large, sweeping, strong ; the creation of a mind that sets recognised rules at defiance by the vehemence of its lyric emotion, the audacity of its fore-shortening, and the force of its allegory. Only that Michael Angelo's world is solemnly, wildly tragic, whereas the world of Aristophanes is dithyrambic, a world of caricatures set in a framework of Greek social conditions.

Compared with Aristophanes, Heine is a private, stay-at-home citizen. Aristophanes holds forth to an audience of thousands in the broad daylight of the theatre ; Heine communes with his public sitting alone in his room. But the scenes that depict themselves simply on the retina of his eye, are aglow with more ardent, passionate life than those which Aristophanes embodied on the stage. And his aims are not the purely local aims of the Greek poet. When he is at his best, he appeals to millions who are not of his nationality, appeals, indeed, to the elect among all who can read. His lyric poetry is more personal, more intense, more nervous than that of any Greek ; his satire is dedicated to the cause of general ideas, which did not exist for Aristophanes. He is not less witty than his Greek forerunner, and he always fought for political progress and personal liberty, whereas the enemy of Euripides and Socrates most frequently fought for a past that was gone beyond recall, a past to which he himself most certainly did not belong.

XVII

HEINE

HEINE'S prose is not on the same level with his verse. In his most famous prose book, the *Reisebilder*, he shows himself to be a pupil of Sterne; in later works, where he has attained to greater independence, he is always witty and lively, but seldom properly qualified to treat the subjects of his choice. Whether he is writing on German philosophy for French readers, or on French art for Germans, he does it in equally dilettante fashion. Judged as journalism, his writing was always excellent, but he is too strong, too great a man to be classified as a journalist.

Too much has been made of Heine's superficiality by the pedants among his detractors. He was not a hard worker, but he was by no means idle, and he possessed a fund of solid and varied knowledge. Still, it is only as a poet that he is great; most of his prose writings treat of the passing topics of the day; and his fame has been actually injured by the publication of his letters, which, as a rule, present him to us in an unfavourable light, namely entirely taken up with his own interests. Pecuniary difficulties are a tiresome subject, even when they happen to be the pecuniary difficulties of a genius.

Heine, as every one knows, did not live to be an old man. He was carried off in the prime of his mental powers by a terrible disease.

He had always been delicate and suffering; in his youth he was plagued by severe headaches, and was obliged to be so moderate in the matter of drink that his friends used laughingly to declare that he contented himself with *smelling* a bottle of Rhenish wine which he kept in his room. His nervous system was undermined while he was still a young man, but it is certain that this was to a much less extent the result of excesses than is generally believed, for Heine is a real *fanfaron des vices*, given to perpetual boasting of his own depravity. He was attacked by the disease which is so frequently the fate of those who have lived lives of unbroken mental productivity. An affection of the spine, with paralysis first of the eyelids and in course of time of almost the whole body, consigned him to that "mattress-grave" in Paris, where he lay for nearly eight years.

His life, which can neither be called a great nor a happy one, falls of itself into two distinctly defined parts—the life in Germany till the Revolution of July, and the life in Paris from 1831 till his death in 1856. It was a life led without calculation, but not without instinctive perception of the direction in which possibilities of development for his talent lay; it is hardly probable that Heine would have attained to his great cosmopolitan fame, or even that he would have become so eminent a satiric poet, if he had lived in his native country all his life.

His youthful years in Germany are passed under the oppression of the reaction—his *Reisebilder* won popularity as an expression of the general political dissatisfaction—but he soon makes up his mind that it is useless to meddle with politics. The Revolution of July puts new life into everything ; Heine goes off to Paris, settles there, and is kept there by the embargo placed upon his works in all the states of the German Confederation. The Guizot Government secretly give him the small pension which enables him to live in comparative comfort. His acceptance of this laid him open to accusations, which, though they were not altogether groundless, were in many points quite unjustifiable. It must be borne in mind that Heine did not understand the art of making money; and even if he had, it would have been of little use to him. Many thousands of pounds must have been made by the sale of his books, but he himself made over the most profitable of them all, the *Buch der Lieder*, to Campe in payment of an old debt of 50 Louis d'ors, and was all his life long dependent on the unwilling assistance of his rich uncle.

N

If he, and if the little Parisian grisette whom he married, had had more idea of economy, it might have been unnecessary for him to accept Government support. The fact of his accepting it no doubt occasionally prevented him from criticising the French ministry freely in German newspapers, but it had no other bad result, and least of all did it induce him to write anything he did not mean.

From French soil he waged uninterrupted, unremitting intellectual warfare with the European reaction. In this respect he may be called Byron's great successor. Only a few years after the sword of sarcasm, wielded in the cause of liberty, had slipped from the hands of the dying Byron, it was seized by Heine, who wielded it for a whole generation with equal skill and power. Yet for the eight last years it was a mortally wounded man who fought.

At no time did he write truer, more incisive, more brilliant verse than when he lay nailed to the low, broad bed of torture in Paris. And never, so far as we know, has a great productive mind borne superhuman sufferings with more undaunted courage and endurance. The power of the soul over the body has seldom displayed itself so unmistakably. To bear such agonies as his in close-lipped silence would have been admirable; but to create, to bubble over with sparkling, whimsical jest and mockery, to let his spirit wander the world round in charming and profound reverie, while he himself lay crippled, almost lifeless, on his couch——this was great.

He lay there shrunk to a skeleton, with his eyes closed, his hands almost powerless, his noble features painfully emaciated ; the white, perfectly formed hands were nearly transparent ; at times, when he spoke, a Mephistophelian smile passed over the suffering, martyr-like face. At last, as in the case of Tithonus of old, all that really remained of the man was his voice ; but it was a voice of many notes, of many whimsies, many jests.

He continued to be mentally active. It was as if the driving-wheel went on turning without steam, as if the lamp went on burning without oil.

It is not true that he reverted to a connection with any church ; but the suffering man clung to a kind of piety and faith in God which was a legacy from the days of his youth. At this faith he himself sometimes smiled. We have such a smile in the words with which on the last day of his life he tried to pacify an excited acquaintance : *Dieu me pardonnera —c'est son métier.*

It is a touching proof of his strength of mind and of his filial affection that during his whole long illness he took the greatest care that all knowledge of his sufferings should be kept from his old mother in Hamburg ; to the last he wrote her cheerful, amusing letters, and he caused any passages that might have awakened her suspicions to be taken out of the copies of his works that were sent to her.

Another pleasant impression of his spiritual condition is conveyed by the circumstance that he, the most wanton-tongued of men and poets on the subject of love, changed during his illness into the tenderest and most spiritual exponent of that passion. The last year of his life was, as is well known, sweetened by the admiration and devotion of the young and beautiful woman who, though German born, made her appearance as a French authoress under the pseudonym of Camille Selden.[1]

She was then about twenty-eight, blue-eyed, fair-haired, and so charming, gentle, and attractive, that she won Heine's heart the first time she visited him. Soon he could not live without her ; he was miserable if a few days passed without his seeing her, though he was often in such pain that he was obliged to request her to delay her visit.

It is in the poems and letters to her, published after Heine's death, that we find that fervency, depth, and fulness of passion which we feel to be wanting in the rest of his love poetry.

He calls her his spiritually affianced bride, whose life is bound up with his by the will of fate. United, they would

---

[1] A. Meissner : *Erinnerungen an Heinrich Heine.* Camille Selden ; *Les derniers jours de Henri Heine,* 1884.

have known what happiness is ; separated, they are doomed
to misery :

> " Ich weiss es jetzt. - Bei Gott ! du bist es,
> Die ich geliebt. Wie bitter ist es,
> Wenn im Momente des Erkennens
> Die Stunde schlägt des ew'gen Trennens !
> Der Willkomm ist zu gleicher Zeit
> Ein Lebewohl ! " [1]

Half laughing, half weeping, he bemoans the compulsory
platonic affection of two lovers, to whom an embrace is an
impossibility :

> " Worte ! Worte ! keine Thaten !
> Niemals Fleisch, geliebte Puppe,
> Immer Geist und keinen Braten,
> Keine Knödel in der Suppe ! " [2]

When, at a rare time, she keeps him waiting, he is
frantic with impatience :

> " Lass mich mit glüh'nden Zangen kneipen,
> Lass grausam schinden mein Gesicht,
> Lass mich mit Ruthen peitschen, stäupen—
> Nur warten, warten lass mich nicht ! " [3]

But the great mystic poem which celebrates the nuptials
of the dead poet with the passion-flower that blossoms on
his grave, is a poem of resignation, resignation in the presence
of Death :

> " Du warst die Blume, du geliebtes Kind,
> An deinen Küssen musst' ich dich erkennen.
> So zärtlich keine Blumenlippen sind,
> So feurig keine Blumenthränen brennen.

---

[1] I know it now. By heaven ! 'tis thou
Whom I have loved. How bitter now,
The moment we are joined for ever,
To find the hour when we must sever !
The welcome must at once give way
            To sad farewell !   (BOWRING.)

[2] Words, empty words, and never deeds !
No roast for us, my puppet sweet,
Not even dumplings in the soup ;
A feast of mind, but not of meat !

[3] With red-hot irons scar my flesh,
Pinch me with pincers glowing hot,
Or have me beat with many stripes—
But oh ! to wait compel me not !

Geschlossen war mein Aug', doch angeblickt
Hat meine Seel' beständig dein Gesichte,
Du sahst mich an, beseeligt und verzückt
Und geisterhaft beglänzt vom Mondenlichte."[1]

These images, these feelings, belong to an insubstantial world, a world like the blind man's, where there are kisses, but not from visible lips, and tears which fall from unseen eyes, a world fragrant with the perfume of flowers that cannot be touched, and illuminated by magic, spirit-like moonshine instead of the light of the sun. There is no substantiality and there is no sound:

" Wir sprachen nicht, jedoch mein Herz vernahm
Was du verschwiegen dachtest im Gemüthe—
Das ausgesprochene Wort ist ohne Scham,
Das Schweigen ist der Liebe keusche Blüthe."[2]

They held noiseless converse, but what they talked of we are forbidden to ask:

" Frag, was er strahlet, den Karfunkelstein,
Frag, was sie duften, Nachtviol' und Rosen—
Doch frage nie, wovon im Mondenschein
Die Marterblume und ihr Todter kosen!"[3]

Heine rises here to a level with Shelley, the sublimest of modern lyric poets. This is Shelley's note—the violin strain of an Ariel, clear and spirit-like and full, and entirely modern in its trembling, thrilling, almost morbid tenderness.

[1] Thou wast that flower, beloved ! I knew thee by thy kisses; no flower lips kiss so tenderly, no flower tears burn so scorchingly. My eyes were fast closed, but my soul gazed steadfastly upon thy face; and in the moonlight's ghostly sheen, blissful and trembling, thou did'st return my gaze.

[2] We said not a word, but my heart felt all thy unspoken thoughts—the spoken word is a shameless thing, silence is love's chaste blossom.

[3] Ask the ruby to explain its fiery glow, ask violet and rose to analyse their perfume, but never seek to know of what the passion-flower and her dead lover talk so caressingly in the pale moonlight.

XVIII

LITERATURE AND PARTY

BÖRNE and many later critics have maintained that Heine was never in earnest about anything, and have condemned him accordingly. Setting aside slighter and unimportant causes, Börne's resentment was really aroused by what appeared to him to be Heine's determination not to espouse the cause of any party. He himself, as far as it was possible in those unparliamentary days, was an extreme partyman in literature.

It is now a generally accepted, trite axiom, that art is its own aim and end, but then people were accustomed to look upon it as the handmaid of the great general aims of the day ; and in all German literary productions of that period, important and unimportant, we feel exactly what it was that induced the writer to take up his pen. Even an author as strongly actuated by a purpose as Heine was, did not satisfy those who, like Börne, lived for their convictions. They applied to him the expression " talented but characterless " (" wohl ein Talent, aber kein Charakter "), which he ridicules so unmercifully in *Atta Troll*. Even in the introduction he alludes jestingly to the consolation for the great majority which is contained in the doctrine that respectable people are as a rule bad musicians, while, to make up for this, good musicians are anything but respectable people—and every one knows that respectability and not music is the important thing in this world.

Elsewhere Heine maintains that it is, as a rule, a sign of a man's narrowmindedness when he is straightway discerned and held in high esteem by the narrow-minded majority as a man of character ; the chief reason for such distinction being that a narrow, superficial, but always

consistent philosophy of life is what the multitude most
easily understands.

Stoic firmness was assuredly not one of the qualities of
Heine's nature. Allowing that in certain given circumstances
he showed want of character, we proceed to what is really
the vital question : Ought the poet to be a party-man ?

At the time when Heine was jeering in *Atta Troll* at those
who in their philanthropic and political ardour imagined
strength of character to be a sufficient substitute for talent,
a serious literary war was being waged in Germany over
the question whether the poet ought to be a party-man
or to take up a position superior to all parties. *Atta Troll,*
which pours such ridicule on Freiligrath's youthful poems,
appeared in the autumn of 1841 ; in November of the
same year Freiligrath, who till then had been best known
by oriental poems in Victor Hugo's style, and who had a
short time previously accepted a pension from the King of
Prussia, wrote, in a poem entitled *Año Spanien* (on Diego
Leon, the Spanish general shot in 1841) the following lines
on the poet as such :

> " Er beugt sein Knie dem Helden Bonaparte,
> Und hört mit Zürnen d'Enghien's Todesschrei :
> Der Dichter steht auf einer höhern Warte
> Als auf den Zinnen der Partei." [1]

This sentiment was condemned by Georg Herwegh in the
poem *Die Partei (an Ferdinand Freiligrath),* the most striking
lines of which are:

> " Partei ! Partei ! wer sollte sie nicht nehmen,
> Die noch die Mutter aller Siege war !
> Wie mag ein Dichter solch ein Wort verfehmen,
> Ein Wort, das alles Herrliche gebar !
> Nur offen wie ein Mann : Für oder wider?
> Und die Parole : Sklave oder frei ?
> Selbst Götter stiegen vom Olymp hernieder
> Und kämpften auf den Zinnen der Partei." [2]

---

[1] He bows the knee to Bonaparte, the hero, yet d'Enghien's death-cry arouses
his wrath: the poet observes from a higher watch-tower than the battlements of party.

[2] What ! not a party man ! Is not strong party feeling the mother of all victory ?
How can a poet calumniate the word in which lies the germ of all the noblest deeds ?
Speak out like a man: Are you for or against us ? Is your watchword slavery or
freedom ? The Gods themselves descended from Olympus and fought on the battlements of party.

A year later, in his poem *Duett der Pensionirten*, Herwegh taunted Freiligrath with accepting a pension from the King of Prussia, whereupon Freiligrath, as is well known, threw up his pension, joined the ranks of the political poets, and developed so rapidly into a Radical and revolutionary, that at the time of the outbreak in 1848, he was looked upon as the representative revolutionary poet in Germany. It is plain, then, that Freiligrath considered Herwegh to be in the right. Still this does not prove him to have been so.

The question whether and to what extent the poet ought to be a party-man is a very complex one. It is so in the first instance because of the ambiguity of the word party, a word which Heine and Börne, Freiligrath and Herwegh employed with a different meaning at different times.

The poet, even if he is a small-minded man, can only lose by pinning his faith to any narrow, political, party programme, to any social or religious theory. How is it possible that his ideals should exactly correspond with the limited, definite aims of any party! Thomas Moore was a Whig poet, Walter Scott a Tory poet, because, with all their great talent, they were not great minds. Byron went more to the root of things than either of them, or than either of the political parties—yet every one instinctively feels that it is absurd to say that Byron, as a poet, did not take a side in politics or religion. He did so even more markedly than Schiller, who also could not be said to belong to any political party, for one reason because there were none in the Germany of his day.

There are certain branches of literature which plainly have nothing to do with party. The poet of love, as such, belongs to no political or religious party ; though it is not impossible that he may belong to an art party, for as soon as there is any question of style in art, we at once encounter party again. But the moment he begins to treat a theme in which there is any trace of theory, of thought, of fundamental principle, he is obliged to choose his side, to rank himself among the disciples of this or that philosophy of life.

When, however, as in Freiligrath's case, we have simply

an assertion of the poet's right to admire Napoleon and yet to be incensed by the death of d'Enghien, party does not come into question at all ; for all that is meant is, that the poet has not dispossessed himself of his right to judge the past with equity and to see the vices as well as the virtues of his heroes. The question of party, strictly so called, is not a question of the judging of the past, but of the shaping of the future ; and no man can proceed in two directions at the same time.

Another difficulty presents itself to us in the word party. It means, generally speaking, part of the population of one's own country. And the poet ought to belong to his country and his people, not only to part of them. Looked upon in this light, party is the narrower, country the wider conception, and if by party an actual political party, corresponding more or less perfectly to its name or its programme, is meant, then as a matter of course country is superior to party.

But if we take the word party in the sense in which we use it when we speak of Schiller and of Byron as party-men, then party is a wider, a grander conception than country. For by country we understand a definitely bounded tract of land, definitely limited interests, a definitely circumscribed history ; but by party in this sense we understand a system of ideas which, from their very nature, are not confined to any place—world-wide thoughts, the great general interests of humanity. And even if the party sided with represents only the great moving ideas of one age, an age is a wider, greater native land than a country ; and the poet does his people a service by extending their horizon beyond their country's bounds.

Börne and Heine were, in my opinion, both strong party-men, but none the less both zealous patriots, their patriotism quite uninjured by their partisanship.

The official press of the day proclaimed Börne to be not only a mad Radical, but a libeller of his country. He had the dangerous habit of expressing all his opinions in such violent terms that they offended, wounded, or incited to action. There was an outcry of indignation when he wrote that any nation had a right to depose its king even if it were only because it had taken a dislike to the shape of his nose. And whole volumes of invective were called forth by his observations on the servility (*Bedientennatur*) of the Germans. He had gone so far as to call them "a nation of flunkeys."

He himself writes: "What can I do with people who really seriously believe that I have advised the nations of Europe to depose their kings as soon as they take a dislike to their noses. . . . If I were to say: Gentlemen! I did not mean you to take me so literally, they would perhaps believe me—but that would avail me nothing. They would say: You ought to have remembered that you do not write for educated readers only, but that a large proportion of your readers are uneducated men. To this I would answer nothing but: Take me to prison! Then when I was brought into court I would say: Gentlemen! The German is a crocodile! (Cries of indignation. Crocodile! Order!) Gentlemen! The German is a crocodile! (Order! Judge: You are abusing your right of self-defence.) Gentlemen! The German is a crocodile—I beg of you to allow me to continue. When I use the word crocodile I am not hinting at savage instincts or crocodile tears. The German is tame and good-natured, and weeps tears that are as sincere as the tears of a whipped child. If I have applied the name of crocodile to the German, it is only on account of his skin, which does resemble that of the crocodile. It consists of hard scales, and is like a slated roof. Anything solid that falls upon it rebounds, anything liquid runs off. Suppose, now, gentlemen, that you wished to mesmerise such a crocodile, with the final intention of curing his weak nerves, but in the first instance of making him so clear sighted that he could see inside himself, discover his own disease, and find out the proper remedy for it. How would you set about it? Would you gently stroke the crocodile coat-of-mail with your warm hand? No, you would not be so foolish; you know that would make no impression on it. You would stamp on it, drive nails into it, and if that were not enough, you would fire a hundred bullets at it, calculating that ninety-nine of them would take no effect, and that the hundredth would bring about just the mild, modest results your mesmerism was intended to produce. This is what I have done." [1]

One sees that Börne's strong language on the subject of German servility and indolence is simply the negative expression of his patriotism. It is a patriotism which as a rule finds only indirect expression, but we feel it as distinctly in his melancholy derision as in the enthusiastic demonstrations of others.

As regards Heine, Börne's charges were, no doubt, to a certain extent well founded. The versatile poet's temperament made the monotonous struggle for a political conviction hard for him, and he was, as we have already shown, drawn two ways and rendered vague in his utterances by feeling himself to be at one and the same time a popular revolutionist and an enthusiastic aristocrat. But his objection to connecting himself with any of the existing political or religious parties was more a proof of his high intellectual standard than of anything else. His raillery in *Atta Troll* at the canting preachers of the Opposition is delightful and perfectly justifiable ; it only shows that he abhorred dogmatism in all its forms.

Börne is wrong in assuming that Heine, the man, was false to his party, taking that word in its greater, wider, signification, namely, the ideas for which he contended. For to these he was faithful, even throughout the eight long years when he lay on his deathbed, with difficulty opening his paralysed eyelids to look for God in that heaven whose emptiness he himself had so sadly and defiantly described.

And Heine was as true a patriot as Börne. Every reader of his works must remember the beautiful passage at the conclusion of the *Reisebilder,* in which he tells how the Emperor Maximilian sate in sore straits in the Tyrol, encompassed by his enemies, forgotten by his knights and courtiers. Suddenly the door of his prison cell was opened, and there entered a man in disguise, whom the Emperor recognised as Kunz von der Rosen, his faithful court jester.

[1] *Letter from Paris,* Dec. 15, 1831.

I feel it to be not only beautiful but true when Heine says : " O German fatherland ! beloved German people ! I am thy Kunz von der Rosen.   The man whose only business it was to amuse thee, to cater for thy mirth in times of prosperity, makes his way into thy prison in time of need. Here, under my cloak, I bring thee thy strong sceptre and thy beautiful crown—dost thou not recognise me, my Emperor ? . . .   Thou liest in fetters now, but in the end thy rightful cause will prevail ; the day of deliverance is at hand, a new time is beginning, my Emperor, the night is over ; look out and see the ruddy dawn."

If we beware of attaching too much importance to single expressions, to the wanton or arrogant outbursts scattered here and there throughout his works, we shall perceive that the feeling which finds classic expression in the words just quoted was very strong in Heine's breast.   Neither his party standpoint, nor the admiration of things foreign which it entailed, affected a very sincere, deep love of his native land, which made exile in many ways a punishment to him.   But he had not the kind of patriotism which he somewhere ascribes to the average German, the kind that narrows the heart, makes it shrink like leather in the cold. His was the patriotism that warms the heart and widens it until it is able to embrace the whole realm of civilisation.[1] How could he help loving Germany !   As he himself has said, and as we all must say each of his own country : " The truth is—Germany is ourselves."   His whole nature and character were determined by his German birth and upbringing.   The second half of his life being spent in an exile that was partly voluntary, partly compulsory—in so far a homeless man, that his works were prohibited throughout the German Confederation—the German language became to him a true, a grander, a real fatherland.   He himself called the German tongue the most sacred of all possessions, the unsilenceable call to liberty, a new fatherland for him whom stupidity or malice has banished from the land of his birth.

[1] Heine : *Werke*, vi. 51.   *Cf.* xiv. 45, and xiii. 16.

XIX

IMMERMANN

ALL who are familiar with Heine's works or letters are aware of the warm friendship and brotherhood in arms that united him in his youth to Karl Immermann. He proposed to Immermann to insert some of his epigrams in the *Reisebilder*, and as a matter of fact there are several pages of them in the book between the divisions *Norderney* and *Das Buch Le Grand*. They satirise various literary personages and events of the day. The attacks on those writers who imitated Oriental forms of poetry incensed Platen, and induced him to write his dramatic satire, *Der romantische Oedipus*, which in its turn called forth Heine's well-known satire.

It was very curious that Platen, in his irritation, should with one blow stamp as Romanticists the two men who, each in his own way, did so much (more than Platen himself) to unswathe from the wrappings of Romanticism a new spirit, a new art—the spirit, the art of modern poetry.

Karl Immermann (born in 1796) was three years older than Heine. He was the son of a correct, austere Government official in Magdeburg, and was himself a man of strong character and solid culture, early imbued with that old Prussian spirit of which there was not a trace in Heine. They were contrasts in almost everything.

Immermann fought in the battle of Waterloo as a volunteer, entered Paris with the army, afterwards retired with the rank of an officer, and studied law at the University of Halle. His strong feeling of justice led him into disputes with the powerful students' union, Teutonia, which had usurped a kind of moral authority over all the students, and enforced its principles, especially that of purity of life, in a domineering, brutal fashion. For several years he continued to oppose the practices of the Union, and more than once during this time was obliged to invoke the power of the law to protect him from the insults and persecution to which he was subjected by his antagonists. The consequence of this was that he was hated by the great majority as an informer—the more so as the political reactionaries took advantage of this opposition to the traditional malpractices of the students' unions, to attack, and, where it was possible, suppress the unions, a proceeding for which Immermann was in no way responsible. From this time onwards he stood alone. Much in his character, much of its dryness and peculiarity, had its origin in this isolation, which also favoured the development of pride and self-esteem.

In 1819, Immermann was given a Government appointment (that of *Divisionsauditor*), in the town of Münster, in Westphalia, an old, strictly Catholic, provincial town, where at first he felt himself out of sympathy with every one and everything. But here, ere long, he made acquaintance with the woman who was to be the most powerful influence in his life.

Elisa von Lützow was the wife of Brigadier-General Adolf von Lützow, the famous leader of the volunteer corps celebrated in Körner's song. By birth she was a Dane, a Countess Ahlefeldt-Laurvig of Tranekjær in the island of Langeland. When Immermann first saw her she was twenty-nine, and, according to the testimony of her contemporaries, a most fascinating woman, graceful, charming, intelligent, of aristocratic bearing, and yet genial. From her earliest youth she had made a deep impression on the men who came within her sphere.

She had grown up the supposed heiress of great wealth, but in an unhappy home ; her father and mother had become estranged from each other, and about the time she was fourteen they separated. Count Ahlefeldt, a favourite of Frederick VI., was a pleasure-loving man, a pasha with a constantly changing harem ; he was a patron of music and of the drama, kept a private orchestra, and entertained companies of French and German actors at Tranekjær ; so

IMMERMANN

hospitable and recklessly extravagant was he that even his great wealth could not stand the drain upon it. What brought Elisa and Immermann together was her applying to him for legal advice when her father not only refused to make over to her what had been left her by her mother, who had died in 1812, but also to pay the yearly income which he had settled upon her.

Count Ahlefeldt long refused his consent to his daughter's marriage with the poor and as yet undistinguished foreign officer, but he gave it in 1810, and when, in 1813, the youth of Prussia joyfully and enthusiastically rose to arms at the call of Frederick William III., and Lützow formed the famous volunteer corps known by his name, his wild and daring riflemen (*die wilde, verwegene Jagd*) found their Valkyrie in their leader's beautiful wife, who was worshipped by the whole regiment as a superior being. Elisa, who appears to have spoken German from her childhood, felt herself at home on German soil, became a faithful daughter of her new fatherland, and identified herself with its interests. She inspirited the brave, nursed the wounded with heroic devotion, was the confidante, helper, and comforter of the best among the young men. After a victory, the choicest of the booty was always presented to her. The lieutenant who first stepped into Napoleon's captured carriage after the fight at Belle-Alliance brought her, as a remembrance, a pair of gloves and two glasses of the Emperor's.

After the conclusion of peace she lived with her husband in the different garrison towns to which he was transferred. In 1817 they came to Münster. The stiff, narrow-minded, bigoted tone of its society was antipathetic to her ; but here, as elsewhere, she gathered round her a circle of enthusiastic admirers, who were charmed by her taste and by the keen intelligence which she displayed, without being a great talker —sometimes only by a smile and a nod.

To Immermann she was like a revelation from a higher, nobler world, for which in his lonely, joyless life he had been longing. Lützow's quarters were in a castle-like building that had been a convent, with high windows and great folding doors. Here, surrounded by flowers, statues, books, birds, dogs, and admirers, she seemed like a noble lady of olden days, or one of those princesses of the Renaissance who attracted poets to their courts and inspired them.

With the year 1825 came a great change in Elisa's life. The good-natured and chivalrous but volatile and impressionable Lützow fell so violently in love with an insignificant flirt that he requested his wife to set him at liberty again. This she was not prepared to do ; but after she happened to overhear Lützow remark to a friend that when he was quite young he had made up his mind to marry a great heiress, a new light was thrown upon the determination he had shown in their early days to win her, and her feelings towards him changed. Her pride was hurt ; she presently informed him that she would no longer stand in the way of his happiness, and agreed to a divorce, the reason of which she kept secret.

Not an angry word passed between husband and wife. The divorce was pronounced in April 1825. Both before and after it Lützow wrote Elisa letters which testify to a most friendly feeling and warm admiration. It was an unlucky day for him when he took the step which separated them. He was universally blamed, and when it came to the point, his capricious enslaver would have nothing to say to him. He repented his delusion when it was too late. Some years afterwards, in order to make a home for himself again, he married his brother's widow, but this lady's temper was so bad that it made the last years of his life most unhappy.

The divorce left Elisa homeless and solitary, and this led to gradually increasing intimacy with young Immermann, who saw in her his ideal, and was passionately desirous to make her his wife. But Elisa shuddered at the thought of a second marriage ; the disillusionments of her wedded life had disgusted her with matrimony in general, and she reflected, moreover, that she was six years older than the young poet. When Immermann, in 1827, was promoted to the appointment of *Landesgerichtsrath* in Düsseldorf, he passionately urged her to accompany him there. She agreed to do this, though she again refused to marry him; both, however, vowed never to think of marriage with any one else.

The lovers inhabited a country house in the village of Derendorf, close to Düsseldorf, where they had their separate suites of apartments. This house, which lay in a great rose garden, they decorated with exquisite taste, and here they lived a full and happy life for a number of years. Düsseldorf was at that time the resort of many of the best artists in Germany, painters like Schadow, Lessing, Hildebrandt. Thither, too, came poets (like Grabbe), composers (Mendelssohn), art amateurs, and critics from all parts. Immermann's and Elisa von Ahlefeldt's house was a rendezvous for all these. In Elisa's circle in Münster, Immermann had distinguished himself as a clever reader of dramatic works ; here he continued to give semi-public readings of the same description. This gradually developed a desire on his part to manage a theatre. He rehearsed a number of trial plays with the Düsseldorf theatrical company; artists from other parts came to his assistance ; the great actor, Seydelmann from Berlin, played Nathan ; Felix Mendelssohn put two operas on the stage for him and directed the performance.

Elisa's father died in 1832. She did not inherit all the wealth that in her youth was expected to be her portion, but the cousin who succeeded to her father's title and property settled a handsome annuity on her. She and Immermann now travelled together—on the Rhine, to Dresden, in Holland ; a tour which Immermann took alone is described in his *Reisejournal*, which consists entirely of the letters he wrote to Elisa. Everything else was written beside her, and subjected to her affectionate but frequently severe criticism.

After an existence of three years, Immermann's theatre, failing to obtain state aid, had to be closed. This was a great grief to him. He sought to distract himself by a tour in Franconian Switzerland. His *Fränkische Reise*, the description of this tour, also consists of letters to Elisa. They were the last he wrote her. For during this absence

O

he met, in Magdeburg, a girl of nineteen, Marianne Niemeyer by name, who made a very strong impression on him. When he rejoined Elisa he once more, to her surprise, asked her to marry him. As before, she refused. It would seem as if he had been pretty certain of the answer he would receive, and only desired to salve his conscience. For immediately afterwards, unknown to Elisa, he began a lively correspondence with Marianne, proposed to her, and was accepted. Elisa heard of his engagement from others, and at once resolved to leave Düsseldorf. She did so in August 1839, Immermann accompanying her and the friend with whom she travelled as far as Cologne. Till this time, in spite of her forty-nine years, she had retained her beauty; now she suddenly grew old. In October 1839 Immermann married; in August 1840 he died. Elisa survived him fifteen years.[1]

It is quite obvious that the connection with Elisa, which for so many years was pleasurable and helpful to Immermann, in the end became burdensome to him. But it is unwarrantable to assert (as Goedeke has done) that it was the breaking off of this connection and his subsequent lawful marriage which first gave Immermann the creative vigour which he displayed in his last important work, *Münchhausen*. It was conceived and executed under Elisa's influence to quite the same extent as his other works.

Her personality and the position in which he stood to her often and in many ways influenced his writings. She is supposed to have suggested his drama, *Petrarca*, which treats of Petrarch's love of Laura, and represents the irresistible strength of a passion inspired by a high-born lady even when the said lady is not free. Her views on the subject of love, and its unqualified justification as such, are said to be recognisable in the drama, *Cardenio und Celinde*. She was probably his model for the heroine of the comedy, *Die schelmische Gräfin*, and certainly the model for Johanne in the novel *Die Epigonen*. But all this is as nothing in comparison with the general development and refining influence which she exerted over him as an author.

[1] Ludmilla Assing: *Gräfin Elisa von Ahlefeldt*, 1857.

Immermann's is a curious fame. Of all his works only one is still read, his novel, *Münchhausen;* and only one part of this novel, the smaller half of it (now separated from the rest and published by itself), will carry his name down to posterity. This one small volume is in reality of more value than all the rest of his work.

In its construction, *Münchhausen,* following the general rule of the Romantic tales, was intentionally disorderly ; the book begins, for example, with the eleventh chapter. The hero, a Westphalian baron, is a descendant of the old lying Münchhausen, and, like him, a fantastic liar. The whole was meant to be a sort of satiric repertory of the various humbugs and nonsensicalities of the day, amongst which the author's humour might play at will. But out of all this irregular play of fancy, which corresponds to the title *Eine Geschichte in Arabesken,* there was gradually developed the great rural romance which has taken a place in German literature under the name of *Der Oberhof.* Its principal characters, the village magistrate (*der Hofschulze*) and the fair-haired Lisbeth, represent a new truth, a new creative art. They live and move on "the red soil" of Westphalia, and in their persons the German peasant is for the first time introduced into literature without the sentimentality of the pastoral idyll or the distortion of the opera ballet, un-doubtedly conventionalised, but with caste and race individu-ality. There is a vigorous, fresh naturalness about these characters, which will never grow old.

Der Oberhof has taken its place as the original type of all the European peasant tales, and in certain points it is superior to any of them, old-fashioned in many ways as it now seems. Hundreds of fantastic threads connect this admirable story with the romance of Romanticism, but it is easy to cut them, and then we have before us as it were the hard crystal into which Romanticism finally condensed itself in Immermann's mind.

It is the custom nowadays to regard the peasant tale as a direct offshoot of Romanticism. Yet it undoubtedly, both in France and in the North, marked the transition to an art which was more true to nature than the Romantic.

It signified a complete change of sphere in German art when Immermann gave up writing historical or fantastic dramas in iambic verse, the scenes of which were laid in countries which he had never seen, and portrayed ordinary human life in the little known province of Westphalia, where he had lived and exercised the functions of a judge. There were no railways in the Westphalia of those days, and no manufactures ; but it was a country of patriarchal, whole-some manners and customs, and he had only to represent it with the faithfulness which illuminates, to produce an effect infinitely surpassing that of any of the earlier arbitrary creations of his poetic imagination.

The wealthy peasant landowner, who is the principal personage in this story, is the prototype of all the sturdy, independent farmers of the German peasant tales, and of many in those of other countries. Excellent as many of Auerbach's characters of this type are, he surpasses them all in what may be called the historic greatness which is imparted to this character by the intimate relation which we feel to exist between it and the far back past of the country. This peasant appears on the background of traditions still in force, which link the present with almost forgotten times.

He is a genuine peasant. He is not in the least amiable ; he has had no time to cultivate amiability ; from his boyhood, life has been too hard to allow of that. His distinguishing qualities are sound common sense, seriousness, obstinacy, pride of position, and permissible self-interest. There is a granite-like foundation to his character. He has the true peasant shrewdness, not to say shiftiness, in business ; he is always ready to advise his neighbours how best to hold their own against the authorities when any forced sale of land is threatened, always on his guard against emissaries of the government, even when their mission is the construction of new roads or some such improvement ; he is cold in his family relations, and has all the prejudices of the rustic.

And yet he is great. He rules, and he always carries his point. He not only reigns over his own large estate like one of the stern, patriarchal kings of old, upholding good old customs, keeping his eye on every one and everything, admonishing in proverbs, rewarding with the honour of retention in his service ; but, unquestionably the superior of all his neighbours, he has induced them to regard him as their leader, and has quietly, without disturbance or revolt of any kind, led them to free themselves from the supremacy of state authorities and to rule themselves under him as a sort of judge of the old Jewish type.   In his district both law-suits and criminal cases are unknown ; no one goes to law with his neighbour ; no one is ever accused of a crime ; one might take it to be an oasis of innocence and peace.   It is far from being that ; but since medieval times the secret courts of justice (*Vehmgerichte*) have existed here, and the peasants, under the influence of this great peasant, have agreed to uphold these, and thus privately provide for the maintenance of equity and justice among themselves.   They assemble secretly at night in a lonely place and settle their own disputes.   The sentences are accepted and executed without dispute.   The only punishment awarded is a sort of excommunication of the malefactor, which is as severe a chastisement as any that could be imposed by a state judge.   A peasant whom all avoid, whom no one will help, with whom no one will have any dealings, suffers from almost as strict isolation as the man confined in a prison cell.

As a symbol of his power and dignity the old " Hof-schulze " treasures a sword, which he believes to be what tradition calls it, the sword of Charlemagne, and which he regards as his most precious possession.   His hand is on its hilt when he pronounces judgment.   This sword, which was dug up somewhere in the neighbourhood, is really a perfectly common weapon, possibly two hundred years old ; and we have an admirable description of how the old farmer is at times tormented by doubts of its antiquity, doubts which, with his peasant shrewdness, he tries to dispose of once for all.   He tempts an antiquarian in the neighbourhood with the sight of a beautiful amphora, and then obliges him to give in payment for it a written certification that the sword had undoubtedly belonged to Charlemagne.

The tragic catastrophe of the story is brought about in this way. A man who is now a vagrant had, in consequence of an intrigue with the daughter of the " Hofschulze," been attacked by her brother and had killed him in self-defence. This vagabond, to revenge himself on the " Hofschulze " for the sentence of excommunication which has ruined his life, steals the sword and hides it where no one can find it. The loss breaks the old man's spirit. All the mysteries of the secret court of justice are divulged, and he is obliged to stand his trial.

Granted permission to make a last speech, he says: " Your Worship ! I have no doubt that the clerk is noting me down in his minutes as a fool, and my sword and secret judgment-seat as foolery ; for so, if I mistake not, I heard the young gentleman call the things that lie nearest to my heart. I would fain give some explanation regarding this foolery." And he goes on to say how, ever since he could think, he has observed that, after calamities such as hail-storms, floods, failure of crops, or cattle-plague, some of those gentlemen came to the district who not only understand how to write reports, but also how to judge everything much better than the people concerned ; they described the calamity after it was past, but were never there at the time to help ; and if a little money happened to be sent, it never reached those who needed it most. " One thing was more astonishing than all else. One or other of these government gentlemen would order things so in the district that we peasants could not refrain from laughing at it all. In a year or two the same gentleman would come driving in a carriage and four, with all kinds of ribbons and orders on his breast, looking as if he had helped to create the world. Thinking over all this in my plain way, I came to the conclusion that the government gentlemen were of little service to us peasants; nor did they come to do us service ; they came to write, and they wrote until they wrote themselves into a carriage and four. . . . And then I thought (for all my life I have been given to thinking) that a steady, industrious man will always get on if he watches the wind and the weather, and attends to his business and is a good neighbour. . . . And first I accustomed myself, even in times of trouble, never to think of help ; I paid my taxes and bore my own burdens . . . and then I accustomed my neighbours to do the same. They followed my example ; we settled our own affairs among ourselves, and many matters about which much ado would have been made elsewhere, were never heard of beyond the bounds of the parish. . . . By degrees we came to settling everything. A peasant has understanding enough to tell who has the best claim to a certain wall or strip of meadow. And when a house has been broken into, the village nearly always knows who has been the thief ; but because it is not always possible to bring sufficient proof, a man well known to be a rascal may impudently and scandalously show his face and enjoy his booty, which its rightful owner never recovers. So we quietly took the law into our hands, and no one could accuse us of anything, for we injured no man ; we only refused to hold any communication whatsoever with the evildoers whom we placed under the ban ; and of this ban men were more afraid than of the judge's sentence and prison."

"And," he concludes, " if other people would but do the same, if the townsmen, the merchants, the noblemen, the scholars, would but manage their own affairs, things would be better than they are. Men would no longer be like stupid children, for ever crying for father and mother, but every man would be like a prince in his own house and among his equals. And the king himself would then be a far mightier monarch, a ruler like no other, for he would rule over hundreds of thousands of princes."

We have the feeling at the end of the story that, now the secret is divulged and the sword stolen, the days of popular justice are at an end. But the author gives us his own opinion on this subject by the mouth of the wise pastor, who declares that the independence which is the watch-word of this peasant and his friends is a reality which cannot be done away with by being divulged, that the idea which has united them, the idea that a man is dependent on his neighbours, not on strangers who stand in a perfectly artificial relation to him, does not require the support of the tribunal under the old lime-tree. In the peasant farmer himself, the mighty old yeoman, he sees the true sword of Charlemagne, which no thief can steal, the true backbone of the country.

Observe that this is written by an author who was a magistrate and the son of a Prussian government official.

A marked contrast to the strong, stern figure of the old peasant, but drawn with as sure a hand, is Lisbeth, the fair-haired, country girl who is the heroine of the tale. Young Count Oswald, who wanders about the country shooting, falls in love with her, and it is the eventful love-story of these two young people which forms the chief attraction of the book. Immermann had in his writings long shown himself to be a firm believer in the unbounded power of love over humanity, but here he tells the story of young love as he had never done before. We have the beat and glow of two innocent young hearts. The youth and maiden meet, full of budding, swelling, healthy presentiments and hopes. No renunciation or disappointment has as yet cooled one drop of their warm blood. The distance between them is bridged over in an original manner. The young sportsman, who has inherited from his parents a taste for shooting, along with absolute incapacity to hit anything, for once in his life succeeds in setting his mark on a living creature; he lodges a whole charge of small shot in the girl's shoulder. The shame and regret he feels give place in time to ardent love. When she has recovered and the two have discovered that they love each other, they go together one day into the wood.

"'I want to ask your wounds to forgive me,' he said —undid her kerchief, and kissed the small red spots between her breast and her white shoulder. She did not resist; her little hands lay folded on her lap, and she sat quite still, a resigned victim of love; but she looked at him bashfully, entreatingly. He could not bear that look; he quickly covered breast and shoulders again with the kerchief, fell at her feet, pressed her knees to his heart, and then walked away a few steps to overcome his emotion."

This suffers in translation. It must be read as it occurs in the original, this little field idyll, in which the lovers play like children ; she stands up against him that he may measure her height ; he plays with her curls ; from time to time she gently whispers : " O du !" but this is all she can say ; they make a meal on apples and bread, which they buy from a woman they meet, agreeing that novel writers lie when they assert that love lives on air ; she eats from his hand and he from hers. It is all as natural and as good as anything of the same style in Auerbach, Keller, or Björnson.

And Immermann's description of the sorrows of love is no less admirable. Nothing in the book surpasses the passage in which the old farmer tells Lisbeth that her lover is a young nobleman, and makes her understand that she must not expect him to marry her. Oswald has concealed his position and given himself out to be an ordinary forester, only with the intention of giving her a joyful surprise later. If she had taken time to think, she would have come to the conclusion that she need have no fear of his proving unfaithful. But the knowledge that her lover has lied is a blow that upsets her equilibrium, and Immermann profoundly remarks, " For love, as long as it is unshaken, is divine penetration . . . but once shaken, once driven to conjecture and surmise, it is madness, which passes cathedrals without seeing them and takes molehills for mountains." This is a profound saying, because it is a true psychological appreciation of a feeling which is the product of unknown causes. Heine's psychology of love was very simple ; when he complains, it is always of faithlessness as a wrong knowingly committed. Immermann here represents what may be called the somnambulistic action of the feeling, the instinct, unerring as that of the sleep - walker, which it possesses when undistracted by disturbing forces.

Both in broad outline and in minute detail this first of the peasant novels is sterling poetry. The influence of fantastic Romanticism is still distinct ; the secret tribunal,

the sword of Charlemagne, the enthusiasm for old customs
are Romantic features ; even Lisbeth's fanciful pedigree—
the fathering of this truthful young being on the old liar
Münchhausen—betrays that the tale is an outgrowth of an
earlier Romantic literature.   All this, however, only throws
into stronger relief the laborious, yet vigorous, process of
condensation by which healthy, modern realistic appreciation and treatment of popular subjects was evolved out
of the arbitrary fantasticality which immediately pre-
ceded it.

Immermann is one of the company of authors, including
Daniel Defoe, l'Abbé Prévost, the Danish poet Wessel,
Chamisso, and Bernardin de St. Pierre, who prove that
a single volume is enough to carry a writer's name down
to posterity, even if everything else that he has written be
quickly forgotten.   As a matter of fact, only this one work
of Immermann's lives.   He wrote mock-heroic poems, such
as *Tulifäntchen*, which was much appreciated in its day, but
is now unreadable.   He wrote works which, for their day,
must be pronounced meritorious, but which are now given
over to moth and rust, such as the drama *Merlin* (1831), a
great Romantic work in well-written verse, a sort of unsuccessful pendant to the Second Part of Goethe's *Faust*
and the historic tragedy which was first known as *Das
Trauerspiel in Tirol* ("The Tragedy in the Tyrol"), but was
re-named *Andreas Hofer*.   The second of these plays is the
better of the two; it is founded on Immermann's own youthful recollections of the formidable resistance encountered by
the French in the Tyrol, and is written with both the ability
and the will to present a faithful and impartial picture of
the two hostile races, so unlike in their character and in
their development.   This work in its original form, as
published in 1826, criticised by Börne in his *Dramaturgische
Blätter*, and satirised by Platen in *Der romantische Oedipus*,
is interesting, especially as a sort of mongrel, the offspring
of Kleist's genius mated with Schiller's muse ; for the hero
reminds us of Schiller's *Wilhelm Tell*, and the love affair
between the Frenchman and the Tyrolese girl, with its tragic
ending, of Kleist's *Die Hermannschlacht*.   But the play was

too devoid of any really profound, impressive originality to live long, and when, in 1831, Immermann re-wrote it, suppressing everything that had given offence or called forth adverse criticism—the whole love-story and the incident (again recalling Kleist) of the sword which the angel restored to Hofer in a dream—he himself took away what life there was in it. Pride, if nothing else, should have made him retain the character which Platen had tauntingly nicknamed the " Depeschenmordbrandehebruchstyrolerin."

It was an unlucky chance which made bitter enemies of two lovers of liberty like Immermann and Platen, and two rare spirits like Platen and Heine. That which gave rise to the whole literary feud, to the clumsy, ugly attacks on Immermann and Heine in *Der romantische Oedipus*, to Immermann's retort, *Der im Irrgarten der Metrik umhertaumelnde Cavalier* ("The Reeling Knight in the Labyrinth of Metre "), and to Heine's crushing attack on Platen in the *Reisebilder*, deadly from its very stench, was such a paltry trifle, such an insignificant though contemptuous distich, that only an arrogant and quarrelsome disposition like Platen's could have made it the occasion of a war with poisoned weapons.

Platen's letters show what dire offence he took at the two lines by Immermann in the *Reisebilder*, which might be construed as referring to his ghazels, and how determined he was to revenge himself ruthlessly. Great and serene in the region of pure art, and a manly champion of political liberty, he displays in his onslaught on the men who had insulted him, an offensively boastful degree of self-admira· tion and an insolence which is partly the arrogance of rank and partly the recklessness of wounded vanity. His letter from Rome of the 18th of February 1828, shows that he really knew nothing about Immermann's *Das Trauerspiel in Tirol*, which he had determined to attack. *Der romantische Oedipus* was almost finished when he wrote to Fugger : " Be sure to tell me something about Immermann's *Andreas Hofer*, something of the plot and any piquant nonsense. I need it for the end of my Fifth Act, where I make him go quite mad." The boundless contempt with which Platen treats Immermann in his play can thus, in spite of his

protests, only be regarded as vindictiveness. As regards
Heine, it is simply his Jewish birth with which Platen
taunts him in both letters and play. In the play everything
turns on this—Heine is the Petrarch of the Feast of
Tabernacles, the pride of the synagogue. So personal is
the satire that Nimmermann is made to say, that though
he is content to be Heine's friend, he would not be his
mistress, for his kisses reek of garlic, &c. From Platen's
letters it is easy to see that he completely underestimated
the strength of the antagonists whom he thus challenged.
He feels that he is capable of "crushing that Jew, Heine,"
whenever he chooses to do so. When his friends try to
persuade him that attacks on Heine because of his birth
carry no weight, he replies, quite unmoved : "That he is, or
was, a Jew is no moral offence, but a comical ingredient.
Intelligent readers will judge whether or not I have turned
it to account with Aristophanic cunning." So sure, so
superior does he feel himself, that even in December 1828,
immediately before he is utterly discomfited by Heine's
return blow, he sees in him nothing but "an impudent
Jew, a miserable scribbler and sans-culotte." His moral
indignation at the first books of the *Reisebilder* was, however,
so great that he calls the author and his like "veritable
Satans." [1] The treatment he met with was not undeserved ;
scorn was returned for scorn, and his under-estimation of
Heine and Immermann was cruelly avenged. The scurrilous
part of Heine's attack injured himself most by exciting the
disapprobation of his own friends and admirers.

The fact that the names Immermann and Platen came to
form a constellation of hate was actually due to the similarity
of their natures, to the feeling of solitariness which, combined
with a self-esteem that was always on the alert, made them
prone to proclaim their own praises and to attack others
with undue bitterness and with insufficient understanding.
These two men, each in his own way, represent the transition from Romanticism to modern liberalism. Platen, who
followed in the footsteps of the Romanticists in his assiduous
cultivation of foreign forms, the oriental ghazel, the southern

[1] Platen's *Werke*. Letters of 18th February, 12th March, and 13th December 1828.

sonnet, the ancient Greek Aristophanic comedy and Pindaric ode, shortly before his early death wrote songs and poems (*Political Poems*, including the *Polish Songs*—posthumously published) which are on the highest level of spirited modern lyric poetry. And Immermann, who all his life had treated tragic or fantastic themes with Romantic extravagance or symbolism, not long before he died impregnated a piece of homely reality with a spirit of true poetry by which the following generation throughout the whole of Europe was influenced.

XX

HEGELIANISM

It was the Hegelian philosophy, in combination with the Revolution of July, which drove thinking men to take their part in the stirring life of modern history and politics. Not that Hegel himself sympathised with the Revolution of July. Such a violent interference with what to him now represented the rational state of things, could hardly appeal to him, in his sixtieth year, as the great Revolution had done. In politics he had long been a strong Conservative.

But none the less certainly did the Revolution of July change the character of the Hegelian philosophy. It was the historical turning point, the historical crisis that was needed to transfer that philosophy from the lecture-room to the arena of life. One of the peculiarities of the philosophy was, that it was capable of diametrically opposite interpretations. From this time onwards we observe it to be one of the most powerful instruments in the remoulding, the reconstruction of life. We saw that it was so in the case of Heine, who never alludes to Hegel's conversion to Prussian Conservatism except to apologise for it ; to him Hegel is always the great philosopher of the new era, the mighty sovereign of the realm of thought.

Until Hegel was called to Berlin he had been unsuccessful as a teacher. He had attracted little attention at the other universities, and in his younger days had often lectured to only three or four students. Now he was at the height of his fame. Unlike Schelling, who reached maturity so early, and became so early barren, Hegel, the man of heavier, slower nature, entered the most momentous stage of his career with his forty-eighth year.

Great expectations were formed of him, and he fulfilled

HEGEL.

them all.   His insight was extraordinary; he seemed
thoroughly to belong to his time, and yet to live as it were
above it—familiar with all its ideas and judging them all
with calm superiority and profound conviction.   Hundreds
upon hundreds of listeners streamed to his lecture-room.

The young student who saw him for the first time
thought him an odd-looking figure.   He had aged early,
his originally powerful figure was bent, and the impression
he produced when he entered the lecture-room was that of
old-fashioned middle-class respectability.   He went to his
desk, seated himself, became absorbed in his manuscript,
turning over the large leaves and looking up and down them
for what he wanted.   His carriage was awkward and characterless, his expression listless, his face worn and wasted,
not by passion but by the most arduous mental labour.
But he had a fine, noble head, and when he turned his face,
with a look of profound, dignified, yet simple earnestness
towards his hearers, the imprint of high intellect was
unmistakable.

He began to speak, cleared his throat, coughed and
stammered, had difficulty in finding his words.   He had a
strong Swabian accent, and a jerky, unrhythmical delivery;
involved himself in long, intricate sentences which he seldom
managed to bring to a satisfactory conclusion; sought long
for the exact word required to express his meaning, but
never failed to find it; and when found, it always struck
his hearers as extraordinarily telling, whether it was a perfectly familiar or a very uncommon expression.   In time
this peculiar delivery simply served to make intelligible to
the listener the extraordinary difficulty and intricacy of the
mental process.   There might be tiresome repetitions, but
if the student let his attention wander and missed a few
sentences, as likely as not he was punished by losing the
thread of the discourse.   For by means of apparently insignificant intermediate steps some thought had been made
to betray its one-sidedness, its narrowness, to involve itself
in contradictions, and these contradictions had to be, or were
already, explained away.

What struck one as peculiarly characteristic of his

lecturing was the combination of two features : the speaker's
concentration in his subject, which made it seem as if he
spoke entirely for its sake ; and his keen anxiety to make
himself plainly understood, which made it seem as if after
all he spoke chiefly for the sake of the hearer.[1]

He was a wretched orator, this professor, but a wonderful thinker and expounder. The technical terms he employed
were bewildering—that extraordinary terminology in which
" an sich " meant according to its constitution, and " an und
für sich," the completed, absolute existence ; but his hearers
became accustomed to it, and soon began to feel as if they
were floating above the earth in abstractions so refined and
so ingeniously complementary that the dialectic of Plato's
Parmenides seemed clumsy in comparison ; at times as if they
were penetrating ever deeper into ever more concrete subjects. The speaker's voice grew stronger, he looked round
with a free, confident glance while, with a few pregnant
words, he characterised an intellectual movement, an age,
a nation, or some specially remarkable individual, such as
that nephew of Rameau's who, without being named, is
described in the *Phœnomenology*.

The novice who heard the famous thinker propound,
without any illustration, the abstract ideas which applied to
everything—spirit and nature, matter and mind—ideas of
which it was said that they enclosed the seen and the unseen
in their mysteriously but methodically woven net—might at
first feel tempted to run away, or at any rate not to come
back again.

But he did come back, for the laborious delivery soon
fascinated him, and he began to feel that he was making
progress. Every now and then a lightning-flash of thought
illuminated the darkness. The pupil began to comprehend
that, in his master's mind, there was no question of this
being a system like other systems, a more profound or
more comprehensive plan of instruction than other plans,
but that the man regarded himself as the originator of an
entirely new science, which comprehended the whole of

[1] Hotho : *Vorstudien für Leben und Kunst*, p. 383. Haym : *Hegel und seine Zeit.*, p. 392. Scherer : *Mélanges d'histoire religieuse*, p. 299.

existence, explained everything, God and the world, and was the completion of everything ; for the thoughts of all earlier thinkers were discernible in his system, as all the lower animal forms are traceable in the human embryo ; everything that had gone before had prepared his way, all endeavours found their fulfilment in him ; from this time forwards progress could only lie in the direction of more special development of the separate sections of the great completed plan.

The pupil was henceforth under the master's magic spell. The very abstruseness of the terminology was now an attraction the more ; difficulties acted as spurs; it seemed to him a point of honour, a matter of vital importance, that he should understand. And with what rapture he understood !—understood that the whole world of sense was only appearance ; the great reality was thought. These separate, individual appearances were not real, not true, only the universal was real. I think, and by inevitable laws the progress of my thought leads me to the complete understanding of myself and of the world. I think my own thought, not regarding it as my own, but as the universal thought, as the thought of all other human intelligences in union with mine ; I deprive them all of the individuality which appears to be essential but is not, and see in all these intelligences one intelligence, and in it the principle of existence. This first principle, which finds its highest expression in man, is that which permeates, which creates the world. This first principle, which works and creates blindly in nature, is in me conscious of itself. The absolute, the idea, that which is popularly known as God, is not a conscious or personal being, for consciousness and personality presuppose the existence of something outside the consciousness and personality; and yet it is not quite unconscious. Man's consciousness of God is God's self-consciousness. I cease to live as a single, fortuitous human being, in order to feel the universal life live and pulsate in me.

Logic, which has been nothing but a sort of childish scholastic discipline, which inculcated self-evident facts by the aid of barbaric formulæ (Barbara, Celarent, Ferio,

Camestres, Baroco), logic, which had languished and died in ignominy long ago, came to life again in the doctrine of the thoughts of existence in their connection and their unity; for the first thought necessitated, produced the second, amalgamated with it into a third, which in its turn summoned up its antithesis, which was at the same time its complement. Thought of necessity produced thought, until the thought-serpent set its tooth into its own tail, thus forming one inviolable circle, from which the realms of nature and spirit again detached themselves, dropping as the rings dropped from Draupner, the ring of Odin.

And all the sciences came and drank of the new meta-physic, as of a fountain of life, and all renewed their youth. And the system gradually rose before the disciple's eye, homogeneous, carefully articulated, severely symmetrical, of an internal infinity, a spiritual Organon, a gigantic Gothic cathedral, every little part of which repeated the whole, every little triad the great Trinity—thought, nature, and spirit. It rose, built upon the granite foundation of thought, all the buttresses and arches of the realm of nature supporting it as it mounted towards the spirit, soaring to heaven in the mighty three-storied tower of which religion formed the lowest, art the middle, and philosophy the highest course.

But even more to the disciple than the system was the method. For the method, the imperative thought-process, was the key to earth and to heaven. It was by virtue of the method that he understood. It was by virtue of the method that he saw the history of the world to be a connected drama, one grand drama of liberation, in which every race had its part, and all the parts were interdependent.

It was, after all, a truly great thought-poem, which men took for a scientific demonstration; a new species of poetry, more dramatic and more masterly in construction than that which Schelling's intellectual perception had revealed to him; a new intoxicant, more subtle and potent than that pro-vided by the natural philosopher. The system has, indeed, collapsed, the machinery of the method, too fine and intri-cate, has come to pieces in our hands; only a few of the great fundamental thoughts remain. But he who in his early youth has passed through the Hegel period in his own mental experience, perfectly understands the rapturous enthusiasm of the youth of that day, and the strength they drew from these cosmic thoughts, world-ideas.

Among Hegel's pupils about the year 1830 there were already master-thinkers like Hotho, Gans, Marheineke, Michelet ; and almost all the men of mark who appeared in the most diverse intellectual domains from this time until far on in the Fifties, belonged at first to the Hegelian school—Rosenkranz and Werder, Strauss and Fischer, Feuerbach, Marx, and Lassalle. Cousin came from France, Heiberg from Denmark, Vera from Naples, to fit themselves for propagating his doctrines in their native countries.

From the professorial chair in Berlin, the Hegelian philosophy spread throughout Germany, throughout the earth. Seldom or never has a spiritual monarch's throne stood so secure. At the time of Hegel's death (by cholera) in 1831, his followers compared him to Aristotle, to Alexander the Great, even to Christ.

On the literature of the following decade, and in especial on the so-called Young Germany, Hegelianism acted as an emancipating spiritual power, a power that destroyed faith in religious dogma and freed the individual from the burden of the Christianity of the State church. We have already observed that even such an essentially lyric nature as Heinrich Heine's took on the tinge of Hegelianism in this respect, quite independently of the fact that his keen understanding was trained in the school of Hegel ; in the peculiar turn of his wit we trace the influence of the Hegelian dialectic, which makes every idea pass over into its opposite (unity of opposites).

But it was as a sort of modern Hellenism that the Hegelian philosophy exercised the most powerful influence upon young minds. What may be called Hegel's Hellenic influence was even stronger than Goethe's.

The reader doubtless remembers the passage in Heine's book on Börne in which he writes on Börne's Nazarenic narrowness. He tells us that he calls it "Nazarenic" to avoid employing the words Jewish or Christian, words which to him convey the same meaning, because he does not use them to designate a faith but a disposition, a nature ; and he places the word Nazarenic in opposition to the word Hellenic, which also to him signifies an innate or acquired disposition and view of things generally. In other words, all humanity is divided for him into Nazarenes and Hellenes, men with ascetic, image-hating dispositions, inclined to morbid spiritualisation, and men of cheerfully realistic temperament, inclined to genial self-development. And he designates himself a Hellene—a name which no Romanticist would ever have bestowed on himself.

Hellenism in this sense emanated abundantly from Hegel. His whole intellectual bent is in the direction of that tendency of the time to present modern matter in antique manner, which we observe in Goethe when he writes his *Iphigenia*, and in Thorvaldsen when he represents the Princess Barjátinska in Greek dress. It was not by mere chance that Hegel and Thorvaldsen were born within a few months of each other in the year 1770. Nor was it a mere accident that Hegel best understood that side of Goethe's nature which turned towards Greece.

Hegel had received his early training in his native country, Würtemberg, under two influences, that of eighteenth century enlightenment with its revolt against theology, and that of classic antiquity. Even as a school-boy he was keenly interested in the study of the Greek language and literature ; as a mere child he was devoted to the *Antigone* of Sophocles, which in later life was to him the typical Greek work of art, and is constantly re-ferred to in his writings. He declared the study of the ancient classics to be the real introduction to philosophy, and his own system as a whole he gradually moulded on the plan of the ancient systems. It stands in the same relation to the Aristotelian structure of thought in which Goethe's *Iphigenia* stands to a play of Euripides, or Thorvaldsen's " Triumphal Procession of Alexander " to the frieze of the Parthenon.

His primary natural disposition towards Christianity is

shown in his studies and researches as a youthful theologian, the substance of which, taken from the original manuscripts, has been given to the public by Haym. In these early writings he maintains that the Greco-Roman religion was a religion for free men, that a free community, a free state, was the highest ideal of the Greek, an ideal to which he consecrated his labour and his life. The God of Christianity was only a substitute for lost republican liberty. Men had lost power; they could no longer will, but only wish and pray. And the more slavish they grew, the more was a God outside of themselves and above themselves a necessity to them. And it is Hegel's opinion that for us, in our days, has been reserved the task of demanding the return of those treasures—the property of man—that were flung up into heaven. In this he anticipates Heine and Feuerbach.[1]

In his youth Hegel always sees Jewish antiquity through classic spectacles. He calls their ancient history "a condition of unmitigated ugliness." The great tragedy of the Jewish nation is, he says, a very different thing from a Greek tragedy; it neither awakens pity nor terror ; for these feelings are only called forth by the fate following on the inevitable errors of a noble nature. He sees the history and fate of the Jews against a background of Sophoclean conception of life and Aristotelian theories. Such ideas as law and punishment are repugnant to him. The Christian doctrine of the forgiveness of sin he can only accept by converting it into the idea of fate reconciled by love. In other words, he can only admire the sufferings of Christ when he looks upon them as he looks upon the sufferings

[1] " Die Objectivität der Gottheit ist mit der Verdorbenheit und Sklaverei der Menschen in gleichem Schritt gegangen, und jene ist eigentlich nur eine Offenbarung dieses Geistes der Zeiten. . . . Ausser früheren Versuchen blieb es vorzüglich unseren Tagen aufbehalten, die Schätze, die an den Himmel geschleudert worden sind, als Eigenthum der Menschen wenigstens in der Theorie zu vindiciren ; aber welches Zeitalter wird die Kraft haben, dieses Recht geltend zu machen und sich in den Besitz zu setzen ? "

The objectivity of the Divinity has gone hand in hand with the slavery and corruption of humanity, and is in reality only one sign of the spirit of the times. . . . Attempts have been made before, but it has been specially reserved for our age to vindicate at least in theory, as the property of man, the treasures which have been hurled up into heaven ; but what age will have the power to enforce this right and to place man in possession of his own?

of Oedipus in Colonos, namely, as a fate overtaking the innocent, not as a sacrifice offered for the sins of others.

All that he rescues for himself from the shipwreck of positive religion is the person and life-story of Jesus—that beautiful divine-human personal life which is to him an equivalent for the citizen-life of the ancient world. But his Jesus is not Jesus pure and simple, but a Jesus-Apollo such as Heine describes in his poem *Frieden*—the giant, who bears the red, flaming sun in his breast for a heart. We have a similar fusion of heathenism and Christianity in the well-known preface to *Romancero*, where Heine talks of his last genuflection " before the ever blessed goddess of beauty, our dear lady of Milo." For this is not Venus pure and simple, but Venus-Madonna.

Thus Hegel himself is the originator of that pagan Hellenism, of which it was the fashion to accuse Young Germany.

And in his philosophy we can even detect the spirit which might evolve such a watchword as " the emancipation of the flesh." This was a French expression introduced by Heine into German literature, which was eagerly taken up by his admirers and imitators, and was specially exe- crated by the enemies and denouncers of the new literature. It certainly might be suspected of an immoral meaning in Heine's mouth and of an ugly meaning in Heinrich Laube's; but amongst the best of the men of the young generation it meant nothing but what Goethe and Hegel, too, had in reality desired. Karl Gutzkow has insisted, and with reason, that only a low mind coupled with this expression ideas of licence for all bad passions. For the word flesh in itself conveyed no objectionable meaning. The New Testament says : " The Word was made flesh." Flesh, in the Christian accepta- tion of the word, means the natural, the unbaptised, the original man. Its emancipation in reality meant to the young enthusiasts of the day nothing more than the re- storing of her rights to nature, war against what is contrary to nature. What they desired was to make the laws of nature the rule of conduct, to release nature from interdict and ban.[1]

---

[1] Karl Gutzkow : *Rückblicke auf mein Leben*, p. 135.

A neo-Hellenism realised in the Hegelian spirit was what was present to their minds.

It did not seem a matter of great consequence to them that Hegel should end his days as a rigid Prussian Conservative, or that his *Philosophy of Right* should recognise all existing institutions as "holy things," and make out the highest ethical conceptions to be "idols." He had underestimated the strength of the scientific doubt of the day.

How many institutions still presented themselves as objects of veneration and faith to the normal mind of the period? Four at most—the monarchy, the church, marriage, and property. As regards these, Hegel's doctrine is as follows:

He does not uphold the monarchy as a guarantee for continuity in the execution of great political plans ; no, the monarch is to him simply the logically necessary pinnacle of the state-building, something like the dot over the i—a most inconsistent position of Hegel's ; to him in all other instances the subjective (the personal) is only a transient form of energy, so that logically the monarch ought to be in time merged in the sovereignty of the State. His defence of monarchy is thus a concession to existing circumstances. Was it any wonder that the following generation drew its own logical conclusion ?

With regard to the Church, Hegel took up the position which was subsequently publicly taken up by his disciple Cousin as French Minister of State. He allowed his followers, the so-called Hegelians of the Left, men like Göschen, to demonstrate the harmony of his philosophy with the Bible and with ecclesiastical Christianity, actually in his review bestowing excessive praise on Göschen's aphorisms. The man who in his youthful letters to Schelling had attacked the philosophy of Kant because it could be made to lend itself to the service of orthodoxy, the man who had adjured Hölderlin never to make peace with dogma, now in his own religious philosophy took the ambiguous course of making out every dogma to be the symbol of a thought, and allowing the dogma to stand, with the explanation that it figuratively expressed the same truth as science. Was it any wonder that his pupils drew their own inferences ?

Marriage, Hegel regarded as an incident in family life, justified to much the same extent as family property. How it was brought about was of comparatively small importance ; arrangement by the parents was probably the most moral way. In his aversion from the arbitary action of the individual, he dwelt on the irrationality of the private individual's capricious fancy for this or that girl ("dass er sich gerade auf dieses Mädchen capricionire "). He spoke on this subject half like an old Spartan, half like a narrow old bourgeois, and the youth of the day, being neither Spartan nor narrow, did not accept his doctrine.

Property Hegel considered morally justified only as the common property of the family. Only when it is not the possession of an individual is what he calls the egotism of greed overcome. Of course he vehemently condemns Communism. But an impetus had been given to logical conclusion-drawing, and the time came when Hegelians like Marx and Engel drew revolutionary conclusions from the philosophy of the apparently Conservative master.

XXI

YOUNG GERMANY AND MENZEL

WHEN, from the all-embracing thought of Hegel, the noble art of Platen, the polished wit of Börne, the lyric and satiric genius of Heine, the classic fulness of Immermann's *Oberhof*, we pass on to the men to whom the name Young Germany was more particularly applied, we feel the change to be in the artistic sense a fall—a fall from the confidence and perfect skill of masters to the immaturity and make-shifts of beginners. And among the men of Young Germany there were those who were destined for ever to remain beginners. More especially is the transition from Heine to his successors felt like a fall from graceful, god-like audacity to clumsy youthful defiance of all established custom, all conventional morality.

And yet the best of these men in their best moments displayed a self-devotion unknown to Heine.

The Young Germany of accepted tradition includes neither Heine, Börne, and their contemporaries (who were regarded as its fathers), nor the circle of young scientific men who expressed their views in Ruge's and Echtermeyer's *Hallische Jahrbücher*, nor the group of political poets who in the Forties gave literary expression to the feelings which found practical expression in the deeds of 1848.

The name in its traditional acceptation has a much narrower signification than that given to it in the present volume.

Its originator was a very earnest, but not specially gifted North German author, Ludolf Wienbarg, born at Altona in 1803. In 1834, under the warlike title of *An Æsthetic Campaign* (a title invented by Campe, the publisher), Wienbarg published a series of lectures which he had delivered in Kiel, and for which he had been deprived of his right to lecture, though their inoffensive matter and their unctuous manner were little calculated to produce excitement of any kind. To this book, which it is a hard task to wade through nowadays, is prefixed the dedication : "To the young Germany, not the old, I dedicate this book" (Dem jungen Deutschland, nicht dem alten, widme ich dieses Buch). This is all that men remember to-day of Wienbarg's lectures. By young Germany he meant all the young German minds that had broken with tradition in art, church, state, and society, and were devoting their literary talents to the furtherance of the reforms which they felt to be imperative.

The programme he proposes for the new literature is alarming in its vagueness. Its conception of life is to be founded on a harmonious union of sensuality and spirituality. He proclaims a new Hellenism, in which the sensual will be more permeated by spirit than in the case of the Greeks, and the spiritual more permeated by the sensual than in the case of the Christians. But before literature can be born again, life itself must be. Not till the life around them has become healthy and harmonious, can the young generation produce a true work of art.

There was, as we see, nothing new in these declamations and prophecies. Heine had already said the same thing in a hundred ways, comic or poetic ; even Menzel in his first period had said the same with all the eloquence of the unsuccessful poet and violent partisan. Here it was expressed in the flowery language and with the rhetoric which seldom fails to produce its effect on immature minds.

The only novelty lay in the fact that now for the first time the exponent of these ideas was a representative of that young generation who regarded Heine as the great author of the age, and that now for the first time expression was given to the theory that prose was the literary form of the new age, and of more value than poetry. Wienbarg's æsthetic theories resolve themselves into glorification of Heine, whom he proclaims to be the great, the greatest prose author. Not till now, he declares, under the influence of French prose, has German prose really been formed. Schiller's style he calls the language of the parade, and

Goethe's the language of the court. All the earlier great authors, even Jean Paul, lived, according to him, within a magic circle, far removed from the stir of the world. What distinguishes the prose of a Heine, a Börne, a Menzel, a Laube, from that of the earlier writers is, in his opinion, the want of tranquillity, of placidity (Behaglichkeit), but it is this want that gives it its superiority, the superiority of life. Heine especially is praised for having disdained "the passing fame" of a lyric poet in order to play upon the colossal, cosmic instrument which lies under the hands of a master of German prose.

First Mundt and then Laube, neither of whom was capable of writing a respectable verse, joined eagerly in this glorification of prose at the expense of poetry, the more willingly as by so doing they entered a protest against the Swabian school of poetry, the tardy offspring of Uhland's branch of Romanticism. Mundt positively elevated this cult of prose to the rank of the newest gospel. How little real ability Wienbarg possessed is clearly shown by his second work, *Zur neuesten Litteratur*, a collection of weak essays, in which the only thing we find to admire is his courageous fidelity to Heine at a time when envious rivals and moral doctrinaires had turned the tide of popular opinion against him.

Wienbarg had called the name Young Germany into existence, but as yet it designated no exactly specified group of authors. Strangely enough it was first applied to definite individuals in connection with a public denunciation and harsh legal proceedings.

The facts were as follows: A number of young authors had gradually brought themselves into notice, who were not exactly in league with each other, but whose common watchword was, spiritual emancipation. They all held aloof from Christianity and dreamed of a new, pantheistic religion for the new era. Many of them desired, under the name of "the emancipation of the flesh" or "rehabilitation of the flesh," the abolishment of the traditional code of morals, and more freedom in the conditions regulating the union and separation of the two sexes. Both the expression of this desire and the desire itself were, in the case of a man like Laube, unpleasantly epicurean, in the case of a man like Gutzkow, unnecessarily defiant and curiously morbid ; with others again, such as Mundt, it took the form of championship of what he vaguely called the emancipation of woman, by which he merely meant more independence in home life and in marriage.   By all these authors certain distinguished women were held in high honour—in France, George Sand, by whom they were strongly influenced; in Germany, Rahel, Bettina, Charlotte Stieglitz.

They all talked much and loudly of the rights of youth, had all imbibed a certain faith in liberty from Hegel, and all owed their general political tendency to the Revolution of July.   Their aim was to identify literature with life, as Hegel had reconciled idea with reality.   They had no really profound sympathy with each other, and they soon went each his own way.   They were widely enough separated as regarded their places of residence.   Heine lived in Paris, Weinbarg at Kiel—entirely isolated ; Gutzkow resided in South Germany, Mundt was in Berlin, Laube in Leipzig ; and the distances separating these places were very considerable then.   Laube was very soon in many ways an opponent of Gutzkow, and a cold, unpleasant critic of Mundt and Kühne.   Mundt attacked Gutzkow.   An accidental meeting between Laube and Gutzkow in the north of Italy in 1833 contributed to their estrangement rather than their reconcilement.   There was no other community between these writers than that usually existing between men of the same age and calling; they were much less a political party than a literary coterie ; nevertheless literature was not to them its own aim and end ; they desired to devote themselves to the service of the spirit of the age.[1]

This was the reason why they did not occupy themselves with the pure forms of literary art, neither with epic nor with lyric poetry, and but sparingly with dramatic.   They all idolised the " Zeitgeist " (spirit of the times), and did homage to it in journalism and fiction, in critical and argumentative

[1] See Ludwig Geiger: *Das junge Deutschland und die preussische Censur*. Berlin, 1900.

KARL GUTZKOW

essays, in fanciful descriptions of travel, after the pattern of Heine's and Prince Pückler-Muskau's, and at times in long-winded novels.

The most able of them all was undoubtedly Karl Gutzkow, born in Berlin in 1811, a man of a tireless, energetic, inquiring spirit, absorbed in the thousand problems of modern life, a cross between an analytical critic and a poet, but a man to whom nothing came of itself and who achieved nothing with ease. His personality had no charm, his youth no freshness, his prose no rhythm. But he was bold, inventive, intelligent, and enterprising. He had the gift of pathos, but not the lyric gift ; his style was effective, but unmelodious. His mind was specially open to ideas, to all the thoughts and spiritual movements that were abroad at that day. By nature he belonged to the ungainly, but his literary enthusiasm was so genuine, his ambition so great, and his will so strong, that he gradually became an intellectual centre and diffused his influence in many directions. There was a time, about the year 1840, when a great part of what was best in German literature took its tone from him and his adherents.

We saw how it was the Revolution of July that awakened in him a desire to write. The following year, the great year of dismissals, imprisonments, and banishments in Prussia, put the pen into his hand. It was a time when every word underwent the strictest censorship ; even the advertisements in the *Intelligenzblatt* were carefully examined, in case they might contain some hidden political meaning.

Gutzkow began by publishing a newspaper, *Forum der Journallitteratur*. He had been brought up on the Hegelian idea of the progress of the world towards ever greater liberty. As Gottschall has expressed it : " There swam before his eyes a constant succession of political sunrises and world-liberating theories." His newspaper reached a circulation of seventy copies, and was then given up.

Wolfgang Menzel, at that time the acknowledged master of German criticism, had repeatedly invited Gutzkow to come to Stuttgart and assist him in the editorship of his *Litteratur-blatt*, as he himself, having been elected a member of the

Würtemberg Parliament, was no longer able to conduct it alone.

In spite of his hatred of Goethe, nay, partly because of it, Menzel, at this period of his career, was revered by the youth of Germany much as Katkóf and Ploug in their first periods were revered in Russia and Denmark. He, above all others, was to them the man of the day, the friend of liberty. One of Gutzkow's aims in his newspaper had been to defend Menzel, the man after his own heart, against the attacks of his enemies—and Menzel had many enemies, for as a reviewer he was disputatious, quarrelsome, and abusive. But he was, or seemed to be, a man of sincere convictions. He urged the necessity for a profounder conception of patriotism and of religion than was then in vogue, but at the same time he was an ardent Liberal in politics, and as such an admirer of Börne and Heine, who looked upon him as a trusty companion in arms ; in Parliament he championed all progressive measures, amongst others the emancipation of the Jews.

Gutzkow, not yet much over twenty, short, slight, fair, and pale-faced, entered the presence of his lord and master, who was thirteen years older than himself, with a bashful reverence which he has compared to that of the student who appears before Mephistopheles-Faust in the first part of Goethe's drama. He saw a man with broad shoulders, a well developed chest, and dark hair, whose clean-shaven face reminded him of a Romish priest's. Round the mouth, with its ugly yellow teeth, a satiric smile played ; the expression of the short-sighted eyes behind the spectacles was half defiant, half dignified. The man's temper seemed to be violent, his will inflexible. An expression of faun-like sensuality would come over his features when he talked of some erotic book, and yet Goethe's worldliness was as hateful to him as his indifference to politics, and he un-critically bowed the knee to men and phenomena that to his mind represented the mysterious. His character was a genuine priestly blend of irony and mysticism. He loved Voltaire, and enthusiastically admired Görres.

Master and pupil agreed well at first, both in their social

and in their business relations.   Gutzkow, who lived now in one, now in another of the towns in the neighbourhood of Stuttgart, indefatigably reviewed the great parcels of books sent him by Menzel.   He soon caught the brisk, sweeping journalistic style, and all went well.   The youthful works which he himself published, naturally found a more than lenient critic in Menzel.   Yet they were poor enough.   *Briefe eines Narren an eine Närrin* (" Letters from a Male to a Female Fool ") are humorous effusions without originality, in a style which is partly an imitation of Jean Paul, partly of Heine ; and *Maha Guru, the History of a God*, the description of the psychological condition of a Tibetan who is made Dalai-Lama and consequently worshipped as a divinity, is a piece of fantastic writing, now totally unreadable.   Yet Menzel, when reviewing this latter book, chose from amongst the vignettes which alternately figured on the title-page of his review, a laurel wreath, and had Gutzkow's name twice printed within its circle.

Gutzkow's intention in *Maha Guru* was to show how the god who is supposed to be incarnated in the Dalai-Lama is subordinated to the man in him, the false divinity being completely thrown into the shade by the true nobility, true divinity of the human being.   But besides this, the book was intended to be a philosophical-satirical romance in the old style, representing home institutions in foreign guise. The Tibetan theocracy was intended to suggest the European hierarchy, the Tibetan polyandry the European emancipation of woman.   The foreign scenery, which Gutzkow had never seen, the foreign customs, which were not described for their own sake, could not interest.   The book was suggested to him by the story of the French atheist, Billaud-Varennes, who escaped the guillotine during the Reign of Terror, took refuge in America, and was there worshipped by the Indians as a god.   His skill in catching, training, and stuffing birds made such an impression on them that they looked upon him as a second creator.   But all this had little to do with Tibet, and the would-be gravity of Gutzkow's theme.

Up to this time Young Germany and its fathers had not

seemed to Menzel to be sacrilegious scoffers or bad patriots. Gutzkow's irreligion so far had not disturbed the good relations between him and his master. Menzel himself praised Börne's *Letters from Paris*, which were attacked on all sides, as manly utterances, and excused their strong expressions as outbursts of feeling which must not be too roughly dealt with ; he compared them to the glow-worms which shine so beautifully on mild summer nights, but which turn into poor little grey insects when seized by rough hands.

But it was inevitable that the tie between Gutzkow and Menzel should soon be loosed. From the first Gutzkow had received warnings not to involve himself too deeply with the Stuttgart author. Hegel himself, who took an interest in the young man, had said to him : " How can any one bind himself to a man like that ? " The first disagreement between them was on the subject of Menzel's attitude to the South German lyric poets, the so-called Swabian school, followers of Uhland, a poet who not only enjoyed the fame which he most undoubtedly deserved, but a far greater. As a good Swabian, Menzel esteemed and supported these men—Gustav Schwab, Gustav Pfizer, Karl Mayer, &c.—as bulwarks of conventional piety and morality. But Gutzkow, with his keen sense of what was the life-idea of the time, Gutzkow, to whom literature was the church militant, had the greatest objection to such Sunday afternoon, gilt-edged poets, men who put into rhyme old, dead ballad themes, or their own petty, sentimental feelings, whilst they were cautiously watching over their interests as government servants aspiring to professorships or consistory counsellorships.

When *Goethe's Conversations with Eckermann* appeared, it became known how severely Goethe had judged his admirer Uhland's poetry. He would hear of nothing but the ballads, considering all the rest unworthy of notice. And a most contemptuously disparaging verdict upon the whole Swabian school, from Uhland to Pfizer, was presently published in *Goethe's Correspondence with Zelter :* he (Goethe) had never expected anything fresh or capable from that quarter ; the fellows concealed their want of genius under the moral-religious-poetical beggar's cloak.[1]

After this Gutzkow took courage and proclaimed that to him also this antiquated pastoral and cloistral Romanticism was an abomination. In an essay entitled *Goethe, Uhland, und Prometheus* he made a violent attack on those poets who sought and " found their creed in their certificates of baptism, their morals in conventionality, their principles in established custom, and their poetry in the poetry of other people." What have you to offer us? he cried. Evening walks in the setting sun. Where is your effort to keep pace with the times?

Meanwhile the reaction against the Revolution of July was in full progress everywhere. The policy of Prussia, as well as that of Austria, was controlled by Metternich ; and when the youth of Germany began to understand on what side the power and the energy were, and probably would be for long to come, they went over to that side. Gutzkow says, that out of every hundred students at the University of Berlin at that time, ninety-seven were strong Conservatives ; and every meeting with an old school or college companion, more especially if he happened to be a civil servant or an officer, left a most painful impression on his mind.

In such circumstances it often happens that high-spirited, able young men lose their heads and commit rash actions for which they are blamed all their lives.

Schleiermacher was dead, laid to rest with great ceremonial, mourned as a father of the Protestant Church, one of the saints of theology. It had long ago been said, and well said, of him, that his character answered to his name (Schleiermacher = veilmaker). By dint of ambiguities and uncertain utterances he had kept himself popular to the end of his days. No one had brought up against him that

---

[1] " Wundersam ist es, wie sich diese Herrlein einen gewissen sittig-religiös-poetischen Bettlermantel so geschickt umzuschlagen wissen, dass, wenn auch der Ellenbogen herausguckt, man diesen Mangel für eine poetische Intention halten muss."

The fellows manage to throw a kind of moral-religious-poetic beggar's cloak so cleverly round them, that, even if the bare elbow shows, we are obliged to consider this defect a poetic intention.

Q

Romantic sin of his youth, the *Vertrauliche Briefe um Lucinde* ("Confidential Letters on the Subject of Lucinde ").

But now Gutzkow, who erroneously concluded that this forgotten book would be omitted from the edition of Schleiermacher's works then in preparation, could not resist the temptation to republish it, and to defend himself and his friends against the perpetual accusations of godless immorality by showing that their erotic views, and even their doctrine of the rehabilitation of the flesh, had been held by that man of God who was the revered lord and master of the theologians.

This might have been a good tactical move if the youth, for he was still only twenty-three, had not written a foolish, boyish preface to the book. In it he addresses himself to the "watchmen of Zion," scoffs at their sanctimoniousness and spiritual coquetry, and thus adjures them :—"For one moment cast your priestly robes from you, forget that a man whom you still perpetually crucify was God, and listen to what happened once on a time elsewhere, in the world of liberty, youth, and fancy!"

What had happened was the publication of Schlegel's *Lucinde*, that lewd skeleton, which in Gutzkow's eyes is glorious and classic, and of Schleiermacher's letters about it, which in Gutzkow's estimation are divine. The Letters speak for themselves. They absurdly over-estimate *Lucinde*, but the genuine human feeling in them is beautiful and courageous. In Gutzkow's preface everything is emphasised in a disagreeably defiant manner. He avers that love is of the nature of genius, maintains that priestly action neither adds to nor takes from the sacredness of marriage, tauntingly declaims against the cold prose of the ordinary marriage, "the water-soup weddings, the sordid procreation of children and struggle for mouldy bread." He winds up flippantly with : "Now tell me truly, Rosalie ! Is it not since you have worn spurs on your little silk boots, since I have taught you how to throw your cloak over your shoulder, since I have invented a new sort of inexpressibles for you, so that every one takes you to be my youngest, dearly loved brother, is it not since then that you know what I meant by : I love you ?" And not content with this female wearer of breeches, who is the realisation of his idea of the emancipation of woman, Gutzkow last of all plays out an atheistic trump ; "Where is Franz?—Come here, dear boy. I know they baptized you secretly. Who is God? What! you don't know, you innocent atheist, you philosophic child! Oh, if the world too had only not known about God, how much happier it would have been!"

No specially acute critical faculty is needed to detect the unreality in this student's braggadocio. The original of the Rosalie who was to follow Gutzkow about in page's dress was more probably the Kaled of Byron's *Lara* than any Heidelberg or Berlin seamstress. It is easy to imagine what effect such a preface to such a book would produce on the general public and on orthodox journalism.

Only a drop was needed to fill the cup of public indignation, and that drop Gutzkow did not fail to add. In 1835 he wrote *Wally, die Zweiflerin* ("The Sceptic"), which is an exceedingly weak story, with a positively burlesque crucial episode, but which nevertheless influenced the course of events more powerfully than any other German literary work of the day.

Strauss's *Life of Jesus* had lately come out, and its resolution of the historical element in that life into myths, bold and fanciful to the verge of folly as the hypothesis was, had violently perturbed the thinking minds of Germany. Indignation was universal. A thousand-voiced cry of condemnation rose from the Eider to Switzerland. For many a year, in the public mind, there was a dark stain on the name of David Strauss.

The book was talked about everywhere, and Gutzkow one evening began to discuss its problem with a young girl to whom he was attached. "Don't let us talk about that," she said, " the very thought drives me mad!" These words made a strong impression on him.

Strauss's book itself had not satisfied him. Rationalist as he was, he felt the need for a historic Jesus, and betook himself to the study of Reimarus's old *Wolfenbüttel Fragments*, to which Lessing before him had devoted so much attention.

He determined to publish a selection from these, but it was in vain that he applied with this intention to the most courageous of the German publishers, Campe. In spite of his bold political attitude, Campe dared not expose himself to the rancour of the Hamburg clergy, Pastor Goetze's successors in the cure of souls.

It was about this time that the noble Charlotte Stieglitz committed suicide. The impression produced by this tragic event combined itself in Gutzkow's mind with the impressions made by his young friend's remark and by Reimarus's Biblical criticism——and *Wally, the Sceptic*, was the result.

It is a childish book, this *Wally*, but it is innocent, honest, and artless. The heroine is a young lady moving in good society, who, in despair at not being able to overcome the religious doubts awakened in her mind by the man she loves, the sceptical, *blasé* Cæsar, kills herself with a dagger.

Gutzkow had been unable to withstand the temptation of reminding the venerable lights and defenders of the Church, the dignitaries of all the different classes of the Order of the Red Eagle, that there had once lived men named Hume, Voltaire, Lessing, &c. There was something fascinating to a young man in the idea of reminding such grand folks of such forgotten existences. But it ought to have been done with talent. In Gutzkow's novel the plot was a mere excuse for ventilating theories, *Wally* was a weak imitation of *Lélia*, the last novel which George Sand had published.

But its author was in the spring-tide of his youth. It seemed to him as if the whole world were growing young again. The glow of Hegel's sinking sun still illuminated the horizon, Bettina arose like a morning star, the ever-young wisdom of Rahel was scattered abroad over the earth after her death like fruitful dew, Lenau's and Rückert's early poems were like the song of the lark, Ruge's first critical articles and Feuerbach's first philosophic writings were like fresh spring breezes that cleared the air——the time seemed to him so sunny, so promising, so laden with fruit, that it was as it were symbolised by the two glorious summers of 1834 and 1835, with their rich harvests of corn and wine. And it was then he committed his first great youthful blunder.

He was not satisfied with embodying his religious hetero-doxy in his book ; he also proclaimed his moral heterodoxy, his defiance of the accepted code of sexual morality—a very clumsy and immature defiance. But the best idea of how very innocently Gutzkow interpreted that watchword, "the emancipation of the flesh," which he himself employs, is to be gained from the notorious scene in *Wally*, which was intended by the author to express his worship of beauty.

Wally loves Cæsar and is loved by him, but they can-not marry each other, because Wally has been obliged to betroth herself to the Sardinian ambassador. Cæsar entreats her that she will as it were symbolically celebrate a spiritual marriage with him by showing herself to him in all her naked beauty the night before her wedding. In an old German ballad, the heroine, Sigune, thus displays herself to Tchionatulander.

No one will deny that Cæsar's request is insane and its fulfilment ridiculous. But the intention of the scene was so chaste and its execution so inoffensive, that only positive low-mindedness could have made it the occasion of calling for the assistance of the police. We read ; "The cloak slips from the young hero's shoulders ; his hair waves freely and luxuriantly. To the left there appears out of the sun-mist an image of intoxicating beauty—Sigune, displaying herself more bashfully than the Medicean Venus hides her nakedness. She stands there helpless, dazzled by the glamour of the love that besought this favour ; her will is gone ; she is the personification of shame, innocence, and self-abandon-ment. And in sign that this is a consecrated, holy scene, no roses bloom, but a high-stemmed lily has shot upwards close to her body, symbolically covering her as the flower of chastity. It all happened in one breathless, silent moment —it was sacrilege, but the sacrilege of innocence and of woeful, eternal renunciation." This is all.

The relations between Gutzkow and Menzel were no longer what they had been. Now and again, in some preface or article, Gutzkow had ventured to make a small joke at the expense of his former patron, or a modest protest against one or other of his utterances. And in a more practical way Gutzkow had for some time past been a thorn in the side to Menzel. His literary supplement to the Frankfort newspaper, *Phœnix*, was a dangerous rival to Menzel's *Litteraturblatt*. But there was worse than this. Gutzkow had gradually got into friendly correspondence with the leaders of the new literature, Laube, Wienbarg, Mundt, &c., men who were rapidly taking possession of all the more important literary organs in Berlin, Leipzig, Frankfort, and Hamburg. When, in 1835, Gutzkow and Wienbarg issued the prospectus of a literary review in the style of *Revue des Deux Mondes*, with almost all the most eminent literary names in Germany on its list of contributors — university professors like Boeckh, influential writers like Varnhagen, not to mention a talented author like Börne and a genius like Heine—Menzel felt the necessity for striking a telling blow.

An invitation to subscribe to the *Deutsche Revue* had been published. It was written by Gutzkow, in flowery, metaphoric language—declares that science is longing to escape from musty class-rooms into the free open air, that the bird of Minerva is no longer the owl, which is afraid of the light, but the eagle, which gazes steadfastly into the sun, &c., &c.

Instead of confining his attack to this programme, which was inoffensive and in some respects promising, Menzel, in his *Litteraturblatt* of the 11th and 13th September 1835, published a general manifesto against the company of young authors headed by Karl Gutzkow. The apology for this action, which he makes as an old man (in his *Memoirs*, p. 304), shows unquestionable proof of narrow-mindedness, but not of any honest conviction. To emphasise the cosmopolitan tendencies and French sympathies of Young Germany, he wrote of it as "La jeune Allemagne." He directed his principal attack against *Wally*, from which book he quoted a few disconnected passages to show that the whole novel was immoral and sacrilegious; the insignificant

sensual element in the story, the Sigune scene, is made its
main feature.

"Only in the deepest mire of immorality, only in
brothels, are such atheistic views hatched.   They were in
vogue among the philosophical parasites of the old French
court.   In the Palais Royal they were translated from the
language of the court into that of the Jacobins.   Herr
Gutzkow has taken it upon himself to transplant once again
into Germany that infamous French ape who, in the arms
of a harlot, mocks at God, but he has done it in an age
which, praise be to God, is more mature and more manly
than the age of Voltaire.   Even then vice was foiled by the
natural disposition of our nation ; now it will be even more
impossible for it to effect an entrance.   Literature will expel
it, public opinion brand it. . . . If such a school for the
most impudent immorality and the most refined falsehood
is allowed to establish itself in Germany, if all the noble
minds of the nation do not set themselves against it, if
German publishers do not beware, but venture to offer such
poison for sale and to praise their wares, we shall soon see
the result. . . . But I will tread down your filth, though I
know that I shall defile myself by doing so ; I will bruise
the head of the serpent that warms itself in the hot-bed of
sensuality. . . . As long as I live, such infamous dishonouring
of German literature shall not go unpunished. . . ."

And Menzel, the practical journalist, was not satisfied,
like the ordinary author, with saying a thing once for all.
He repeated his accusations in one number after another
of his paper with growing emphasis, more abusive language,
more venomous imputations, appealing more and more
plainly to the State to interfere while it was yet time.

On the 26th of October he wrote: "I know that their
war against Christianity, against morality, against marriage
is of no more significance than the war of young owls against
the old sun.   But a spark may give rise to a conflagration. . . . Upon the new literary judgment-seat in Frankfurt, Venus vulgivaga will be enthroned in place of justice
. . . never will these men, who only believe in the flesh,
these priests of foulness, forgive an author for being purer

than they are. . . . Is it possible to sit still and allow them to propagate French morality among us by word and deed ? Under the mask of French republicanism, this libellous, infamous new Frankfurt school is introducing the most frightful immorality. The flesh, unbridled sensuality, the abolition of marriage, are their watchwords, and they not only write obscene books themselves, but serve up the old ones afresh. . . . They are to a certain extent disciples of Saint-Simon, they proclaim a still more dissolute republicanism, without any virtue, a hetæra-republic on the grandest scale. . . . As yet these principles are confined to the narrower, aristocratic circles of literature. . . . But to what do these doctrines appeal but to the bestiality and ferocity which, though they are still slumbering, would be so easily aroused in the great capitals and manufacturing towns, with their obscene haunts of drunkenness and depravity."

On the 11th of November Menzel directly denounces the Prussian university professors who have been rash enough to promise Gutzkow their co-operation in his review : " Are the universities not State institutions ? Does the Prussian State no longer protect Christianity, morality, marriage ? We have heard so much of the moral, religious, Conservative spirit that prevails in Prussia. Are we now to see the most eminent professors of Berlin, Königsberg, and Halle following at the heels of an obscene Marat, who, like the real Marat, literally preaches the sacrament of ' the irresistible moment' and a republic of sans-culottes and sans-chemises ? Are we to hear them raving with him against Christianity, morality, marriage, the family, modesty, against God and immortality, against German nationality and the established order of things ?" And he concluded his outburst by applying the designation of a Jewish party to the good Germans, Gutzkow, Wienbarg, Laube, Mundt, and Kühne, because of their sympathy with the ideas of Börne and Heine. Young Germany, he declared, was in reality Young Palestine.

As a consequence of this denunciation, Karl Gutzkow was arrested on a charge of blasphemy and lewd writing, and Menzel was dishonourable enough to go on exciting public indignation against him whilst he was in confinement and the case was being tried at Mannheim. The sentence pronounced was, however, only ten weeks' imprisonment for attacking the existing religious institutions of Baden.

But fear of the revolutionary movements which Menzel maintained would be the result of the teaching of Young Germany, induced the German Confederation to take action, and on the 10th of December 1835 the Federal Diet passed a resolution, which aimed at nothing less than the annihilation of the whole group of authors, young and old, which it comprehends under the designation Young Germany. It reads as follows : " In view of the fact that a school of literature has lately come into existence in Germany, a school now known by the name of 'Young Germany,' or 'the young literature,' whose aim is, by means of belletristic writings, accessible to all classes of readers, impudently to attack the Christian religion, to discredit the existing conditions of society, and to subvert all discipline and morality, the Council of the German Confederation (Bundesversammlung) . . . has unanimously passed the following resolutions : (1) All the German Governments bind themselves to bring the penal and police statutes of their respective countries and the regulations regarding the abuse of the press in their strictest sense to bear against the authors, publishers, printers, and disseminators of the writings of the literary school known as 'Young Germany' or 'the young literature,' to which notably belong Heinrich Heine, Karl Gutzkow, Heinrich Laube, Ludolf Wienbarg, and Theodor Mundt, as also by all lawful means to prevent the dissemination of the writings of this school by booksellers, lending libraries, or other means," &c., &c.

It was in this manner that the appellation Young Germany first became familiar to the general public. It was the German Police-Confederation which, constituting itself a critical authority, stigmatised a group of authors, mentioned by name, as an immoral and injurious "school"— and this on the information of one single rival of these men in the favour of the reading public.

Menzel was to Young Germany what Southey in his day was to the "Satanic school" in English literature, *alias* Byron and Shelley, or Katkóf, a generation later, to the "traitorous school" in Russian literature—Herzen, Ogarev, and Bakunin. In disturbed times the informer is as necessary an appendage to the foreground figures as the envious rival and spy was to the hero of the old tragedies.

XXII

GUTZKOW, LAUBE, MUNDT

THE determination of the Federal Council to suppress the writings of Young Germany not only nipped the *Deutsche Revue* in the bud, but also put an end to the existence of Mundt's *Litterarischer Zodiacus*, published in Leipzig, and prevented the publication of Laube's *Mitternachtszeitung*, which was to have appeared in Brunswick. Immediately after Menzel's first attack on Gutzkow and his friends, Mundt, with the valour of the prudent man, had written a series of severe articles against Heine, Gutzkow, and Wienbarg—but all to no purpose ; his fate was sealed.

It seemed for a time as if the resolution were intended not only to affect everything that the proscribed authors had already written, but everything that they might write in the future.

An edict of the Prussian Government, dated 11th December 1835, expressly provides that "the *future* literary productions of Heinrich Heine, wherever they may be published and in whatever language, are to be subject to the same regulations as the writings of Gutzkow, Wienbarg, Laube, and Mundt." And not only was every possible measure taken to silence the obnoxious authors, but (as in Russia, when a man is in disgrace with the Government) it was made illegal, even for those who desired to write disparagingly of them, to print their names. Mundt's name was erased from the list of contributors to the *Berliner Jahrbücher für wissenschaftliche Kritik*, and in the announcements of Varnhagen and Mundt's edition of Knebel's *Literary Remains*, Varnhagen alone might be named as editor.

Excessively strict precautions were at the same time taken with regard to foreign publications. A few inoffensive English and French newspapers were countenanced. In the case of all the others the expedient was resorted to of requiring the same postage to be paid for them as for letters, thereby raising the cost of such papers to at least 500 thalers (£75) per annum.[1]

To the leaders of Young Germany the Government thus offered the compulsory choice between biding their time in defiant silence and purchasing other conditions for themselves by disowning their past and making humiliating promises for the future. No one who has had any experience of the average valour of the denizens of the literary world can feel surprised that few stood this test, that many accepted the second alternative. Neither Heine, Wienbarg, nor Gutzkow gave in; but many others made pitiable exhibitions of themselves. Crowds of the young authors who had plumed themselves upon their revolutionary - philosophical, their oppositionist-political ideas, now hastened to prove their philosophic commonplaceness, their political innocuousness. The name "Young Germany" had been an honourable name; but now that those who had borne it found themselves the objects of special police surveillance, they refused to acknowledge it, each declaring that he, at least, did not belong to the party, and that if he ever had done so, it was an old story, and he had since then become a most respectable member of society. In this case, as so often, it was proved that modern high-class education only provides desultory knowledge, does not form character, and least of all amongst those who make their living by their pens.

August Lewald, who to all intents and purposes belonged to the group, procured the annulment of the prohibition of his periodical, *Europa*, by making a declaration that he had never printed anything inimical to the Government, to religion, or to morality, and was consequently in no wise compromised by any of the mischievous proceedings of Young Germany. Eduard Duller, who had been co-editor with Gutzkow of the paper, *Phœnix*, publicly disclaimed all sympathy with the aims of Young Germany and declared his principles to be perfectly different from those of his

---

[1] A. Strodtmann: H. Heine's *Leben und Werke*, 1874, ii. 174, &c.

former fellow-workers. Theodor Mundt professed that he had always kept clear of "that manufactured category," Young Germany, as it was plain that such an appellation must sooner or later become a literary nickname (Ekelname); and in the preface to his new periodical, *Dioskuren für Wissenschaft und Kunst*, he declared that his aim was to counteract the literary excesses of recent times by the display of a settled conviction devoid of any principle of destructiveness (*worin nichts Verheerendes wuchert*).

Meekest of all, perhaps, was Heinrich Laube, he who had been the most daring and defiant of the Young Germans, he whom Heine had called "one of those gladiators who die in the arena"—an appreciation which now seemed somewhat ridiculous. He affirmed, in the *Allgemeine Zeitung*, that in promising Dr. Gutzkow to contribute to his new review, he had never dreamt of aiding and abetting the party known by the name of Young Germany in its attacks on the existing conditions of society, much less in its attempts to disturb and overturn them. On the contrary, he had from the first plainly signified that he did not identify himself with the movement.

On New Year's day, 1836, in the announcement of his *Mitternachtszeitung*, which he had obtained permission to publish on condition that his name did not appear as editor, he wrote that he had become another man, that literature was no longer to him an expression of political desires, that it was not his intention to take any part in the literary disputes of the moment, "the rough-and-tumble fights with uncombed hair and unwashed hands"; no, it had long been his idea to form "a neo-Romantic school," and in it he would have no disintegrating, destructive elements. He would support the existing, not make war upon it. He would not · identify himself with Menzel (actually!) but neither could he take part with the so-called Young Germany. He who had been the most daring of them all was the quickest and most adroit in wheeling round.

Day after day, too, as was to be expected, the newspapers contained declarations by the different university professors who had been incautious enough to promise their co-operation in the *Deutsche Revue*. Ulrici, Eduard Gans, Hotho, Rosenkranz and Trendelenburg, Hegelians and Anti-Hegelians, all, one after the other, cleared themselves from the charge of complicity. They repented with their official souls. They vied with each other in their utter repudiation of Gutzkow.

Heine did not belong to the number of those who lose their courage or their heads in a difficulty. And in any case, partly because of his established reputation, partly because of the personal security ensured by his residence abroad, this interdict was not such a serious blow to him as to the others. On the 28th of January 1836, after receiving intimation of the prohibition of his books, he addressed a solemn protest to the Federal Diet, a proceeding about which he immediately afterwards jokes in a private letter to his publisher. In this · protest he expresses his astonishment at having been judged without a trial, and without having been given any opportunity to defend himself. He reminds the Federal Diet that Martin Luther did not meet with such treatment at the hands of the Holy Roman Empire—not that he would think of comparing himself with Luther, " but the pupil naturally appeals to the precedent of his master." But what he especially desires to protest against is his compulsory silence (which he was privately determined to break as soon as possible) being taken for an admission of culpable intentions, or even for a disavowal of his earlier writings. To Laube, of whose new attitude he was still ignorant, he wrote about the same time that, in the matter of politics, it was, for the present, allowable to make any number of concessions, political forms being of no consequence as long as the conflict for the highest life-principles was still going on ; but they must hold to their right of free discussion of religious and moral topics, or there would soon be an end of all Protestant liberty of ·thought. Laube, as we know, finding himself obliged to give in to a certain extent, gave in all round at once, struck simultaneously his political, religious, and moral flags.

It was a slight consolation to the sufferers that the

informer did not go unpunished. Heine wrote *Ueber den Denunzianten* and Börne wrote *Menzel der Franzosenfresser* (" The Frenchman-eater "), which is with reason regarded as his wittiest and at the same time most warm-hearted production.

But the more severe punishment came from Heine, who threw himself upon his victim with all his tiger-like strength, and shook him till there was nothing left of him but a shapeless, ridiculous bundle.

Heine points out how carefully Menzel has chosen the time for making his accusations, a time when the leaders of the movement were either in exile, or silent, or in safe keeping behind bolts and bars. He exposes Menzel's hypocrisy, showing how, as long as he was connected with Gutzkow, he looked on silently, though he knew Christianity to be in peril of its life. He is quite ready to give him credit for " a certain physical morality "—for a man can be virtuous alone, but to be vicious he must have a companion. Herr Menzel's personal appearance stands him in good stead when he is desirous to flee from vice. Heine has far too high an opinion of the good taste of vice to be able to believe that it would run after a Menzel. Poor Goethe was not so fortunately gifted in this particular. Of Menzel's political opinions Heine is afraid to speak for political reasons. Nor can he say what he thinks of his private life (as if by a printer's error *Privatschelmenleben* is substituted for *Privatmenschenleben*), in the first instance for want of space.

Never did Heine write anything at once so insulting and so crushing.

And how did matters stand with Gutzkow, who at the early age of twenty-four had become a kind of centre of literary events, and upon whom " the Goliath of the Philistine army " had fallen ? For a moment he was astonished and cast down. It was his first instructive experience of life. His sin was that he had expressed his feelings naïvely and honestly in a second-rate novel, and its result was that he now found himself denounced as a plague of society, mocked at by his enemies, forsaken and disowned by his friends. With perfect calm he heard himself compared to the men who had prepared for the enormities perpetrated at Münster under Jan van Leyden—division of property, marriage with twelve wives, &c. He was inexperienced enough to look forward to the legal proceedings against him with expectations of victory, and when he was arrested at Mannheim, he went to prison with a feeling of relief. In prison he did not hear the yelling of the press ; he heard nothing but the squeaking of the mice that ran over his bed. He could lead a peaceful life, a life of uninterrupted, quiet production. He wrote his novel *Seraphine* and a work entitled *Philosophie der That und des Ereignisses* (" Philosophy of Action and Event "), a kind of criticism of Hegel's *Philosophy of History*. When he came out of prison he took up his life-work again with firm determination, but for a time wrote anonymously and expressed himself more cautiously.

About a year before this he had fallen in love with a young girl in Berlin, and become engaged to her. But the Berlin newspapers called him an atheist. The young lady's mother was a foolish, hysterical woman. One day she would embrace Gutzkow, the next threaten to throw a knife at him and shriek to her daughter, " Choose between him and me ! " As the wisdom of allowing her daughter to unite her fate with Gutzkow's became more and more questionable, the mother's amiable days became fewer, the unamiable more frequent, and in the end the young lady, as an obedient daughter, drew back altogether. This episode had made a tremendous impression on Gutzkow's young heart. It had taught him that to hold convictions contrary to those of the people one lives amongst isolates a man even in private life, and that he who sets the opinion of his neighbours at defiance cannot expect to be successful in life or in love.

His friends behaved no better to him. No sooner was he released from prison than he was overwhelmed with reproaches and complaints by persons to whom he had previously promised literary employment, and who were now not only disappointed in their hopes, but compromised by the patronage he had extended to them.

His first disappointment in love led to one of his best shorter stories, *Der Sadducäer von Amsterdam*. And the disappointment, combined with the general disillusionment, produced the frame of mind which characterises the dramatised version of the story which he published many years later under the title of *Uriel Acosta*—undoubtedly his best drama, probably his best work.

The hero is a historic personage, Gabriel, afterwards Uriel Acosta, born in 1594, a religious philosopher of Jewish nationality. His parents were baptised Christians, but he himself, on account of his disbelief in Christianity, was obliged to leave his native land, Portugal, and take refuge in Holland. Then he threw in his lot with the Jews, but soon began to publish works in which the Jewish doctrines were as freely criticised as the Christian. For this he was condemned to pay fines, and in the end was sentenced to a most humiliating penance. After public acknowledgment and recantation of his errors, he was to lie on the ground at the threshold of the synagogue and allow himself to be trodden under foot by the whole congregation of the faithful. After seven years of persecution he submitted to the sentence, but immediately afterwards, in despair at having retracted his opinions, shot himself (in 1647). He was the forerunner, and, if we may believe tradition, the teacher of Spinoza.

In the little old-fashioned story, *Der Sadducäer von Amsterdam*, the most important personages of the future drama are outlined. Judith, the vacillating and finally faithless woman, beloved of Acosta, was very evidently suggested by the inconstant Berlin lady. The style is artless and weak. Spinoza is introduced as follows : " She called, and her only child, a boy of seven, came running up to his uncle, whom he easily recognised in the moonlight. Bare your heads ! That boy was Baruch Spinoza ! "

What attracted Gutzkow as a young man to this theme was evidently its pathos, its being the story of the first martyr for free-thought.

In our days we read of such a life without being remarkably impressed by it. The spiritually emancipated know that all the advance that has been made amounts to this, that they are now tolerated. The life that they have lived has so accustomed them to hear all that they hold highest

R

condemned, and all that they regard as base or foolish extolled, that no story of this kind affects them much.

It was different with the generation of 1830 in Germany. Even the fact that Uriel Acosta sued for pardon and recanted did not lessen Gutzkow's interest in him. In the novel he writes : "We who have been, as it were, born into a state of constant martyrdom for the sake of our convictions, who have lived in it all our lives, must refrain from condemning a man who had the courage to protest against the dogmas of a fanatical, intolerant religion, but who, nevertheless, was capable of cringing beneath the hand that had chastised him." He depicts the confusion in Uriel's soul : Faith is the blind man's staff ; his eyes are suddenly opened ; but they are utterly unaccustomed to distinguish objects ; they cannot, like the staff to which he has been so long accustomed, save him from falling ; and so he gropes more helplessly than before.

After the storm raised by Menzel had passed in all its fury over Gutzkow's head, the story of Acosta inevitably acquired quite a new significance for him. Considering it now, he saw not only its purely dramatic possibilities, but the correspondence of its main features with the main features of his own life story. He, too, had been placed under ban and interdict ; he, too, after being cursed, had been deserted ; he, too, had paid the penalty of intrepid thought ; he, too, had been flung on the ground before the threshold of the injured Church, and the whole multitude had passed over him and trampled on him.

In 1846, in Paris, under the influence of the acting of great tragedians, Gutzkow dramatised the story. He made various alterations in it. To increase the interest of the plot, he idealised the chief female character. In the tragedy of *Uriel Acosta*, Judith is the betrothed of another ; Uriel is her master. But when the Rabbis, with solemn ceremony, pronounced the terrible curse, when all draw back from him and he is left alone on one side of the stage, whilst the words :

> " Fluch dem Freund
> Der Dir im Elend je die Treue hält !
> Nie giebt sich Dir ein liebend Herz des Weibes," [1]

---

[1] Cursed be the friend who is faithful to thee in trouble ! Never shall a woman's loving heart cherish thee.

are being spoken, she crosses the stage and places herself by his side with the famous and beautiful speech ending with the line :

"Er *wird* geliebt !   Glaubt besseren Propheten !"[1]

Of a personage who hardly appears at all in the novel, Gutzkow made an imperishable character, the best and most original in the drama, the aged Chief Rabbi, Ben Akiba. This old man has in reality only one conclusive speech, which he repeats again and again to Uriel and to the others:

"Es war alles da."
(This has all been before.)

Admirable words ! Ben Akiba is age, that has seen all these things before, seen the Church attacked, seen the Church triumphant, seen sceptics and champions arise, seen them humiliated, defeated, dead, and buried. The others believe that this is something new ; it is all old, it all leads to no result. Ben Akiba is dogmatic conservatism in human form ; he is experience, shaking its heavy head. If youth were to listen to him, despairing indifference would be the inevitable result.

Uriel lets himself be persuaded to recant. He does it for his mother's and Judith's sake. His old, blind, believing mother comes to him, and in a scene which never fails to affect the audience, persuades him to recant and submit to the ignominious punishment—persuades only by her silent dignity and the strength of her love, without a single entreaty to do this or anything else for her sake. Uriel takes the step, hoping that it will remove a weight from his mother's heart and make it possible for him to marry Judith. But whilst he is still in prison preparing for the penance, his mother dies, and Judith is forced to marry Ben Jochai. He degrades himself in vain. Judith poisons herself, and he (the drama in this point keeping to fact) shoots himself.

By reason of its theme, the tragedy of *Uriel Acosta* occupies a unique place in the German literature of the day. It is a tragedy of free-thought, a drama that gives us a better

[1] He *is* beloved !   Trust better prophets !

idea than anything else does of the period which produced it—a period of energetic struggle for liberty, and of still more energetic oppression—and of the spirit of that Young Germany which was so gallant in advance, but so prone to defection and retractation. It is a play, too, which bears unmistakable testimony to its author's qualities of head and heart. Any one who compares Gutzkow's *Uriel Acosta* with Heine's *Almansor*, will subscribe to the affirmation already made, that the best men of Young Germany in their best moments displayed a manly earnestness which we do not find in Heine.

On the German stage *Uriel Acosta* has now long been a favourite play. The pure style and the treatment of the subject remind us of Lessing's *Nathan der Weise*, but in energy and pathos Gutzkow in this case surpasses Lessing. In spite of some weak parts, such as the Spinoza scene, the dramatic construction is excellent.

Of all Gutzkow's works, this play has had the widest circulation. It has been translated into all the Slavonic and all the Latin languages, into English, Hungarian, and Swedish.

In Germany it was for a time, as Gutzkow himself aptly remarked, a sort of barometer indicating the state of public opinion. When the ecclesiastical reaction was in the ascendant, it was prohibited in many of the theatres. When there was a change of system, the prohibition was cancelled. It is significant that in Austria its performance was always permitted in the provinces, but that the Concordat with the Pope stood in the way of its being played in the Burg Theater of Vienna. As was to be expected, the play was long in reaching Denmark ; it was first played there in the Nineties.

After 1835 Gutzkow writes nothing childish or crude. From this time onwards he is the great, indefatigable literary worker; a student and critic who possessed the faculty of discerning and explaining the relation in which all characters, past or present, stood to the requirements and problems of his day ; an acute distinguisher of the various drifts of the times ; a psychologist distinguished for his understanding of individual character. His *Goethe* (1836) is a thoughtful little work, in the first instance a protest against Menzel ; his long series of portraits (*Zeitgenossen*, afterwards *Säkularbilder*) show qualities which somewhat later stood him in good stead as a novelist ; his *Life of Börne* (1840) is a tribute to the memory of that progenitor of Young Germany and a challenge to Heine, whose injudicious and ungenerous work on Börne had lowered him in the estimation of the young generation.

A special interest attaches to Gutzkow's dramatic attempts from the fact that he and Laube were the first German authors of any position since the days of Kleist to connect themselves with the theatre and to win an honourable place for themselves on the German stage. Gutzkow makes a laboured beginning with sentimental dramas that no longer satisfy the public taste. His *Richard Savage, oder der Sohn einer Mutter* (1839) is from beginning to end a high-flown extravaganza. A talented English poet, who has grown up in ignorance of his parentage, discovers his mother in a beautiful, brilliant, aristocratic woman of the world, who refuses to acknowledge him or to have anything whatever to do with him. The play is a series of representations of his fruitless attempts to win this mother's cold heart. *Werner, oder Herz und Welt* (1840), is a pathetic, middle-class drama, turning on a theme on which Gutzkow rang many changes, the struggle in a man's heart between an old attachment and a more recently formed connection. Heinrich Werner has allowed himself to be adopted by people in a position above his own. He has been ennobled under the name of von Jordan, and has deserted a poor but charming young girl in order to marry a lady of position. But in his new, affluent circumstances, ne misses his former plain, studious life, and, most of all, Marie Winter, the girl to whom he had been engaged, and whom he cannot forget. He suddenly meets her again as governess in his own house. He is long distracted between his duty to his wife and his attraction to this girl, whom he is determined to love only platonically, but whom he really loves above everything. At last things come to a crisis. The wife asserts her rights, rights that Heinrich refuses to acknowledge. His morality is a higher, a freer than hers. She "shudders at his principles." The knot is finally cut by a *deus ex machinâ.* A young friend of Heinrich's comes to an agreement with Marie that he and she will marry, and so prevent the breaking up of the family. The tragic motive is thus, we observe, deprived of its point.

The first of Gutzkow's plays that it still gives one a reasonable amount of pleasure to see is *Zopf und Schwert* ("Pigtail and Sword"), written in 1843. It is a play which has kept its place on the German stage, but which never gained a firm footing outside of Germany from the fact of its being a species of national drama. The beat of a Prussian's heart is felt in it. Gutzkow's aim was to represent Frederick William I. and his court in a comedy like those which Scribe was bringing out so successfully about the same time. The historic appreciation is, however, far from being so superficial as in Scribe's comedies. Gutzkow had an eye for the admirable as well as for the comical qualities of the miserly family tyrant, the monarch of Spartan severity. But the very fact of the play being a comedy made a really profound study of the character an impossibility. And it was not Gutzkow's habit, and still less was it Laube's, to investigate into historical characters and situations until they arrived at the historic, as opposed to the traditional truth. Their history was simply the vehicle of a more or less cleverly concocted plot. We have only to open the first volume of Carlyle's *Frederick the Great* to find such an immensely more powerful and impressive picture of the eccentric Prussian king with his tall grenadiers, that Gutzkow's in comparison shrinks into a mild pleasantry. And we have only to look at a few pages of the Memoirs of Gutzkow's heroine, Wilhelmine of Bayreuth, to see that in the relations between her and her father there was no suggestion of comedy. But, putting aside all thought of historical correctness, we have a very pretty intrigue-play, with a historic colouring which cannot fail to appeal to lovers of Prussia. *Zopf und Schwert* is a species of light-hearted pendant to Kleist's serious *Prinz von Homburg.*

Of the other plays written by Gutzkow in the Forties, *Das*

Urbild des Tartüffe ("The Prototype of Tartuffe") has been the most successful, but it is a much over-estimated work. A very charming little work is *Der Königslieutenant*, an unassuming play, written for Goethe's centenary, and treating of him in his youthful days.

The long historical novels, *Die Ritter vom Geist* ("The Knights of the Spirit"), *Der Zauberer von Rom* ("The Roman Magician"), &c., which Gutzkow wrote during the reaction period after 1848, and which immensely strengthened his hold over the minds of his contemporaries, do not come within the scope of the present work. They were the forerunners of Spielhagen's long series of novels.

Next to Gutzkow, Heinrich Laube (born in Sprottau, in Silesia, in 1806) was the most eminent member of the new group. He is a clear-cut type, a man with plenty of fresh, vigorous talent, exuberant spirits, an intuitive perception of what is effective, a gift of slight, but in most instances adequate character delineation, and, to start with, many daring but shallow and second-hand ideas. He is not devoid of feeling, nor totally devoid of earnestness, but his distinguishing quality is his brisk, energetic practicalness. Between 1826 and 1832 he studied theology at Halle and Breslau. In 1832 he embarked on the career of a journalist in Leipzig. In his unpedantic literary style, as also in his outward appearance, there was something that seemed to point to Slavonic blood in his veins. As a student he loved to go about in a Polish braided coat, and eccentric caps and cloaks of his own invention. He wrote with a fluency and vehemence, with a crude naturalness and a want of exactitude which were not German. His blood was hot and flowed quickly ; he had the sanguine, choleric temperament, without a touch of melancholy.

As a member of a student's union (Burschenschaft) and because he had given too free expression to his sympathy with the Revolution of July and its results in Germany, he was, in 1834, expelled from Saxony and sentenced to nine months' imprisonment in Berlin. In the introduction to his drama, *Monaldeschi*, we find an account of his life in prison, of the monotony of that beautiful summer of 1834, which he spent in his cell, without a book—nothing but a bed, a table, a stool, and a pitcher of water. He also gives an indirect and more effective description of the same experience in the Third Part of *Das junge Europa*, where Valerius, upon scraps of paper procured with the greatest difficulty, writes his impressions during a long confinement in a Prussian prison.

We know what his conduct was after the Federal Council had prohibited his writings as belonging to the Young German school ; but to judge him fairly we must remember that this blow came upon him immediately after his release, and that, in spite of his subsequent cautious behaviour, he was again, soon after his marriage in 1837, condemned to imprisonment for participation in the doings of the Burschenschaften. This time the punishment was mild, thanks apparently to the protection of Prince Pückler - Muskau. The place of imprisonment was a country house on the Prince's property of Muskau ; for a cell he was given a hall ; instead of a skylight he had eight windows, looking in three different directions. Even a short daily walk in the famous park was permitted. He might read and write as much as he chose. His wife shared his imprisonment. From this time onwards he shows extreme moderation in politics. When, in 1848, he is elected a member of the German National Assembly, he sides, not with the republican, but with the " hereditary-imperial " party.

Laube makes his début in literature as a disciple of Heine. His *Reisenovellen*, a long series of volumes, are the direct offspring of the *Reisebilder*. But along with the influence of Heine we trace that of Heinse. From Heine Laube takes liveliness and ingenuity of style, and also to a certain extent the personal coxcombry by which we are sometimes very unpleasantly affected ; but it is from Wilhelm Heinse, for whom he had an extreme admiration, and whose works he edited, that he derives the undisguised sensualism which displays itself in a positive cult of woman's outward charms constantly and loudly proclaimed. In Heinse's case this worship of female form and colouring, this adoration of the fleshly, is more primitive, more naïvely Bacchanalian, more sincerely religious, than in Laube's. Laube at times offends by coarseness, at times by an almost personal boastfulness of woman-killing qualities, and at times it is too perceptible that he is writing for the purpose of annoying his respectable neighbours.

When, in his old age, he began to republish his youthful works, the new generation were astounded by the breaches of good taste which youthful readers some forty years before had admired, and many assented to the severe judgment which had lately been passed on him by Emil Kuh in the chapter on Young Germany contained in his book on Hebbel. But it is unfair to allow a little coarseness and want of taste here and there to keep us from estimating Laube's work in its integrity.

In the *Reisenovellen*, in spite of the off-hand way in which they are written, there is little originality. At the very beginning, in the division entitled *Leipzig*, with its French sympathies and its reverence of Napoleon, there is too strong a suggestion of the *Reisebilder*. Laube, like Heine, in his childhood saw the great Emperor ; so he gives us to understand, but in such an uncertain manner that we are left in doubt as to whether it was in a dream or in reality ; and Laube, too, has—in the person of Gardy the dragoon—his drummer Legrand.

Those who wish to get a real, full impression of what Laube was as a young man, ought to read his novel, *Das junge Europa* (4 vols. 1833–37). A whole, long stage of his development is placed clearly before us in this now pardonably forgotten book, which retains its interest only for the historian. Its three parts—the Poets, The Soldiers, The Citizens—are three works differing very much from each other in kind and in quality.

In the First Part the author is completely under the influence of Heinse's *Ardinghello*. "The Poets" is a sort of prose hymn to female beauty and free love, in the old-fashioned form of a novel in letters, which communicate the love fates of about a dozen people. When the reader has struggled through them, there is left on his mind an impression of the wild ecstatic desire of young, vigorous, hopeful men, and of the resolute self-surrender of young and daring or tender women, the impression of a generation in whose veins glows a desire for liberty—political, social, erotic— which breaks down all forms and all conventions. We see into an imaginary, romantic world, the world of Laube's youthful dreams, where there is abundance of power and of life, and of illusions as to the renovation of the world by means of revolutions of various kinds. It is a romance of beautiful bodies and beautiful souls, male and female, the essence of whose being is revolt against Christianity and against marriage.

Between the First and the Second Part, a considerable change has evidently come over the author's views ; he has received his impression of the strength of the reaction ; he has ripened into a man. In the First Part one could hardly help mixing up the characters, for the men were only distinguished from each other by their more or less fiery, erotic, uncontrollable temperaments, the woman only by the dissimilarity of their physical charms ; in the Second Part we are introduced into a world where a real struggle for national and political liberty is going on. The letter form is abandoned, and there are comparatively few characters.

It is the revolt of Poland which is described ; Valerius, one of the principal characters in the First Part, is led by his enthusiasm for liberty in general to join the Poles. The subject-matter is interesting, though here and there we have too much of the purely historical. The Poles as a people are described impartially and with a sure touch ; their characteristics—the strong patriotic feeling inspiring high and low, the prejudices and tyranny of the nobility, the savagery and vigour of the lower classes—are depicted as they mirror themselves in the mind of the German volunteer. The distrust with which he, as a foreigner, is received, the want of liberal-mindedness in the devotees of liberty, which he observes more especially in their conduct to his friend, a Polish officer of Jewish descent, gradually dissipate the illusions which he had cherished of a golden future for Europe, the final outcome of the Revolution of July. There is a tragic tone throughout the book. We are shown how fruitless the rebellion of the Poles is, how it ends, as it was fated to end, in crushing defeat ; and we are shown how the young Jew, Joel, in spite of his valiant endeavours on the battlefield to gain for himself those rights which his aristocratic countrymen enjoy, can never rise from his position as the pariah of Polish society. The woman he loves dares not give him her hand ; a common peasant disdains his sympathy. After the revolt is suppressed, he puts off his uniform in despair and shoulders the pedlar's wallet. The Christians repudiate him, the Jews he himself long ago alienated by his alliance with the Christians, his humanity gives him no rights ; there is nothing for it but to forget his learning, his philosophy, his scientific and military talent, and to wander from village to village, selling ribbons, as his forefathers did.

This character has a special interest for Danes, as it evidently suggested to Goldschmidt some of the leading characteristics of the hero of his novel, *En Jöde* (" A Jew ") ; he, too, becomes a Polish officer during the struggle for liberty, and he too, repulsed everywhere, in the bitterness of despair ends his career as a money-lender, outside the pale of society.

The Third Part of *Das junge Europa* (" The Citizens ") is an inferior production. Its chief interest for us lies in what it tells us of two of the most enthusiastic, indomitable heroes of the First Part, Hippolyt and Constantin. Hippolyt is finally driven to despair by the civilisation of the modern world, which leaves no room for the great exception, but requires all to be alike small. The bold Constantin, who fought in the streets of Paris in the Days of July, makes his appearance not very many years later as a Prussian judge, inflexibly, fanatically severe in his dealings with political revolutionaries. Constantin enters into long explanations of the influences that have wrought the change in his convictions (this character was evidently drawn from the life) ; but the author is still so possessed by the ideals of his own youth, that he makes this man commit suicide in despair at having been unfaithful to these ideals.

From the year 1849 till his death in the Eighties, Laube, as is well known, devoted all his powers to the theatre. He speedily became the best and most highly esteemed theatrical manager of Germany and Austria. As such he always retained a preference for the French drama. What he himself wrote for the stage is what will keep his name longest in remembrance.

Of the many historical dramas which he produced, the most important—*Monaldeschi* (1834), *Struensee* (1844), and *Die Karlsschüler* (1847)—are suggestive of the ideals of Young Germany as they took shape in Laube's mind. The last-mentioned play became popular and is still often put on the stage ; the others are effective pieces in a style that is now obsolete.

The character of Monaldeschi is a vigorous conception. He is the bold, unscrupulous adventurer, who has no higher aim than to make his way and to enjoy life to the full, but who understands the meaning of power, and desires to use his power worthily—the Hippolyt of *Das junge Europa* in historic costume. With Queen Christina's more complex feminine character, Laube has not been so successful, though his representation of her has elements out of which a good actress could make a telling part. But the play as a whole is overweighted by the intolerable sentimentality of the love scenes (Monaldeschi has a romantic attachment to a certain Sylva Brahe), and it suffers as a work of art from its author's dread of offending a Philistine public's sense of propriety. The real relations between Christina and Monaldeschi are smoothed down into indistinctness. The sharp edges of historic fact are filed away to make the subject fit into the mould of theatrical Romanticism.

In *Struensee,* the second of Laube's dramas in which the action passes at a Scandinavian court, still greater liberties have been taken with history and historical characters. Laube makes Struensee the noble, liberty-loving reformer, whose only fault is an excessive German humanity, which shrinks from shedding blood. Had he only been a trifle less high-minded and scrupulous, he might easily have remained in power. The weakness that is his ruin is his chivalrous, platonic devotion to Caroline Mathilde, who returns the sentiment in an equally innocent manner.

Christian VII. is represented as an estimable, somewhat taciturn monarch, subject to attacks of melancholy. Struensee's fall is brought about entirely by Germans, who are partly envious of him, partly enraged because he will not comply with their unreasonable wishes ; and the bitter moral of the play is, that the worst enemies of a German intellectual hero are his own countrymen—Germans have always had to suffer most from Germans, who show their want of patriotism even in their relations with foreigners.

Quite apart from the historic inaccuracy of the character, the sentimentally erotic Struensee, with "his enthusiasm for all that is noble and beautiful," is a very impossible parvenu minister of state. Laube has tampered with facts to the extent of representing Struensee's death as the result of a shot fired, by order of Guldberg, at the moment of his arrest in the castle on the 17th of January 1772. The chief reason, and at the same time excuse, for all this perversion of facts lay in the necessity for presenting them in such a shape that the censorship might not forbid the play on account of the possibility of its giving offence to a friendly power. We get some idea of how severe this censorship was, when we read that, in spite of Laube's precautions, the performance of *Struensee* was for many years prohibited in Prussia, out of consideration for the feelings of the Danish royal family.

It is, nevertheless, impossible to understand why such a perfectly harmless and studiously, punctiliously, inoffensive play as *Die Karlsschüler* should, immediately after its appearance in 1846, have been prohibited throughout Austria, Prussia, Hanover, Würtemberg, Hesse-Cassel, all the Grand Duchies and several of the Duchies. It is in reality nothing whatever but a panegyric on the youthful Schiller, in a representation of the well-known difficulties he got into as a young regimental surgeon in the service of Duke Karl of Würtemberg, ending with his flight from Stuttgart to Mannheim. It forms a parallel to Gutzkow's Goethe comedy, *Der Königslieutenant,* which it surpasses in dramatic vigour. In this case, too, Laube has sacrificed strict historic truth. Duke Karl's character is softened and toned down exactly as King Frederick William's was in Gutzkow's *Zopf und Schwert.* This is not only art which is compelled to be cautious, but art which has come into being under the oppression of a tradition which has insinuated itself into the very disposition of the artist.   But the disposition was a cheerful, buoyant one, and the hand that wrote these scenes was light and skilful.   Something of the lustre that surrounds its hero's name is shed upon the play.   It is probable that as long as Schiller retains his great popularity in Germany, Germans will enjoy seeing this transcription of his youthful history—though they know many facts concerning that history now that were not known at the time *Die Karlsschüler* was written.   Such a play is not calculated to produce much effect out of Germany.

After Gutzkow's and Laube's, Mundt's is the name that occurs most frequently when mention is made of the leaders of Young Germany.   It is about the year 1835 that Mundt is most distinctly the mouthpiece of the feelings and ideas of that school.   In 1835 he published *Charlotte Stieglitz, ein Denkmal,* the only one of his historical delineations which had any real influence on the minds of the youth of the day.   This work, no doubt chiefly owing to its subject, but also to its pathetic, affectionately reverent treatment of that subject, took thousands of hearts by storm.   In the same year appeared his *Madonna, Unterhaltungen mit einer Heiligen* ("Converse with a Saint"), which, more than any other of his works, gives expression to the sentiments of Young Germany, and a clue to the character of its author.

Theodor Mundt, born at Potsdam in 1808, was a man capable of enthusiastic, yet clear-sighted devotion to causes and to persons.   He had Wienbarg's enthusiastic temperament (though not his bravery), with a much more highly gifted, many-sided mind.   And yet there was no edge or pungency in his wit, no grace in his whimsicality, no method in his works, no conciseness in his style.   His book on Charlotte Stieglitz is the only one of his works that has survived him, and it has done so thanks to its subject. He could be caustic and biting and unjust, as weak natures are apt to be, but even his most caustic tirades are not the expression of any warlike inclination ; they are only penned in self-defence and self-assertion, are called forth by some misunderstanding on the part of an opponent, and are no more dangerous than the thrusts of an angry wether.

It is surprising to the modern reader that a work like Mundt's *Madonna* can ever have been considered a dangerous book. To understand how this could be, we must keep in mind that those in power at the time of its publication stood in terror of shadows. It is, however, a book which must not be overlooked by any one who is making a study of the period, for there is something typical in its expression of the thoughts and enthusiasms of the youth of the day.

In its very formlessness, *Madonna* is characteristic of Mundt, and of those whose literary taste was identical with his. It contains prose lyric effusions, descriptions of travel, personal confessions, world-revolutionising theories of the rehabilitation of the flesh by means of a hitherto unknown mystic creed—all this grouped round a central female figure and interwoven with her story.

The book opens with a " post-horn symphony," well written in the old Romantic style, but not Romantic in tendency. It is a glorification of " movement," the shibboleth which Mundt invented and fell in love with. Movement is to him what progress and the struggle for freedom were to others—the watchword of the new era. He talks of the party of movement ; the new literature is to him the literature of movement (*Bewegungslitteratur*) ; in a postscript to *Madonna* he calls that book *ein Bewegungsbuch*. We perceive that the expression is perfectly neutral and innocent.

The only readable part of *Madonna* nowadays is the heroine's narrative of her life experiences. The author meets her in a little Bohemian village ; when he first sees her, walking in a Roman Catholic procession, he is tremendously impressed by her extraordinary beauty. Later in the same day he accidently makes his way into her father's cottage, wins the narrow-minded, bigoted old man's heart (in a very improbable manner) by the unction with which he tells him the story of Casanova, who had at one time lived in that neighbourhood in the castle of Dux, receives an invitation to supper, and spends part of the night in a sentimental conversation with the daughter, whom he discovers to be a woman deserving, in his estimation, the name of saint— a secular or worldly saint (*eine Weltheilige*)—and who, in that capacity, embraces and kisses him, weeping hot tears. He is obliged to leave the neighbourhood next morning, but soon afterwards receives from her an immoderately lengthy letter—*Die Bekenntnisse einer weltlichen Seele* ("The Confessions of a Worldly Soul")—in which she makes a frank revelation of herself and all her experiences.

This beautiful girl is an unfortunate victim. She has been enticed by a relative, a depraved woman, to leave Teplitz, her native town, where she lived in poverty with her parents, and come to Dresden. There, under the pretext of providing for her future, this woman educated her for a rich debauchee, a man of high position, whose prey she was to become as soon as she was grown up. The time comes; all preparations are made; at night she is locked into a room with her benefactor and pursuer, whom she loathes. She forcibly breaks away from him, manages to get out, and, in her despair, seeing a light in the room of a young theological student who lives in the same house, takes refuge with him. She has long loved this young man and he her. Now with chaste passion she gives herself to him, and he cannot find it in his heart to repulse her. But on the following day, repenting as a Christian of his sin, he commits suicide. The young girl has to make her way on foot from Dresden to her native village in Bohemia, where, after her experience of the life and variety of a great town, she pines in sadness and loneliness. Her old father, with whom she lives, is a cripple and a fanatically bigoted Roman Catholic.

The point in this story evidently lies in the innocence of the young. girl's self-abandonment, innocence which the world calls guilt. To the author his heroine is a saint, a Madonna, the type of lovable womanliness. She is a carnal saint, undoubtedly; but it is his creed that we can conceive of nothing more holy, that there exists nothing more spiritual, than the carnal. And he propounds a neither new nor remarkable, but somewhat peculiarly formulated theory of the necessity for a fusion of flesh and spirit, for the abolition of the distinction between spiritual and carnal. "The world and the flesh must be reinstated in their rights, in order that the spirit may no longer have to live in the sixth storey, as it does in Germany." And he brings the narration of a very lengthy Bohemian legend of Libussa to a close with the jubilant cry : "The free woman ;is sovereign ; let her decide, let her speak, for she has the right to speak ! And sweet is the happiness of free love ! "

Mundt began as a Hegelian, but his Hegelianism has, as we see, turned into a sort of fantastic mysticism. Christ declared that his kingdom is not of this world, and yet he came to us and himself became world. God, out of love, entered into the flesh, and the world's flesh has become holy since it became God. Hence the kingdom of God flourishes over the wide earth, and yet it is, as Christ declared, not of this world, that is, not of the world which is flesh only, and which sets its face against the free " movement " of thought. Like an insufficiently trained pedant, Mundt involves himself in lengthy and confused polemics against " the beyond" which is without " the here," and against " the here " which refuses to know anything of " the beyond." He ends by enthusiastically proclaiming the praises of what he calls " the image " (as distinct from both spiritless matter and immaterial spirit) : " O ye philosophers ! what you want is the image. . . . I contend for the re-habilitation of the image."[1]

If there ever was a man unsuited to be a leader and teacher of other men, it was this unctuous proclaimer of self-evident truths. *Madonna* was followed by a long series of historical novels (a still longer series came from the pen of Mundt's wife, who wrote under the pseudonym of Louise Mühlbach), and a considerable number of critical and historical writings. Amongst these latter one of the best is his *Geschichte der Litteratur der Gegenwart* (" History of Present Day Literature "), 1842, because in it he treats a

---

[1] Th. Mundt : *Madonna*, pp. 142, 274, 326, 374, 406.

S

subject with which he has a thorough acquaintance ; but it, too, like all his other works, is formless, full of undigested material, and spoiled by would-be profundity. He reads, for instance, a special meaning into the fact that Hegel died of cholera. Hegel's system, he writes, was, like Casimir Périer's, a universally levelling *juste-milieu* system : hence he, like Casimir Périer, was fated to die of this universally levelling malady. It was a malady which must be regarded as the physical expression of the general anguish of the times. Troubled and restless, the body had attacked its own intestines, and was at last obliged to pay the penalty of its craving to know and understand itself, by performing the last possible process of self-examination, that of vomiting itself up.[1]

In a work entitled *Das junge Deutschland*, consisting for the most part of letters to the publisher, Feodor Wehl, the well-known theatrical manager, has endeavoured to give the reading world a more favourable idea of Mundt than that prevalent in our days ; and he has succeeded in producing the impression that Mundt was a man with excellent intentions, many acquirements, and no small degree of enthusiasm in the causes that were sympathetic to him. He is not, and never will be considered, a great writer.

The authors of the second rank, the rearguard of Young Germany, men like Gustav Kühne, Hermann Marggraff, and Alexander Jung, are in reality his equals. Their gifts lie, like his, partly in the direction of journalism, partly in that of creative authorship. They are men of character, cultivation, and distinct literary ability, animated by the same fundamental ideas as the men in the front ranks.

The reader who takes up Kühne's *Weibliche und männliche Charaktere* (1838) will be agreeably surprised by the vigour and brilliancy of his delineations, and by his accurate appreciations of public personages. His heroines are those of his school—Rahel, Bettina, Charlotte Stieglitz ; but he sees them with his own eyes and describes them with unpretentious enthusiasm. Among the poets, who are the subjects of his laudatory criticism, are not only the great

---

[1] Mundt : *Litteratur der Gegenwart*, p. 353.

Radicals of a former generation like Shelley, not only all
the singers of freedom of his own day, from Anastasius
Grün to Karl Beck, but tranquil spirits like Rückert and
Chamisso. He is not remarkably original, but he is impartial
and unprejudiced.

The same can be said of Hermann Marggraff. Though
his book *Deutschlands jüngste Litteratur- und Culturepoche*
(1839), is written in the spirit of Young Germany, its
author always reserves his right to perfectly independent
judgment. He is a thoughtful, earnest critic and a good
writer, always natural, at times brilliant. His errors are
much more due to Conservative tendencies than to excessive
modernity.

Unless we single out the *enfants perdus* of this new
school—and there are such in every school—it cannot be
said that its members gave any real occasion for the violent
attacks made upon it. It is not Young Germany, but its
assailants, who uniformly show the worst taste and exaggerate
most grossly.

Such an assailant was Tieck, now an elderly man.
Several of his tales contain thrusts at Young Germany ;
that in which it is satirised most directly is *Der Wassermensch ;*
but the caricature is so overdone that it loses all effect.

Florheim, the representative of Young Germany, is half
crazy with enthusiasm for Frenchmen and Jews. He poses
as the democrat and friend of freedom in a manner which
we should consider foolish in an ordinary schoolboy. He
maintains that in every concert programme the Marseillaise
ought to have a place, to keep people from forgetting what
is the one thing above all others. He would have portraits
of the great heroes of liberty, Mirabeau, Washington,
Franklin, Kosciuszko, &c., inserted in every printed book,
even in cookery books. In every almanac, if he could have
his will, July should be printed in red letters, to keep the
glorious Revolution of July in ever fresh remembrance.
And he hopes that all the truly noble will unite in insisting
that the nouns, prince, lord, king, count, squire, &c., shall
be written without capital letters, in order to show contempt
for their signification.

When the Privy Councillor (Geheimrath), the representative of intelligent Conservatism, asks Florheim how he and his (" Sie, die Sie sich das junge Deutschland nennen "—you who call yourselves Young Germany) hope to carry out their plans and plots against the existing order of things, he answers naïvely : " By perpetual abuse of all that stands in our way." And he goes on to show how it was thus they treated Goethe in the last years of his age—an assertion which is quite contrary to fact—and how, now that they are the " party of movement" and already in possession of the most important newspapers, they are in a position to form an invisible and yet open league spread over the whole of Germany, which shall ruin every author who is not of their way of thinking, and make the reputation of its own members by means of unscrupulous mutual laudation.[1]

The reality was very different from this. The caricature has the double fault of not being like and not being amusing. Mundt took an ingenious revenge some years later by suggesting the performance of Tieck's fairy-tale comedies in Berlin.

---

[1] L. Tieck: *Gesammelte Novellen*, Breslau, 1855, i. 38, 79.

XXIII

RAHEL, BETTINA, CHARLOTTE STIEGLITZ

THE representation of the relation between literature and politics, the history of literary events, and the delineation of the characters and work of the most eminent of the men who constituted Young Germany, do not sufficiently reveal to us the spirit, the psychical condition of the time.

What is done, and what happens, is its outward manifestation. In books, effect is a first consideration ; what is represented in them must be to a certain extent exaggerated, thrown into relief, if only for the sake of distinctness. To find the clue to the intellectual life *lived* at any given period, we must get as close as possible to the living, feeling, individual, and we must not neglect to supplement the impression received from an observation of the leading men of the time by a study of its typical women.

It is where there is more feeling than action, where, in spite of great originality, the formative, the fashioning power is too slight entirely to separate the production from the personality, that the student comes into closest contact with the life-springs of a period. A letter from a highly gifted woman tells us more of the living human being and its real emotions than a political speech or a tragedy.

Not one of the few great women who ruled men's minds during the period under consideration produced a work of art ; not one of them even attempted to. They neither wrote novels nor essays. Their literary influence was a directly personal influence, and their power of stirring men's minds was evidently due to the fact that something of the inmost essence of the period was expressed in their personalities. Their natures are unplastic, evasive ; the contours of their spiritual lives are blurred and indistinct ;

this makes it difficult to delineate their characters, but makes it all the easier to feel the pulse of the time in their utterances.

They help us to arrive at the result that the idea which shapes the lives of the most noble characters of this period, and which makes itself felt in the resistance they offered to the worship of rule and the tyranny of custom, is the idea that the one course worthy of a thinking, feeling, human being is independently and unconventionally to interpret human life, human relations, for himself, and to base his conduct on his own interpretation. This is not a new idea ; it originated in Germany with Herder, descended from him to all the preachers of the gospel of Nature, including that Heinse who had such a strong influence upon some of the leaders of Young Germany, but was more especially developed and applied in all the relations of life by Goethe. A careful study of the characters of the most remarkable women of the time shows that the subterranean, hidden secret of the period between 1810 and 1838, what had happened deepest down, was that Goethe's theory of life had, point by point, displaced the Church theory and taken possession of all the men of great instincts, of all the really gifted minds of the day.

Rahel Varnhagen von Ense is, beyond all comparison, the greatest of the women who occupied the attention of intellectual Germany in the Thirties and Forties. She died in March 1833, and in 1835 her husband published the three volumes of selections from her letters and journals which revealed to the great reading public what manner of woman she had been. This publication was followed by many others, of which she was the main theme.

A less innately great, but much more talented woman than Rahel was Bettina von Arnim, who, in 1835, published *Goethe's Briefwechsel mit einem Kinde* (Goethe's Correspondence with a Child), a work which created a great sensation and was most favourably received.

Rahel's name is remembered by the quiet, powerful influence she steadily exercised for so many years ; Bettina's shines with the lustre of her brilliant talent and sparkling wit ; the third woman who made a deep impression on the men and women of that day is remembered by one action, her suicide. This was Charlotte Stieglitz, who committed suicide in December 1834, and whose biography, diaries, and letters were published by Theodor Mundt in 1835. She was at once made the subject of studies and panegyrics by the new school. Gustav Kühne, in particular, wrote an admirable notice of her. It was her death which, as has been already mentioned, suggested Gutzkow's *Wally*.

Rahel Antonie Friederike Varnhagen (family name originally Levin, afterwards Robert) was born in Berlin in 1771. She would thus seem to belong to quite another epoch than that of the Revolution of July ; but it was not until after her death that she became a public personage, and entered, by means of her written words, into relations with the literary public. She was one of those rare beings whose inexhaustible vigour and freshness of mind enable them to understand everything and every one, to sympathise with the most dissimilar individuals and tendencies, to penetrate to the core of things ; and whose wide and untiring sympathy wins for them all their life long the affection and admiration of the élite of their time, young and old. Rahel received the same homage from Karl Gutzkow that she had received from Schelling and Friedrich Schlegel, from Schleiermacher and Wilhelm von Humboldt. She had shown herself a fervid patriot during the war of liberation, superintending hospitals in Berlin and Prague ; and she was admired by Heinrich Heine, who dedicated the Lyric Intermezzo in the *Buch der Lieder* to her when she was fifty. She, who had been the intimate of the famous men of the beginning of the century, the Prince de Ligne, Fichte, Prince Louis Ferdinand, Fouqué, and many others, surprised every one by her enthusiastic appreciation of Victor Hugo's *Les Orientales*, and the writings of the Saint-Simonists. There is something great about such a life, undramatic though it be.

It gives us a feeling of the many-sidedness of her character to remember the long list of persons, differing from each other in every possible way, with whom she was on intimate terms. There are depths in her nature which still surprise us, and vaguenesses quite incomprehensible to the modern mind. The magic of her nature lay in the spoken word, the momentary impression, the opportune utterance : so it is not easy to reconstruct. A strong influence emanated from her, yet her real life was introspective ; she was a woman of distinctly aristocratic instincts and sentiments, and yet so tender hearted that her sympathies extended far and wide.

The daughter of a rich Jewish merchant, as a girl plain-looking and without talent of any description, she grows up in her father's house in Berlin at a time when as yet the Jews had none of the rights of citizens. At the age of twenty-five she has already become an influential member of the best society of the capital, and from the age of thirty till her death her house is the intellectual centre of Berlin, and one of the intellectual centres of Germany. Her great attraction was her perfect originality and unconventionality. All human beings desire and love to see themselves mirrored in the mind of a greater human being, all crave for sympathy, all would fain be understood. And those who approached Rahel—princes and nobles, diplomats and philosophers, poets and scientists—felt instinctively that this young girl with the slight, graceful figure, the beautifully formed limbs, the thick, waving hair surrounding a face with an expression of suffering, but with a deep, steadfast look in its dark eyes, was worthy of their confidence, and this for the one and sufficient reason, that she was innocent of all prejudices.

She gladly associates with a charming hetæra like Pauline Wiese, Prince Louis Fredinand's friend ; is her and her cynical husband's and her princely lover's confidante. She has a sincere regard for a reactionary sensualist like Friedrich Gentz, warmly congratulates him when he, at the age of sixty, wins the affections of Fanny Elsler, sees in him the distinguished prose writer and the politician who had been of national importance at a critical moment. Human beings are to her, in Goethe's sense, natural products.

That she, with her strict personal morality and Liberal tendencies, should have been able to rise to such a height of freedom from prejudice and gain such a wide horizon, was primarily due to her having been born in a sort of sanctuary outside the pale of society, that is to say in the house of a wealthy Berlin Jew.

In intolerant, stiff old Prussia, the alien, despised, hook-nosed money-lenders had sat behind their counters for some centuries, with no thought for anything but money—piling thaler upon thaler, buying bills, and lending money even to princes. With all their wealth they were ignorant, orthodox, superstitious. But during the period of enlightenment the influence of Moses Mendelssohn thoroughly aroused them. Their piety became a noble rationalism, and they comprehended the meaning of knowledge and culture. By the close of the eighteenth century they were giving their sons a perfectly new training, and society was also beginning to look upon these sons as men to whom reparation for a wrong was due.

It was in the generation of these sons that the Jewish houses all at once opened their long closed doors, revealing interiors which in no way resembled the cramped middle-class German houses—spacious rooms with rich Oriental carpets and hangings; here and there a valuable painting, made over to father or grandfather by some prince in pecuniary difficulties; on the dinner tables gold and silver plate, the finest crystal sparkling upon lace-edged linen, choice viands, and the rarest wines. The mistress of the house and her daughters had received a higher and more refined education than others in their rank of life; they were deeply interested in theology, philosophy, and music; they had developed quickly under the influence of the mixed society which now frequented their house.[1]

For here, as upon neutral ground, met all those whom society usually separated, members of all its different ranks and castes, and many whom it altogether excluded; German and foreign actresses had the entrance of no other middle-class houses in Berlin; here they were received on the same footing as the other guests. The princes frequented no

---

[1] Karl Hillebrand: *Zeiten, Völker und Menschen*, ii. 5. *Aus dem unzünftigen Schriftthum Deutschlands.—La société de Berlin. Revue des deux mondes.* 1870.

other middle-class houses, if it were for no other reason
than that the company they met there bored them. To
these houses they came, attracted by the easy tone and by
the wit of the women. It was a refined Bohemia. It
was the first development of the cosmopolitan spirit in
the Berlin of old Prussia.

It is in these circles that Rahel grows up, early distinguished by her friendship with Prince Louis Ferdinand,
the hero of the young generation of that day, son of
Frederick the Great's youngest brother. He was about
Rahel's own age, chivalrous, artistic, loose in his morals,
brave to foolhardiness, a first-rate musician, and a first-rate
cavalry general. Goethe describes him in his book on the
campaign of 1793. Like all the princes of that day, he
had been educated like a Frenchman, to the extent (as we
know from some of his published letters) of not being able
to spell German correctly; nevertheless he was an ardent
enemy of Napoleon, and burned to match his troops against
the great Emperor's. Like the Prince of Homburg in his
day, he disobeyed an order to retreat, and, infuriated by
the defeat at Saalfeld, refusing to flee, refusing to yield, was
cut down by the French hussars. He confided his wild
love adventures to Rahel, and found comfort, when suffering
from the treachery of a faithless lady love, in tranquil,
serious conversation with his sisterly friend.

But Rahel was not always in a position to comfort
others. In her young days she stood sorely in need of
comfort herself. By nature she was of such an irritably
nervous temperament that as a child she was with difficulty
kept in life: " Let the air be too dense or too rare, too
warm or too cold, and I am ill at once. And the slightest
excitement has a still worse effect. I cannot imagine any
one more sensitive." In nearly all her letters, immediately
after the date, we find a detailed description of the weather
and temperature: " Friday, 14th March, 1828.—A grey
day, with south-west wind, damp and yet spring-like, though
not inviting for a walk. Pigeons are flying. Every now
and then a blue window appears in the sky; at this moment
sunlight is coming through one of them." " 23rd March,

1829.—The sun has broken through the clouds and is shining brightly ; a cold, sharp, unmistakable north-east wind ; impossible to go to the Thiergarten, where there is still ice and it is as cold as in a cellar." " 17th April, 1830.—Noon ; spring weather after rain ; the trees turning green. To me the best time of the whole year—no flies or mosquitoes, no heat. Spring is approaching, wafting to us a thousand memories, and a thousand hopes which can never be fulfilled, but which are a necessity to us."

Such natures deserve and arouse as much compassion as admiration. Her friend, W. von Burgsdorf, writes to her : " When I saw you for the first time, it struck me at once that you must have been educated by long suffering." It was true ; she had had an infirm body, a melancholy youth, a severe father, and had early suffered humiliation. Her Jewish birth was the cause of great unhappiness to her —an unhappiness almost unworthy of her ; she calls it a sword thrust into her heart by a supernatural being at the moment of her birth. Not one fibre in her nature attached her to the religious community to which by birth she belonged. The memory of its fanaticism and of the fanatical enmity displayed towards it was still fresh. As lately as 1756 the Jewish community in Berlin had expelled a child from the town for having carried a book for a Christian. And on the other side, even Moses Mendelssohn could not go out with his children without having stones thrown at them.

With all the power of his intellect and will, Rahel's father had striven to overcome the sickly child's independence of character, and only her unusual elasticity and strength of mind enabled her to preserve her originality. When young she felt as if she had suffered so much there could not possibly be anything left in her to be bent or broken.

It was inevitable that a woman with this passionate nature should love passionately and should suffer agony through her love. And she did not escape her fate. Twice, when she loved most ardently, she experienced as it were the feeling of being struck down with an assassin's knife and of living for years with the knife in the wound.

At the age of twenty-four she formed a very strong attachment to Count Karl von Finckenstein, the son of a Prussian minister, a man a year younger than herself. They became engaged, and Rahel lived for some years solely for this love. Finckenstein was good-hearted, very much in love, and sincerely devoted to her, but his character was weak. He told her what he had to bear from his family, whose pride revolted against an alliance with a person of inferior position, and who were endeavouring to make him give her up. Rahel's pride was deeply wounded, and she gave him back his word. In character and intellect his superior, she could easily have vanquished his scruples if she had made up her mind to do so, but instead of this she set him free at once, and he was weak enough, attached though he was to her, to take the liberty she offered. She never overcame this first great humiliation.

Three years passed, and she fell in love again, this time passionately, soul and senses, and the feeling was returned. Her second engagement was to Don Raphael Urquijo, a particularly attractive young attaché of the Spanish embassy in Berlin. The engagement lasted for a year. They were passionately attached to each other, but their characters were too unlike, he was too decidedly her inferior. He tormented and insulted her with his jealousy to such an extent that to preserve her self-respect she parted from him ; but she did it with a feeling of crushing, maddening grief, a feeling of loneliness, of being left exposed to all the coldness of life without that shelter from it which she, with her woman's heart, could so ill dispense with.

After Finckenstein's desertion, it had been proposed that she should make a *mariage de convenance.* Her answer was : "I cannot marry, for I cannot lie. Do not imagine that I am proud of myself for this ; I cannot do it, just as I cannot play the flute. . . . He must have no prejudices, otherwise I could not stand it. . . . And he must not be stupid and compel me to lie and pretend that I admire him. I must be able to say exactly what I choose."

For long the needs of her heart were only incompletely satisfied, and she applied herself all the more ardently to intellectual pursuits. It was a great hindrance to her that she had acquired so little knowledge. She herself talked about her dense ignorance. She was, of course, very far from being ignorant, but so much is certain, that she never acquired any real insight into what science is, and never thought a scientific thought.

She had been taught as little Jewish dogma as history and geography. She says that she grew up like a tree in the forest, and that it was as impossible for her to learn religion as anything else. So she evolved a religion of her own, which, as Karl Hillebrand correctly observes, has something akin with Schopenhauer's doctrine ; her ideas of a will in nature, of the misery of the world, of compassion as the only source of morality, are akin to his. She was a great admirer of Angelus Silesius and Saint-Martin ; like Goethe she was an ardent Pantheist. She copies the German mystic's lines :

> " Alle Tugenden sind eine Tugend.
> Schau, alle Tugenden sind ein ohn' Unterschied.
> Willst du den Namen hör'n ? Sie heisst Gerechtigkeit," [1]

and writes beneath them :

" Weil sie Wahrheit ist. Einfachheit, Unparteilichkeit, Selbstlosigkeit, Austheilung für Alle." [2]

She saw everything in its unity, its entirety. There was something of the Delphic priestess in her nature. It is a pity that her words, disconnected from her personality as we have them, are so often dark oracular sayings.

She was, says Karl Hillebrand, full of leniency towards the culpable, of sympathy with the slighted and humble, of compassion for the poor ; the one thing she despised was correct mediocrity, and her contempt for this she displayed openly, even when by so doing she made enemies.

Time passed, and she grew into the old maid ; but years made no change in her appearance and did not diminish

---

[1] All virtues are one virtue ; yea, verily, they are all one and the same. Wouldst thou know its name ? Its name is justice.

[2] Because justice is truth. Simplicity, fairness, unselfishness, a share for all.

her wonderful power. For ten years she carried on a tender correspondence with her future husband, Varnhagen von Ense. He was fourteen years younger than herself, was first a brave officer, then a clever diplomatist, and finally an excellent, very aggressive writer; he had to distinguish himself in both war and peace before he could appear in the character of her fiancé without being entirely overlooked. She married him when she was forty-two, and had a perfectly happy married life for nineteen years.

Rahel owes her literary distinction to the fact that she was the first in the literary circles of Berlin to comprehend and to proclaim Goethe's real greatness. Long before any decisive opinion on this vital question in German culture had been arrived at, Rahel, fully persuaded of Goethe's genius, completely under the spell of its power, proclaimed to all with whom she came into contact that this man was not to be compared with other men; that he stood alone— the loftiest intellect, the wisest counsellor and judge in all the affairs of life. This was at a time when Goethe as an author was only one among the crowd, and when others were ranked high above him. Long before the criticism of the brothers Schlegel established his position beyond dispute, Rahel had introduced the cult of the great, uncomprehended, misjudged genius in her circle in Berlin, had everywhere proclaimed the praises of his illuminating word, and declared his name to be a holy, a consecrated name.

In 1795, when she is only twenty-four, she is so fortunate as to meet him at Teplitz. We learn from a letter from David Veit to Rahel, what Goethe said about her: "Yes, that now is a girl of remarkable intellect, a girl who is always thinking—and as to feeling—where is the like of her to be found? We were constantly together, and were on the most friendly, intimate terms." To Franz Horn, Goethe said: "She is a girl with a loving heart; she feels everything very strongly, and yet expresses herself very gently—we admire the originality and are charmed by the amiability. . . ."

When Rahel is told this, she writes: "How can he know that I have feeling? Never in my life was it so difficult for me to show myself as I am. But why write thus? He is Goethe. And what he feels and says is true. I believe what he says of me. . . . When you see him, Horn, greet him from one who has always worshipped him, idolised him, even when no one else praised, understood, admired him. And if he wonders at a staid young woman sending him such a greeting, make him understand that her excessive reverence for him prevented her telling him how she reveres him. Tell him that this is not affectation, but true, tender feeling (*Pflaumenweichheit*). It is not my fault that others affect what in my case is serious earnest. Am I not right? Yes, yes! I worship him."

Nothing further happens; there is not the slightest attempt on Rahel's part to keep up the acquaintance with Goethe, by correspondence, or any other means. She never mentions his person, only his genius. Twenty years pass, during which she sees nothing of him. Once, in 1811, Varnhagen sends Goethe some appreciations of his poetry written by Rahel. Goethe is much struck by them, pronounces the author to have a remarkable gift of instantaneously grasping, comprehending, connecting, helping, completing; but he never learns—Rahel having forbidden Varnhagen to tell—who the author of the manuscript is. In 1815, in the neighbourhood of Frankfort, Rahel sees Goethe again. There is something touching about this meeting. Goethe is now sixty-six. He is visiting his friend, Marianne von Willemer (the Suleika of the *Diwan*) at Willemer's country house " die Gerbermühle." Rahel, who is in Frankfort, accidentally sees him driving with his hosts, and in her sudden joyful surprise calls loudly: "There is Goethe."

Twenty years, as already mentioned, have passed. It is a quarter past nine on the morning of the 8th of September. Rahel, who had been suffering from an affection of the eyes, has got up later than usual, and is standing half-dressed, brushing her teeth, when the landlord comes to say that a gentleman wishes to see her. Her maid hands her his card. It is Goethe. And out of pure respect, that he may not have to wait, she does not take time to dress herself properly, to make herself look presentable : " I told them to ask him to walk into the sitting-room, and only kept him waiting the time that it took me to put on a dressing-gown (*Unterrock*). It was a black quilted dressing-gown. I sacrificed myself so as not to keep him waiting one minute. It was my one thought. I did not even excuse my dress ; I did nothing but thank him. I did not excuse myself, for it seemed to me that he must know that *I* obliterated myself, that *he* was my one consideration. Such was—alas !—the first impulse of my heart. Now, with the most passionate, most comical, most torturing remorse, I think otherwise."

The feeling of being unsuitably, unbecomingly dressed, depressed her ; she said nothing that was worthy of her. After all these years of love for him, of living in him, and longing for him, she saw him once and once only in private for a few minutes, and this was the turn things took. " But you must hear to the end how ridiculous I was," she writes to Varnhagen. "When he had gone I dressed most carefully and beautifully. I wanted to make up for everything. I put on a lovely white dress with a high collar, a lace veil, my Moscow shawl. . . . Now I can say as Prince Louis wrote : ' My market value has risen ten thousand thalers. Goethe has visited me.' "

Rahel, after twenty years of waiting, after the worship of a lifetime, receiving Goethe in a quilted dressing-gown rather than keep him waiting ten minutes—this every one will confess to be a supreme expression of feminine heroism. After the perusal of many volumes of Rahel literature, this scene is what remains in one's mind as definitely characterising her. It gives the measure of her reverence, her understanding, and her capability of overcoming even the most justifiable vanity of her sex.

It is to be regretted that a being with such rare attributes should have been entirely destitute of talent, of all creative, plastic power. Her ingenious and profound thoughts are scattered, as mere observations, throughout private letters and records which otherwise are of little interest to us nowadays. Probably none but enthusiastic devotees of the women's rights theories are capable of reading much of her at a time.

Her nature was not the artistic nature. Its essence was truthfulness. She herself says : " In the great universal misery of this world, I have consecrated myself to one God, truth ; and every time I have been saved, it has been by him." She was a staunch, reliable friend, yet, even at the risk of sinking in the estimation of others, she frankly and without shame confessed when the feeling of friendship had ceased to exist. Closely connected with her truthfulness was her simplicity ; she made no pretence of being above common weaknesses, no secret of her love of sweets and her keen interest in the latest Paris fashions. And she was fortunate enough to feel what she deserved to feel, an undisturbed inward harmony, partly innate, partly acquired, a perfect consistency of her spiritual life with her convictions. This was what gave her her great and justifiable self-confidence. " Pedantry cannot exist within thirty miles of where I am," she used to say.

We have seen how great her moral tolerance was ; in intellectual matters she was equally forbearing. She neither demanded moral purity nor marked ability in those she esteemed ; what she did demand was unaffectedness. She was unique in her keen recognition and appreciation of whatever was natural and original, however unassuming ; and she herself, in spite of her searching intellect, was as naïve and fresh in perception and expression as a gifted child.

When she was at the zenith of her reputation she was obliged to make herself unapproachable, to surround herself with all sorts of social barricades, that she might be free to choose her associates. She invariably chose individuals of markedly original character.

One of her intimates, Count Tilly, writes to her : " I have a thousand polite messages to give you before I close. One person admires you ; a second is devoted to you ; a third is astonished by your words of wisdom ; a fourth is grieved to say farewell to you, even when it is only a letter that must be brought to a close. It is I, myself, who am all these different persons." This little pleasantry serves to give us an idea of the varied impressions she produced.

T

Rahel often reflected on the subject of originality. She writes : " If a person were to say, ' You imagine it is easy to be original—on the contrary, it costs no end of trouble and exertion,' he would be thought crazy. And yet the assertion would be a true one. Every one could be original, if only people did not carelessly cram their heads with half-digested maxims, which they pour forth again as carelessly."

There had been eminent and interesting women in German intellectual society before Rahel. The latest were Caroline, Dorothea, and those others known to fame through the Romanticists. Rahel is the first great modern German woman, and the first to be completely conscious of her originality.[1]

The pursuit of originality in her day was not without its accompanying danger. It is not the danger of affectation that I allude to. In all days and times there have been affected creatures who imagine that they are original when they help themselves to soup with their shoes. But the perpetual self-inspection and self-examination prevalent in Rahel's day produced a dangerous tendency to impute singularity to very ordinary feelings and impressions, a liability to become unaffectedly unnatural, like the beautiful Henriette Herz and many of her friends, whose outpourings have a haunting flavour of lamp-oil and ink. The fire-writing of originality is something very different.

This is to be found in Bettina's *Goethe's Correspondence with a Child*. Bettina's letters are written in the fiery characters, the " singing flames " of passion.

Bettina von Arnim, a sister of Clemens Brentano, wife of Achim von Arnim, by family and marriage connected with the Romanticists, nevertheless belongs as an authoress to the Young German school. Rahel admired and worshipped Goethe timidly, with a beating heart, a quiet, dignified seriousness. Bettina's admiration showed itself in an insinuating, half-sensuous, half-intellectual devotion, a determined bur-like adhesiveness, and flights of the wildest enthusiasm.

Rahel, ein Buch des Andenkens für Freunde, i.–iii. *Briefwechsel zwischen Varnhagen und Rahel*, i.–ii. Varnhagen : *Gallerie von Bildnissen aus Rahels Umgang*, i.–ii. Ludmilla Assing : *Aus Rahels Herzensleben*.

In 1807, when she, as a native of the same town, made Goethe's acquaintance through his mother, she must have been twenty-three, but in her ways she was still a child, or rather a being midway between child and woman. She comes to Weimar, provides herself with a superfluous letter of introduction from Wieland, holds out both her hands to Goethe as soon as she sees him, and forgets herself altogether. He leads her to the sofa, seats himself beside her, talks about the Duchess Amalie's death, asks if she has read about it in the newspaper. " I never read newspapers," said I. " Indeed! I understood that you were interested in all that goes on at Weimar." " No, I am only interested in you, and I'm far too impatient to be a newspaper reader." " You are a kind, friendly girl." A long pause. She jumps up from the sofa and throws her arms round his neck.

This little anecdote suffices to show the difference between her position to Goethe and Rahel's. From her childhood she had been distinguished by a youthful daring more often met with in boys than girls. At Marburg they still show a tower to the top of which she climbed, drawing the ladder up after her, so that she might be alone. Along with the agility of a young acrobat, she had something of Mignon's childlike, innocent devotion. She is Mignon in real life, as charming as ever, and far less serious.

In 1835, when her *Goethe's Briefwechsel mit einem Kinde* came out, Bettina was fifty. Arnim had died in 1831, Goethe in 1832. She had got back the letters written by herself to Goethe between 1808 and 1811, when an end was put to their intercourse by an act of discourtesy on her part towards Frau Goethe, and had taken even greater liberties with these letters than Goethe took in *Dichtung und Wahrheit* with the experience of his past life. She expressed in them not only all that she had felt, but much that she now thought she ought to have felt ; she gave to their intercourse a more passionate colouring than really belonged to it, and yet in the profoundest sense she was truthful. The letters were at first accepted as genuine. But strong suspicions were presently awakened by the fact of Bettina's having published poems, which were undoubtedly addressed to other women, as if they had been written to her ; and there came a time when her letters lost all credit as historic documents, and everything in them was considered to be fictitious. In 1879, however, Loeper published the genuine letters written by Goethe to Bettina, and it was then seen that in them she had made almost no alteration ; a few greetings were omitted and *thou* was substituted for *you*— nothing more. In only one of the original letters is she addressed as *thou*, but that letter is the only one which Goethe did not dictate, but wrote with his own hand, so Bettina's alteration was not altogether unjustifiable. Goethe was in the habit of enclosing in his letters any poem which he had just written. Bettina was conceited enough to imagine that poems addressed to Minna Herzlieb (even those which played upon the name Herzlieb, and were consequently incomprehensible to her) and to Marianne von Willemer, were meant for her. This was an absurd but excusable mistake. It was inexcusable of her to transpose these poems into prose and incorporate them in her earlier letters, thereby producing the impression that Goethe had simply put her thoughts and feelings into verse.

What she tells us of her intercourse with Goethe's mother, of her eagerness to gather from that mother's lips information about Goethe's childhood which might serve as an introduction to *Dichtung und Wahrheit*, and also what she tells about Beethoven and the relation in which she stood to him, is in all essentials absolutely true.[1]

No one with any feeling for poetic enthusiasm who has read Bettina's book in his youth will ever forget the first impression produced by her style. There is a vitality about it, an animation, a refined wildness, a rhythmic ring and flow, which astound and fascinate. Turning from Rahel's dark hieroglyphs, which suggest a thousand secrets to us, but which we seldom really understand, because the living life which was the commentary is no more, it is refreshing to bathe in this clear spring of naïve and charming devotion. Rahel is more profound and more realistic. But talent is

---

[1] *Briefe Goethe's an Sophie von la Roche und Bettina Brentano nebst dichterischen Beilagen.* 1879.

such a marvellous thing. The pleasure it gives is great. We can and must excuse much for its sake.

In these letters Bettina is twenty-three to twenty-five years old, Goethe fifty-eight to sixty. Hence her passion is not the ordinary human passion of a young woman for a young man. She has grown up with it ; it is an inheritance from her mother, Maxe Brentano, who partly suggested Werther's Charlotte. She loves Goethe's mother, as a young woman always does love the mother of her beloved ; she is grateful to her for having borne him—" how else should I have known him ! " Her devotion to the son finds expression in letters to the mother, till she meets him ; then she writes to himself.

After that first embrace she looks upon him as her own. She writes to his mother : " It is possible to acquire a kind of possession of a man which no one can dispute. This I have done with Wolfgang. And it is what no one ever did before, in spite of all these love affairs you have told me about. Love is the key of the universe ; through it the spirit learns to comprehend and to feel everything. How else could it learn ! "

These letters have been compared to ships laden with rich cargoes. Goethe is the guiding star on all their voyages.

All her thoughts of him are thoughts of enthusiastic devotion : " I would I were sitting at his door like some poor beggar child, so that he might come out to give me a piece of bread. He would read in my eyes what I am, would take me into his arms and wrap his cloak round me to warm me. I know he would not tell me to go again ; I should have my place in his house ; years would pass, and no one would know where I was ; years would pass and life would pass ; I should see the whole world mirrored in his face, and more I should not need to learn.

" Last May, when I saw him for the first time, he picked a young leaf from the vine at his window and held it against my cheek and said : ' Which is softer, the leaf or your cheek ? ' I was sitting on a stool at his feet. How often I have thought of that leaf, and of how he stroked my forehead and my face with it, and played with my hair, and said: 'I am a simple-minded man; it is easy to deceive me; there would be no glory in doing it.' There was nothing brilliant in these words, but I have lived that scene over again a thousand times in my thoughts; I shall drink it in all my life, as the eye drinks light—it was not intellectual converse, no! but to me it surpasses all the wisdom of the world."

There is poetry in this exaltation and in the way in which she tells of his constant presence with her, of her longing for him, of her dumb jealousy of the famous women who came, as Madame de Staël did, to make his acquaintance; there is poetry in her distress at her inability to be of any use to him, and in her vivid appreciation of her own capacity.

"I must tell you what I dreamt about you last night. I often have the same dream. I am going to dance for you. I have the feeling that my dance will be a success. A crowd has gathered round me. I look for you, and see you sitting alone, straight opposite to me; but you don't seem to see me. With golden shoes on my feet, my shining silver arms hanging listlessly by my side, I step forward in front of you, and wait. You lift your head, your eyes involuntarily rest upon me; with light steps I begin to trace magic circles, and you keep your eyes upon me. You follow me through all my bends and turns; I feel the triumph of success. All that you dimly feel I show you in my dance; you marvel at the wisdom it reveals. Presently I fling aside my airy mantle, and let you see my wings, and away I fly, up to the heights. It rejoices me that your eyes follow me, and I float down again and sink into your open arms."

This symbolic description is both graceful and felicitous. In Bettina's Goethe-worship there is something of the same love of mounting and climbing that she displayed in her childhood. She climbed up on to the shoulder of the great Olympian's statue—a statue she was perpetually modelling —drew the ladder up after her, and sat there alone, revelling in the pleasure of being so near him. But it was not her Goethe-worship merely as such which made Bettina an ideal character, a Valkyrie, in the eyes of Young Germany. What won their hearts was the political liberalism to which she gave expression in her letters, and with which she in vain tried to imbue the sage who sat aloof in Weimar, her ardent admiration for the brave resistance of the Tyrolese to the domination of France, her eager desire for the well-being of humanity, for the extermination of poverty and all the other ills of society. It made a powerful impression when she, a worshipper of Goethe, but a more independent-minded one than Rahel, extolled Beethoven's republicanism as greater, worthier than Goethe's submissive loyalty. She tries to bring Goethe and Beethoven together ; she wishes she could send Wilhelm Meister to the Tyrol, to Andreas Hofer, that he might learn to feel greater enthusiasm and to do manly deeds.

In the commencement of Frederick William's reign she was in favour at court. There was a frank, friendly intimacy between her and the king ; she had almost as much influence upon him as Humboldt, when there was any question of assisting talent or alleviating misery. But before long her feelings led her openly to declare socialistic principles. In 1843 she published *Dies Buch gehört dem König* (" This Book belongs to the King "), a work in which she calls upon Frederick William to relieve the distress of his subjects. From her youth she had looked upon herself as the natural champion and advocate of the distressed. " The forsaken and unhappy possessed a magnetic attraction for her," says Hermann Grimm, who, as her son-in-law, knew her intimately. Her natural inclination to help others, and the early impressions made on her mind by the French Revolution, produced those political sympathies to which she unhesitatingly gave utterance, in the naïve expectation of receiving support from royalty.

In 1831, when the cholera raged in Berlin, she went fearlessly among the sick and suffering. Judging from the hard lot of the Berlin working classes, she came to the conclusion that the whole nation was in a bad way and in need of help. To her, liberty had always been a magic word. She believed that whenever the words " Let there be light ! "

resounded from the right quarter, liberty would manifest itself, and all the feelings and dreams of humanity would take shape in harmonious music, to the strains of which the peoples would march joyfully onwards.

Her book, which in a little introductory parable she dedicates to the king, is written in the form of conversations. Goethe's mother is the chief speaker. There is much warm feeling in the book, and a considerable amount of information on the subject of the distress among the lower classes, but too little political insight to make it readable nowadays.

The authoress reaches a climax with the words: "Our sign is the banner of liberty; its brightness lights up the black darkness of the times; its brilliancy dazzles and terrifies those who are on the shore, but we are glad and rejoice. . . . Dangers? Liberty knows no dangers! To it everything is possible. The storm itself, the wildest of all storms, is the captain of our ship." [1]

Such sentiments were not likely to meet with a favourable reception at the Prussian court of that day. The book created a sensation, but put an end to the good understanding between Bettina and the king. It naturally only increased the political discontent of the masses, and a pretext was found for seizing her next book (on Clemens Brentano), because a repetition of the same sort of thing was feared.

Long before this, however, Bettina had received the unanimous homage of the younger generation. Those interested should read Gutzkow's account of his first visit to her, Mundt's description of her, Kühne's poetical appreciation. Even Robert Prutz, severe as he is on all the representatives and models of Young Germany, numbers himself among her admirers. "Bettina's letters are," he says, "the last bright blaze of Romanticism, the sparkling, crackling fireworks with which it closes its great festival; but they are at the same time the funeral pile upon which it consumes itself, the pillar of fire which rises from its ashes—and shows us the way."

The third woman whose life and character made a deep

---

[1] *Dies Buch gehört dem König*, p. 531.

impression on the generation of 1830 was Charlotte Stieg-
litz, the daughter of a Leipzig merchant named Willhöft.
As a child Charlotte was quiet and thoughtful, as a young
girl there was something nun-like about her. In 1822
Heinrich Stieglitz, then in his twenty-first year, came to
Leipzig to study philology. From no fault of his own he
had been mixed up in the prosecution of the demagogues in
Göttingen. He was a handsome young fellow, audacious,
and, to judge by his looks, passionate ; and he was a poet.
Charlotte was then a beautiful girl of sixteen, whose appearance suggested the possession of that supernatural quality
which the Germans in olden days ascribed to those women
whom they believed to possess the gift of prophecy. She
had a high, open, intellectual forehead, curly brown hair
piled up in a tower-like coiffure, a thin, aquiline nose, a
beautiful mouth, large, star-like brown eyes that looked
brightly and bravely out into the world. She spoke low,
but sang with a full, clear voice.

Whatever else modern poets may have neglected, they
have not neglected to impress upon all, but more especially
upon women, that a poet is a superior being. When Charlotte fell in love with the handsome young Stieglitz, who
was fascinated by her, she felt that she had learned what
happiness is. The very idea of being the beloved of a poet,
a real, living poet, was bliss. And to this poet of hers she
consecrated her every feeling, her every thought, from the
first time she saw him until, twelve years later, she stabbed
herself to the heart for his sake. Even before they were
engaged, the desire was ever present with her to be able, all
unknown to him, to do something really difficult, really
great for him. She had the feminine helpfulness, the
motherliness, the housewifely understanding, and the brave
cheerfulness which are among a woman's best qualities.
The impression she produced was that of gentle high-
mindedness.

And this noble woman was unfortunate enough to mistake an effeminate Leipzig student for the ideal man of her
day-dreams—a poet of inferior, perfectly mediocre talent, for
a great artist. In order to be able to marry, Stieglitz was

obliged to find employment. In 1827 he became a teacher in the Berlin Gymnasium and at the same time assistant librarian in the Royal Library, groaning immoderately over the restraint imposed on him by these occupations. He was gloomy, passionate, eager to distinguish himself as a poet, but any artistic gift he had was purely bookish and unrealistic ; he had no perseverance or power of resistance in the struggle of life, but was one of those whom adversity prostrates. He had the outward appearance of a genius ; in reality he was but a dull fellow.

It was a tragic misunderstanding on Charlotte's part. She believes that he has an untamable, uncontrollable temperament. " You need not deny it," she writes; " you ought to have been a brigand-chief." And she calls him her dark, wild, poniard-wielder with the flashing eyes. During their long engagement they live in different towns. His letters are genial, natural, and affectionate ; but one feels in them that he is not unhappy away from her. She, more warm-blooded, pines for him, for his personal presence. Hers was the uncontrollable temperament—he was the genuine bookman, as unlike a robber-chief as any librarian on the face of the earth. About the same time as Victor Hugo in France, he feels the poetical attraction of the East, and, sitting in his library, makes as careful a study as he can of Oriental literature and civilisation. From this study result the *Bilder des Orients*, three volumes produced with much toil and trouble. There is a great deal of pretty and graphic writing in them, and it was unjust that they were so entirely overlooked ; but the feeling which animates these Turkish and Persian poems, these Stamboul tragedies and scenes from Ispahan, these more than passable verses on the Greek war of liberation, is too commonplace, too tame ; the marked individuality, the savagery which Charlotte saw in Heinrich Stieglitz is exactly what is wanting in them. It is all too literary.

Shortly before their marriage in 1828, Charlotte, at her *fiancé's* request, bought a poniard for him to wear on their wedding tour, the weapon with which, six years later, she took her own life. It was but a short time of unmixed happiness that she enjoyed after their marriage. But she completely identifies herself with her husband, and is miserable because he, the genius, is compelled to spend so much of his time and energy on his library work and teaching. She devotes much of hers to writing letters to their rich relations in Russia, who are ministers and privy-councillors, and to other patrons and friends, in the hope of improving his position. She encourages him indefatigably ; she knows every one of his poems by heart, parodies one of them with affectionate playfulness. A certain scene in his tragedy, *Selim III.*, is costing him much time and trouble. One day when he comes home, she leads him smilingly to his desk, where he finds it lying, completed—the fine scene between the Sultan's mother and the physician in the Third Act.

From time to time there came over her what she calls her champagne-mood ; she grieves that this is no longer the case with him. She writes a poem to him, with a present of six quills, exhorting him to be energetic and determined, and not to reflect too long before he begins :

> " Giess ein Füllhorn aus mit Früchten,
> Blüth und Früchte gieb zugleich,
> Weisheit sei in deinem Dichten,
> Witz und Jugend mach' es reich.
>
> Menschen lass uns drinnen finden,
> Menschen die gelebt, gedacht,
> Lass von Lieb' dich warm entzünden
> Und von Zorns Gewitternacht." [1]

She firmly believes in the existence of mighty Titanic thoughts and imaginations in his soul, which it is difficult for him to persuade his lips to utter. Alas ! he is not only uncommunicative, he is barren, and on the verge of insanity, at times possibly over the verge. He listens to her exhortations with indifference. She writes : " O Heinrich, for God's sake let us be inconsistent at times, let us blaze up wildly, despair madly, rise to the bliss of heaven, sink to the depths

[1] Pour out thy horn of plenty ; give us blossom and fruit together ; let there be not only wisdom, but wit and youth in thy words. In thy pages let us find human beings, beings who have lived and thought ; let love, let anger's lightning-flash kindle thy Muse's flame.

of hell—anything but be stolidly indifferent!" We feel the spiritual kinswoman, the admirer of Rahel, in these words.

Harassed by the drudgery of his daily life, troubled by the sterility of his overrated talent, he was sometimes irritable, sometimes gloomily stolid. She tries every means to brace him. At one time she fancies that he is too lonely, that he requires the stimulation of more female society—and she is not jealous. She writes (October 1834): "I wish, Heinrich, that you could have more intercourse, either personal or by correspondence, with clever, womanly women. They are the poet's true public. It would be of interest to you to learn, frankly and truthfully, what they think of you and your works. Such intercourse would be both instructive and refreshing, a useful and agreeable diversion for you."

She is determined that they are to travel, to go far afield. He throws up his appointments and they go off to St. Petersburg and Finland. But it is all in vain.

As she and Stieglitz stood looking at the waterfall of Imatra in Finland, in July 1833, she spoke the following memorable words: "Is not this like a great thought which has strayed into these mountain solitudes? Feelings like mighty billows, thunderstorms, a hurricane, would be a suitable accompaniment to this tumbling, foaming water. How poor the song about the little violet would sound here, pretty as it is in itself! Like the mighty waterfall, this foaming, wildly excited time cries for mighty song. You will give what it demands. . . ."

In October 1835, when he was making perpetual complaint of the small pin-pricks of life, she said to him (as he himself has noted): "My careful observation of you has led me to the conclusion that whoever wishes to do you real service must provide a real, great sorrow for you. Nothing would do you so much good as that; nothing would so surely bring out your powers."

Like most people whose minds are affected, Stieglitz had periods of violent excitement, after which he relapsed into his ordinary state of silent, almost animal-like brooding. Once when they were on a walking tour, he was so lost in his own thoughts, so indifferent to all else, that she left him and went off by herself, hoping that this would rouse him ; but he did not even notice it. It was a kind of warning that her *final* desertion of him would be of no avail ; but it was a warning that she did not understand.

Entirely possessed by the latest ideas of the day, persuaded that a poet ought to live in the world, to influence and be influenced by it, it was her constant desire to drive him to action. She said to him one day : " I long for your spiritual regeneration. You will be born again ! I know you will ! Would that I could hasten that birth—even if it were by artificial means ! But how if my surgical operation miscarried ! " And in December 1834 she writes in her diary that Goethe's life becomes fuller from the moment that Schiller enters into it, but that Goethe ought to have profited more by his friend's death, and would have done so, if he had not, according to his custom, determinedly refused to sorrow ; if he had allowed the sorrow to enter into him, to become part of himself, the result would have been a renewal of youth as far as his poetical productivity was concerned.

It was in this same month of December, 1834, that Stieglitz's disgust with life reached a sort of climax. His malady took the form of intellectual stagnation, of absolute incapacity to express himself. Charlotte begged him, as if he had been a child, rather to rave and storm as of old than to collapse in this terrible manner ; but she begged in vain. It was then that she determined to employ the last means in her power, to take that step which she, with her innocent, high-flown ideas, felt it obligatory to take, in order that a great, simple sorrow might enter into his life, reawaken his genius, and give his poetry new themes.

On the evening of the 29th she came home, knowing that she would have two hours to herself, threw her short fur cape and boa on the hall floor, hurried into her bedroom, locked the door of communication with the kitchen, undressed, washed herself, put on a clean night-dress, wrote a few lines to Heinrich expressing her belief that new life for him would arise out of this misfortune, and exhorting him

no longer to be weak, but calm and strong and great. Then
she lay down on the bed and with a firm hand plunged the
dagger of their wedding tour into her heart.

One's first impression is that these women, Rahel, Bettina,
and Charlotte, who all three became famous in the year
1835, have nothing in common. Rahel dies in 1833 at
the age of sixty-one, and her real life-work, the first energetic
vindication of Goethe's pre-eminence, belongs quite as much
to the eighteenth as to the nineteenth century. Bettina, who
is fourteen years younger, does not come before the public
till a year after Rahel's death ; she combines the exalted
enthusiasm and the unreality of Romanticism with the
reforming tendencies of Young Germany. Charlotte's only
achievement was to kill herself, a thing which has been done
by women times without number, though probably never for
the same reason.

But when we look a little deeper, we find that they have
many traits in common. They are all restless, with the
restlessness distinctive of their day, which manifests itself,
not in outward hurry and strain, but in strong emotions,
not in the nervousness prevalent in our own day, but in
perpetual introspection. Then there is the peculiarity
that none of them transgress the laws of society, though
none of them have any respect for these laws. And there
is the wonderful, ideal fidelity which they all display. Rahel
is Goethe's, from the first breath she draws as a grown-up
woman to her last. Bettina is Goethe's, with such absorbing
devotion that the scheme of erecting a colossal monument
to him which she advocated in her first published work (a
monument which she herself planned and had executed in
miniature), becomes in her old age an *idée fixe*. Charlotte so
entirely belongs to the man on whom her choice falls when
she is sixteen, that she not only lives for him, but dies
for him.

Another thing they have in common is enthusiasm.
Rahel's burns like a steady, sacred flame ; Bettina's breaks
out in a pyrotechnic display of ideas and visions ; Charlotte's
manifests itself in the resolute, uncomplaining sacrifice of

her life. It is genius that they all worship ; they have the enthusiastic German appreciation of poetic genius ; their great desire is to do what in them lies to promote its recognition and glorification, or its development and emancipation ; to this task they devote their lives, regardless of the worthiness or unworthiness of the object of their choice. Lastly, the thoughts and feelings of all three are remarkably original. These women resemble no other women. Never, to our knowledge, has there been such another reflective emotionalist as Rahel, such another sylph-like enthusiast as Bettina, such another suicide as Charlotte's, a suicide inspired by a lofty though false æsthetic principle.

Those who look deeper into the matter and view these characters in the light of history, see in Rahel's introspection and self-reflection, the first form which woman's self-emancipation necessarily took in the Germany of this century ; this height of intellectual independence had to be attained before the women in a country where they for centuries had been relegated to simple domesticity could rise to anything above it. In Bettina's triple enthusiasm, for Goethe, for the ideas of political liberalism, and for social reform, the student of history descries the transition stage between the era of art and the era of liberalism and socialism. And in Charlotte's suicide he sees an expression of the desire of the women of her day to snatch the men from their literary quietism and place them face to face with the seriousness, the tragedy of life. The whole era speaks when she says to Stieglitz that the song of the violet cannot be sung to the accompaniment of a great waterfall. None of these women could have developed as they did at any other period, and at no other period would they have been understood and appreciated as they were. To-day, already, we find it difficult to understand them.

It is characteristic that the word *work* finds no place in the description of their lives. They never learned anything methodically, and in their fear of being unfeminine are proud of this—as we observed in the case of Rahel. Even that accomplished linguist, Henriette Herz, is deeply offended because Jean Paul in one of his letters used the expression,

" M. Herz and his learned wife." Charlotte Stieglitz has not the faintest idea that talent is developed by work, by obstinate industry, and not by bereavements. And Bettina, the bayadere, who imitates Mignon's egg-dance, has nothing whatever to do with work. This fact impresses itself on us when we are annoyed by the slovenly composition and the want of any real understanding of politics in her book for the king.

About the year 1848 it began to be recognised that all this intellectuality would have been more solid, more real, more lasting, if these women had known something, had followed some course of study, taken up one or other branch of science. All this soaring thought would have been doubly valuable if it had in the first place been subjected to regular discipline. To soar without previous training is often mere waste of power. If Rahel had had a solid foundation of knowledge to build upon, she would have had a very different influence upon posterity. As it is, her ideas, obscure and lucid, chaff and seed-corn, are scattered to the winds.

In the Thirties men still believed in an inspiration that could dispense with knowledge, in a morality of the heart which rendered any reform of the old social morality unnecessary, in a defiance of law which allowed all laws to hold good, but kept clear of them all. This state of matters Young Germany was bent upon altering.

During the Forties men had arrived at the persuasion that there was something of greater value than sudden inspiration and a life of pure intellectuality. There was humble and daring work to be done in science and in politics. We see German philosophy develop in the direction of radicalism, and we come upon poets whose aim it is to prepare the way for political liberty.

XXIV

FREDERICK WILLIAM IV. OF PRUSSIA

WITH the year 1840 the literary movement enters upon a new, more philosophic, and more political phase. Yet another generation had arisen, a generation which owed its profoundest culture to Hegel, and which, strangely enough, he had influenced chiefly in the direction of politics. Schelling in his day had declared art to be the highest manifestation of intellect. His principle, and that of the Romanticists, was that the artist is the true man. What art had been to Schelling, history was to Hegel—history, that eternal progress of the idea of liberty, that great liberty-epic. And what the work of art had been to Schelling, the State was to Hegel. To him the true, the perfect human being is not the artist, but the citizen of a constitutional State.

This youngest generation was inspired by the Hegelian philosophy to make the reform of the State its aim. It held the adherents of the Young German school in light esteem, being of opinion that they had not stood bravely by their colours, either in philosophy or politics, that they were too belletristic, too epicurean. It would not join in the old cry for the rehabilitation of the flesh, would not even listen to it. Heine, in *Atta Troll*, had told the young generation that a man of character without talent was no better than a bear ; the young men retorted that a man of talent without character was nothing but a monkey—possibly a very amusing monkey, but nothing more.

That the Hegelian philosophy had again become a guiding principle was made plain when the periodical known as the *Hallische Jahrbücher* was brought out by Ruge and Echtermeyer in 1838. This organ of the Hegelians of the Left disseminated the ideas which moulded not only the politicians but also the poets of the day. In all essentials the principles were the same as those in whose name Young Germany had taken the field, but they were now proclaimed with more scientific precision and more resoluteness. The elder men had to choose between joining the Young Hegelians and reprobating the principles of their own youth, as now proclaimed by others. As was only natural, they did not recognise their own opinions as propounded by these bellicose youths, and there was many a collision between the youngest generation and Gutzkow, Laube, and Mundt.

The idea of the State now became the central idea of the day, the idea of the State as a living organism, realised in the consciousness of all its citizens. In the many philosophical, theological, æsthetic feuds waged by this new generation, the State and the necessity for its reform is always the burden of their cry. This was the season of preparation for that absorption in the idea of the State which is so characteristic of the Germany of later days, and which caused even a revolutionary (but a Hegelian revolutionary) like Lassalle to exclaim: " Do not malign the State! The State is God!" It is a sign of the nature of the literary development that the *Hallische Jahrbücher* began as a philosophical, but was suppressed as a political periodical.[1]

The new political ideas with which the nation was impregnated presently broke forth in poetry and song. The first political poetry appears in the same year as the *Jahrbücher*, and spreads political free-thought in far wider circles. At first it was for the most part rhetorical, and devoid of artistic value, but the common national feeling of the German countries had slumbered so long that the mere watch-words "liberty" and "fatherland" produced an electrical effect.

On the 7th of June 1840, Frederick William IV. ascended the throne of Prussia. The new king presented in every respect a marked contrast to the man who, succeeding in 1797, had wielded the Prussian sceptre for forty-two years. Frederick William III. had been the born soldier; his

[1] *Cf.* R. Prutz: *Vorlesungen über die deutsche Litteratur der Gegenwart.*

son was an artist by nature, with mediocre half-suppressed talents, a dilettante in art and science. The father had been a sober, modest, steadfast character ; the son was a fanciful enthusiast, as impressionable as a woman. The father had been the devotee of duty, an upright, dry, narrow-minded man, the son was full of romantic ideas, clever, famous for his witty sallies. The father had been tall, slender, soldier-like, in his bearing and dress ; the son had soft, rounded features, not unlike Queen Louisa's, was fat rather than muscular, quick and jerky in his movements, communicative, sociable, very talkative. The father had been a reliable man, the son was an interesting one.

Though Frederick William IV., as Crown Prince, had had the best of instructors in all the branches of a military education, he did not take the lead in military matters. He was fond of calling himself a Prussian officer, but the strict, pedantic discipline inseparable from military service in time of peace, was wearisome to him, and at times he, a Hohenzollern, was even known to jeer at State parades. Now and again, however, it happened that he grew wildly enthusiastic. At a review, the music, the clash of weapons, the loud commands, the firing, produced in him a sort of poetic excitement. Carried away by military enthusiasm, he once, on the occasion of a big sham-fight, led the troops right into Berlin, regardless of the confusion thereby produced, and of the hundreds of window-panes shattered by the volleys fired in the streets.[1]

But for the most part it was with men of science and artists that the Crown Prince consorted—scholars such as Humboldt, historians like Ranke, painters like Cornelius, sculptors like Rauch. He was much interested in architecture, made a study of the antique styles in their application to ecclesiastical architecture of the Byzantine type, sketched plans, tried to produce imposing effects by means of colonnades and halls. He projected ideal landscapes, resembling scenes on the Italian shores of the Mediterranean. He criticised music and poetry. He specially encouraged and patronised the study of ancient German customs and of

[1] Prutz: *Zehn Jahre*, i. 77.

all ancient art which had devoted itself to the service of religion ; and all this occupation with the past increased his distaste for the time in which he lived, and developed his inclination to restore the old order of things, or at any rate to oppose reforms inspired by the modern spirit.

This inclination could not but be strengthened by the young prince's intercourse with clergymen, and with the small circle of romantically disposed aristocrats who were his familiar associates. From his childhood he had been religious. As a boy he had, during the war with Napoleon, learnt to believe in the sacredness of the old system of government, in the divine right of kings, and in the mission of Austria as heir of the Holy Roman Empire. He adopted the whole system of ideas and enthusiasms of which Joseph de Maistre was the first and ablest exponent. He studied Haller's *Restauration der Staatswissenschaft*. Ere long he came to look upon the crown as a mystic jewel, a combination of the priestly fillet of old with the dictator's golden wreath ; the kingly office became in his eyes a sacred calling, the king himself a divinely inspired being. His ideal was a patriarchal relation between the king and his people, much the same ideal as that which was aimed at during the same period by the so-called Young England, the followers of Disraeli.

Frederick William IV. was received by his people with all the confident expectation with which a nation that is still in its political childhood welcomes a new king. They believed of him what is believed of all crown princes, that his principles were more liberal than his father's. The hopes and expectations of the nation surrounded him with a sort of halo. He began, as kings are wont to do, with an act which appeared to justify the popular estimate of his character ; he proclaimed a general amnesty for political offences. This led all to hope that he would fulfil the political desire of the country, that he would confer on Prussia that benefit which was regarded as a necessary condition of all progress, constitutional government.

As already stated, the Prussian people were in possession of a distinct, definite, royal promise of a constitution, a promise the fulfilment of which had been dishonestly delayed. This made their hope all the stronger; they felt sure that this promise would now be redeemed.

Soon after the new king's accession, the Estates of the Provinces of Posen and East and West Prussia were summoned to meet at Königsberg, for the purpose of paying homage to him. The Estates of East and West Prussia replied to the announcement of this meeting by sending in a most humble petition to the king, in which they besought him to maintain and to complete the system of representative government inaugurated by his glorious father, who, in this as in all else faithful to his promise, had introduced representative government in the provinces, but had left the completion of the work to his royal successor "whom the nation loves with the truest devotion, and on whom its dearest hopes are set" (in welchem die treueste Liebe und die innigsten Wünsche des Landes sich begegnen).

The lower classes of citizens, all those who hoped that their trades and industries would profit by the approaching festivities at Königsberg, were highly incensed by this proceeding, which they considered calculated to offend the king. The higher classes, on the contrary, imagined that their gifted monarch would at once gladly accede to the legitimate desire of his people; no one was in a better position than he to understand the defects of the old system of representation. But neither those who dreaded an outburst of royal indignation nor those who expected a manifestation of royal liberal-mindedness proved to be right.

Frederick William's vague answer was to the effect that the constitution of the Estates rested upon a national, historic foundation, that the king took a deep interest in the said institution, that he was firmly determined to pursue the path entered on by his predecessors, and that his faithful Estates might "place absolute confidence in his intentions" with regard to the institution of the Landtag (Parliament).

Little of positive assurance as there was in this message, it was received with joy; it relieved one party from the dread of a stern rebuff, and encouraged the sanguine hopes

of the other. The festival at Königsberg went off successfully, and was marked by general enthusiasm. Its most
imposing incident occurred immediately after the deputies
had repeated, word for word, the oath of allegiance read
out to them. Hardly had the echo of the loud Amen pronounced by the four hundred voices died away, when the
king was seen to rise from the throne, which stood upon
an open balcony, come forward to the rails, raise his arm
as if he were taking an oath, and begin to address the
assembly. Every word of his speech was clearly audible.
He promised to be a just judge, a faithful, painstaking, and
merciful ruler, a Christian king like his ever-to-be-remem-
bered father. The concluding sentence bears witness to his
literary gift: "May God preserve our Prussian fatherland,
for its own sake, for Germany's, and for the world's—our
fatherland, which is made up of many parts, and yet is one
whole, like that noble metal, a mixture of many others, but
itself one metal, liable to no rust but the beautifying rust
of centuries!"

Astonishment that a King of Prussia should thus of his
own free will give a promise to his people in return for
theirs to him, combined with the impression produced by this
ostensibly improvised address from such an animated and winning royal personage, to create a feeling of excited jubilation.
Above on the balcony the queen burst into tears, down below
the people wept, smiled through their tears, and pressed
each other's hands. In the transport of the moment it was
not observed that there was no definite political promise in
the speech, nothing but liberal generalities and romantic
phraseology.

But the Königsberg festival was only a prelude to the
great one held in Berlin. In the minds of the inhabitants of
his capital a halo of golden promises still surrounded the
person of the king. They were determined to do everything in their power to show their devotion, and to give the
festival a character that was likely to be agreeable to him.
The military element was not allowed to preponderate;
something in the style of a medieval German municipal
pageant was aimed at. The different guilds, numbering in

all about 10,000 men, marched in procession, carrying their banners and emblems. As an agreeable little surprise for the king, a great projecting piece of masonry at the Rathaus (town hall) with which his carriage had come into collision one day when he was Crown Prince, was altogether removed.

In the interval between the two festivals an incident occurred which could not but awaken in the mind of the nation a suspicion of the king's fickleness. On the 4th of October 1840, a royal order in council was published which intimated, to prevent any misunderstanding, that the king, in expressing his appreciation of the loyalty of the Estates, had by no means declared himself to be in favour of a representative constitution as formulated in the ordinance of the 22nd of May.

The princes and nobles were to take the oath of allegiance in the palace, the citizens were to pay homage in the great square outside the so-called Lustgarten. But from early morning rain fell in torrents. For two whole hours the citizens stood outside the square, getting soaked through, whilst the king listened, indoors, to the speeches of princes, nobles, and clergy, and gave the rein to his own eloquence.

At last he stepped out on the balcony. But on this occasion people were prepared to hear him speak ; there was no question of improvisation. Berlin would have felt itself insulted if the king, who had made a speech at Königsberg, had received its homage in silence. And speak he did. Every one could see the motion of his hands, but the size of the square and the sound of the wind and the rain prevented his words being heard. Every time he stopped speaking, the attentive crowd, imagining that the speech was concluded, broke forth in loud acclamation ; but the king waved his hand, and proceeded. The rain poured, but still he spoke. All watched his gesticulations. Four times the multitude shouted " Hurrah ! " in the belief that he had done, and four times he began again. He promised to rule as one who feared God and loved man, with his eyes open when attending to the needs of the people and of the times, closed when called on to do justice

—but the antithesis was lost in the whistle of the wind and the rush of the rain.   He shouted : " Will you promise, while I am striving so to do, to stand by me, in prosperity and in adversity ?   If so, give an answer in that plainest, finest word of our mother-tongue, an honest ' Ja ! ' "   Shouts of " Bravo ! bravo ! " from the square.   They thought he had finished.   But the king waved his hand and continued. At last he concluded by turning the downpour of rain to account in his peroration, by taking it as a favourable omen— though this also was lost on the audience.   " So help me God, I will keep the promises which I have made here and at Königsberg !   In sign hereof I raise my right hand to heaven. Proceed we now with our high festival, and may God's blessing fall like his fertilising rain upon us this day ! "

But God's fertilising rain completely extinguished the festive spirit, poured its chilling prose over both audience and orator.

No one could observe that any promises were kept, but neither could any one name any particular promises that had been made by his Majesty.   The new king and his government soon showed themselves in their true light.

Eichhorn was nominated Minister of Public Worship (*Kultusminister*) in place of the late Count Altenstein, the patron of Hegel and the Hegelians.   Eichhorn had already shown Pietistic leanings ; it was reported that he intended to introduce strict regulations regarding the observation of holy-days, and possibly also rules of church discipline binding on all Government officials.   The indignation roused by this report was so great that advantage was taken of the first possible opportunity to display it.   Racine's *Athalie* was put on the stage by the king's special request.   There was no fault to be found with the play itself, but it had a religious subject and had been originally written for the inmates of a convent.   On the occasion of its first perfor-mance, January 4th, 1841, it was hissed by the audience, a demonstration the meaning of which every one understood. People were much more exasperated with the minister than with the king ; for no one doubted that the king was a sincerely religious man, whereas the life Eichhorn had lived and the company he had kept led them to conclude the opposite of him. And when it came to his making public use of the expression, "the Christian state," that is the state of which the unorthodox cannot be reckoned true citizens, war was waged against this "square circle," as the expression was called, with all the weapons of sober earnest and of mockery. Unfortunately the king had, a few months before this, in one of his fits of political liberalism, possibly influenced by his appreciation of wit, abolished the censorship of caricature-drawing. So now Eichhorn was to be seen everywhere, in the shape of a squirrel (*Eichhorn* = squirrel) gnawing leaves, cracking the empty nut of the Christian Church, &c., &c. The ungrateful caricaturists did not even respect the king; and Heine, the greatest caricaturist of the age, ridiculed royal indecision in the following lines of *Der neue Alexander :*

> "Ich ward ein Zwitter, ein Mittelding, das weder Fleisch noch Fisch ist,
> Das von den Extremen unserer Zeit ein närrisches Gemisch ist.
> Ich bin nicht schlecht, ich bin nicht gut, nicht dumm und nicht gescheute,
> Und wenn ich gestern vorwärts ging, so geh ich rückwarts heute." [1]

But Eichhorn was not content with Christianising the State, he aimed at Christianising science. He was particularly desirous to oust known Hegelians from all good and influential appointments, the Hegelian philosophy being distasteful to the king, because it left no play for his imagination.

It was by the king's wish that Schelling was brought from Munich to Berlin to fill the professorial chair left vacant by the death of Hegel, that from that vantage ground he might propound his new philosophy, that *Philosophie der Offenbarung* (Philosophy of Revelation) which, like some quack remedy, had been kept secret for years, and yet puffed as if it were to introduce a new era. He received a larger salary than had ever before been given to a Prussian

---

[1] I'm neither fish nor flesh, neither this nor that, but a queer compound of the extremes of the day; I'm not bad, I'm not good, not stupid and not clever; if I walked forwards yesterday, I'll walk backwards to-day.

university professor (it was declared that he was almost as well paid as a *première danseuse*) ; and it was certainly not the king's fault that, in spite of all Schelling's endeavours, there seemed no possibility of eradicating Hegelian unorthodoxy. As a matter of fact, Schelling was a failure. He could not but feel that he was regarded with contempt by the whole youth of a nation. Ch. Kapp wrote a clever description of the court thinker's various metamorphoses since the days of his youth, his apostasy from himself, the humbug in his reconciliation of faith and thought ; and Ludwig Feuerbach, in his energetic language, styled him the philosophical Cagliostro of the nineteenth century, and his philosophy a theosophic farce.

Eichhorn proceeded to take a variety of measures to counteract the progress of science. He set a fixed limit to the number of teachers at all the different Prussian universities, thereby reducing the number of private lecturers and increasing the influence of the Government. Professor Hoffman (von Fallersleben) was dismissed from the University of Breslau, because of some harmless jests at politics in his *Unpolitical Songs* — jovial, catching verses, which so exactly chimed in with the Liberal ideas of the middle-class citizen that they alarmed the authorities. The Biblical critic, Bruno Bauer's, two books on the authenticity of the Four Gospels cost him his post of lecturer at the University of Bonn. The servile Faculties carried out the wishes of the Government : they approved of free scientific inquiry, but could not approve of Bruno Bauer as a lecturer on *theology*. The Hegelian theologian, Marheineke of Berlin, undauntedly declared that he, too, was desirous that Bruno Bauer should be relieved from his post as lecturer, because he considered that such an eminent critic, a man of such thorough scientific training, should be promoted to a really influential appointment. But Bauer's fate was sealed. The Halle students petitioned that David Strauss might be appointed professor at their university. The answer to their petition was a reprimand, and the three students whose names headed the list of petitioners were expelled. After Gans's death, the noted reactionary Stahl (author of

Umkehr der Wissenschaft) was appointed to his professorship in Berlin. It was somewhat humiliating for the Government that the students refused to listen to Stahl's first lecture ; they drummed him out of the lecture-room.

In the summer of 1841 there appeared in Switzerland a little book, entitled *Gedichte eines Lebendigen* (" Poems of a Living Man "). It contained many an astounding verse ; among others :

> " Reisst die Kreuze aus der Erden !
> Alle sollen Schwerter werden !
> Gott im Himmel wird's verzeihn.
> Lasst, o lasst das Verseschweissen,
> Auf den Amboss legt das Eisen,
> Heiland soll das Eisen sein." [1]

And :

> " Brause, Gott, mit Sturmesodem durch die fürchterliche Stille,
> Gieb ein Trauerspiel der Freiheit für der Sklaverei Idylle !
> Lass das Herz doch wieder schlagen in der Brust der kalten Welt
> Und erweck ihr einen Rächer und erweck ihr einen Held ! " [2]

The collection was prefaced by a poetical challenge " To the Dead Man," namely Prince Pückler, who had written under this pseudonym. He was chosen as the representative of the careless pleasure-lovers who seek distraction in travel. The attack was unjust, but how fine it sounded !

The anonymous author, whose name soon became public property, was a young man of twenty-four, Georg Herwegh, born in Würtemberg in 1817, and educated at the well-known Tübingen Institution. While serving his time in the army, Herwegh quarrelled with an officer, and was

---

[1] Tear the crosses from the graves ;
'Tis the sword alone that saves ;
   God forgives the deed ye do.
Leave, oh leave your rhyming trade ;
Steel on anvil must be laid—
   Steel shall bring us safely through.

(JOYNES.)

[2] Let thy tempest blow, O God, and put an end to this terrible calm ! Give us a tragedy of liberty in place of this idyll of slavery ! Set the heart of the clay-cold world beating again ; raise up for her an avenger ; awaken for her a hero !

obliged to take refuge in Switzerland, where he lived for
several years, associating with other refugees and other
youthful Radicals. His poems, with their fresh, energetic,
and yet vague Radicalism, at once made their mark, and
attained an immense circulation in the course of a few
months. The sentiment of these poems is somewhat mixed.
Now it is with tyrants, now with Philistines, that their author
is at war ; at one time he discovers the enemies of the good
cause in Germany itself, at another abroad ; now he writes
as a staunch Republican ; again, following the example of
Platen, he appeals earnestly, imploringly to the King of
Prussia, warning him, but at the same time assuring him
that it is not too late :

> " Du bist der Stern, auf den man schaut,
> Der letzte Fürst, auf den man baut." [1]

·The public of that day overlooked the young poet's want
of consistency ; his enthusiasm was infectious, his melodious
lyrical rhetoric irresistible. He was the first lyric poet who
had taken men's hearts by storm since the days of Goethe
and Schiller. From the Alps to the Baltic the young men
sang : *Reisst die Kreuze aus der Erden !*

In the autumn of 1842 Herwegh took a tour through
Germany, with a practical aim in view. The work which
he had begun as a poet, he desired to carry on as a
journalist, a political writer ; his journey was undertaken
for the purpose of securing contributors to a monthly
magazine to be entitled *Der deutsche Bote aus der Schweiz* (" The
German Messenger from Switzerland ") ; but it became a sort
of triumphal progress ; he was entertained at banquets in
Cologne and Leipzig, and serenaded by the students of
Jena ; never before had such homage been paid to a German
poet.

Towards the end of October he arrived in Berlin, where
he could not expect to make as great a sensation, especially as he had followed the advice of his companion, Ruge,
and refused the advances of a very unprosperous Radical

---

[1] Thou art the star to which we turn our eyes,
Of monarchs all the last in whom our hope yet lies.

association.   But something happened which made far
more impression on the public mind than any popular demonstration could have done—the king expressed a wish to
make Herwegh's personal acquaintance.

So far the only public manifestation of Frederick
William's æsthetic sympathies had been his patronage
of Tieck and Rückert, both of whom he had invited to
Berlin.   Ludwig Tieck, now an old man, crippled with
rheumatism, occasionally read aloud at Court and put plays
on the stage ; Friedrich Rückert was expected to assist in re-
organising the study of Oriental languages at the University,
but proved unfit for the task.   Unprejudiced judgment in
literary matters was certainly not traditional in the Hohenzollern family.   There was only one possible precedent for
the audience granted to Herwegh, and that was to be found
in the present king's own private reply to the ode in which
Platen conjured him to embrace the cause of unhappy
Poland.   In a cordial letter to the poet, Frederick William,
then Crown Prince, expressed his hearty sympathy with the
Poles and bewailed his inability to help.   The ode addressed
by Herwegh to the king implored him to put down
clericalism ; it was an agreeable surprise to find that this
had given no offence.

The audience took place on the 19th of November 1842.
Herwegh was very silent, depressed by the situation.   The
king was, as usual, eloquent and communicative.   He is
reported to have said : " You are the second enemy whom I
have received this year ; the first was M. Thiers (who had
threatened war in 1840, because of the support given by the
great powers to the Sultan in his quarrel with the Egyptian
Pacha) ; but it gives me greater pleasure to see you.   We
have our vocations, you and I ; mine is to be a king, yours
to be a poet.   I shall be faithful to mine, as I trust you will
be to yours.   Nothing is more abhorrent to me than vacillation ; I esteem an Opposition which is actuated by real conviction (wenn sie nur gesinnungsvoll ist)."   Referring to
Herwegh's youth, he prophesied " a Damascus day " for
him, concluding with the words : " Until then, let us be
honourable enemies."

Such particulars of this meeting of king and poet as reached the ears of the public awakened feelings either of childish envy or childish indignation among the oppositionist writers of the day. It was considered that Herwegh ought (*à la* Marquis Posa) to have taken advantage of the opportunity to demand political liberty for Prussia.

A few days after the audience, Herwegh left Berlin. At Königsberg, where he was again entertained at a banquet, he was surprised to receive the news that his projected periodical, before its appearance, had been declared contraband in Prussia. It was a prohibition for which he might well have been prepared, for all books published abroad (his own poems included) were contraband, except those for which special licence had been granted. But already irritated by accusations of treason brought against him in one and another Radical newspaper, he was completely upset by this rebuff, and at once addressed an awkward, unmanly, would-be pathetic letter to the king.

He pleaded the king's promise of honourable enmity, a promise which he declared to be broken by this prohibition; he would not ask the king to revoke this edict, though it was hard for him to see the child of his Muse menaced while yet in its mother's womb, and hard to have to live in a state of constant warfare with the law of the country; not that the prohibition did him any harm, for he was fortunate enough to be at that moment preparing the fifth edition of his poems, also a prohibited book; but he felt impelled to address a last, honest, impassioned appeal to the king; an appeal which, though private, was not merely his own, but that of thousands, &c., &c.

The letter itself was stupid and indiscreet; its publication in a Leipzig newspaper a few weeks later was a piece of folly that avenged itself. In Stettin, Herwegh received orders to leave the country; policemen escorted him to the stage-coach, from which he was forbidden to alight in Halle. He had received a festive welcome in Prussia, but his leave-taking was of the coldest.

The arch-scoffer Heine, in his poem, *Der Ex-lebendige*, has the following lines:

> " Aranchuez ! in deinem Sand'
> Wie schnell die schönen Tage schwanden,
> Als ich vor König Philip stand
> Und seinen uckermarkschen Granden.
>
> Er hat mir Beifall zugenickt,
> Als ich gespielt den Marquis Posa,
> In Versen hab' ich ihn entzückt
> Doch ihm gefiel nicht meine Prosa." [1]

And in *Die Audienz* he jeers more mercilessly still at the Swabian suckling :

> " ' Ich will, wie einst mein Heiland that,
> Am Anblick der Kinder mich laben,
> Lass zu mir kommen die Kindlein, zumal
> Das grosse Kind aus Schwaben.'
>
> So sprach der König, der Kämmerer lief
> Und kam zurück und brachte
> Herein das grosse Schwabenkind
> Das seinen Diener machte.
>
> Der König sprach : ' Du bist wohl ein Schwab ?
> Das ist just keine Schande.'
> ' Gerathen ! erwidert der Schwab, ich bin
> Geboren im Schwabenlande.'
>
> .   .   .   .
>
> ' Erbitte dir eine Gnade,' sprach
> Der König.   Da kniete nieder
> Der Schwabe und rief : ' O geben Sie, Sire !
> Dem Volke die Freiheit wieder.'
>
> Der König stand erschüttert tief ;
> Es war eine schöne Scene.
> Mit seinem Rockärmel wischte sich
> Der Schwab' aus dem Auge die Thräne.
>
> Der König sprach endlich : ' Ein schöner Traum !
> Leb' wohl und werde gescheidter !
> Und da du ein Somnambülericht bist,
> So geb' ich dir zwei Begleiter.

---

[1] O my Aranchuez ! how the days flew that I spent amidst thy sands ! those days when I stood in the presence of King Philip and his Uckermark grandees. He nodded approval to me when I played Marquis Posa ; my verses charmed him, but my prose he could not stand.

Zwei sichre Gendarm', die sollen dich
  Bis an die Grenze führen.
Leb' wohl, ich muss zur Parade geh'n,
  Schon hör ich die Trommel rühren.' "[1]

It was not only humour that laughed, but envy and vindictiveness as well. Men wreaked vengeance on their own former enthusiasm. The Herwegh catastrophe was, moreover, attended by disastrous practical results. The *Leipziger Allgemeine Zeitung*, the Opposition newspaper most widely read in Prussia, was suppressed the day after it published the letter to the king. The *Rheinische Zeitung*, the principal Liberal paper published in Prussia, itself very soon received

[1] "I will, as my gracious Saviour did,
    Find the sight of the children pleasant ;
So suffer the children to come, and first
    The big one, the Swabian peasant."

Thus spake the monarch ; the chamberlain ran,
    And return'd, introducing slowly
The stalwart child from Swabia's land,
    Who made a reverence lowly.

Thus spake the king : "A Swabian art thou?
    There's no disgrace in that, surely?"
"Quite right ! I was born in Swabia's land,"
    Replied the Swabian demurely.

.   .   .   .

"One wish I will grant thee," the monarch said—
    Then the Swabian in deep supplication
Knelt down and exclaimed : " O sire, I pray grant
    Their freedom once more to the nation !"

The monarch in deep amazement stood,
    The scene was really enthralling ;
With his sleeve the Swabian wiped from his eye
    The tear that was well-nigh falling.

At last said the king : "In truth a fine dream !
    Farewell, and pray learn discretion ;
And as a somnambulist plainly thou art,
    Of thy person I'll give the possession

To two trusty gendarmes, whose duty 'twill be
    To see thee safe over the border—
Farewell ! I must hasten to join the parade,
    The drums are beating to order."
                                    (BOWRING.)

its death-blow. And in Saxony, at the request of Prussia, Arnold Ruge's *Deutsche Jahrbücher* (first known as the *Hallische Jahrbücher*), the leading periodical expressing the opinions of the reflective youth of the day, was also suppressed.

One lesson the young generation learned from what had happened. It was no momentous matter that a young poet should have shown himself embarrassed and then unmanly in his relations with a king. But the men of this day had imagined themselves to have taken a great step in advance of the men of the Thirties ; they believed that they possessed strength of character, whereas their elders had only been gifted with talent. Now it was borne in upon them, not only that poets are little calculated to make good political leaders, but also that the whole generation must discipline itself severely if it were to stand any firmer in the day of trial than its predecessors had done.

So now thinkers and politicians by profession (in almost too many instances professors) took the lead. And the fact that the generation which now revolutionised the mind of Germany failed so miserably in the close of the struggle of 1848, is to be ascribed, not to want of strength of character, but to that idealism which is bred in the minds of men who have never ruled, to their belief in the irresistible powers of ideas and ideals to realise themselves, and to their contempt for that external brute force, which in theory was of minor importance, but which, vanquished in the first brush, calmly allowed itself to be disdained, and awaited the moment when, with renewed vigour, it returned to the attack.

There was considerable difference of opinion as to the advisability of the various measures taken by Frederick William's ministers, but for the most part they were unfavourably criticised. Under every other question smouldered the question of the Prussian Constitution. The king's attempt to dispose of it by a rebuff had been unsuccessful, and the means which he and his advisers employed to put down the movement were extremely infelicitous. In the Silesian Landtag (Parliament) the chief magistrate and other representatives of the town of Breslau had proposed an address from the Silesian Estates on the

x

subject of a general assembly of the Estates of the whole kingdom—a Reichstag. The king replied by a special announcement of the procedure to be observed on the occasion of his approaching visit to Silesia, intimating that no arrangements need be made for his festive reception and entertainment in Breslau, as he would accept nothing from that town. This in May, in reference to a journey to be taken in October, and festivities of which there had as yet been no offer! And the king entered Breslau in state and was fêted after all, though the festivities were not held specially on his account, but on the occasion of the hundredth anniversary of the incorporation of Silesia with Prussia. He contented himself with deploring the absence in the invitation sent him of " expressions which would have given him heart-felt pleasure," and with declining to stay longer than a day or two on account of want of time.

Yet the king stood in need of the consent of the Estates of the realm to the carrying out of a project of the utmost importance for the whole country. The time of railways had come, and two matters had to be arranged, a loan of the money needed for the construction of State railways, and a State guarantee to the constructors of private lines. According to a law passed by Hardenberg in 1820, the consent of the Estates of the realm was imperative in both cases. The king evolved an impossible plan ; he proposed to convoke an assembly of six hundred representatives chosen from the different provincial Landtage, and to let this assembly play the part of Reichstände (Estates of the realm). Metternich was obliged to interfere, and prove the utter impracticability of the scheme.[1]

It was at this juncture that a small pamphlet, *Vier Fragen eines Ostpreussen* (" Four Questions by an East-Prussian "), made a sensation throughout the whole of Germany. The little book appeared on the spiritual horizon like the first distant flash of lightning that preludes the storm. Purporting to be printed in Mannheim, it was scattered abroad everywhere in the end of February 1841. Such careful arrangements had been made that it found its way into the

---

[1] Sybel : *Die Begründung des deutschen Reiches*, i. 107.

booksellers' windows of every town in Prussia on the same day—every town except Berlin, where it appeared a little later, a precaution taken to prevent confiscation before the general distribution.

The Four Questions which it contained foreboded the downfall of absolute monarchy. They were : What did the Estates ask ? What right had they to make such a request ? What answer did they receive ? What remains for them to do ?

The book's answer to the first question was that, as things now stood, the people had almost no share in their own government, although the general high level of education made it natural that they should wish it. And their desire for a representative constitution, for a national parliament, was made more ardent by the fact that they possessed no other means, such, for instance, as a free press, of expressing their opinions, and that they thoroughly distrusted the king's ministers because of their arbitrariness, servility, and pietistic tendencies. To the question : What right had the Estates to make such a demand ? the author replied : The right of authority, an authority declared and recognised on the 22nd of May 1815. To the third question : What answer did they receive ? the reply was : A recognition of their loyalty, a rejection of their proposal, and comforting promises of some vague future indemnification. The answer to the fourth question : What remains for the Estates to do ? only occupied a line and a half. It was : To demand now as a demonstrable right what they had previously solicited as an act of grace.

The earnest, impressive tone of the pamphlet, its appeal to the people's sense of justice and self-respect, aroused a keen desire to know the name of the anonymous author. He himself had sent his book to the king, with his name written on the title page : Dr. Johann Jacoby, physician in Königsberg. The king at once ordered criminal proceedings to be instituted against him. It appeared that he was a man of means, and a very highly esteemed physician. In 1831, during the first and most violent epidemic of cholera in Poland, he had gone there to study the disease. At a later period he had had a protracted quarrel with a Warsaw doctor, a regular quack, who, when the cholera broke out again in 1837, advertised his discovery of an infallible remedy for "this trivial, easily curable disease." Jacoby wrote a short scientific article in disparagement of this man. The quack wrote an answer full of insulting imputations, which he published in the Berlin newspapers. By the help of influential friends he not only managed to secure the prohibition of the publication of Jacoby's retort, but also to defeat the latter's successive appeals to the Berlin censor's superior, to the highest council of censorship, to Rochow, the Secretary of State, and to the king himself. The publishers in Hamburg, Leipzig, Grimma, Basle, and Berne, one and all refused to print the documents throwing light on this affair. Any other man would now have given up the attempt to get his reply to an attack in a contemptible newspaper article published. Not so Jacoby. Month followed upon month. The manuscript travelled thousands of miles, and was published at last in Paris, under the title of *Contribution to a Future Historical Account of the Censorship of the Press in Prussia.*

Such was Jacoby's character. Here at last was found what Young Germany so sorely needed, what even Youngest Germany with its Herwegh had not produced, that first essential in public life—a man. At last the Germany of the Forties had found a strong political leader——not a statesman in the proper sense of the word, for time showed that he was incapable of accommodating himself to circumstances, that he could not be satisfied with aiming at the attainable ; but a man of inflexible will, of absolute integrity, who with indomitable couragepressed onwards to his goal.

The Government organs, the libellous press, began a systematic attack upon him. There was nothing to lay hold of in his blameless personality, but he was of Jewish descent. In a little pamphlet published by the local magnates of a small town in the neighbourhood of Königsberg under the title of *Stimme treuer Unterthanen seiner Majestät des Königs von Preussen* ("Voice of a Few Faithful Subjects of his Majesty the King of Prussia"), we read : "Not from

German, not from Christian lips did these words proceed.
. . . East-Prussia would be disgraced if her sons had
expressed such sentiments. . . . The seed of Jacob did not
hearken to the voice of God, did not acknowledge his only-
begotten son, but put him to death ; therefore they were
cast off for ever, and scattered abroad among the nations of
the earth." Presently, however, in all the booksellers'
windows the portrait of Jacoby was to be seen ; his face,
with its clear-cut features, was surrounded by four marks of
interrogation ; he held his pen like a lance poised for attack.

The significance of the man who thus made his appearance was felt by the poets, even by those with least strength
of character, even by Dingelstedt, who was then preparing
to barter his oppositionist principles for the title of *Hofrath*
(Privy Councillor). In Dingelstedt's fine collection of poems,
Nachtwächters Weltgang, we find one with the heading :
? ? ? ?, evidently addressed to the King of Prussia :

> " Du weisst, was das bedeuten will ? Du wirst sie mir nicht streichen ?
> Es sind ja nur unschuldige—vier kleine Fragezeichen.
> Die wurzeln tief, die ragen hoch ; wie die gerühmten Eichen
> Des freien deutschen Volkes stehn vier kleine Fragezeichen.
> Du wolltest sie zwar nimmer sehn in deinen weiten Reichen,
> Doch drängen sie sich immer auf, vier kleine Fragezeichen.
>
> . . . .
>
> Und einst, wenn du gestorben bist, als Stempel dann und Aichen
> Stehn gross an deinem Monument—vier kleine Fragezeichen." [1]

Herwegh, too, sang Jacoby's praises, as if he had a prevision
that this was a man who, placed face to face with the King
of Prussia, would play a more manly part than he himself
had done. And the prevision was correct. In November
1848, when the king replied to the deputation that waited
on him to demand a change of ministers : " I will not listen
to any communication on this subject," it was Jacoby who

---

[1] You know the meaning of these marks? You would never dream of erasing
them—four innocent little marks of interrogation ? Yet they strike deep root, they
mount towards heaven, like the oak, the emblem of the great, free German nation.
You have done your best to annihilate them throughout your wide realms. but they
persistently appear again, these four little marks of interrogation. . . . In years to
come, when you are dead, there will stand as sign and symbol on your monument—
four little marks of interrogation.

stepped forward and said : " It is the great misfortune of kings, that they will not listen to the truth." Herwegh's poem, which has a J. as headings, begins :

> " Und wieder ob den Landen
> Lag jüngst ein schwerer Bann :
> Da ist ein Mann erstanden,
> Ein ganzer, deutscher Mann.
> Ein deutscher und ein freier,
> Wer hätte das gedacht !
> Dass selbst die deutsche Leier
> Aus ihrem Schlaf erwacht." [1]

The proceedings against Jacoby were carried on with extraordinary vigour. In less than four weeks he was brought up for examination twenty times ; ninety-six witnesses gave evidence, shop-women, cooks, and school-children among the number. His real misdemeanour was merely a transgression of the press-laws, namely circumvention of censorship. But he was accused of instigation to disaffection— for which the punishment was two years' imprisonment and disfranchisement ; of lese-majestie—for which the punishment was four years' penal servitude ; and of high treason —punishment, " death, with application of the most severe and deterrent pains and penalties."

It was in his native town, Königsberg, that Jacoby was brought to trial ; but the court there declared itself incompetent to deal with the case, seeing that it was one of high treason, and passed it on to the Kammergericht in Berlin. The Kammergericht, aware that the charge of high treason was untenable, also declared itself unqualified, and sent it back. The king was obliged to issue an order in council, requiring the Königsberg court to proceed with the trial. It was altogether to Jacoby's advantage to be tried by his fellow-citizens ; but he disdained the idea of an illegal acquittal, and obstinately demanded to be tried by the Kammergericht in Berlin, since he was accused of high

---

[1] Our country in these latter days lay under a heavy ban ; but, behold ! there arose to deliver her one who with truth could be called a man. A German, and a freeman—who could have dreamt it ? who could have looked for this awakening of the German lyre ?

treason. His wish had to be complied with. He was condemned to two and a half years' imprisonment with hard labour and disfranchisement. But three years later the highest court of appeal pronounced a full and free acquittal.

In the meantime all over Germany money was collected to present him with a civic wreath ; subscriptions poured in ; the names of eminent men headed the lists. Once more the Government was obliged to take action ; the subscription lists were seized, the subscribers summoned, and a stop put to the whole proceeding. While the police and the censors were thus struggling to suppress the agitation for a free constitution, there was issued, on the 11th of August 1842, the most absurd regulation of which there is any record in the annals of an autocratically governed country—one of the country's own existing laws was added to the list of prohibited writings; it was forbidden to reprint the law of the 22nd of May 1815 (that relating to the institution of Estates of the Realm), because of its tendency to excite discontent.

In September 1842, those Prussians who had hoped to see their country under the new king shake itself free from its humiliating relations with the Emperor Nicholas, learned that Frederick William IV., in Platen's day the warm, if platonic, friend of Poland, the hater of Russian tactics, was preparing for a journey to Warsaw to meet the Czar. On the return journey the king stopped at Kalisch to inspect the monument erected there in memory of the meeting between the sovereigns of Russia and Prussia in 1813. A Russian officer, General Berg (the future castigator of Poland), translated the inscriptions for him. One of them was : "May the Almighty give His blessing to the alliance and friendship between Russia and Prussia, that it may advance the peace and prosperity of both countries and inspire fear in their common enemies !" On hearing this inscription read, the king hastened up the steps of the monument and in the dust upon its side wrote with his finger the word : Amen !1

1 Prutz: *Zehn Jahre* i. pp. 237, 367, 516, &c. ; ii. 379, &c.

XXV

THE NEUTRAL LITERATURE

NEVERTHELESS, Frederick William IV. was, and remained, the most intellectually gifted monarch of his day ; his conversation gave evidence of both intelligence and imagination. It was a principle with him that all his feelings ought to be kingly ; his published letters to Humboldt, written in amusing court jargon, are bright and clever; his sayings show quickness of apprehension, easily awakened compassion, ready wit.[1] Nor can it be said that he was out of touch with the German intellectual life and literature of the day ; he showed favour to all the " good " writers, and disfavour to the " bad " ; but it was not long before all Oppositionist writers were included in the latter class.

In the beginning of the reign, Humboldt's was the dominating literary influence at court. Alexander von Humboldt, now eighty, the most famous scientist of the day, and a man of world-wide celebrity, kept the king well posted up in all the latest intellectual and scientific movements. His brother Wilhelm's liberal political theories had fallen into complete disrepute ; to his own he dared not give expression at court ; holding both superstition and reaction in abhorrence, he was a silent witness of much that

---

[1] Examples of Frederick William's style of wit : When the king was at the play, lackeys stood in attendance outside the door of the royal box. One evening, when his Majesty, provoked by the tiresomeness of a new play, left his box before the close of the performance, he found one of the lackeys sitting on the floor of the passage, sound asleep, his head leant against the wall of the box. Instead of being angry, the king said : " Der hat gehorcht " (means both : He has listened, and : He has obeyed). In 1848, in the palmy days of the Revolution, the king was obliged to receive one deputation after another, sometimes of very pretentious and presumptuous common people. He addressed the members of one such deputation, one after the other. What are you ?—A silk and woollen cloth warehouseman, your Majesty.—Most interesting occupation. And you ?—A medical student.— Excellent preparation for taking part in the government of the country ! And so on, all the time with a most polite, if ironical, smile. (Told me by an eye-witness.)

was repugnant to him, though he now and again spoke his mind.[1] Honoured by the king and his intimates as the ornament of the court and the pride of his country, he took advantage of his position to further the cause of science and to say an occasional helpful word for this or that persecuted author. Published letters show that, before 1848, the king treated Humboldt with a sort of playful familiarity, though there was no real, deep sympathy between the two men. After 1848, when the Kreuzzeitung party became all-powerful, Humboldt gave expression to his annoyance at having lost his influence, in such remarks as, " It is no longer possible to amuse the king ; " or, " the king persists in wasting fruitless affection on persons whom he has taken into favour." Amiability was not his characteristic at court ; he was often sarcastic, and became angry when Ranke's political opinions found more favour than his. He was disliked by many, amongst others by the queen, who disapproved of his attachment to Louis Philippe and his family. He was in the habit of reading aloud all varieties of literature, but never his own writings ; most frequently he read the *Journal des Débats*, whilst the king sat planning landscapes and architectural drawings.

Another of those who read aloud to the royal family was Tieck, whom the king had brought to Berlin from Dresden. Though Tieck was considerably younger than Humboldt, court life was a burden to him because of his bodily infirmity. Shakespeare and Kleist were the authors he most frequently read from. The king ordered Tieck's own old fairy play, *Puss in Boots*, to be performed in Berlin. It was like the appearance of some antiquated spectre. At the king's instigation Tieck put the *Antigone* of Sophocles on the stage, and Mendelssohn composed music for it. But Tieck was only one of literature's invalided soldiers. When

---

[1] The king was at one time deeply interested in the mysteries of table-turning, but it was long before any of the palace tables could be persuaded to perform, a fact which did not surprise Humboldt. At last the king received him one morning with the exclamation: " Aha ! what do you say now ? We sat round the table for a full half-hour last night before it would move, but at last off it went, round and round, faster and faster. How do you explain that ? " " Why, your Majesty, in all disputes it's the wiser of the two that gives in." (Related by Humboldt himself.)

the court dined in the garden of Sans Souci, he was afraid of draughts, even on the warmest days.

Another once famous author of the Romantic period whom the king called to Berlin was La Motte Fouqué. Though not much over sixty, this writer had completely outlived his reputation. His romances seemed to the younger generation to belong to a pre-historic period. People were tired of tales of chivalry and the service of love (*Minnedienst*) told in a conventionally childish style ; his unhistorical conception of past times and his sanctimoniousness aroused derision. Had it not been for the king's support, he would have died in want and oblivion.

In 1841, chiefly on the recommendation of Varnhagen, the king invited to Berlin a great poet who did not belong to the Romantic school. This was Friedrich Rückert (1788–1866). Rückert was only fifty-three, but he did not belong to the period in which he lived ; he was the expression in the literature of the day of that German universality which is unaffected by circumstances, of the gift of appropriation, absorption and imitation of the peculiarities of all other races. All his life long he shook poems out of his sleeve with a truly astonishing skill. As a young man he was initiated by Joseph von Hammer into the literatures of Arabia, Persia, and Turkey, and in 1826 he was appointed lecturer in Oriental languages at the University of Erlangen, but his duties as lecturer he constantly tried to evade.

There is something about him which reminds us of Goethe in the Divan period, and something which he owes to the Schlegels and their indefatigable study and translation. The essay on philology, *Ueber das Wesen der Philologie*, which he wrote in 1811, shows the influence of Friedrich Schlegel's work on the wisdom of ancient India ; for he starts from the idea of a "universal poetry," for which he considers the German language the most sympathetic vehicle. And universal, cosmopolitan poetry is exactly what this great master of style has given us. He, as the German patriot, makes his début with *Geharnischte Sonnette* ("Armoured Sonnets"), polished and rather mannered verse. This book is followed by volume after volume of love-poems to various young women (five to six hundred poems). In the last and largest of these volumes, *Liebesfrühling*, inscribed to his fiancée, Louise Witthaus, feeling is predominant; everywhere else he is the didactic poet employing lyric forms, here he is the singer. But even here, set forms—as in the *Canzonets of the South*—stand in the way of the simple, natural outburst of feeling, and already Rückert's inclination to display his mastery over language shows itself in a hitherto unexampled free invention of new words and ease in interlacing within the limits of metre:

> " Welche Heldenfreudigkeit der Liebe,
> Welche Stärke muthigen Entsagens,
> Welche himmlisch erdentschwungene Triebe,
> Welche Gottbegeistrung des Ertragens !
> Welche Sich-Erhebung, Sich-Erwiedrung,
> Sich-Entäussrung, völl'ge Hin-sich-gebung,
> Seelenaustausch, Ineinanderlebung ! "

There is more of philological and technical than of purely poetical interest in such verse as this. But Rückert *was* the philologist as poet. His predominating gift is the gift of language in its two developments—the capacity to learn languages and penetrate into their spirit, and the capacity, due to his profound penetration into the mysteries of his own language, to reproduce in German the best poetry written in other languages. He delighted in creating linguistic difficulties for himself to overcome. At one time we have him writing in the old German style that corresponded to his Albrecht Dürer curls, at another as a young officer of the time of Napoleon; now he is a Bedouin telling us Hariri's tales with marvellous skill, and again a Persian weaving his rhyme in the form of Ghazels or recreating the epic of Rustum and Sohrab. He appears before us as a Turk in caftan and turban, as a Chinaman with slippers and pig-tail; but most frequently and with most pleasure he sits as a Brahmin on the banks of the sacred Ganges, proclaiming in sonorous verse the thousand golden rules of a happy philosophy of life. It is said of Théophile Gautier that he was, intellectually speaking, equally at home in ancient Egypt, in the Russia of to-day,

in Constantinople, and in Seville.   This is only true to the
extent that he was well acquainted with the climatic characteristics and the monuments of many foreign lands.   It
may be said with much profounder truth of Rückert, who
comprehended the human beings through their literatures,
understood their language and thought in their spirit.   He
never saw the foreign lands with his bodily eyes, therefore
he has neither Gautier's colour, nor his power of graphic
presentation ; he views them all calmly, reflectively, with
the eye of the mind, and gives us the mental pictures in
an astonishing variety of metrical forms.   Whoever desires
to make acquaintance with excellent specimens of his art
should read *Hariri's Makamehs* (more particularly the division entitled *Jungfrau und Junge Frau*) or *Weisheit der
Bramanen.*

These works had gained Rückert a wide circle of readers
and admirers in Berlin ; but the town, with its restlessness,
was antipathetic to him.   He was to lecture on Oriental
languages at the university, and his first lectures were
attended by a curious crowd ; but this crowd soon dwindled
down to an audience of two or three, and Rückert gave up
going to the university.   He sat in his room in the third
flat of a house in the Behrenstrasse and wrote poems in
which he expressed his detestation of Berlin and its agitated,
modern life.   Even the Berlin of the royal romanticist was
too modern for these celebrities of past days.

At a somewhat later date the king extended his patronage
to Christian Scherenberg, whose poems, more especially the
battle-pieces *Waterloo* and *Abukir*, were much admired at
court—the author himself had to read them aloud.   Even
as an octogenarian, Scherenberg retained his place as a
favourite in Berlin society.   He was born in 1798.   His
life had been a hard struggle.   After the dissolution of his
unhappy marriage, he lived, from 1833 to 1840, in rooms
in a small house at the corner of the Bendlerstrasse, looking
towards the Zoological Gardens, in such poverty that he
could not afford to buy firewood, and had to send his
children to gather sticks in the Gardens.   He wrote poems,
tragedies, and comedies, for which he could never find a

publisher ; nevertheless he was so successful in his attempts
to keep up the appearance of a gentleman, that his relations
in Stettin believed he had won fame under an assumed
name, and begged him to "remove his mask" and let them
into the secret. All that his pen brought him was what
he received for composing begging letters and for copying ;
the rest of his living he gained by acting as tutor to the
families of the gardeners who lived in the neighbourhood,
giving lessons which, according to agreement, were paid for
in potatoes. A pretty story is told by Fontane in his *Life
of Scherenberg*. Great hopes had been entertained in the
Bendlerstrasse that a certain long-deferred payment would
be made at Easter in the shape of a juicy roast of veal ;
but in place of this, the pupil, in his innocent desire to give
pleasure, appeared with a lark in a little green cage. On
Easter morning, 1840, Scherenberg himself carried the cage
out to an open field, set the lark free, and wrote the sweet
poem, one verse of which runs :

> " Du, Vöglein, singst, das ist das Deine,
>   Hub leise ich zur Lerche an,
> Ich geb' dich frei, das ist das Meine,
>   Ein Jeder bete, wie er kann." [1]

The poor, struggling poet let the lark go, but kept its little
clay water-dish as a remembrance, promoting it to be his
ink-pot.

At last his poems caught the fancy of the public, and
the king, delighted with the originality and rugged energy
of the battle-pieces, took their author into favour. The
only thing connected with the time when he read aloud at
court that Scherenberg could be persuaded to talk about,
was the pleasure of the half-hour before the reading, spent
in his friend Count Bismarck-Bohlen's room, where men
joked and smoked, and afterwards drenched themselves with
Eau de Cologne, because the king disliked the smell of
tobacco. Many years later there was another potentate in

---

[1] O little bird, to sing 'tis thine,
    I gently to the lark began ;
  I set thee free, that deed is mine ;
    We all must pray as best we can.

Berlin at whose court Scherenberg was an attendant. This was Ferdinand Lassalle. At his house the poet met livelier companions, in whose society he not infrequently permitted himself to make fun of his royal and aristocratic patrons. It was in his nature to suit himself to his company ; his court friends knew his weakness and excused him.

Another favourite at the Prussian court, as indeed at all the courts of Europe, was Prince Hermann Pückler-Muskau, who from time to time came to Berlin to visit the wife whom, though divorced from her, he still loved. He was a handsome man, aristocratic in appearance and manners, accomplished and versatile, a favourite with men because of his spirit and gaiety, irresistibly charming to women ; the list of famous women who were devoted to him is a long one ; it includes Sophie Gay, Henriette Sontag, Bettina, and Ida Hahn-Hahn. In much the same manner as the Prince de Ligne before him, Pückler-Muskau belonged, by right of his intellectual qualities, to the international aristo-cracy of Europe. His desire to shine did not lead him to over-estimate his powers, did not even preclude real modesty. He was a brilliant vagabond, a master of the art of living, and a skilled professional in one department of art strictly so-called, namely, landscape gardening. He was the first in Germany to desert the stiff, French style of laying out a garden, and to reinstate nature in her rights. His garden at Muskau soon became the model garden of Europe.

There were many strange episodes in his life. Nothing could be much stranger than the story of his marriage. He was in love at the same time with two young girls, daughters of Count von Pappenheim, whose wife was a daughter of Chancellor Hardenberg. This lady, who was forty, nine years older than Pückler, herself conceived such a violent passion for him that she infected him with it. She gave up everything to become his, and he married her, but with the proviso that he was to be at complete liberty to dispose of his affections as he chose. The marriage turned out happily. But after they had lived together for ten years the couple amicably arranged a divorce, in the hope that the prince might find and marry a rich heiress, and thereby repair his fallen fortunes. With this aim in view he first visits London, then travels about in Germany. He writes daily to his divorced wife, his Lucie, keeping her faithfully informed of the progress he makes and of the difficulties he encounters in his pursuit of an heiress. Unable to capture one, he returns to Lucie, and they again live lovingly together for some years. After this he travels for six years, returning at the end of that time with a beautiful little slave, named Machbuba, whom he instals at Muskau. With this arrangement the princess was not altogether satisfied, though she had made it a rule never to plague him with jealousy. At the age of seventy she still loved and worshipped him, and in his intercourse with her he was always personified kindness, frankness, and cordiality.

Prince Pückler had never had any serious thought of taking up the profession of author, but in 1830 he determined to publish anonymously the letters which he had written to Lucie during his travels in search of an heiress. They had a great success. There was a society tone about them very uncommon in German literature, an attractive carelessness of construction, due to the fact that they were not written for publication, a pleasing mixture of wisdom and frivolity. As already mentioned, many ascribed their authorship to Heine. Their writer was modern in the extreme, thoroughly blasé, an advanced Liberal, a free-thinker in the literal sense of the word.

For readers of to-day the four volumes of *Briefe eines Verstorbenen* (" Letters of a Dead Man ") have much the same value as Madame de Girardin's attractive five volumes, *Lettres parisiennes du Vicomte de Launay*. She is fresher and writes infinitely better than the prince. He has cosmopolitan experiences of classes and of countries that she knows nothing about. As a specimen of his style, those interested should read the unassuming account of his conversation with Goethe in Weimar, to be found in the third volume of the Letters. Pückler's enthusiastic reverence for Goethe has a genuine ring, and the same may be said of Goethe's answer to Pückler's polite speeches. Goethe at once begins to talk about Muskau (referred to in letters as M.), and commends attempts like Pückler's to awaken the feeling for beauty, dwells on the fact that the welfare of all would be rapidly advanced if only each in his own sphere, great or small, would work faithfully and lovingly—that is what Pückler is doing in Muskau, and he himself has done no more.

Pückler's later volumes of travel, many in number, leave us quite cold. They lack the spontaneity of the Letters, and are still more destitute of that which could alone replace it, namely, literary talent. But until about the year 1840 they stood as high in the favour of the reading public as his first books, and their author's popularity was unbounded ; he was, like Franz Liszt, known and admired everywhere. As late as 1854 Heine dedicates his *Lutetia* to him in an enthusiastic preface, in which he calls him "mein hochgefeierter und wahlverwandter Zeitgenosse" (that highly honoured contemporary, to whom I feel myself spiritually akin). And in Varnhagen's diary for July 7, 1839, we read: "Prince Pückler's name acts like magic. It needs but to be mentioned, and the great world of all countries listens in suspense. His fame is stupendous, and the cleverer men are, the more they appreciate him."

In 1834 Varnhagen had said of him that he possessed one quality in common with Young Germany, and that the most important, namely, absolute freedom of thought ; at a later period he said that Pückler represented the upper house, Heine the lower house in modern German literature.

Puckler's attitude to the House of Hohenzollern was one of chivalrous devotion. He never came to Berlin without waiting on the king. He appreciated Frederick William IV.'s culture and wit, but, being a pronounced Voltairean, to whom every priest was a hypocrite and all vague piety an abomination, the romantic strain in the king's character repelled him. Like Humboldt he often fled from the court and took refuge with Varnhagen, the keen observer and critic, who sat forgotten in his corner, writing in his Journal (a diary kept in Sainte-Beuve's manner) the history of the times. And in later years Pückler, too, was a regular guest at Lassalle's small dinner-parties, where he often did most of the talking; it is said that he was the only person privileged by Lassalle to do so.[1]

To the authors already named we have only to add the aged Arndt, who in his day had been persecuted as a demagogue, and we have the complete list of the romantic, conservative, neutral, or aristocratic writers whom the most powerful king in Germany succeeded in attaching to his person. We see the length and the strength of the attachment. The Opposition attacked every author who had the very slightest connection with the court or with those in power. We have seen how Herwegh begins his first book with a defiant attack on Prince Pückler. He jeered even at Arndt—called him a sunset glow, incapable of illuminating the young world—and received a poetical reproof from Freiligrath for so doing.

Freiligrath was the only one of the young poets whom the king at once (1841) placed under an obligation (Geibel was taken into favour a year or two later). General von Radowitz, who admired Freiligrath's poem " Löwenritt," in spite of its unnaturalness, induced the king to look favourably on its author and to grant him a pension of 300 thalers. Herwegh, not content with making merry at Freiligrath's expense in such lines as the following, where *Freiligrath* is substituted for *Mühlenrad* (mill-wheel) :

> " Mir wird von alle dem so dumm,
> Als ging mir ein Freiligrath im Kopf herum," [2]

wrote in his *Duett der Pensionirten :*

> " *Geibel :* Bist du's ?
> *Freiligrath :*   Ja, willst du mich kennen ?
> Ja, ich bin es in der That,
> Den Bediente Bruder nennen
> Bin der Sänger Freiligrath." [3]

---

[1] A. de Reumont: *Aus König Fr. Wilhelm IV. gesunden und kranken Tagen. —Briefe Alex. v. Humboldt's an Varnhagen von Ense.—Varnhagen von Ense's Tagebücher.*—Hillebrand: *Zeiten, Völker und Menschen II.*

[2] All that is going on makes me as stupid as if a mill-wheel (a Freiligrath) were turning in my head.

[3] *Geibel :* Is this you ?

Freiligrath : Yes ! will you recognise me ? Truly it is I ; servants now call me brother, yet I am the poet Freiligrath.

This was more than Freiligrath could stand.   He threw up his pension, a step which was soon followed by his complete conversion.   His volumes, *Ein Glaubensbekenntniss* (" A Confession of Faith "), published in 1844, and *Ça ira*, published in 1846, show a steadily increasing passion of devotion to the revolutionary cause.   He became the most honoured poet of the party.   Immediately after the publication of *Ein Glaubensbekenntniss* he was obliged to flee the country, going first to Brussels and then to London, where he earned his livelihood as a merchant.

The following anecdote shows how popular he already was : From Brussels he had taken an excursion to Antwerp. There he and his friends went on board a barque that was lying in the river, ready to sail for Canton.   While the boatswain was showing them over the ship, the captain, with some friends, came out of the cabin.   Freiligrath's party made many excuses, but the courteous sailor bade them welcome, and invited them into the cabin.   On one of the shelves of the little book-case stood Freiligrath's Poems. "Are you not pleased that your poems are going out to Canton?" asks one of his companions." "Eh !" says the captain.   "This is Freiligrath ?   The real Freiligrath ?" On his question being answered in the affirmative, the captain rushes to the speaking-tube: "Hoist the flags ! Man the yards ! and serve champagne on deck !" [1]

The fermentation throughout Germany was rapidly becoming more violent.   Ever since 1842 the Hungarians under Kossuth had been defying Metternich ; in Bavaria the prestige of royalty had suffered from King Ludwig's amour with the ballet-dancer, Lola Montez ; in German Switzerland the Radical and Jesuit parties were engaged in stern conflict.   In Prussia the authority of the State Church was being vigorously asserted ; Roman Catholicism was favoured, but all other dissenters were harassed.   It was not only the Free-Catholics, a sect founded by Ronge, and the so-called Friends of Light, another free sect, founded by Wislicenus, that were regarded with disfavour ; even Pietists were objected to, as not orthodox enough to

[1] Schmidt-Weissenfels : *Freiligrath.*

suit the State requirements. One protest after another
reached the king from those whose liberty in matters of
conscience was threatened. And purely political agitation
was on the increase too. The leaders of the opposition
parties in all the States of Germany decried with one voice
the old Federal constitution (*Bundesverfassung*). Louder and
louder rose the cry in Prussia (the king having laid no great
restrictions on the liberty of the press) for the promised new
constitution. From abroad too came revolutionary impulses.
Since 1846 Pius IX. had been giving himself out as a
Liberal and an Italian patriot. Insurrections were breaking
out all over Italy ; Metternich was unable to prevent them,
and they were destroying his prestige. German emigrants
in Switzerland and North America did their best to fan the
flame in Germany.

Meantime the King of Prussia occupied himself with
the institution of the new Order of the Swan and with
architectural plans. He proposed the erection of a great
Hermann monument on the Rhine, as a demonstration
against constitutional France ; and he set the builders to
work again on the Cathedral of Cologne, after a pause of
300 years. This latter undertaking was considered symbolical, not from the national but from the ecclesiastical point
of view. It gave Heine occasion for various protests and
erroneous prophecies in *Deutschland, ein Wintermährchen*, and
also gave occasion to Strauss's clever pamphlet, *Der Romantiker
auf dem Trone der Cäsaren*, in which he manages to describe
Julian the Apostate as the enthusiastic religious reactionary,
in such a way that the parallel with Frederick William IV.
suggests itself without being pointed out.

The new literature, to which the king was distinctly
inimical, soon began to return his enmity with interest. He
established Tieck, the fretful, crippled old man, at Sans
Souci as poet-laureate, and Schelling, the mystifier, in
Berlin as *summus philosophus*. He caused the *Antigone* of
Sophocles and the *Medea* of Euripides to be performed in
the theatres of Berlin and Potsdam, in hopes of thereby
counteracting the spirit of unrest in German literature. But
that literature went its own way.

XXVI

POLITICAL POETRY, PHILOSOPHICAL REVOLUTION

IN Anastasius Grün's (Count Alexander von Auersperg's) volume, *Spaziergänge eines Wiener Poeten* ("Walks of a Viennese Poet"), there is a poem, the title and the refrain of which is: Why? When new prohibitory enactments are pasted on the notice-board at the town-hall, a little man comes and reads them and quietly asks: Why? When the priests from their pulpits groan and howl at the sunlight, he asks: Why? When men go out to fight sparrows with halberts and spears, and use cannons to shoot larks, he asks: Why? And when they try, condemn, and execute himself, from his very grave is heard the question: Why?

Something of this kind happened in Germany as soon as the patriarchal faith in monarchy was thoroughly shaken. When an act of violence, or a stupid act, or a subterfuge on the part of the Government killed a hope, out of the grave of that hope grew a Why. And every Why gave birth to others. The four questions of the East-Prussian were inadequate now; questions grew and multiplied like those invisible but dangerous animals which in an incredibly short time can undermine an organism. Why revere? Why trust? Why endure? And, first and foremost, why keep silence? When they are going to shake off the yoke, men begin by refusing to bear it silently. Suffering and wrath, desire and longing, now found vent in words, in song.

Political verse, of which there had been occasional specimens among the work of Platen and Lenau, Uhland and Heine, now concentrates and crystallises itself into a separate species of poetry, a separate form of art. Political song of every variety is heard throughout the land. It is a time of growth ; men of talent come to the surface in crowds—Hoffmann and Herwegh, Dingelstedt and Prutz, Freiligrath and Max Waldau, Karl Beck and Moritz Hartmann—such a rich and fragant bloom as had never been seen in this domain before. Old Romanticists expressed their contempt for prose (*i.e.* political) poetry, dogmatic æsthetes declared these poets to be possessed of rhetoric and not of lyric talent ; but all to no purpose ; the very number of them, and the way in which they spontaneously fell into position as a group, showed that they had the very best, the only unchallengeable reason for coming into existence, namely, that they could not help it, that the spirit of the times was making its voice heard through them ; and soon they also proved that they possessed the one and only right to exist, for they were able to hold their ground, they took their position as literary men, and gained the popular ear.

They had had a single forerunner in the Thirties, the above-mentioned Austrian poet, Alexander Auersperg. His verse was imposing, somewhat overloaded with imagery, at times wanting in taste ; nevertheless it had the true ring, and his pathos was genuine. Joseph II. is Auersperg's hero, and it is from the "enlightenment" standpoint that he regards that political liberty which he so eagerly desires. It is the power of the priesthood that specially arouses his wrath ; but he distinguishes between *Pfaffen* and *Priester*, attacks the worthless and sings the praises of the high-minded among the clergy. Upon lines like :

" Stoss in's Horn, Herold des Krieges : Zu den Waffen, zu den Waffen !
Kampf und Krieg der argen Horde heuchlerischer, dummer Pfaffen !" [1]

follow others which extol the virtues of the really saintly priests. Still we feel that in his opinion more of the former than of the latter are to be found in his own day. He regards it as one of the signs of the times that the fat, animal priest has been succeeded by the lean, intelligent, ambitious one :

---

[1] Sound the trumpet, herald of war ! To arms ! To arms ! War to the death with the wicked horde of stupid, hypocritical priests !

Die Dicken und die Dünnen.

"Fünfzig Jahre sind's, da riefen unsere Aeltern zu den Waffen,
  Krieg und Kampf den dicken, kugelrunden, feisten Pfaffen !
  Auch in Waffen stehn wir Enkel ; jetzt doch muss die Lösung sein :
  Krieg und Kampf den dünnen, magern, spindelhagern Pfäffelein !" [1]

In spirited verse the courageous poet attacked now
Metternich, now the detective police, now the censorship.
His poems display a frank, vigorous spirit of opposition, no
hatred, no wild resentment ; one feels that they are animated by anticipation of a glorious future and enthusiasm
for the great men of the past.   But Auersperg's plastic
power is slight ; he too often loses himself in a maze of
allegory.   The best of the political poetry of the Forties
is, both intellectually and artistically, much superior
to his.

About a year after his famous journey, from the effects
of which he had completely recovered, Georg Herwegh published a second volume of *Gedichte eines Lebendigen* (" Poems
of a Living Man "), in which some new and valuable qualities
are combined with those characterising the first.   There is
more confidence and more fire, and both enthusiasms and
animosities are less vague.   We have fewer illusions, and a
clearer understanding of ends and means ; no more appeals
to a king to lead the onward march of his people, or to God
to give freedom and happiness to all the nations of the earth.
Frederick William IV. had extinguished Herwegh's faith
in princes, and Ludwig Feuerbach his faith in God.   But we
gain the impression that the dawning light in men's minds
has broadened into the light of day.

In the old dawn-songs, which Shakespeare has imitated in *Romeo and Juliet,* the young girl always tries to
keep her lover with her by declaring that it is not sunlight
but moonlight that he sees, not the lark but the nightingale
that he hears.   This idea is cleverly reversed in the poem
Morgenzuruf (" Cry of the Morning ") :

---

[1] Fifty years ago our parents declared war against the fat and flabby priest ; we,
their children and grandchildren, have, like them, taken up arms against the cloth ;
but our cry is : Death to the lean and lanky priestlings !

" Die Lerche war's, nicht die Nachtigall,
Die eben am Himmel geschlagen :
Schon schwingt er sich auf, der Sonnenball,
Vom Winde des Morgens getragen.
Der Tag, der Tag ist erwacht !
Die Nacht,
Die Nacht soll blutig verenden.
Heraus wer an's ewige Licht noch glaubt,
Ihr Schläfer, die Rosen der Liebe vom Haupt,
Und ein flammendes Schwert um die Lenden ! " [1]

Unglückliche Liebe (" Unhappy Love ") is an epigram
pointed against kings :

" Nicht an den Königen liegt's—die Könige lieben die Freiheit,
Aber die Freiheit liebt leider die Könige nicht." [2]

The tone of Herwegh's previous volume, even in its
apparently irreligious utterances, had been theistic. On
the adjuration to tear the crosses from the graves and use
them as swords, follows the line : " God forgives the deed
ye do." But in this new volume we find a poem in which
Feuerbach's praises are sung because he has attacked the
doctrine of immortality, and a Song of the Heathen, which
is more daring in its mockery than any similar poem of
Heine's :

" Die Heiden—'s ist doch Schade um solch Ingenium.
Sie hiessen Vier gerade und nahmen Fünf für krumm.
Auch hatt' die Jungfernschaft ein End, sobald die Magd ein Kind gebar,
Dieweil das neue Testament noch nicht erfunden war."

And, unlike Auersperg, who makes a distinction between
the good and the bad priest, Herwegh holds the whole
brotherhood in derision, mocks at Catholic and Protestant,
shorn and unshorn, in the witty, untranslatable epigram :

" Ob sie katholisch geschoren, ob protestantisch gescheitelt,
Gleichviel—immer geräth man den Gesellen in's Haar."

---

[1] 'Tis the lark, not the nightingale, that sings so clear ; the great sun-ball is rising
fast, borne by the winds of the morning. It is day ! it is day ! The night will end
in blood. Awake, all ye who believe in the light eternal ! Tear the rose-wreaths of
love from your heads, and gird yourselves with swords of flame !

[2] 'Tis not the fault of the Kings—*they* are all lovers of freedom ;
But their misfortune is this : Freedom has no love for them.

He had pricked before, now he stung; the singer of liberty had developed into a herald and preparer of the approaching revolution.

If these powerful poems did not greatly move men's minds, it is to be ascribed to the fact that the deficiencies of Herwegh's personal character were subtly influencing his verse. They betray themselves in a certain straining after effect, in his evident satisfaction with his own witty sallies, and in his intellectual barrenness in every domain except that of polemics. This second volume of poems is not a collection which suggests that its author has any store of ideas, of imagination, to draw upon. When we read it, we understand his life; and his life helps us to understand this book, with which his career as a poet practically came to a close. All that he subsequently wrote, and he lived for thirty-two years longer, is contained in one small volume, published after his death. The poems of this last collection are full of wit and full of enthusiasm for liberty; they are written—hardly four in the year—by a man who to the day of his death remained faithful to his revolutionary youth.

Though faithful enough to his past, Herwegh was no worker in the service of liberty. The latter part of his life was spent in idleness. His career as a poet and critic began in 1839[1] and culminated with *Gedichte eines Lebendigen*. He married a rich young Jewess, an enthusiastic admirer of his poetry. After the Revolution of February he took up the position of a leader in Paris, and invaded Baden at the head of a body of republican German and French workmen; on the 27th of April they were defeated by Würtembergian troops; thanks to his wife's courage, Herwegh escaped. Heine has given a bitingly sarcastic, but very unfair description of this campaign in *Simplicissimus I*. The simple, truthful account which Herwegh's wife has published since, of all the incidents of the revolt, and of the part which her husband played in it, proves that, even if he lacked the tactical skill which he laid no claim to possessing, he was a brave man. Herwegh now became a member of the

[1] His youthful writings are collected in *Gedichte und kritische Aufsätze*, 1845. 2 vols.

emigrant colony in London, and lived the emigrants' per-
niciously idle life; they had literally nothing to do but
concoct futile plans for new revolutions and fall in love
with one another's wives. He afterwards lived in Paris and
Zürich, always the same inactive life, persistently dissatisfied
with the progress of events in Germany. Like Kinkel and
like Moritz Hartmann, Herwegh was unable to the day of
his death (1875) to reconcile himself to the great development of power attained by Germany at the expense of
liberty. He never relinquished the ideals of his youth;
retained a manly admiration even for Heine, who had held
him up to derision.

Being such as he was, it was only natural that Herwegh
should from the very first be on the watch in the matter of
his brother poets' fidelity to their flag and the genuineness
of their liberalism. His attacks on Geibel and Freiligrath
have already been noticed. He next turned upon Anastasius Grün (Auersperg), who had gone to Vienna in hopes
of obtaining the appointment and rank of Chamberlain; his
wife, by birth a Countess Attems, was invested with the
Order of the Star of the Cross, and he wished to be able
to accompany her to court. In stirring words Herwegh
entreated him to retrace his steps:

> "Darf man den Tempel um ein Weib entweih'n,
> Mit einem Weib um goldne Götzen tanzen," &c.[1]

Dingelstedt retorted, defending Count Auersperg in a
pretty poem:

> "O, sie will es nie begreifen, ihre Prosa und Gemeinheit,
> Das ein Geist wie Du, ein Name, bürgt für der Gesinnung Reinheit,
> Nur das Schlechte glaubt sie willig," &c. [2]

The retort evaded the attack instead of repulsing it.
No one seriously believed in a man like Auersperg having
changed his convictions; the ground of Herwegh's attack

---

[1] Would you desecrate the temple for the sake of a woman, dance with her before
golden idols, &c.
[2] Prosaic vulgar-mindedness cannot, will not, understand that thy name, a mind
like thine, is a security for integrity of purpose; it is ready to believe only what is
bad, &c.

was that, holding such convictions, he had solicited a court appointment. It was his own future position that Dingelstedt defended ; he was the next poet upon whom Herwegh turned, with a satire that was all the fiercer because it was silent, or at least only indirectly expressed.

Dingelstedt, like Herwegh, had been obliged to leave Germany to escape the consequences of writing political poems. The two poets met in Paris. There they one evening amused themselves by trying which could write the better verses on the subject of his own imaginary political conversion. Herwegh wrote the poem " Wohlgeboren," the burden of which is : What is the use of all this talk of liberty and fatherland, of all this enthusiasm, all this meddling with politics ? What good has it done me ? No, no ! for the future I will be a quiet, respectable citizen :

> " Du sollst, verdammte Freiheit, mir
> Die Ruhe fürder nicht gefährden ;
> Lisette, noch ein Gläschen Bier !
> Ich will ein guter Bürger werden." [1]

This last line forms the refrain of all the verses. To outbid his friend, Dingelstedt wrote the poem " Hochwohlgeboren," which begins :

> " Ein guter Bürger willst du werden?
> Pfui Freund !—Ein guter, Bürger—Du?
> Das also war dein Ziel auf Erden,
> Dem stürmten deine Lieder zu ?
> O nimm's zurück, das ekle Wort,
> Wer mag sich so gemein geberden !
> Nein, nein, mich reisst es weiter fort :
> Ich muss Geheimer Hofrath werden ! " [2]

In this poem, too, the last line of the first verse serves as refrain to all the others.

Two years later Dingelstedt was Privy Councillor,

---

[1] No longer, damned Liberty, shalt thou disturb my peace of mind. Lisette ! another glass of beer ! For the future I'm a respectable citizen.

[2] A respectable citizen ! You an ordinary respectable citizen ! Shame on you, my friend ! Was this your aim in life ? Is this the end of all your passionate song ? Take back the offensive word, I pray ; just imagine displaying such vulgar-mindedness ! Mine is a nobler ambition : I am determined to be a Privy Councillor !

librarian, and reader at the court of the King of Würtemberg. Herwegh contented himself with reprinting the two poems side by side.

Franz Dingelstedt (born in 1814) represents one of the most curious types of the day. He is a revolutionary who ought to have been born in the purple, a Prince Pückler in the guise of a poor schoolmaster, a satirist who cannot dispense with appearances, a man of first-rate abilities with neither serious vices nor serious enthusiasm, but with ready wit and frequent poetic inspiration ; early blasé, he retains a certain practical activity of mind to the last. He was born in the worst-governed country in Germany, Hesse-Cassel, under the hated administration of Hassenpflug, became master at one of its grammar-schools, aroused dissatisfaction by his emancipated opinions and conduct and the liberal tone of his poetry, was transferred and perpetually interfered with, and sent in his resignation in 1841, when he was twenty-seven. Only one year after Herwegh he published his first collection of political poetry, *Lieder eines kosmopolitischen Nachtwächters* (" Songs of a Cosmopolitan Night-Watchman "). Good verse, clever poems, a good idea. The watchman in his uniform, armed with his spiked mace, his horn in his hand, goes his nightly round, and, pausing outside the houses, tells us what he sees and imagines within.

He is a genuine night-watchman—thoroughly weary of the old woman at home, who is so ugly and so wrinkled, yet with whom he manages to live peaceably, for she sleeps by night and he by day ; a genuine night-watchman, who sings the watchman's song about lights and fires ; looks up at the prisoners, the political prisoners, peering through the iron bars and shaking them ; shudders as he passes the cathedral with all its relics, where the wind is howling so loud in the organ pipes ; and then laughs at himself for shuddering. It is twenty years since he was inside the building, he is none of your seat-holding church-goers.

And yet he is not a genuine night-watchman. He has feelings and opinions which are not those of a man in his station. In one house a ball is going on ; he listens to the music, and describes the dancing and the behaviour of the

fashionable company. What a sensation it would create if
he, lantern and mace in hand, snow on his cloak and cap,
his cheeks burning and frost on his beard, were suddenly to
appear among all these shadows! Outside another house
stands the carriage of the great, the all-powerful, Minister of
State. The coachman is wrapped in furs, but the poor uncovered horses are trembling with cold whilst their master
is playing cards within—just as if they could not revenge
themselves when he comes :

> " Ich rathe dir, lass die Karten ruhn,
> Und hüte dich fein, Ministerlein !
> Du hast es mit vier Hengsten zu thun,
> Bedenk', dass es keine Bürger sein." [1]

There are many pathetic passages. In one of the
suburbs the watchman passes a house where a poor wretch
lies in his last agonies ; he passes the lunatic asylum, and
the dread of madness that always seizes him here is mingled
with a strange feeling of attraction ; he passes the cemetery,
where his poor father, who took his own life, lies in a disdained, neglected corner ; and on his way back he passes
the palace, where the prince tosses sleeplessly on his pillow
of down, while the sentry sleeps soundly standing in his box.

A night-watchman might easily have had some of these
feelings—he would never have expressed them thus ; the
mask is perpetually falling off. There are one or two most
masterly and natural expressions of popular indignation,
for example the tirade occasioned by the sight of light in
the sickroom of a cringing courtier whose extortions have
impoverished his country :

> "Warum er nicht schläft ? warum er in Wuth die Spitzen am Hemde
> zerissen ?
> Ein gutes Gewissen schläft überall gut, und nirgends ein schlechtes
> Gewissen.
> Er hat an des Landes Mark, die Schlang', sich voll gefressen, gesogen,
> Er hat—ein Menschenleben lang !—gestohlen, gelogen, betrogen." [2]

---

[1] My advice to you is to drop the cards and look out for yourself, O minister !
Remember that you have to do with four stallions, not four citizens !

[2] You ask me why he lies sleepless ? why in his rage he tears the lace from his
pillow ? A good conscience sleeps well everywhere, a bad conscience nowhere.
He has sucked the blood of his country, gorged himself with its substance ; during
a whole long life he has stolen and lied and deceived.

But there are also expressions of hatred and exasperation which we feel belong to another class of society. We actually find the watchman giving frivolous advice to a beautiful young lady who has been married to an old reprobate, telling her how she may best revenge herself upon him. At times his thoughts and reveries take a higher flight. He is leaning on an old cannon, which stands on the rampart, shining and dumb. Once its wheels rolled over dead and living on the field of victory ; once it gave the signal for the dread onslaught, for beside the touch-hole there is an N. surmounted by the imperial crown. Now its voice is only heard when some wretched prisoner has escaped from his dungeon, or on the occasion of his Majesty's birthday, or when a princess is born. " Patience ! " cries the watchman to the cannon ; " it may be that ere long thou wilt once more pour thy balls upon the enemy ; but keep silent in the meantime, old veteran, or they will spike thee as they are gagging us." Here the mask is completely thrown off.

After Dingelstedt had left Hesse-Cassel, he published *Nachtwächters Weltgang* (" The Night-Watchman's World Patrol "), in which the poet is no longer the unsophisticated night-watchman—but the cultivated revolutionary. He falls foul of bad kings, of the governments of Hesse-Cassel, Prussia, and Hanover, and of false German patriotism : " What, gentlemen, is a German patriot ?—A man who serves the Lord on Sunday and the king on week-days. What are the objects of his desire ?—Office, a title, and a ribbon for himself, bread for his lawful offspring, and legitimate sovereigns for his country.—Away with you, German patriot ! The temple is no place for you ! You are a Judas, whose treacherous kiss has been the death of liberty ! "

A few months later Dingelstedt was a Privy Councillor and Councillor of Legation—held office, had a title, wore a ribbon. Naturally no one believed in any genuine conversion, and it is not surprising that his conduct was severely, and in some quarters spitefully, judged. The numerous documents relating to his character and life which have

been published of late years (especially Julius **Rodenberg's**
articles in the *Deutsche Rundschau* of 1889–90) throw a
more favourable light upon his action than that in which
his contemporaries saw it.   There was a want of fine feeling
about it, it was unseemly, but it was not base.   There was
nothing wrong in the actual fact of his accepting the post
of reader to a cultivated and amiable sovereign, the fault
lay in his having so shortly beforehand proclaimed all sorts
of democratic and radical principles which he was not
prepared to stand by,

He had the true artist's temperament, and yet was distinctly practical ;   he was pleasure-loving and ambitious,
unable to bear permanently the humiliation of being poor
and consequently ignored ; he was above all else impressed,
strongly impressed, by the belief that in following the path
he had entered upon he was pursuing a *métier de dupe.*
What did he gain by refusing, because of his principles, to
accept good appointments and influential positions !   What
did the world gain by clever men on principle leaving titles,
money, office, orders, and posts of honour to the stupid men !
Was this the best way to improve matters ?   His great
desire was to play the sovereign in some domain of art,
to solve great scenic problems, to direct great theatres, to
be the favoured of beautiful women.   Was he at all likely
to attain it as the exiled schoolmaster, the correspondent of
the *Allgemeine Zeitung?*   Who would permanently hold in
esteem the poor, independent journalist ? who would not,
in course of time, esteem the influential courtier ?   Of
course there would be an outcry when he accepted the
call—if only he had not written that wretched poem to
Herwegh !—but what was needed was cool courage, ironical
impenetrability, smiling indifference, and the calm superiority
which allows one's opponents to bawl till they are tired ; and
these gifts he possessed.

He became, as every one knows, not only a courtier,
but in course of time manager of one court theatre
after another—Stuttgart, Munich, Weimar—ending his
career as the influential director of the Burgtheater in
Vienna.

Heine, who was not strict, but witty, wrote the incomparable poem "Verhofrätherei," which begins :

" Verschlechtert sich nicht dein Herz und dein Stil,
So magst du treiben jedwedes Spiel,
Mein Freund, ich werde dich nie verkennen,
Und soll ich dich auch Herr Hofrath nennen." [1]

It expresses a mournful understanding of Dingelstedt's conduct, and bitter contempt for the public to whom both he and Dingelstedt addressed themselves.

Any one who desires to get a distinct and correct idea of Dingelstedt's intellectual personality should compare the clever, graphic account of his life, entitled *Münchener Bilderbuch*, with his own cyclus of poems entitled *Ein Roman*. These poems show us far more of his inmost nature than the verses of his early youth. But he had early experienced the mingled feeling of attraction to the great world and contempt for it. In the poem "Krähwinkel," he wrote of fashionable society :

" Sie lügen, sie krakehlen, sie hassen sich bis auf's Blut,
Zum Morden oder Stehlen fehlt ihnen nur der Muth.
Sie möchten gern und wagen's nicht, das heisst denn Recht und Pflicht ;
Die denken können, sagen's nicht. Die Meisten denken nicht." [2]

Now he tells the story of a society amour. In England, at a ball, the poet meets a lady of Hindoo blood, but English in every other respect. She is spiritually akin to himself, gloomy and cold and weary of life. They fall in love :

" Wir klammerten uns, ob aus Zeitvertreib,
Ob aus Verzweiflung, an einander an,
Sie, ein verlornes, neugebornes Weib,
Ich, ein verlorner, neugeborner Mann." [3]

---

[1] If heart and style remain still true,
I'll not object, whatever you do.
My friend, I never will mistake you,
E'en though a Councillor they make you.
(BOWRING.)

[2] They lie, they squabble, they hate one another with a deadly hatred ; it is only want of courage that keeps them from robbing and murdering. They dare not do the things they long to do, and so they talk much about right and duty. Those that think keep their thoughts to themselves ; most of them do not think.

[3] We clung to each other—was it to pass the time, or was it in despair ? she a lost, new-born woman, I a lost, new-born man.

The word "Zeitvertreib" (pastime) is a little too weak, the word "Verzweiflung" (despair) is a shade too strong. There is German puerility in this insistence upon fashionable frivolity and blank despair. So much is certain; the two fall in love. We have plenty of passion, hot and wild— more of sensuality in it than love, voluptuous nights, secret pleasures, and coldly cynical front shown to the world; then separation, farewell, and oblivion; until one day in a conservatory in Amsterdam the decaying smell of a dead lotus-plant makes him feel faint. He is reminded of her, and presses one of the dead leaves to his lips as if it were the hand of a corpse.

Such characters as Dingelstedt significantly illustrate their age, they do not create it. They are not the builders of the palace, they are its gilders. No doubt the work of the gilder first attracts the eye, and attracts far more eyes than the work of the builder, who in laying the foundation of the palace determines its whole construction; but there is also no doubt as to whose work is of the more importance.

These pleasure-loving poets, often disillusioned so young, with no principles except the political convictions of which they sing and boast, and to which they generally prove unfaithful, are of social importance from the fact that they create the opinion of the moment, general political opinion, and thereby accelerate the slow reorganisation of society. But this outward reorganisation is not itself the principal matter; political opinion is not the prime mover. The outward revolution is a result of movements going on much deeper below the surface. Perhaps the most powerful impulse is given by philosophy with its quiet revolutionising of the religious view of life.

In this domain of philosophic agitation there appeared in the summer of 1841 (the year in which Dingelstedt's first book was published, the year following the publication of Herwegh's first) an epoch-making thinker. In the work entitled *Das Wesen des Christenthums* ("The Nature of Christianity") he formulates great thoughts, founds and expounds a philosophy of life which makes its influence

felt in the spoken and written words of all who come
after him, all at least whose minds attain their fullest
development. Ludwig Feuerbach is the foundation-stone
upon which for the next twenty years every one builds,
everything is built.

When I say of him that he was great, a great man and
a great thinker, I myself resent the platitude. Great is a
term which we hear so constantly applied to this, that, and
the other thing, that we have come to be unaffected by it.
There is not even any very keen appreciation among us of
the quality of greatness. The sense for it is deadened by the
cold, clammy manner in which the intellectually great are
handled by those who write learned treatises on their work.
Take up a history of philosophy, and you will find them all
arranged and labelled, one looking exactly like the other.
There they stand in a row, all treated with the same respect,
and regarded with the same interest—Schelling, who was a
genius and a charlatan ; Trendelenburg, who accepted his
appointment from Eichhorn and improved his opportunities
after the death of Altenstein ; Strauss, who was a second-
rate thinker, and a bit of a pedant ; Karl Vogt, who was
a gifted gourmand ; Lotze, who was an excellent professor
of philosophy, but nothing more ; and amongst the rest
Feuerbach, one of a list, possibly labelled as inferior, one-
sided men, calling themselves ideal realists or something of
the sort. The effect is demoralising.

He was great. This means that there is a wide, open
space round him on every side. It means that if we would
understand him, we must separate him clearly in our minds
from all those men, all those facts that jostle him in lesson-
books and hand-books. That he was great means, that he
is altogether upon another level. The moment we catch
sight of him as he stands there alone, reverence takes
possession of us.

Simply natural as he was in intercourse with friends,
there was yet something awe-inspiring about the man.
Look at that face, in every feature of which there is genius
and character—obstinate, energetic character. There is
character in the mighty brow, in the small eyes, in the big,

z

fan-shaped beard. There is power in it all, power and nobility, and manly beauty, stern as though cast in bronze.

Himself a genius, he belongs to a notably talented family ; the father one of the most distinguished criminal jurists of Germany ; brother, sister, nephew, all gifted. He is born at Landshut in 1804 ; studies at Heidelberg ; turns his attention to theology, first from the orthodox, afterwards from the critical standpoint ; then to philosophy, first abstract, afterwards realistic, ever more realistic. He publishes his *Gedanken über Tod und Unsterblichkeit* ("Thoughts on Death and Immortality") anonymously. The book is at first confiscated, but subsequently allowed to circulate. After it becomes known that he is the author, he applies in vain for professional appointments at several of the South German universities, and similar attempts made somewhat later in Berlin, France, Switzerland, and Greece prove equally fruitless, in spite of the support of noted savants. From 1836 onwards he lives a retired life in the country—till 1860 at Brückberg, near Ansbach, afterwards at Rechenberg, near Nuremberg. In his later years it is the life of a hermit. He corresponds with friends of his own class and stamp, and also with men of the people (such as Konrad Deubler of the Salzkammergut), who sometimes understand his writings better and feel them more deeply than the so-called cultivated class. In 1837 he married the love of his youth. It was not without influence on his life that, in the beginning of the Forties, a young girl, daughter of one of his friends, was for a time passionately attached to him, an attachment which he returned.

His only course of lectures was delivered in 1848, at Heidelberg, but not at the university ; there he was dreaded and shunned. In 1842 his friends had tried to get him appointed professor at Heidelberg ; he at first took kindly to their plan, but afterwards frantically opposed it. "To try to make me a professor and that, too, in the ordinary way, the way in which any blockhead can be made one . . . is to place me on a level with the fools that are posing as professors now, is to insult, to disgrace me. . . . The professor's desk is no place for a man with a head like mine.

Do you know the proper place for my head ? Guess ! The block : for my brain is as keen and as peremptory as the executioner's sword, and I have no desire, no courage to do any deeds but those for which men risk the loss of their heads." [1] His friend had been advising him rather to call his work *Wesen der Theologie* than *Wesen des Christenthums.* He answers: " I take no interest whatever in the overturning of theology. I concern myself only with great world-entities (welthistorische Wesen). . . . One must deal a mortal blow, must deny on principle. To act means to take life— with the determination, if necessary, to give one's own life in return."

This is more resolute language than the poets used ; these views are very different from theirs. Saint-René Taillandier animadverted on the fact that Feuerbach, hold-ing such views, did not take part in the revolutionary move-ment of 1848. Feuerbach answered : " M. Taillandier ! When another revolution breaks out and I take part in it, know, to the dismay of your godly soul, that that revolution will be victorious ; the last day of the monarchy and the hierarchy will have come. Alas ! I shall not live to take part in that revolution. But I am playing an active part in another great and victorious one, the results of which will not be evident till centuries have come and gone. For, according to my philosophy—which you know nothing about and presume to judge without having studied—according to my philosophy, which ignores gods, and, consequently, miracles wrought by means of political measures, space and time are necessary conditions of all being, all thought, and all action. It was not, as has been asserted in the Bavarian Reichsrathskammer, because the Parliament of Frankfort con-sisted of unbelievers that it was such a complete and shame-ful failure ; as a matter of fact the majority of its members were believers—and surely God, too, respects a majority ; it was a failure because it was destitute of the sense of place and time." [2]

Notwithstanding the number of different stages through

---

[1] *Briefwechsel zwischen Feuerbach und Christian Kapp*, 1876, p, 176.
[2] *Wesen der Religion*, p. vii.

which Feuerbach passed in his progress towards realism,
notwithstanding all that can with justice be said of the
diversity of the positions he took up, his ground-thought,
the key-stone of the vaulting upon which the whole rests,
is as simple as it is great.   It is this : Man cannot be
conscious of a being that is higher than himself.   If it
were possible for man to be conscious of himself—that is,
his being or nature—as finite, compared with another being
apprehended as infinite, he would by this consciousness
limit his own being, *i.e.* deny it.   His consciousness would
extend beyond the limits of his being, which is impossible,
for consciousness is simply the self-affirmation of being.

Instead, therefore, of saying with Hegel : Man's consciousness of God is God's self-consciousness, we are
compelled to say : Man's consciousness of God is man's
self-consciousness ; religion is man's first and indirect
self-knowledge.

It is universally acknowledged that the idea, God, can
only be formulated by the aid of human predicates—God
is love, God is goodness, knowledge, power, &c.   The
subject here is nothing but the personified predicate.   The
predicate is the original.   What religion really means is
this : Love is divine, *i.e.* of absolute worth, deserving of
adoration ; goodness, knowledge, power are divine.

Hence belief in a God is belief in man as the essential
being.

The apparent axiom of religion is : I am nothing,
measured with God ; its real axiom is : Everything else is
nothing measured with me ; everything serves my purposes.
By means of prayers and miracles, with God as intermediary,
I have everything at my disposal.   God is the creation of
man's desire.   The main desire of Christianity being un-
limited happiness, bliss, God is the means whereby bliss is
attained, or, more correctly, bliss and God are one.

In a word : theology is anthropology, the theological
problem is a psychological problem—which Feuerbach has
solved in all essentials for all time.

Viewed thus, his life-work is seen in its unity.   Though
it is not possible to express the whole in a few words, yet

it is easy to feel that it is one single great thought, for which humanity is his debtor.

When a young man stands in the Pantheon in Rome, lost in admiration of its dome, the most beautiful in the world, his most natural thought is : O, like the builder of this temple, to have, were it but once in one's life, an idea, simple and great as that which produced this cupola —to conceive some single fundamental principle, some simple and yet composite formula, capable of expansion to a whole scheme, of dimensions as grand as this firmament in miniature ! One such thought, simple in its beginning, stupendous in its development, would give greatness enough to any human life.

Feuerbach's was one of these fundamental thoughts.

XXVII

REVOLUTIONARY POETRY

THE profoundest characteristic of that literature which in the Forties still continued to be known by the name of *Bewegungslitteratur*, is its utter want of connection with official Germany. It is the absence of any such connection that gives it its strength and its freshness. Official Germany is not to be taken here in the narrow sense of German officialdom ; it means all that part of the people—German or any other—which in normal circumstances appears to be the whole people, and as such sets the stamp of nationality on all that is produced by that people, the same stamp which it has set on all that has emanated from it in the past. With what a later period has called *Bildungsphilisterei* (cultured philistinism), the most eminent literary men of the period in question have no connection whatever. There is no corresponding group of personalities and writings in Scandinavian literature. Even the Radical poetry of the Scandinavian students became official in the course of a very few years.. The most gifted of the German poets of the day are independent, or make themselves independent, of official Germany, and bear like men the consequences of the position they take up.

Among those who declare their independence, the most interesting figure is Freiligrath, born in Detmold in 1810. Fair, blue-eyed, massively built, and shaggy-maned, he is the true son of Westphalia. His father, a schoolmaster, educated him against his will as a merchant, and to his commercial education and pursuits are to be ascribed his freedom from classical reminiscences, his exclusively modern literary culture, his understanding of the foreign climes and countries with which commerce brings us into communication, and his distinctly modern turn of thought.

Freiligrath is not, like Hoffmann von Fallersleben, his predecessor in the field of political poetry, only a prolific song writer ; he is a genuine, inspired poet. Hoffmann, who had made a study of the old German songs and ballads, and was himself a man of simple, popular tastes, poured forth an inexhaustible stream of polemical verse, directed against the squirearchy and bureaucracy, but he repeated himself with the monotony of the popular poet. Freiligrath wrote comparatively little, but every one of his poems has its distinct individuality. He is influenced by that modern French and English poetry of which he has given us so many admirable translations, and makes his début as a descriptive poet of the Victor Hugo school, but soon develops a distinct literary individuality. He possesses in a very high degree two qualities which are seldom found united, the faculty of picturesque description and intensity of feeling. The former leads him to depict themes from foreign lands, full of glowing colour, the latter displays itself when he sings of home and fatherland. In his revolutionary period his warm feeling became powerful pathos, and his gift of graphic delineation was exclusively devoted to the service of hostility and ire.

In his youth, in Amsterdam (1831), the sea and the shipping made a deep impression on him. In his dreams he followed all the vessels that glided out of the harbour bound for Africa, for India, for Turkey, for America. He was seized by the desire to describe these foreign climes as they appeared in his imagination, and Hugo's *Les Orientales* not only suggested the colours to be employed in the treatment of such themes, but also the metrical form. Freiligrath alone among German poets tried to master the alexandrines beloved of Frenchmen, despised in Germany, and to vindicate their beauty. Strangely enough, in spite of his usually correct ear, he so entirely misapprehended the peculiarity of this metre that he always writes it in pure iambics, a practice which Germans have continued.

He was possessed by the longing to roam—out into the wide world, across the great ocean. Instead of German " garret poetry," he wrote, in his garret, scenes laid in the deserts of Africa and the primeval forests of America. He attempted tropical local colouring, which was at times successful, at times unnatural; his linguistic specialty was new and remarkable rhymes, produced with the assistance of resonant foreign words like "Sykomore," "Tricolore," &c. His good verses were like living, his bad, in their lifeless splendour, like stuffed humming-birds.

But this African Freiligrath is not the best Freiligrath. Freiligrath, the Liberal patriot, is greatly his superior. After Herwegh's political challenge had roused him, he took himself to task, tested with simple-minded fairness those sympathies and tendencies of his nature as to which he himself was not yet absolutely clear, and discovered in the depths of his being an unquenchable desire for liberty and a sympathy with the oppressed which on occasion could develop into burning indignation and hatred. His genius chose the revolutionary path, pursued it at full speed, and finally spread its wings and flew. *Marseillaise* after *Marseillaise* came from the poet's pen. O these hymns of 1848 ! they are enthusiasm itself, the enthusiasm that begets enthusiasm. In the earlier ones we have fierceness, faith, revolutionary piety, fiery sarcasm, the intoxicated jubilation of victory; in the later, noble despair, sublime in its expression.

But the poems which anticipate the Revolution and incite to it are also worth reading. Take, for instance, the volume entitled *Ça ira*, published in 1846. In each of the poems of which it consists a symbolical picture is graphically elaborated. In the first, a ship is setting sail ; her name is Revolution, she is the black fire-ship that sends her rockets aboard that hypocritical craft, the Church, and then points her guns at the silver fleet of Wealth. In another we have a symbolical idea borrowed from Thomas Moore : the ice-palace of despotism, which will crack, and break up, and melt away as soon as spring comes. In *Wie man's macht* (" How the Thing is Done ") the poet describes the storming of the arsenal of a capital with such infectious ardour, so dramatically and vividly, that we see it all, are ourselves in the thick of the fray. As the Revolution which he foresees draws nearer and nearer, his poetry becomes more and more up to date. He describes a Rhine steamer, which has the King and Queen of Prussia on board. The steamer is a picture of German society. The company on deck are enjoying the fresh air, the bright sunshine, the beautiful scenery of the Rhine ; but down below in the engine-room stand the proletariat, in the shape of engineer and stoker, masters of the volcano that drives the ship onwards. One push, one blow from them, and the whole edifice of which the king is the crown, collapses ; the deck is blown to fragments, the flames mount to the clouds—but not yet, thou angry element, not to-day ! In such a poem as *Freie Presse* the course of events is anticipated : the insurrection is on the point of breaking out ; one day more, and there will be fighting in the streets. Ammunition being short, the owner of the printing works orders his workmen to melt down all the alphabets. And presently the hissing, glowing mass is flowing into the bullet moulds. The times are such that only in the form of bullets can the types emancipate humanity.

The days of Young Germany were over, but now it seemed as if Germany herself had grown young.

Robert Prutz (born in 1816 at Stettin) received that classical education which had been denied to Freiligrath. A critical student of philosophy and history, he wrote upon many subjects, but it is only as a political poet that he has any abiding significance. He was one of the young men who ardently vented their opinions in Ruge's *Hallische Jahrbücher*, the result in his case being banishment. He is the Feuerbachian as poet. His political poetry, from the absolute directness with which it follows its aim, is apt to be somewhat dry and unimaginative, but his sober and yet warm love of liberty attracts us. If you once learn to like him, it will be a thorough liking ; you will even highly prize his latest collection of poems, *Aus der Heimath*, a book which has been foolishly condemned as sensual ; it cannot be denied that he showed bad taste in dedicating it to his wife.

In his best work, a little Aristophanic masterpiece entitled *Die politische Wochenstube* (" The Political Lying-in

Room "), Zürich, 1843, Prutz, Holberg's warmest German admirer,[1] has succeeded in epitomising the wit, the irony, the endeavour, and the hopes of the younger generation.

It was only natural that a poet with Prutz's classical training should adopt the Aristophanic method, the pity was that he followed it too closely. His play became in consequence a jewel of price for a select circle of readers instead of food for the multitude. It is the production of a young, hopeful dreamer, whose faith in a glorious future for Germany was quite as lively and as strong as the pleasure he felt in demolishing with his sarcasm what was decrepit and decayed ; the burlesque figures and conceits stand out against an idealistic golden background because the poet sees the sun of the future rising and shining behind them.

The action passes partly in, partly outside of the house of a doctor who keeps a kind of private lying-in hospital, where young ladies of the upper classes at times take refuge. Of late his business has not thriven. It had flourished when Pietism flourished in Königsberg ; much pious embracing had gone on then, which, with God's blessing, had borne fruit ; but now that the State Church has set itself to suppress Pietism, his wards stand empty. He will soon be driven to apply for a post on the staff of the Prussian official newspaper ; those who are fit for nothing else can always earn their bread in its service. The Doctor's servant, Kilian, who is famishing, asks for food. The Doctor advises him to have his stomach removed, takes out his knife to do the operation, tells him that he will never feel hungry again, and that he will confer an inestimable benefit on humanity if he can show himself as a living proof that the operation is possible. For what is the rock on which virtue splits nowadays ? Why did Freiligrath take a pension ? Why did Dingelstedt allow himself to be branded. The stomach, and nothing but the stomach is to blame for everything.

In the meantime Herr Schlaukopf (Mr. Sly) has come

[1] The name of one of Holberg's best known comedies is *The Lying-in Room* (" Barselstuen ").

on the scene, disguised as a beggar. He declaims some patriotic sentiment, in the style of the Niebelungenlied, on the subject of Hermann the Cheruscan, and then asks for a contribution for the statue of that national hero. The Doctor is incautious enough to call the statue a scarecrow, a hideous sentry brandishing a spit, on which Schlaukopf declares that he shall pay for these words by at least twelve years' imprisonment with hard labour. They fight, the Doctor pulls off Schlaukopf's false nose, and thereupon recognises in him the friend of his youth, the quondam socialist, singer of liberty, republican, and regicide, now advanced to the post of "Wirklicher-geheimer-königlicher Leibspion" (Real Private Royal Body-spy). They fall into each other's arms, and Schlaukopf tells his errand, but not till he has assured himself that the Doctor holds no awkward or seditious political beliefs. The Doctor, recognising the importance of the man with whom he has to do, falls on his knees and swears that he believes nothing except that crown-pieces are round. Then Schlaukopf divulges the secret : "Germany, our mother-country, the Germany of Frederick and of Luther, the fair-haired queen, is with child."

The Doctor is at first incredulous. Is it not dropsy, the result of all the water-drinking introduced by these new total abstinence associations ? No, she is pregnant, and the only surprising thing about it is that the fact has not been announced in the newspapers, which usually inform the public when queens and princesses are in that condition. And now Schlaukopf communicates the joyful intelligence that the Doctor, as an experienced accoucheur, has been chosen to attend Germania ; he, and no other, is to deliver her. The Doctor dances for joy, demands that he shall be rewarded with perquisites and an order, requests Schlaukopf to bring the lady—but see, she comes !

Slaves, who represent the enthralled people, bear her in in a golden chair. She is fair, with a fat, amiable face, a wide mouth, and eyes of watery blue. All salute and do homage to her as Germania. But from a confidential conversation between her and Schlaukopf we learn that she is not the person she gives herself out to be. He asks her if she is really pregnant; she replies that he ought to know best, he and the others whom he has introduced to her. It seems that he has taken her from the street and trained her to play her part. She is the official Germania—and she has done everything that her artful masters have ordered her to do, has bowed, and knelt, and pattered prayers at command. And now, at command, she is pregnant. Schlaukopf abuses her, and threatens to beat her ; she taunts him and threatens in return to run away and leave him to find another Germania where he best can.

Meanwhile in the darkness of night a stranger has appeared in the street in front of the house, a woman with a harassed, hunted look, who declares that she knows not where to lay her outlawed head. "I," she says, "the legitimate queen, must, like a common vagrant, hide my royal head in the darkness of night, whilst she who has been exalted in my stead and impudently allows herself to be called by my name, sleeps voluptuously on silken pillows. Ye stones, be my pillow ! For my people, like their queen, have to lie on stone."

Through the night comes a cry, "Germania !" The woman in the house and the woman on the street answer at the same moment. Wrangling and confusion ensue, the gendarmes arrive, and an attempt is made to discover which of the two has taken a name that does not belong to her. " Not I ! " cries the stranger to Schlaukopf. She maintains that he has stolen her name and decked his brazen-faced paramour with it, and concludes: " Shame on you both ! I alone am the real, the true Germania !" Kilian finds it impossible to believe that any one so slender and emaciated can be Germania, but the serfs are thrilled to the heart by the sweet sound of her voice. The diplomatic Schlaukopf alone keeps his countenance :

> " Allein, so thut ein wenig nur die Augen auf,
> Zu sehen braucht Ihr diese da und jene nur,
> So ist's ja klärlich, welche hier die Rechte sei :
> In Lumpen jene, diese jedoch im seidnen Rock ;
> Die abgemagert, hungerbleich, ein Schattenbild,

Verbannt zu Bettlern, selber eine Bettlerin;
Höchst stattlich diese, wohlgenährt, anmuthiglich,
In hoher Herren ehrender Festgenossenschaft,
Ja selbst gesegneten Leibes ist, wie Ihr seht."[1]

To this comparison between her rival's magnificence and her own poverty the stranger answers with dignity:

" Wohl spotte mein ! In meine Wunde lege du
Die blutbefleckten, diebsgewandten Finger mir !
Auf meine Lumpen speie du, und rühme dich
Weil ich ein armes, heimathlos vertriebnes Weib ;
Du weisst am besten, wessen Hand mein Blut vergoss,
Und wer vom Haupt die Krone mir gerissen hat.

Ihr bautest du Paläste, mir Gefängnisse.
Ihr schmeichelten deine Schergen, mich verfolgten sie—
Dir aber sag ich, Schattenkönigin, o du,
Die du mit Zittern meines Namens dich erfrechst :
Hinweg ! verbirg dich ! Räume du den Platz, der mir
Allein gebührt ! Denn eure Herrscherin bin ich."[2]

And the serfs bend low in homage to the woman who comes, not in regal purple, but in rags like their own, saying to each other: " May not this be the long-looked-for redresser of our wrongs, she who is to break our yoke asunder and awaken the sleeping world with the lightning flash of liberty ? "

But now the two women are called upon to prove their respective claims. Schlaukopf exclaims : " It is the legitimist principle we are called on to defend ! " and proceeds to prompt official Germania. That fat, fair lady, who boasts that she bears the future of Germany in her womb and

---

[1] To know which is the true Germania, you need but use your eyes. Look first at one and then the other. Is not the one in rags, the other clad in silk ? the one starving and pale, a mere shadow, driven to house with beggars, herself a beggar ; the other stately, plump, and pleasant to the sight, consorting with right honourable gentlemen ; with child moreover, as you plainly see?

[2] Yes, mock at me ! Put your pilfering, blood-stained fingers into my wounds ! Spit on my rags, and proclaim me to be a poor, banished, homeless woman. You know best whose hand shed my blood and tore the crown from my head. . . . Fo: her you built palaces, for me prisons. Your menials flattered her, me they persecuted. And you, trembling phantom queen, who have the effrontery to call yourself by my name, away ! hide yourself ! make room for the rightful sovereign ! make room for me !

claims in consequence to be treated with consideration and reverence, repeats a long rigmarole, supposed to be the story of her life: In the gray of eld she lay on bear-skins in the forest, drinking foaming mead and eating beech-nuts and acorns. "Beech-nuts and acorns!" cry the Doctor, Kilian, and Schlaukopf. "It is she." Then she tells how she was sent to school to the priests, had her nose flattened against the crucifix, became *christlich-germanisch*, endowed monasteries, built churches, kissed the Pope's toe, &c., &c., and once more the Doctor, Kilian, and Schlaukopf cry: "It is she!" She tells what a peaceable, governable disposition she developed, how she allowed any one that liked to box her ears, how her loyalty has now reached such a pitch that if her master but whistle, she comes, stands on her hind legs, fetches the stick—"In a word, I am a well-trained poodle." And again we hear the jubilant chorus: "It is she!" She concludes: "God and the king willing, I shall be in the future what I have been in the past. By government order I am now, as you see, with child. O gendarmes, take my part! Recognise me as the one, true, Germania, as the thoroughbred German, and be assured that in return I will bring up my son as a gendarme!"

The gendarmes are of opinion that she has made out a good case, and Schlaukopf is beginning to boast that the vagrant has been silenced, when she in turn lifts up her voice. She does not understand the art of self-praise, she says, nor has she much to praise herself for; the future will show what she is. "I cannot deny," she continues, "that she who stands there is a Germania; she is official Germany, the Germany of the Government, of the Federal Diet; but the Germany of the German people she is not; they do not know her, they do not care a straw for her rotten genealogical tree. If you would know which is the true Germania, ask these fettered serfs!" At this moment the other Germania is seized with violent pains. She suddenly explodes with a loud report and disappears in a cloud of smoke, which, as it gradually disperses, takes the shape of pilgrim monks, of romantic poets who sing the praises of the holy Middle Ages, of geese who lament that the Order of the Swan is not yet instituted, of moderate Liberals singing the chorus :

"Immer langsam voran, immer langsam voran !
Dass der preussische Fortschritt nachkommen kann !"[1]

Then the serfs break their chains, cast themselves on the ground before the poor stranger, and do homage to her as the true Germania, who is still a virgin, but who one day will give birth to the ruler of the future.

The emblematical picture is a very fine, powerful one, and moreover it is true. The German Empire of to-day is not the offspring of the oppressed, divided Germany that was then extolled as pregnant with future greatness ; it is the outcome of the much-despised, the harshly suppressed endeavours after liberty and unity. It is a mistake, however, to have represented the true Germania with no past, with all her power and glory in the future ; though such a break of historical continuity did not in those days seem the impossibility that it does in ours.

One of the truths proclaimed by this Radical polemical poem admits of no controversion, namely, that the official fatherland, the official country, everywhere lays claim to all that the genius of the people in times past has produced, to all their great men, even those whose lives were one constant rebellion against it. It banished, imprisoned, executed them—no matter ; now it wears their portraits next its heart. And the official fatherland claims, and always has claimed, to bear the future in its womb. It not only maintains that the present existence of all and of everything is inseparably bound up with its existence, but that it is pregnant with the new age and is consequently entitled to receive the respectful care that is the due of a pregnant queen. For the thinking men of any people there is, besides this fatherland, another, one that is not re-cognised, that is often disowned. It does not deck itself with the national colours ; for it the national song is not sung.

[1] Slowly onward, slowly onward in the race !
That Prussian progress may be able to keep pace !

It exists wherever people feel and act in the spirit that has been the spirit of the best of the country's sons. It has the allegiance of all the thinking youth. Those of low degree have more part and lot in it than those in place and power. To it alone the future belongs.

XXVIII

REVOLUTIONARY POETRY

THERE were real poets, aspiring spirits, who did not follow the general trend of literature at this period. There were men like Eduard Mörike (born in 1804), the last scion of the Swabian School, who broke the bounds of its narrow tradition, and in his lyric verse may rather be regarded as an offshoot of the Goethe stem—a genuinely gifted poet, the idyllic, arch, melancholy singer of the inner life, author of the immortal poem, *Denk es, o Seele!* And there were men like Otto Ludwig, the Thuringian, and Friedrich Hebbel, the Ditmarschian, the two most robust originals in modern German literature, who were both born in 1813, and both developed their very dissimilar peculiarities after 1848—two gnarled, leafy oaks standing without the forest's bounds. The only mark of the period in which they were youths is the peculiar defiant gloom which lies deep down in both natures. Specially their own is a kind of melancholy keen-sightedness, inclining towards bold realism. They are the heralds of the realism of a later, unpolitical age. But they have not the characteristic common to all the political poets of their own age—sunny enthusiasm, a natural bias towards public life, towards the radical reform, or, if necessary, the complete revolution of society.

This bias, in combination with the philosophic lucidity due to the influence of Hegel and Feuerbach, is perhaps most remarkably observable in an author whose writings are, undeservedly, beginning to be somewhat neglected nowadays, an author who, dying at the early age of thirty-one, did not live to see the Revolution of March. This is Friedrich von Sallet, a young German officer of extraordinary strength of character, whose solid, comprehensive culture was due to his own unaided efforts. In him the profound

2 A

thought of his age is united with its extreme, passionate Liberalism. After his dismissal from the army in 1831, he devoted himself entirely to literature.

His best known work is his *Laien-Evangelium*, a kind of devotional book for free-thinkers, a series of poems in which he gives a symbolical modern interpretation to the various events of the Gospels. He begins each poem with some story or lesson from the Bible, and then proceeds to show the living, eternal kernel in it, and to cast away the historical or mythical husks. The interpretations are at times rather far-fetched, and the employment of but one metre throughout the whole book undeniably tends to monotony. In its general conception the work reminds us of another, older book, Leopold Schefer's *Laien-Brevier;* but the contrast is great between Schefer's comfortable satisfaction with the divine government of the universe, and Sallet's impatient inclination to interfere with the natural course of events. We are also slightly reminded of Rückert's *Weisheit der Bramanen;* but Sallet's wisdom is a wrathful wisdom, no peaceful collection of golden rules of life like Rückert's, but fiery denunciation of deceit and stupidity. In his introductory poem Sallet compares those who had written Oriental poetry before him to the Kings of the East, who offered gold, frankincense, and myrrh to the Light of the world, and then fell back again into their Oriental dream-life. Now, he says, light is once more dawning, thought is once more rousing from their slumber both East and West. In his eager advocacy of his ideals, he is too indifferent to colouring, too Western ; his book is spoiled by its too modern, directly didactic tone.

The collection of poems known as *Gedichte* is a much finer one. Here again the political poems are the most important.

He describes a sleeping giant, on whose head and breast foolish dwarfs are disporting themselves. They sit on chairs in his open mouth and pay compliments to each other ; spread their tables and dine upon his stomach ; declare that it is his duty to sleep—if he does not, they will punish him with pin-pricks. They believe that God has created the great giant solely that they may disport themselves merrily on the top of him, the truth being that if he were to awake and rise there would be an end of them. The poet himself is tickling the giant's nose with his paper in hopes that he will perhaps sneeze ; that alone would play the deuce with them. He cries : "Awake and see how they are daring to behave ; it will be an easy matter for you to drive them away." And he concludes : "I know perfectly well what the giant's name is, but I have my reasons for not divulging it."

In another poem, *Ecce Homo*, instead of appealing to the people as a people, he appeals to man as man : "There stands the old, grey cathedral, and there the old, fortified royal castle, looking down on wandering humanity passing beneath them, one generation after another. Song is heard from the one, fealty is sworn in the other, from century to century ; we seem, in comparison with them, but insects of a day. And therefore fools preach veneration for these houses of cards. For what are they but card-castles, built for himself by man in his childhood ! He built them, and he can knock them down, and build others in their stead. Heaven and earth are but soft clay, which man can mould as he inclines."

At times Sallet writes in a lighter, more playful tone : "What is the name of the old man to whom people everywhere, but these good Germans in particular, are devoted, though he has never done anything worth doing ? He stands in the pulpit, he drills the soldiers, he administers justice, he lectures at the universities, and his voice carries weight in the councils of the State. Taking a hundred steps to do what could be done with one jump is called in his language 'the good old ways and customs' ; this is what he approves of, but if you produce anything original and great, his wrath is aroused and he scolds and storms till men begin to be afraid of you. He is wanting both in brains and backbone, the old gentleman, and yet he rules almost absolutely, and to oppose him successfully one would need to be as strong as a lion. There is no reason for concealing his name : it is Old Routine."

Among the *Gedichte* are also clever parodies, such as the one in which the poet attacks the censor, by whom he was perpetually worried :

> " Kennst Du das Land, wo Knut und Kantschu blühn,
> Den Steiss von Zarenliebe machend glühn,
> Wo man das Zeitungsblatt schwarz überstreicht,
> Dass preussisch' Landtagsgift in's Volk nicht schleicht,
> Kennst du es wohl ? Dahin, dahin,
> Möcht' ich mit dir, geliebter Censor, fliehn."

He is even more wroth with the cowardly prophet than with the censor: "Ever so slight a blow with your hand," he says, "and the mummy falls to pieces, once it has been brought up from the airless subterranean halls to the light of day ; it will stand intact so long as no hand is raised against it." He is furious with those who declare that things will happen of themselves, that historical evolution, &c., will bring them about. Nothing irritates him so much as to hear people say : "A change *must* come; things *cannot* go on as they are doing." "Since the beginning of the world," he says, "nothing has ever happened of itself."

He could not, on account of the censorship, attack monarchy directly, but he gives us, in excellent verse, the parable of the bear. Much in the same manner as wolves are kept in the Capitol in Rome, the bear is kept in Berne as the emblem of the city. On this practice Sallet founds his fable: "The people of the Canton of Berne in days of old kept a bear. They let him live on the fat of the land, but they took good care to keep his claws cut in case he should take it into his head to tear them to pieces. When asked to explain what good the bear did them, they answered with surprise : 'Explain ! Why, what should he do ! He eats his fill, he moves about majestically, he growls—he is our bear, and that is enough.' If questioned as to why they kept him, they gave answer : 'Because our fathers did. If the race were to die out, all would be over with us.' If any one ventured once again to ask why, they only shouted : 'Hold your tongue, or we'll beat out your brains.'

"One day loud cries were heard throughout the town ; the citizens thronged together—the bear lay dead. He had died suddenly ; they had no new bear ready to take his place, and everywhere the dolorous cry resounded : ' It is all over with the Canton of Berne ! Up and away, brave hunters ! Get us a new bear ! '

" In vain the hunters explore the mountains and the ravines ; they cannot find a bear. But in spite of this, wonderful to relate, corn and grapes ripen, fruit grows on the trees—it seems as if nature were utterly indifferent to the woe of Berne. The sun, though it saw the bear lie dead, still rises every morning—the world still stands. What can be the meaning of it ? "

Witty as the fable is, it will hardly convince any supporter of monarchy of the uselessness of that institution. Sallet only attacks the foolish worship of the supposedly indispensable symbol, without making any attempt to dispute the most frequently employed argument in favour of monarchy, namely, the benefit which results from the withdrawal of the highest of all positions from competition. He puts his whole soul into another poem, *Aut—Aut*, a poem which became a sort of watchword for the youth of the day. Its most characteristic verses are :

> " Die ihr den grossen Kampf der Zeit
> Ausfechten wollt, herbei ihr Ritter !
> Sprecht, welcher Sach' ihr euch geweiht,
> Sprecht frei durchs offne Helmgegitter !
> Entweder—oder !
>
> Für Fürstenmacht, für Volkesrecht ?
> Für Geisteslicht, für Pfaffendunkel ?
> Republikaner oder Knecht ?
> Ja oder nein ! nur kein Gemunkel !
> Entweder—oder ! " [1]

And the poem concludes with an allusion to the time now fast approaching when the last on one side or the other with cloven skull will bite the dust.

Sallet did not live to take part in the great, decisive

---

[1] Ye knights who have made ready to take part in the great battle of the day, lift your visors and speak clearly : On which side are you fighting ? Either—or !

Is it for the power of the sovereign or the rights of the people ? For spiritual light or priestly superstition ? Are you republicans or thralls ? No evasion ! Answer plainly ! Either—or !

encounter for which he so ardently longed. He died in 1843. Not long after his death the storm-clouds begin to thicken and the birds to fly low. We are approaching 1848.

Literature follows in Sallet's path. From all parts of Germany comes the cry : " Let deeds follow upon words ! " We hear it not only from the poets of North Germany, the Rhineland, and Switzerland ; three poets of far-off Austria, Karl Beck, Alfred Meissner, Moritz Hartmann join in the chorus.

Karl Beck, the son of a Hungarian and a Hungarian Jewess, born at Baja in 1817, first studied medicine in Vienna, but gave that up, devoted himself to literature under the auspices of Gustav Kühne, and produced a succession of poetical works which attracted attention by their faithful and vivid delineation of Hungarian scenery and Hungarian national character. As regards this aspect of his work, Beck may be classed with the Hungarian national poet, Petöfi, a man five years his junior ; but as the poet of liberty, he must be regarded as a disciple of Börne—the only one who was of any importance as a poet. Like Börne he is the champion of the Jewish race, of the proletariat, and of political liberty. In his writing we have the Old Testament style and pathos combined with the influence of the newest French and German oppositionist literature. In Austrian poetry Anastasius Grün and Lenau are his immediate predecessors. He had not the culture of a Prutz, but his writing is distinguished by fervid colouring, emotional glow, graphic power, and wrathful enthusiasm. He was, however, one of those who, hailing the outbreak of the Revolution with joy, changed the key-note of their song after the victory of the reaction. After the magnificent revolt of Hungary had been crushed, he addressed a poem to the Emperor of Austria in which he flatters the victor, and entreats him to have mercy on the captive heroes. This poem enraged his old companions in arms. They called to mind that he who was now playing the part of a loyal subject of the Emperor of Austria had, before the collapse, been a republican and a socialist.[1]

[1] Cf. Moritz Hartmann: *Reimchronik des Pfaffen Mauritius.* Chap. v. " Apostel und Apostaten."

Alfred Meissner (born at Teplitz in 1822) and Moritz Hartmann (born at Duschnitz in 1821), Bohemia's two best lyric poets, are both inspired by the most ardent desire for political liberty.

It is unfair to allow the unpleasant ending to Meissner's literary career to blind us to his unquestionably genuine poetical talent. It is both pitiable and monstrous that one of Germany's best lyric poets should, after an honourable youth, have descended so low as to buy the manuscripts of an inferior novel-writer and publish them under his own name, but it does not detract from his worth as author of the fine poems which undoubtedly are his own. As specimens of a revolutionary eloquence which was, and with reason, irresistible to the youth of the Forties, read his glowing lines to the memory of Byron and George Sand.

Moritz Hartmann, Meissner's countryman and contemporary, is a figure cast in different metal ; there is no flaw in him ; he is a hero as well as an unusually gifted poet. No other German poet has loved liberty so faithfully and passionately from his earliest youth to the day of his death, or risked his life for it so daringly and so often.

Hartmann, who was one of the handsomest men it is possible to imagine, was born of Jewish parents in the little town of Duschnitz. The family was of Spanish origin, the name Hartmann being a translation of Duros. Moritz was sent to school in Prague, where, as a boy, he witnessed the banished King Charles the Tenth's melancholy entrance into the town. At the early age of thirteen he emancipated himself from the religious faith of his family, and while still a mere child was deeply affected by the news of the discomfiture of the Polish revolutionists. As a student he became acquainted with Lenau, to whom he devoted himself with the enthusiasm of a boy and a disciple. From his childhood he spoke both Czech and German, and his first book of poems, *Kelch und Schwert* (" Chalice and Sword "), contains abundant indication of his love for the Czech language, which he ranks with Polish, and extols as superior to Russian. But when it comes to the question of Czech political sympathy with Russia and hatred of everything German, he is entirely the German.

In *Kelch und Schwert* (1845) the Bohemian predominates. The little introductory poem tells us as much:

> " Der ich komm' aus dem Hussitenlande,
> Glaube, dass ich Gottes Blut genossen,
> Liebe fühl' ich in mein Herz gegossen,
> Lieb' ist Gottes Blut—mein Herz sein *Kelch*.
>
> Der ich komm' aus dem Hussitenlande,
> Glaube an die fleischgewordnen Worte,
> Dass Gedanken werden zur Kohorte
> Und jedwedes Lied ein heilig *Schwert*." [1]

A native of that country from which the emancipating doctrines of Huss have been banished, he feels himself a Hussite, and interprets the old Hussite war-cry, the right of the laity to receive the chalice in the sacrament of the Lord's Supper, in a modern spirit, almost the spirit of Feuerbach. In a poem on the German "songs of liberty" he tells the lyric poets of Germany that song is not the hammer that will shatter a prince's heart ; also that liberty is a woman, and not to be won by words alone. He feels for the Poles as if he were himself a Pole. We are made aware that he loves a Polish lady, and that through his love to her he has become in his heart her countryman. The poem, *To C——a*, is one of the most beautiful that sympathy with Poland has produced. Hartmann can at times be prolix and commonplace, but much more frequently he is concise and dramatic. Some of his scenes impress themselves indelibly on the reader's mind. Read, for instance, *Die Drei*, the poem of the three exiles who meet in a lonely inn on the plains of Hungary. They are sitting silent over their wine in the stillness of night, when some one suddenly raises his glass and cries: "Our country !" Of the three, one is a gipsy, one a Jew, and one

---

[1] I, who am of the land of the Hussites, believe that I have drunk the blood of God ; love has been poured into my heart ; love is God's blood, my heart his *chalice*.

I, who am of the land of the Hussites, believe in the word made flesh, believe that thoughts become armed cohorts, that every song is a holy *sword*.

a Pole. They have no country ; they look at their glasses and sit silent as before.

Even more impassioned than his pity for Poland is his pity for Bohemia, "the poor stag that is bleeding to death in the depths of a forest." Nothing is left to the Bohemians but their music, that sweet music which awakes compassion for them everywhere, which sings and sobs and melts men's hearts with its mysterious melodies.

We may say of this first book of poems what the poet himself has said of the following: "Not a song in it but has been kissed on the brow by liberty, the most beautiful and noble of all muses." He already gives frank expression to his hatred of Metternich's Austria, that Austria which in 1848, in his *Reimchronik des Pfaffen Mauritius*, he was to call the Bastille of the nations, within whose walls the silence of death is only broken by the clank of fetters.

The sensation created by *Kelch und Schwert* meant exile for Hartmann. He had, in the first instance, transgressed the laws of Austria by publishing in a foreign town a work which had not been submitted to Austrian censorship. He knew that if he were to return from Leipzig, where he had been living for some time, in intercourse with Kühne and Laube, he was liable to be arrested on the frontier. But he could not resist the desire to see his mother again, and succeeded in making his way secretly to his native town. It was not possible to conceal his presence there ; a traitor betrayed him, and he was obliged, before many days had passed, to make his escape by a back-door while the police were forcing their way into the house. In his *Zeitlosen* there is a set of poems entitled *Heimkehr und Flucht*, in which he describes this youthful escapade, and thus proudly delineates his own character :

> " Und als der Verrath mich ausgewittert
> Und als die Häscher herangekommen,
> Da hat die bleiche Mutter gezittert,
> Der Schwester Aug' in Thränen geschwommen.
> Ich aber sprach : Die Thränen verwischet,
> Wir müssen scheiden und von einander,
> Und da mich rings die Gefahr umzischet,
> In Flammen werd' ich zum Salamander.

> Ich bin geboren, ich, für Gefahren,
> Sie lauern immer auf meinem Gange
> Wie Wegelagrer in dunklen Schaaren;
> Doch kenn' ich nimmer die Furcht, die bange.
> Ich bin zu Gefahren bestimmt und geboren,
> Sie lieben mich, wie Löwen den Meister.
> Ich hab' sie alle heraufbeschworen,
> Sie dienen mir, wie dem Zaubrer die Geister." [1]

On account of the prologue which he spoke at the Schiller Festival at Leipzig on the 11th of November 1847, a festival which was in reality a demonstration in favour of the liberty of the press, Hartmann was accused of high treason and of offering affront to the Emperor of Austria. In 1848, as soon as the revolution broke out, he hastened to Prague. He and two friends, of whom Alfred Meissner was one, were sent as a deputation to Vienna. He has given an exquisitely humorous account of their audience with Archduke Franz Karl, who received them because his brother, the Emperor, was ill, and who was perfectly unable to understand what they wanted.[2] When the rabble, during the disturbances in Prague, attempted to storm the Jewish quarter and slaughter its inhabitants, it was Hartmann who rushed to the university, persuaded a body of armed students to accompany him, and with their assistance defended the quarter against the maddened crowd until the grenadiers arrived.[3]

In the Parliament of Frankfort Hartmann voted with the extreme Left; his aim was the unity of Germany as a republic. He spoke seldom, but attracted much attention; he was known as the handsomest man in the Parliament. Kinkel describes him at this time as a handsome,

---

[1] The traitorous friend had tracked me down, the minions of the law had come; my mother turned pale and trembled, my sister's eyes were bathed in tears. But I said: "Dry these foolish tears; my time has come and I must go; the flames of danger hiss around me—I become a salamander in their fiery glow."

I was born for danger; dangers, thick and dark, beset my path, yet I know no fear; are they not my destiny? They love me as the lion loves his tamer; 'tis I who have conjured them up, and they serve me as spirits do the magician.

[2] Moritz Hartmann: *Gesammelte Werke*, x. p. 16, &c.

[3] Alfred Marchand: *Les poètes lyriques de l'Autriche*. Hartmann: *Gesammelte Werke*, x. p. 23, &c.

amiable man, with firm convictions ; " the Southern imagination of the Austrian gave him fluency of speech, his German training had given him solidity; with Jewish cosmopolitanism he combined a steadfast patriotism which not unfrequently found utterance in proud words." At first he took part enthusiastically in the proceedings of the Parliament. Afterwards, when these became both tedious and barren, and the assembly showed its incapability of laying any great and lasting new foundation, his disappointment found vent in the witty, impressive *Reimchronik,* a work written in the metre of Hans Sachs. Hartmann, however, was not only a man of words, but a man of deeds. In the engagement in the streets of Frankfort on the 18th of September, he exposed himself a hundred times to the bullets of both parties in his endeavours to arrange a truce. After the revolution had broken out in Vienna, he and Froebel went there as deputies from Frankfort to the provisional government to express the sympathies of the national assembly, and Hartmann entered the army of the revolution as a common soldier. When Vienna was defending itself desperately against the Croats, he one day, with apparently certain death before him, joined a party that were determined to march through a severe fire to gain possession of a mill, and was made officer and leader when the original leader fell. After the fall of Vienna he escaped, thanks to the protection of a lady of high position, who procured him a falsified passport. He returned to his duties in the Parliament of Frankfort, and, when it broke up, went with the protesting party to Stuttgart. There this last remnant of the Parliament was dispersed by force of arms.

All Hartmann's work, including the youthful poetry written before 1848, bears the mark of his resolute character. In the volume, *Neuere Gedichte,* published in 1847, which as a whole is unpolitical, we find in the division *Ost und West* wild omens of the coming European storm —for example, the irate poem to the King of Prussia, in which Hartmann, deprecating Platen's and Herwegh's respectful attitude, cries shame upon him for delivering up the Poles to the Russian knout, and that other very touching poem, *Hüter, ist die Nacht bald hin?* ("Watchman, is the Night nigh past?"), which is one long sigh of impatient desire for the dawning of the new era.

And now that Bohemia and Hungary, Franconia and North Germany, were lifting up their voices in one great chorus—the voices of thinkers and of poets blending in unison—the youth of the country, as soon as they awakened to intellectual life, were impelled to join that chorus; from the boy on the school-bench to the oldest student, their minds were re-attuned, attuned to the key of revolution. Now they suddenly began not only to imbibe a revolutionary spirit from the works of the revolutionary writers of the day, but to read one into the writings of approved neutral and conservative authors long since dead. At a given moment it became their persuasion that all literature called to arms, even that old classic literature which was living its immortal life in handsome bindings on the bookshelves. A certain frame of mind is the result of our reading of all books.

What had he been, that Schiller whose writings had been put into their hands when they were children? What but a revolutionary, the motto of whose first book was the famous saying that what medicines cannot cure, cold steel cures, and what cold steel cannot cure, fire cures. Did the spirit of his works in any single point harmonise with the royal Prussian or the Austrian imperial spirit? What had Goethe's youthful attitude been but one of Titanic defiance? Did not even the work of his old age, the second part of *Faust*, end with the wish that he could see a free people on free soil? He had loathed the Berlin of Frederick II., would not his detestation of the Berlin of Frederick William IV. be greater still? From the writings of Hegel, who had begun life as a revolutionary and ended it as an ultra-conservative, they drew all the conclusions which he himself had left undrawn. Feuerbach had declared that he would have nothing to do with politics, nevertheless they transposed his philosophic decapitation of the historical state into the region of practical politics.

Yes, the clouds were gathering. In place of the swallows, the heraldic eagles of Prussia and Austria were flying low. The monarchs attempted in vain to exorcise the tempest. Frederick William IV. convened a general Landtag (Parliament) in April 1847. With his convictions he could not do otherwise than open it with a speech in which, in spite of all concessions, real and apparent, he made it clear that he was not prepared to take the decisive step which his people demanded of him.

" No power on earth," he cried, " will make me consent to the exchange of the natural relation between a king and his people for a conventional, constitutional relation ; never with my will shall a written paper interfere between Almighty God and this country, rule us with its paragraphs, and supercede ancient, sacred loyalty." [1]

The time had come. The assembly demanded annual Parliaments and complete fulfilment of the promises made in 1815 and 1829. Jacoby, Heinrich Simon, Gervinus, and others criticised the king's proposals and rejected them.

Then the storm broke—first in Switzerland, where in November 1847 the Liberal cantons armed and suppressed the Jesuitical *Sonderbund* (league of the Catholic cantons), then with overpowering force in Paris, then in all the German and many of the other European capitals. As thunder in a mountainous country echoes from hill to hill, so the thunder of the revolution echoed from one European country to another in the mad and holy year, 1848.

[1] Keiner Macht der Erde soll es gelingen, das natürliche Verhältniss zwischen Fürst und Volk in ein conventionelles, constitutionelles zu verwandeln, und nun und nimmermehr werde ich es zugeben, dass zwischen unserm Herrgott im Himmel und dieses Land ein geschriebenes Blatt sich eindrängt, um uns mit seinen Paragraphen zu regieren und die alte heilige Treue zu ersetzen.

XXIX

THE REVOLUTION

" Im Hochland fiel der erste Schuss—
Im Hochland wider die Pfaffen !
Da kam, die fallen wird und muss,
Ja, die Lawine kam in Schuss—
Drei Länder in den Waffen !
Schon kann die Schweiz von Siegen ruhn :
Das Urgebirg und die Nagelfluhn
Zittern vor Lust bis zum Kerne !

Drauf ging der Tanz in Welschland los—
Die Scyllen und Charybden,
Vesuv und Aetna brachen los :
Ausbruch auf Ausbruch, Stoss auf Stoss !
—' Sehr bedenklich, Euer Liebden ! '
Also schallt's von Berlin nach Wien
Und von Wien zurück nach Berlin—
Sogar dem Nickel graut es ! (Nickel, *i.e.* **Czar Nicholas.**)

Und nun ist denn auch abermals
Das Pflaster aufgerissen,
Auf dem die Freiheit, nackten Stahls
Aus der lumpigen Pracht des Königssaals
Zwei Könige schon geschmissen. . . ." [1]

THUS sang Freiligrath in February 1848, a few days
after the revolution in Paris. A long shudder, of pain and
at the same time of relief, passed through the whole of

---

[1] 'Twas in the mountains the first shot was fired—in the mountains, against
the priests ! That shot loosened the avalanche—three countries sprang to arms !
Switzerland can already rest on her laurels; the eternal mountains are trembling
to their centres with joy.

The sport soon spread to Italy—Scylla and Charybdis, Vesuvius and Etna broke
loose ; explosion upon explosion, blow upon blow ! " This is becoming serious, my
royal, my imperial brother ! " is the message from Vienna to Berlin, from Berlin to
Vienna ; even Nick begins to tremble.

And now the paving-stones are once more torn up, the stones of those streets on
to which ere now two kings have been ruthlessly flung by armed liberty.

Germany. It was as if a window had been opened, and air had reached the lungs of Europe. Example, the one power that can do miracles, was forcing the German people to action. They were also impelled by the fear that absolutism would now venture its last move, would declare Germany to be endangered by the revolution in France, and compel the people of Prussia and Austria to take up arms against the French republic.

In Austria intolerance had gone as far as it could go. In 1846 Metternich's government had actually placed the *Herzensergüsse* of the Emperor Joseph II., collected and published by a banished patriot, on the list of contraband books. And now the disturbances in the Austro-Italian provinces, which were endangering the credit of the state and the industries of the country, brought dissatisfaction with Metternich's rule to a climax. The decisive defeat he had met with in Switzerland, namely, the collapse of that Jesuitical "Sonderbund" which with all his might he had supported against the Radicals, had given the last blow to men's faith in his invincibility. In one of the provinces of Prussia, Silesia, bureaucratic misgovernment had just produced terrible consequences. Typhus, the result of starvation, had raged for months among the miserably poor industrial population before those in power had made any attempt to remedy the state of matters. Hundreds of dead and dying lay by the roadsides. In the cold of January, poor, solitary wretches starved in their hovels, and naked children pined to death beside the corpses of their parents ; no one came to their aid, for the ignorant local authorities had, in order to prevent the spread of infection, made it a punishable offence to enter any infected house. All this time the government officials only appeared to collect the taxes, which they did with harsh regardlessness of circumstances ; and when the Governor was attacked because no remedial measures had been taken from August 1847 to the end of January 1848, he answered that no formal appeal for assistance had been made.

In such circumstances the political leaders of the middle classes found it an easy matter to rouse their own class to

action, and the working classes, hoping to improve their
position, and exasperated by arbitrary police regulations,
everywhere followed in the footsteps of the middle classes.

It is difficult for the present generation to enter into the
feelings of the men of 1848. The frame of mind which
prevailed in Denmark at that time cannot be regarded as
typical. There, as elsewhere, it undoubtedly was the instinct
of national self-preservation and pride that asserted itself.
But whereas the other countries rose in revolt against
hereditary rule and coercion, in Denmark a revolt was suppressed by the power of the hereditary monarchy and of
insulted national feeling. There was no thought of revolution in the minds of the Danes; it was for old rights they
fought, not for new ideas.

Everywhere else in Europe the oppressed peoples revolted. It was long since anything but evil had fallen to their
lot, since they had witnessed the triumph of anything but
wrong, use-and-wont, and falsehood. Actual and detestable
had with them come to be almost synonymous terms. But
they had a faith that could remove mountains and a hope
that could shake the earth. Liberty, Parliament, national
unity, liberty of the press, republic, were to them magic
words, at the very sound of which their hearts leaped like
the heart of a youth who suddenly sees his beloved.

The aspiring spirits of the generation of to-day do not
feel thus. They know that stupidity is a ferocious animal,
and the hardest of all to kill—that cowardice, the agile slave
that stands at the beck of power, is as strong as courage
itself when there is any question of defending ancient privilege—that what is known by the name of progress is a feeble
snail. The simpleton in the fable bought a raven that he
might see for himself if it was true that ravens live for two
hundred years. The friends of progress in our days know
beforehand that all the raven-black lies and raven-trickeries
of all the privilege-rookeries, great and small, will outlive
them—for how many hundred years they cannot tell. At
a rare time they have seen good victorious, but never
have they heard it acknowledged that it is *their* good
which has triumphed. They have always seen truth first

abused, then if possible killed—if that proved impossible, maimed and recognised. Therefore they have little hope. Many of them, indeed, have killed hope in their own breasts, as we kill a nerve that gives us too much pain. They have been disappointed too often.

The men of 1848 had never relinquished their hope in the future. They had been oppressed, and they had suffered so long that they had grown accustomed to see brute force and hypocrisy triumphant, accustomed to live in a sort of spiritual twilight. But they believed in the coming day. And now, suddenly, they saw it. First a gleam, then a ray, then a flame, then the whole horizon, as far as the eye could reach, a sea of light. For the first time they heard loud, ringing voices proclaim liberty to be the right of the people, without a voice raised in opposition ; and for the first time, with wondering eyes, they saw power, that hitherto immovable mass, the giant bearer of oppression and falsehood, begin to stir like some gigantic elephant, writhe and turn and shake itself, throw off its riders, and move ponderously in the direction of the high-spirited, ardent friends of liberty, the men of the new day, who stood ready to fling themselves on its back and force it to trample down all the ancient abuses.

For the younger men especially it was a moment without compare, a sight that intoxicated them, that drove them wild. They shouted, they sang, they rejoiced, and in their wild exultation they felt it a necessity to act, to risk all, to give their lives if need be—anything, everything, except be behindhand in greeting and ushering in the dawning day of liberty.

True it is that democratic illusions held high revelry ; true it is that there prevailed a touchingly naïve belief in the infallibility of popular instincts; and true it is that the ability of theorists to settle practical difficulties was greatly overestimated. But the first impulse was irresistible, the original instinct was correct. Those who really possessed capacity became leaders, took the command without any fuss or parade, and were obeyed, not because of their outward authority, but because their real superiority was felt by all.

The score of students who commanded on the barricades in Berlin may be given as an instance. Many a so-called very ordinary man for a few days of his life showed himself to be a hero. During the first months some of the finest qualities of humanity displayed themselves and shone with astonishing lustre.

It was in Austria that the revolutionary movement began, immediately after the arrival of the news of the Revolution of February in Paris. A speech made by Kossuth in the Hungarian Parliament on the 3rd of March, demanding constitutional government for all the provinces of the Empire, inaugurated the revolution both in Buda-Pesth and Vienna. On the 11th of March a similar demand was made by the Czechs in Prague, and before this, on the 6th of March, the Austrian Industrial Union had presented a petition to Archduke Franz Karl, the presumptive heir to the throne, requesting Metternich's dismissal, and also demanding liberty of the press, the right of voting supplies, of taking part in legislation, &c.

On this followed what has been called the petition storm. Every day, every hour new petitions to the Emperor poured in. On the 12th of March the students held a great meeting at the University, the result of which was also a petition to the Emperor, demanding liberty of the press, religious liberty, and liberty of instruction. The Emperor received the deputation the following day, but gave an undecided answer. In these unforeseen circumstances the 13th of March, the opening day of the Lower Austrian Convention of the Estates, arrived and found the Government unprepared. The populace crowded into the enclosure of the assembly hall, where Kossuth's speech was read aloud amidst excited rejoicings and shouts of "Hurrah for the constitution!" A party forced their way into the hall and began to smash the furniture and throw it out on to the heads of the soldiers; even Archduke Albrecht, who was in command, was struck by a block of wood. Then the order was given to fire, and the first Revolution of Vienna broke out. The Italian troops fired, but the Austrians unscrewed their bayonets amidst the joyful shouts of the crowd. At the Castle the gunners, instead of shooting, placed themselves in front of their guns—as we read in one of the poems of the day, Rick's *Das Lied vom braven Kanonier*:

> " Vor der Burg in glühender Front,
> Des blutgen Befehls gewärtig,
> Vor der Burg in glühender Front,
> Da stehn die Kanonen fertig.
> Schon zittern die Thore, sie brechen schier,
> Jetzt gilt's, du braver Kanonier !
>
> Und du trittst vor die Mündung hin,
> Als wolltest du fesseln den Würger—
> Und du rufst mit begeistertem Sinn :
> Erst mich ! dann den wehrlosen Bürger !—
> Dann schweigt das Commando, beschämt vor dir.
> Hab Dank, du braver Kanonier ! " [1]

Towards evening it became clear to Metternich that no concessions would now avail. He who for forty years had led the policy of Austria hurriedly gave in his resignation and made his escape in disguise in the imperial laundry cart. At nine o'clock the same evening the troops were withdrawn from Vienna (exactly a week before the same thing happened in Berlin), and citizens and students mounted guard everywhere. The arsenal was opened, and in one day arms were served out to 25,000 men.

There was some severe fighting in the outskirts of the town. So fiercely resolute were the populace that, all unarmed, they pressed in upon and disarmed two companies of grenadiers who were defending the entrance to Metternich's villa. Those who resisted were trampled under foot.

That same evening the abolition of the censorship and liberty of the press were publicly announced. The intimation produced a feeling of intense relief—it was as if a gag had been removed from the mouth of the nation.

---

[1] In front of the castle in threatening line stand the cannon, awaiting the word of command—the gates are shuddering and yielding—the moment has come, brave gunner !

Forward to the muzzle he goes, as if the order had been to stop the mouths of the destroyers; fearlessly he cries : " First me, then the defenceless citizen !"—No farther command is given. Thou hast shamed them ! All thanks to thee, brave gunner !

The newspapers, as a matter of course, instantaneously began to give expression to the popular political ideas. It had hitherto been impossible to treat even in poetic form any subject with a social or political tendency ; Austria had resembled a forest where the voices of the birds were silent. Now suddenly pipe and call, whistle and song, were heard from every bush and tree, a mighty and confused chorus.[1]

Poems of liberty were published in all the languages of Austria—German and Czech, Slavonian and Croatian, Hungarian, Polish, and Italian. So eager were men to make use of their new liberty that a whole bevy of poems, superscribed *Erstes censurfreies Gedicht* (" First poem printed after the abolition of the censure "), appeared simultaneously.

The one generally accepted as the first is Frankl's *Die Universität*. During the night between the 14th and 15th of March, one of the professors, fearing an outbreak of the prisoners, requested the armed students to despatch a guard to one of the prisons. Twenty students were at once sent, under the command of Ludwig August Frankl. Whilst he stood on guard that young man gave expression to the feelings of the day in the song:

> " Was kommt heran mit kühnem Gange?
> Die Waffe blinkt, die Fahne weht,
> Es naht mit hellem Trommelklange
> Die Universität.
>
> Das freie Wort, das sie gefangen,
> Seit Joseph arg verhöhnt, verschmäht,
> Vorkämpfend sprengte seine Spangen
> Die Universität."

In 1890, on his eightieth birthday, Frankl published a large volume of able poetry ; during his long life he has been an unusually productive poet and writer of biography ; he has been presented with the freedom of Vienna and of three other European and Asiatic towns ; but this song, of

[1] Frhr. von Helfert : *Wiener Parnass im Jahre* 1848.

which in course of time at least a hundred thousand copies were printed, was what founded his reputation.

It was not, however, really the first poem printed after the abolition of the censorship, for on the previous night Castelli had written his song of the *Garde-National.* In the German language alone there are three or four poems which lay claim to the same distinction. One of these is the song of the Vienna student brigade, *Erwacht, erwacht o Brüder! Ein grosser Morgen tagt* ("Awake, awake, O brothers! a great morning is dawning"), and another is Fr. Gerhard's *Die freie Presse,* which begins:

> "Die Presse frei! Die Glocken lasst ertönen
> Und läutet Jubel überall!
> Und ruft's hinaus zu Deutschlands fernsten Söhnen
> Die Presse frei, erstürmt der Freiheit Wall!" [1]

Simultaneously with these poems, which express such an innocent, exuberant delight at being able to speak and write without restraint, there appeared others full of the most childish gratitude to the weak-minded Emperor. In them he is "the good Emperor," "our good Ferdinand," &c., &c. People were ready to forget immediately that every single concession had been, not granted, but forcibly extorted, or else they believed naïvely that this was the way to make their late oppressors forget it. In one of the many songs in praise of the Emperor we read:

> "Heil dir, mein Kaiser! in all der Lust
> Zu der sich dein Volk ermannt hat,
> Sei Dir vor Allen ein Heil gebracht,
> Den es immer als edel erkannt hat." [2]

On the 16th of March the Hungarian deputation, 150 magnates with Kossuth at their head, rode into Vienna, through the Prater, welcomed with deafening cheers and showers of flowers. That day the number of armed citizens

---

[1] The press is free! Peal the bells! sound the glad tidings far and wide! Proclaim to the farthest-off of Germany's sons: The press is free, the ramparts of liberty are stormed!

[2] All hail to thee, my Emperor! Full of joy in their accomplished work, thy people greet thee, whom they have always known to be of noble mind.

had risen to 60,000. In the afternoon a herald appeared on the balcony of the Castle and read the following proclamation : "We, Ferdinand the First, by the grace of God Emperor of Austria and King of Hungary and Bohemia, of Lombardy and Venice, of Dalmatia, Croatia, Slavonia, Galicia, Illyria, &c., have now, in agreement with the wishes of our faithful people, decided to take certain steps." On this introduction follows the announcement of the liberty of the press, the formation of the National Guard, and the convention of an assembly of deputies for the purpose of drafting "that constitution which we have determined to bestow on our country."

Saphir sang:

> " Schwert aus der Scheid, aus dem Herzen das Lied !
> Stimmt an das Lied der Lieder !
> Jauchzend ertön' es durch Reihe und Glied,
> Jauchzend durch jubelnde Brüder !
> Blank wie die Waffe und hell wie der Stahl
> Klinge das Lied von der Garde-National." [1]

Even the mocking-birds, we see, on this occasion ceased from mocking and found voice to join in the universal chorus. In the persistent employment of the French word, *Garde Nationale*, we have an example of the importation and imitation which so largely characterised the movement.

In turning over the pages of a collection of the German political poems, several thousand in number, which were published in 1848 in Vienna alone, we come upon many unknown names, but also upon almost all that were well known at that time and on many that were destined to become famous. We are struck by a poem of Bauernfeld's, *Wien an die Provinzen*, weak from a literary point of view, but significant from its indication of the first sign of reaction, namely, an attempt made in the provinces to shake off what was called the tyranny of the capital ; in other words, to counteract the influence of the example set by victorious, free Vienna. Friedrich Uhl, at a later period

---

[1] As your swords leap from their scabbards, let a song, O my brothers, come from your hearts ! Let the song of songs resound through your rejoicing ranks— bright as burnished armour, clear as ringing steel, the song of the Garde-National !

editor of the *Wiener Abendpost,* the official organ of the Government, writes a lament for the fallen revolutionary heroes:

> " Das schwarze Band, den schwarzen Flor
> Lasst in den Lüften wallen,
> Den Todten singt ein Klagelied,
> Die für die Freiheit gefallen." [1]

There are poems to Lenau, the most popular of living Austrian poets, bewailing that the singer of liberty is now insane and silent, his ears deaf to the victors' joyful shouts. Richard Wagner, as yet unknown to fame, sends a " Greeting from Saxony to Vienna ":

> " Ihr habt der Freiheit Art erkannt ;
> Nicht halb wird sie gewonnen ;
> Ist uns ihr kleinstes Glied entwandt,
> Schnell ist sie ganz zeronnen.
> Dies kleinste Glied ist unsre Ehre,
> Ehrlos ist, wer es lässt,
> Mit hellen Waffen, guter Wehre,
> Drum hieltet Ihr es fest." [2]

Amongst the writers of serious poems we find name like Grillparzer and Hebbel ; Saphir and Dingelstedt write mock-heroic elegies on the last of the censors, both of them parodies of Schiller's *Nadowessische Todesklage ;* and there are no end of satiric thrusts at the King of Prussia, who, curiously enough, was considered to have acted heretofore in a more reactionary spirit, and now to be granting concessions more unwillingly than the Austrian Emperor.

Since the beginning of March Berlin had been in a state of the wildest excitement. Directly after the Revolution of February the *Kreuzzeitung* published an article advocating war with France. It awakened extreme anxiety ; people asked each other if long-suffering Prussia was actually to be compelled to take up arms against the French Republic.

---

[1] Let the black draperies flutter in the wind, and let a sad lament resound for those who have laid down their lives in the cause of liberty.

[2] Ye have rightly understood the nature of liberty ; we cannot half possess her ; if we but let her little finger be taken from us, she will soon be gone. That little finger is our honour. Who lets that go knows not what honour is. Therefore with strong arms and good swords ye have defended it.

It was in these days that all Germany began to deck itself in black, red, and gold, the colours symbolising unity and liberty. Freiligrath wrote of them :

> " In Kümmerniss und Dunkelheit
> Da mussten wir sie bergen,
> Nun haben wir sie doch befreit,
> Befreit aus ihren Särgen ;
> Ha, wie das blitzt und rauscht und rollt !
> Hurrah, du Schwarz, du Roth, du Gold !
>   Pulver ist schwarz,
>   Blut ist roth,
>   Golden flackert die Flamme ! " [1]

On the 7th of March the first great public meeting was held at In den Zelten. It was resolved to present an address to the King, demanding that he should immediately convene the Landtag and grant a constitution. The address ended with the words : "No war with France ! Lawful liberty in our own country ! Fraternal union of the whole great German nation !" On the 12th of March a regiment of cavalry charged the crowds at In den Zelten and dispersed them, but they collected again in town, built barricades, and attempted to seize a gunsmith's shop in the Jägerstrasse. Two men were killed in front of the Opera House. Under the windows of the Castle the people shouted " Liberty ! Liberty of the press !" and insulted the sentries. On the 14th of March a general Landtag was summoned. So far things had been managed on the whole peaceably ; but on the 15th of March the soldiers, who were worn out with night-watching, and with having to hold themselves in constant readiness in the barracks, began to behave roughly to the crowd, to strike with the butt-ends of their guns, &c. Small barricades which some boys had erected at the corner

---

[1] In secret hiding-place and gloom
   Long time we have concealed it ;
But now at last the day is come,
   The day that has revealed it.
Ha ! how the smoke is round it rolled !
Hurrah ! thou Black and Red and Gold !
    Powder is black,
    Blood is red,
    Golden glows the flame ! (JOYNES.)

of the Kurstrasse and the Gertraudenstrasse were charged by
the Cuirassier Guards from Potsdam, and the boys were
cruelly handled.

At one o'clock on the 18th of March a royal proclamation was read in front of the Castle. It declared
that Germany was to be from henceforth not a federation
of States, but one federated State (Staatenbund—Bundes-
staat), with a common Parliament, a common army, free-
trade, liberty of emigration, and liberty of the press. At
the end of each sentence the crowd answered with thun-
dering hurrahs. Cries were heard of "Away with the
soldiers!" and some stones were thrown. The famous
General von Pfuel, who was in command, forbade the
soldiers to fire, ordered the dragoons to dismount, and
praised the discipline they showed in obeying at once,
furious as they were. When the town seemed quiet he
went home for a short time.

During his absence, in consequence of an order given,
no one knows by whom, though the embittered populace
during the following days laid the blame of it on the Prince
of Prussia, the future Emperor William, a regiment of
dragoon guards arrived. The crowd shouted "Away!"
The dragoons wheeled round, and the crowd were beginning to cry "Bravo!" when suddenly the soldiers charged
in amongst them with naked swords. At the same moment
a battalion of infantry marched out at the Castle gate, drew
up in line, and also charged with levelled bayonets. Some
shots were fired—possibly by accident. With loud shrieks
the crowd instantaneously dispersed. Only a moment before
joy had been at its height ; strangers had been embracing
each other, waving their hats, and shouting "Hurrah for the
King"; now, as if at a preconcerted signal, barricades sprang
up, as they had done in Vienna, over the whole town. There
were two hundred of them, built of paving-stones, gutter-
planking, and carts. The town was a camp. Men fired on the
troops from every roof ; those who could not get guns, threw
stones. Every axe, every thick stick became a weapon.[1]

[1] *Des deutschen Volkes Erhebung im Jahre* 1848, *sein Kampf um freie Institu-
tionen und sein Siegesjubel. Von J. Lasker und Fr. Gerhard.* Danzig, 1848.

The roofs were torn off corner houses, and paving-stones were carried up in baskets. The students met, armed, in front of the University, fastened tri-coloured cockades in their caps, and proceeded to man the barricades. Powder and shot, axes and iron bars, were provided by the merchants. On the evening of the 18th, the artillery opened fire in the Königstrasse. The King looked on from the windows of the Castle, incensed by the deputations that came entreating him to withdraw the troops, but at times condescending to jest; what specially annoyed him was the sight of the tri-coloured flags waving on the barricades. He was ready, he said, to concede much to entreaty, nothing to illegal violence.

Varnhagen, in his Diary, describes what he saw and heard from his windows that night: "A small body of citizens under trusty leaders held the streets, doubly watchful because their numbers were so few. For a number of hours absolute darkness and silence prevailed; then, towards morning, the sound of far-off drums was heard; troops were evidently approaching. The citizen combatants were instantly on the alert; we could hear them whispering. A youthful voice gave the word of command: 'To the roofs, gentlemen!' and every man went to his post. This calm, determined command, given with noble simplicity, rang terrible and yet inspiring through the darkness. One felt the dangers which those who obeyed it were braving, for the general resistance was becoming weaker, and it seemed as if they were doomed, after a fruitless struggle, to meet an ignominious death, either by a fall from the roof, by the soldiers' bayonets, or by the hand of the executioner." Varnhagen concludes: "The heroic courage and determination of these daring youths was most undoubtedly worthy of all admiration"—weighty words, coming from the pen of an old, experienced officer.

On the night between the 18th and 19th of March, wherever barricades were being erected or repaired, the windows were illuminated. But the moment troops entered the street all was darkness. The soldiers hewed and sabred right and left in the houses which they entered, and showed mediæval brutality in their treatment of prisoners. Towards morning the arsenal of the Garde-Landwehr regiment was captured by the insurgents ; they found that the locks of the guns had been destroyed, but all the smiths of the quarter set to work and repaired the damage.

At last, in the course of the morning, a royal proclamation headed *An meine lieben Berliner!* was circulated, in which an attempt was made to explain the events of the day before as being the result of an unfortunate misunderstanding. " It had been necessary to clear the square in front of the Castle with cavalry, ordered to advance at a walking pace and with sheathed swords (*im Schritt und mit eingesteckter Waffe*); two infantry muskets had about this time gone off by accident, fortunately injuring no one ; a company of evil-disposed individuals, chiefly strangers, had taken advantage of this unfortunate occurrence to stir up ideas of revenge in the minds of the excited crowd ; the troops had used their weapons, but not until driven to do so by being repeatedly fired at. The King promises that the troops shall be withdrawn from Berlin, and concludes with the hope that both parties will forget what has happened. [1]

Meanwhile the struggle raged on with frightful exasperation on both sides. In treating with the deputations that waited on him on the morning of the 19th of March, the King attempted to make his promise of withdrawing the troops conditional on the dismantling of the barricades. But in the end everything was conceded — change of ministry, release of the prisoners taken during the night, and withdrawal of the troops. Amidst the shouts of the rejoicing crowd, to muffled beat of drum and Choralemusic, the soldiers were marched off to Potsdam, feeling that they had sustained a deadly insult at the hands of their royal commander-in-chief.

An enormous crowd thronged to the Castle, partly con-

---

[1] Eine Rotte von Bösewichtern, meist aus Fremden bestehend, die sich seit einer Woche, obgleich aufgesucht, doch zu verbergen gewusst haben, haben diesen Umstand im Sinne ihrer argen Pläne durch augenscheinliche Lüge verdreht und die erhitzten Gemüther von vielen meiner treuen und lieben Berliner mit Rachegedanken um vermeintlich vergossenes Blut erfüllt und sind so die greulichen Urheber von Blutvergiessen geworden.

sisting of those who hoped by the force of numbers to
exercise pressure on their vanquished rulers, partly of
curious idlers ; all the funeral processions from the streets
where there had been fighting also made their way there.
The corpses were borne on biers, or, where the numbers
were too great, conveyed in open waggons, decorated with
flowers, ribbons, and scarves, the corpses too being decked
with flowers.

Every available space in the neighbourhood of the
Castle was closely packed. The crowd demanded to see
the King. With a pale face he stepped out on the balcony.
"Set the prisoners free !" shouted the crowd, and he was
actually obliged to order the release of all those who were
confined in the cellars of the Castle. The next proceeding
was the carrying of many of the most severely wounded
insurrectionists into the Castle, where their wounds were
dressed. Now the funeral processions began to arrive,
a sight by which the crowd was thrown into a state of the
wildest agitation. Whilst the corpses were being carried
into one of the apartments on the first floor of the Castle,
one orator after another addressed the people. The speech
which met with most approval was one made by Karl
Gutzkow, the refrain of which was "general arming of the
citizens." This the newly appointed ministers, who were
moving about among the crowd, vainly attempting to pacify
them, were loth to concede, but they were soon compelled
to do so, for a scene which occurred at this juncture made
it impossible to resist the demands of the people.

A new funeral procession arrived—four corpses were
borne on flower-decked biers through the crowd, their
bloody wounds exposed to view for the purpose of rousing
the beholders to revenge. The biers were deposited below
the King's balcony, and the bearers raised a wild shout of
"The King! The Queen!" which found a thousand-fold echo
among the crowd. Two of the new ministers, Schwerin
and Arnim, tried in vain to gain a hearing ; their voices
were drowned in the cry of "The King! The Queen!"

When the King and Queen actually appeared on the
balcony the people's frenzy knew no bounds. The King

attempted to speak, but the bearers held high the biers with their bloody burdens, and the crowd yelled " Off with your hat ! " And as each corpse was carried past the King was obliged to uncover.[1] In Freiligrath's grand poem, *Die Todten an die Lebenden*, written in the following year, the year of disillusion, we read :

> "Die Kugel mitten durch die Brust, die Stirne breit gespalten,
> So habt Ihr uns auf blutgem Brett hoch in die Luft gehalten !
> Hoch in die Luft mit wildem Schrei, das unsre Schmerzgeberde
> Den, der zu tödten uns befahl, ein Fluch auf ewig werde !
> Dass er sie sehe Tag und Nacht, im Wachen und im Traume—
> Im Oeffnen seines Bibelbuchs und im Champagnerschaume !
> Dass wie ein Brandmal sie sich tief in seine Seele brenne :
> Dass nirgendwo und nimmermehr er vor ihr fliehen könne !
> Dass jeder qualverzogene Mund, dass jede rothe Wunde
> Ihn schrecke noch, ihn ängste noch in seiner letzten Stunde ! "[2]

On the 21st of March, at noon, the King rode out at the Castle gate with a black, red, and gold band on his arm, and himself distributed black, red, and gold favours. He was followed by the royal princes and the Ministers, who were in despair at the humiliating proceeding ; at his side rode a veterinary surgeon, Urban by name. One of his generals had in vain attempted to dissuade him from taking this step. He answered : "Non, non, c'est décidé, nous allons monter à cheval." Presently he drew rein and spoke as follows : " I am usurping no man's right when I declare that I believe myself called to be the saviour of the unity and liberty of

---

[1] *Des deutschen Volkes Erhebung*, p. 54. Varnhagen : *Tagebücher*. Adolf Streckfuss : *Erinnerungen aus dem Jahre* 1848 ; *Der Zeitgeist*, 1889, Nr. 51.

[2] With bullets through and through our breast—our forehead split with spike and spear,
So bear us onward shoulder-high, laid dead upon a blood-stained bier ;
Yea, shoulder-high above the crowd, that on the man that bade us die,
Our dreadful death-distorted face may be a bitter curse for aye ;
That he may see it day and night, or when he wakes or when he sleeps,
Or when he opes his holy book, or when with wine high revel keeps ;
That ever like a scorching brand that sight his secret soul may burn ;
That he may ne'er escape its curse, nor know to whom for aid to turn ;
That always each disfeatured face, each gaping wound his sight may sear,
And brood above his bed of death, and curdle all his blood with fear !

(JOYNES.)

Germany—that unity and liberty, based on a free constitution, I will defend with the aid of German loyalty." At the University he called for the professors and students, and said to them: "Schreiben Sie sich's auf, meine Herren! Write down my words to you, for they are for posterity. I place myself at the head of the German nation ; with its unity and liberty the existence of Prussia is henceforth inseparably bound up. Write that down!" At the arsenal, when he was again pouring forth promises, a piercing voice suddenly cried : "Don't believe him, he is lying ; he has always lied, and he is lying now. Tear me in pieces if you like, but I say he is lying—don't believe him!"

In Vienna, a few days later, the following poem appeared :

"PREUSSISCHE MISSVERSTAENDNISSE.

Im grossen ungläubigen Altberlin sind nun die Wunder zu Hause,
Da wird geschossen, gestürmt, gebrannt zwei Tage ohne Pause,
Bis tausende liegen im rothen Sand. Den König betrübt die Wendniss :
Die Flinten gingen von selber los. Das war nur ein Missverständniss.

Durch's grosse, ungläubige Altberlin gehn wunderbare Witze,
Ein König hüllt sich in Schwarz-Roth-Gold und stellt sich an Deutschlands Spitze,
Ein König wird Ober-Demagog mit deutsch—einheitlicher Sendniss,
Doch Deutschland lacht und ruft mit Macht : Das ist ein Missverständniss."[1]

Another poem that bears witness to the irritated, sarcastic feeling provoked by the events of these days is entitled *Erlkönig*, and begins :

---

[1] PRUSSIAN MISUNDERSTANDINGS.

The big, incredulous town of Berlin has become the home of miracles. For two whole days they have been shooting, storming, burning there without a pause ; thousands are lying in the bloody dust. The King is distressed by what has occurred ; he says : "The guns went off of themselves ; the whole has been a misunderstanding."

In the old, incredulous town of Berlin strange tricks are being played ; a King decks himself in black, red, and gold, and declares himself to be the leader of Germany, the arch-demagogue, chosen of heaven to bring about German unity. But Germany only laughs and shouts : "This is a misunderstanding."

"Wer schiesst noch so spät auf's Volk ohne Wehr
Es ist ein König mit seinem Heer.
Er hält sein Volk so treu im Arm,
Er fasst es so sicher mit seinen Gendarmes.

O Bürger, o Bürger, o hörest du nicht
Was Erlkönig in der Zeitung verspricht," &c.

The Revolution of March in the capitals of Germany did not call forth any particularly fine poetical effusions ; it gave rise chiefly to street songs, inflammatory and ephemeral verse ; but the counter revolutions, the terrible re-capture of Vienna in October and of Berlin in November 1848, inspired a whole host of fine poems. The poets also found inspiration in the martyr deaths of individual liberationists, who either fell in fight or were murdered judicially after the suppression of the revolution. The insurrection of Hungary, too, with its suppression by the Russian army, awakened a sympathy which found expression in touching poems.

The enthusiastic ecstasy in Vienna was of short duration. The democrats did not consider the free constitution free enough. A central political committee was formed as a sort of check on the government. The existence of such a body was declared to be illegal, but popular pressure compelled the government to retract this declaration and to suspend the constitution. In the beginning of May the Emperor fled to Innsbruck. An attempt was made to disband the student brigade, but as this led to a renewal of barricade fighting, the ministry were obliged to desist. The Emperor returned in August. During all this time the capital was in a most excited state ; the revolution had put a stop to every kind of business, and the want of employment increased discontent and restlessness. A deep impression was made by the intelligence of the events of June in Paris, Cavaignac's victory being regarded as equivalent to the suppression of the revolution in France. About the same time came the news that Jellatschitsch, the Ban of Croatia, was preparing to invade Hungary. Intercepted letters showed that in this proceeding he had the support

of the Court of Vienna and of Latour, the Minister of War ;
and the consequence was that Count Lamberg, Latour's
envoy, was torn to pieces by the mob on his arrival at
Pesth (September 28), and Latour himself, having declared his intention of despatching troops to Hungary, was
killed (October 7) by the enraged populace of Vienna.
In his poem, *Der 7 Oktober,* which is a eulogy of the murdered man, Dingelstedt takes the opportunity to dissociate
himself from the revolution and all its doings.

The Emperor now fled from Vienna for the second
time.   Whilst Radetzky suppressed the insurrection in
Lombardy, Windischgrätz, who had been appointed commander-in-chief, surrounded the capital with his troops.
In a struggle which lasted from the 24th to the 29th of
October the outworks and outlying parts of the town were
captured, and the city had already been driven by want
of provisions and ammunition to agree to the unconditional
capitulation demanded by Windischgrätz, when the cry was
heard in the streets : "The Hungarians are coming."   They
had been seen from the tower of St. Stephen's Church.
There was great rejoicing.   The agreement to surrender
was disregarded, the arms which had already been given
up were again seized at the arsenals, and sorties were made
to support the Hungarians, whose cannonading was now
heard.   But the Hungarian army was completely routed
by Jellatschitsch.   Windischgrätz entered Vienna on the
31st of October, followed by Jellatschitsch on the 2nd of
November.   A state of siege was proclaimed, and court-
martials, sentences of death, and executions became the
order of the day.

Simultaneously with the elections for the first German
Parliament in Frankfort-on-Main, elections went on in
Prussia for the Prussian Constitutional Assembly, which
was opened by the King in May.   This body numbered
few eminent members, the best men having been sent to
Frankfort.   Berlin was in an almost anarchic condition ;
the arsenal was stormed and plundered, the political clubs
terrorised and coerced the Assembly.   It rejected the constitution proposed by the government as not sufficiently

democratic. The result of this was a first change of ministry. The new ministry made proposals which coincided more closely with the wishes of the Assembly, but found themselves unable to agree to the demand of the majority that it should be made a point of honour with all officers who disapproved of the new constitution to leave the army. A third ministry, with Pfuel for its leader, was formed. On the last day of October, while the Assembly was debating an appeal to the government "to support, by every means in its power, the cause of popular liberty, at present endangered in Vienna," a mob broke in on the meeting, attempted to influence its decision by violent means, and insulted the Pfuel ministry. Then this ministry too resigned, and on the 2nd of November the King put the reins of government into the hands of a war ministry, with his step-uncle, Count Brandenburg, at its head. This new government decreed the transference of the Assembly from Berlin to Brandenburg, and brought the troops that had just returned from Denmark under General Wrangel to Berlin. The citizens were disarmed and a state of siege was proclaimed.

The revolutions of Vienna and Berlin had been fruitless ; alike fruitless were the proceedings of the first German Parliament (Reichstag), which met at Frankfort on the 18th of May 1848, and was forcibly dispersed by troops at Stuttgart on the 18th of June 1849. The President it chose, Archduke John, did his best to subject it to the domination of Austria ; it made a vain offer of the imperial crown of Germany to Frederick William IV. in April 1849 ; its sacred inviolability was disregarded as early as November 1848, when Windischgrätz ordered the execution of one of its members, Robert Blum, at Brigittenau ; it lost importance as a representative assembly by the gradual desertion of its conservative members. When it was dispersed at Stuttgart, the reaction was once more triumphant throughout Europe :

" Da sah man die letzten der Getreuen,
Die ausgeharrt beim Heiland, zerstreuen
Sich, wandernd nach allen Seiten und Winden,
Das Wort des Heiles zu verkünden,

2 C

Wohl wissend, dass ein langes Exil
Und Armuth, Noth und Dulden ihr Ziel,
Und Qual und Tod und Kerkermauern.
' Das Wort des Heils wird sie überdauern'
Das merkt euch, ihr Knechte und blutigen Horden :
Das Wort ist Fleisch und ist Gott geworden." [1]

Thus sang Moritz Hartmann, one of the last of the faithful. He rightly felt that the ideas survived the outward changes.

By the end of 1848 the poets of the revolution had nothing left to sing of but fallen heroes and extinguished hopes. Among these poets Freiligrath and Hartmann rank highest, and as typical of the elegies written on the fallen heroes, we may take the verses composed by these two authors on Robert Blum, whose firm, gentle character, simplicity, and prudence, stamped him in the minds of his contemporaries as the ideal of a popular leader.

In his *Reimchronik* Hartmann writes mournfully :

" So ruhe sanft und gut, mein Robert !
Nicht braucht's der Wunsch, dass leicht dir werde
Die blutgetränkte Wiener Erde,
Der Boden, den du dir erobert.
Du bist nicht todt, trotz aller Klage
Des deutschen Volks, trotz aller Lieder.

. . . . . .

Ein Mythus geht : der Robert lebt,
Der Robert Blum, den sie erschossen
Und jedes deutsche Herz erbebt :
Das theure Blut ist nicht geflossen—
Die Hoffnung raunt uns in die Ohren :
Entflort, entflort die Trikoloren,
Noch, noch ist Deutschland nicht verloren.

. . . . . .

Allüberall ist der dabei !
Er wendet mit den Geisterhänden
Und fängt mit seiner Brust das Blei,
Das uns die Fürstenväter senden.

. . . .

---

[1] Then the last of the faithful, who had remained true to their saviour, scattered to the four winds of heaven, to proclaim the word of salvation, knowing full well that what awaited them was exile and poverty, want and suffering, torture, imprisonment, and death. " The word of salvation will survive them "; note this, ye slaves, ye bloody hordes : The word has become flesh, has become God.

Und wandeln muss er, bis entrafft
Das deutsche Volk sich dem Verräther
Bis er entfürstet und entpfafft
Den heilgen Boden seiner Väter." [1]

And a week after Blum's death, Freiligrath writes the
magnificent verses on the commemoration service in the
Cathedral of Cologne, where the mighty organ pealed forth
Neukomm's requiem music :

" Und heut in diesem selben Köln zum Weh'n des Winterwindes
Und zu der Orgel Brausen schallt das Grablied dieses Kindes.
Nicht singt die Ueberlebende, die Mutter, es dem Sohne :
Das ganze schmerzbewegte Köln singt es mit festem Tone.
Es spricht : Du, deren Schoos ihn trug, bleib still auf deinem Kammer !
Vor deinem Gott, du graues Haupt, ausströme deinen Jammer ;
Auch ich bin seine Mutter, Weib ! Ich und noch eine Hohe—
Ich und die Revolution, die hohe, lichterlohe !
Bleib du daheim mit deinem Schmerz ! wir wahren seine Ehre—
Des Robert Requiem singt Köln, die revolutionäre.
 . . . .
Was greift ihr zu den Schwertern nicht, Ihr Singer und Ihr Beter ?
Was werdet Ihr Posaunen nicht, Ihr ehr'nen Orgeltuben,
Den jüngsten Tag ins Ohr zu schrein den Henkern und den Buben ?
Den Henkern, die ihn hingestreckt auf der Brigittenaue—
Auf festen Knien lag er da im ersten Morgenthaue !
Dann sank er hin—hin in sein Blut—lautlos !—heut vor acht Tagen !
Zwei Kugeln haben ihm die Brust, eine das Haupt zerschlagen." [2]

---

[1] Rest peacefully, rest well, my Robert ! No need is there for us to wish that
light upon thy breast may lie the blood-drenched earth of Vienna, the soil thy valour
captured. Thou art not dead, despite the loud laments and songs of mourning of the
German people. . . . From mouth to mouth spreads the report : " Our Robert lives,
that Robert Blum the tyrants shot "—and every German heart beats high. That
precious blood has not been shed ; hope whispers in our ears : " The tri-coloured
standard is trailed in the dust, but Germany is not lost." . . . He is with us everywhere ! With his spirit hands he turns back the bullets, or receives them in his
breast—these bullets rained on us by our paternal rulers. . . . A wanderer he,
until the German people have released themselves from the betrayer's grip, until he
has cleared the sacred land of his fathers, of princes and of priests.

[2] In this same city of Cologne, 'mid moaning winds of winter wild,
To-day in deepest organ-tones resounds the grave-song of this child.
'Tis not the mother bow'd in grief who sings it o'er her fallen son ;
Nay, all Cologne bewails the death of him whose toil too soon is done.
With solemn woe the city speaks : Thou who didst bear the noble dead,
Remain to weep within thy home, and bow to earth thine aged head ;

It is to Hartmann's *Reimchronik des Pfaffen Mauritius* that we must have recourse if we desire to view all the successive events and impressions of 1848 in the mirror of poetry. Many of the details of this poem have become difficult to understand ; the reader of to-day comes upon lists of names, of whose owners he knows little or nothing —men like Bassermann, the parliamentary debater, and Hansemann, the financier, in their day famous members of the Parliament of Frankfort, now forgotten—but from parts of it, without the assistance of any commentary, he gains a vivid impression of men's feelings, of their exalted frame of mind, in that year of revolution. Very affecting is a final outburst, in which the poet bewails the want of men :

> " Ich seh' Gelehrte und Professoren
> Und Präsidenten und Assessoren,
> Weinküfer seh' ich und Redakteure
> Superintendenten und Accoucheure
> Und Börsenleute und Zeitungsschreiber,
> Astronomen und Steuereintreiber,
> Lumpenhändler und Alterthumskenner,
> Biedermänner, Hansemänner, Bassermänner—
> Allein wo sind die *Männer*, die *Männer?* " [1]

When Hartmann wrote these words he was living on the shores of the Lake of Geneva, a banished man, and the best

I also am his mother ! Yea, and yet a mightier one than I,
I and the Revolution's self, for whom he laid him down to die.
Stay thou within and nurse thy woe. 'Tis we will do him honour here ;
'Tis we will watch and requiem sing for thy dead son upon his bier.

.   .   .   .

Why grasp ye not your swords in wrath, O ye that sing and ye that pray ?
Ye organ-pipes, to trumpets turn, and fight the scoundrels with your breath,
And din into their dastard ears the dreadful news of sudden death,
Those scoundrels who the order gave, the cruel murder dared to do—
The hero leant him on his knee in that autumnal morning's dew,
Then silent fell upon his face in blood—'tis eight short days ago—
Two bullets smote him on the breast, and laid his head for ever low.

(JOYNES.)

[1] I see scientists and professors, presidents and assessors, wine merchants and editors, superintendents and accoucheurs ; I see financiers and journalists; I see astronomers and tax-collectors, rag merchants and antiquarians ; I see Messrs. Biedermann, Hansemann, Bassermann—but where are the *men*, the *men?*

men of Germany and Austria who had survived the great
discomfiture were either in prison or, like himself, in exile.

1848 is a year of no decisive political significance,
although it was in this year that the old order of things
was for the first time disturbed simultaneously in almost
every country of Europe. The local revolutions of 1789
and 1830, whatever they resulted in, were successful revolutions, but the general European revolution of 1848
was nothing in any single country but an unsuccessful
attempt.

Yet 1848 is a year of great spiritual significance.
After it men feel and think and write quite otherwise
than they did before it. In literature it is the red
line of separation that divides our century and marks
the beginning of a new era. It was a year of jubilee,
like that instituted by the old Hebrew law, that fiftieth
year, in which the trumpet was to be sounded throughout
all the land, which was to be hallowed, and in which
liberty was to be proclaimed "throughout all the land
unto all the inhabitants thereof" (Lev. xxv. 8, &c.). This
year, with its quick heart-beat, its all-subduing youthful
ardour, was, like that Bible year of jubilee, a year of returning into possession, a year of redemption, in which "they
that had been sold were redeemed again." To this day we
imbibe youthful enthusiasm from its days of March and
learn important lessons from its days of November.

It is the year of jubilee, the year of mourning, the
boundary year.

XXX

CONCLUSION

IT is a mighty panorama, this, which the study of the feelings and thoughts of Germany, first oppositionist, then revolutionary, between 1815 and 1848, unrolls to our view. We see the spirit of Metternich, a spirit of shallowness, brooding over Austria and the whole of Germany. We follow the new intellectual movement from the time when it first finds expression at the Wartburg Festival in 1817. We see how the assassination of Kotzebue gives occasion to the open persecution of Liberalism and introduces a long period of ruthless reaction and oppression, during which Goethe is regarded as the Quietist foe of liberty and lauded or denounced as such, and German philosophy under the auspices of Hegel becomes, in a rather questionable manner, conservative. The oppositionist tendency finds occasional expression in the writings of poets like Chamisso, Platen, and Heine, but the general intellectual condition is one of depression, relieved by outbursts of self-ridicule. The state of stagnation is put an end to by the news of the Revolution of July 1830, which electrifies public feeling and gives both poets and prose writers new courage and fresh inspiration. The remembrance of Byron's life and death influences men in the same direction, and the Polish revolt awakens sympathy and enthusiasm in spite of the part that Germany takes in the annihilation of Poland as a nation. Börne becomes the most eminent advocate of Liberalism in politics, holds high the banner of liberty and justice, shows a noble example in the matter of strength of character and conviction, but at the same time displays a naïve and fanatical optimism which proves that his is not the temperament required in a statesman. In Heine, the greatest poet of the period, we feel the vibration of its every nerve. In him modern poetry casts off the swaddling-clothes of Romanticism. In love, in appreciation of nature, in his political, social, and religious views, in his descriptive, poetic, and satiric style, he is the man of our own day— fitter, as we pointed out, than any other to grapple with modern life in its hardness and ugliness, its charm and its restlessness, and its wealth of violent contrasts. About the same time, in a different and yet kindred manner, Immermann, in his best book, marks the transition to a more realistic style of art.

The Revolution of July had not only changed the tone of literature, it had also altered the character of the Hegelian philosophy, which from this time onwards is to be regarded as one of the strongest influences in the revolutionising of men's conception of life ; from the doctrines of the master who died such a strong Conservative, his pupils draw reformatory or revolutionary inferences and principles. And now, with the echoes of the Revolution of July sounding in their ears, appear a group of young authors ; they are influenced by the philosophy of Hegel and the poetry of Goethe, this last interpreted as anti-Christian ; Heine and Börne are their masters, Rahel and George Sand their muses ; they come to be known by the name of Young Germany. They desire to assimilate literature with life, to subvert existing religious and moral doctrines, to introduce a freer morality in the matter of marriage and divorce and a new species of pantheistic piety. The impeachment of these men by Menzel in 1835 is the signal for a new series of persecutions directed against all that in that day went by the name of the literature of movement (Bewegungslitteratur). Very few of the representatives of the young generation show strength of character when thus put to the test, but both the highly gifted men (Gutzkow) and those of moderate ability (Laube, &c.) develop their talents amidst these persecutions, and works are produced which accurately mirror the hopes and struggles of the age, the thoughts and feelings, emptations, mistakes, and victories of the individual.

Between the years 1830 and 1840 something has been happening quietly, deep down in men's minds——Goethe's poetry and Goethe's philosophy of life, at first championed exclusively by enthusiastic women, have been steadily gaining influence over the cultivated, making them proof against theological impressions but receptive to all great human ideas. The cult of Goethe leads by degrees, even in the case of women, to the cult of political liberty and social reform.

In 1840 German philosophy begins to develop in the direction of Radicalism, and the poets begin openly to advocate the cause of political liberty. The men of this new generation, too, owe their philosophic training to Hegel, but they have metamorphosed his doctrine into an atheistical, anti-monarchical doctrine. They regard the standpoint of Young Germany with contempt as being purely belletristic, and busy themselves with the nature of Christianity and the idea of the state.

On the throne of Prussia at this juncture sits a king with a curiously complex character and many talents, a typical transition figure, whose personality, especially in ts relation to the literature and intellectual life of the day, s of great interest. In the south of Germany it is Metternich, in the north it is Frederick William IV., who outwardly regulates the course of events. We see literary and political celebrities being attracted by him, coming into collision with him, and rebounding from him. The invalids of literature, men like Tieck and Schelling, pass their last days under his protection ; Herwegh and Freiligrath are first attracted and then repelled by him ; Jacoby attacks him, Dingelstedt ridicules him.

And now we follow the development of political poetry, from its founder Anastasius Grün to Herwegh and Dingelstedt, observing what a deep impression such a thinker as Ludwig Feuerbach makes on the intellectual life of his contemporaries. Men like Freiligrath and Prutz, Sallet and Hartmann, are the petrels that foretell the storm ; in 1848 we hear the song of certain gifted poets high above the roar of the political hurricane, and we also notice that these unexampled occurrences transform men of minor or undeveloped talent into organs of the great movement of the hour.

During our study of this fragment of literary history we have passed in review a whole gallery of remarkable figures, devoting careful attention to the most important or most typical.

We saw how Napoleon's great personality, in its legendary form, exercised almost as powerful an influence on men's minds as Byron's. Of the great intellectual forces of the eighteenth century, Goethe, Jean Paul, Heinse, and Hegel are those by which our period is most perceptibly influenced. Some of the Romanticists influence as teachers and masters (Wilhelm Schlegel, Brentano, Chamisso), others as antagonists (Tieck). Börne and Heine, geniuses of most dissimilar types, by virtue of that polemical quality which was an essential characteristic of both, influence the whole period.

What a wealth of remarkable, original characters! Glance at our gallery of women—Rahel and Bettina, the friends of Goethe ; Börne's friends, Henrietta Herz and Jeannette Wohl ; Heine's La Mouche, Immermann's Elisa, and Princess Pückler and Charlotte Stieglitz—gifted women and devoted wives! Or let your eyes wander over our collection of male portraits—authors and men of the world, like Varnhagen and Pückler ; stiff, stately figures, like Platen and Immermann ; others that are all life and fire, like Börne and Heine ; manly eccentrics, like Jacoby ; kingly figures, like Feuerbach ; grimacing fanatics, like Menzel ; independent poets great and small, like Rückert, Hebbel, Ludwig, and Scherenberg ; agitators, like Wienbarg and Gutzkow ; men of pliant talent, like Laube and Mundt ; weak desponders, like Stieglitz ; bold singers of liberty, like Hoffmann and Freiligrath ; immature characters, like Herwegh ; problematic characters, like Dingelstedt and Meissner ; brave men, like Sallet, Hartmann, and Prutz. Even when their productions are not of the highest quality, we study the men themselves with interest.

And yet what is presented in this volume can only be fully understood by those who read it in its connection with the earlier volumes of the work of which it forms a part,

2 D

who regard it in the light of the last act of a great historic drama. The plan of the work is indicated in the introduction to the first volume, and is strictly adhered to throughout all six.

The author's intention, as explained in the first lines of his work, was, by means of the study of certain main groups and main movements in European literature, to outline a psychology of the first half of the nineteenth century. The year 1848, which, as a historical turning-point, marks a conclusion for the time being, was indicated as the point to which he intended to pursue his subject. The six groups which, according to the original plan, have been portrayed, are, the French Emigrant Literature, German Romanticism, the French Reaction, English Naturalism, French Romanticism, and Young Germany. Each one of the six parts of the work has in the course of years either been re-written or revised.

The author's first proceeding was to separate and classify the chief literary movements of the first half of the century, his next to find their general direction or law of progression, a starting point, and a central point.

The direction he discovered to be a great rhythmical ebb and flow——the gradual dying out and disappearing of the ideas and feelings of the eighteenth century until authority, the hereditary principle, and ancient custom once more reigned supreme, then the reappearance of the ideas of liberty in ever higher mounting waves. The starting point was now self-evident, namely, the group of French literary works denominated the Emigrant Literature, the first epoch-making one of which bears the date 1800. The central point was equally unmistakable. From the literary point of view it was Byron's death, from the political that Greek war of liberation in which he fell. This double event is epoch-making in the intellectual life and the literature of the Continent. The concluding point was also clearly indicated, namely, the European revolution of 1848. Byron's death forming the central point of the work, the school of English literature to which he belongs, became as it were the hinge on which it turned. The main outlines now stood out clearly: the incipient reaction in the case of the emigrants, held in check by the revolutionary ideas still in vogue ; the growth of the reaction in the Germany of the Romanticists ; its culmination and triumph during the first year of the Restoration in France ; the turn of the tide discernible in what is denominated English Naturalism ; the change which takes place in all the great writers of France shortly before the Revolution of July, a change which results in the formation of the French Romantic school ; and, lastly, the development in German literature which issues in the events of March 1848.

It is self-evident that the standpoint here adopted is a personal one. It is the personal point of view, the personal treatment, which presents literary personages and works thus grouped and ordered, thus contrasted, thus thrown into relief or cast into shadow. Regarded impersonally, the literature of a half-century is nothing but a chaos of hundreds of thousands of books in many languages.

The personal standpoint is not, however, an arbitrary one. It has been the author's aim to do justice, as far as in him lay, to every single person and phenomenon he has described. No attempt has been made to fit any of them into larger or smaller places than they actually occupied. It is no whim or preconceived intention of the author that has given the work its shape. The power which has grouped, contrasted, thrown into relief or suppressed, lengthened or shortened, placed in full light, in half light, or in shadow, is none other than that never entirely conscious power to which we usually give the name of art.

THE END

COMPLETE INDEX TO
THE SIX VOLUMES OF
MAIN CURRENTS IN
NINETEENTH-CENTURY
LITERATURE

A

INDEX

INDEX

4

INDEX

9

INDEX

INDEX

INDEX

INDEX

22

INDEX

23

INDEX

INDEX

26

INDEX

INDEX

INDEX

Riall, Major, *iv.*, 154
Richard, III., Shakespeare's, *v.*, 340
Richardson, Samuel, *ii.*, 61
Richelieu, *i.*, 185 ; *iii.*, 117 ; *v.*, 48 ; De Vigny's exaltation of, *iii.*, 287
Richepin, *vi.*, 132
Richter, *v.*, 24—*see* Paul [Richter] Jean
Riddere, De Sorte, Ingemann, *ii.*, 217
Riemer, v., 172
Righi, Cloud effects on Mount, *iv.*, 302, 303
Right, Hegel's Philosophy of, *vi.*, 5, 6
Rights of Kings and the People, De Maistre on, *iii.*, 104
Rights of Man, Declaration of the, *iii.*, 8, 18, 24, 25, 49
Rights, On the Origin and Main Principles of, Gentz, *ii.*, 317
Rinaldo Rinaldini, Vulpius, *ii.*, 35
Rioult, Gautier's art master, *v.*, 294
Ritter vom Geist, Die, Gutzkow's (The Knights of the Spirit), *vi.*, 75
Rizzio, D., *v.*, 22
Rob Roy, Sir W. Scott's, *iv.*, 53, 120
Robert, Leopold, *ii.*, 131 ; *v.*, 389
Robert Guiscard, Kleist, *ii.*, 259, 261
Robert le Diable, opera by Meyerbeer, *ii.*, 149 ; *v.*, 11
Robespierre, Maximilien, *i.*, 5 ; *ii.*, 94 ; *iii.*, 19, 53, 54, 78, 135 ; *v.*, 74 ; champions the Jews, *iii.*, 10 ; and French Revolution, 19 ; draws up Declaration of Rights of Man, 24 ; advocates restoration of belief in God and of the soul, 28 ; fear of atheism, 53 ; love of order, 75
Robespierre, The Fall of, Coleridge and Southey, *iv.*, 33, 73
Robinson Crusoe, Defoe, *ii.*, 205
Rocca, Albert de, marries Mme. de Staël, *i.*, 111
Roche, Sophia von la, *ii.*, 26
Rochefoucauld, La, *ii.*, 185
Rochow, General Theodor H. von, *vi.*, 11
Rococo style, French-Italian, *i.*, 161
Rodenberg's articles in *Deutsche Rundschau*, Julius, *vi.*, 350
Rogers, Samuel, *iv.*, 280 *n*, 281 *n*, 334
Rohan, Abbé de, *v.*, 364 ; Duc de, *iii.*, 208
Roi s'Amuse, Le, Hugo's play, *v.*, 97, 98, 350, 367
Roi de Bohème et ses Sept Château, Le, Nodier's, *v.*, 40
Roland [de la Platiere], *iii.*, 14
Roland, Mme. Manon Jeanne, *i.*, 153 ; *iii.*, 44, 92 ; letter to the Pope, *iii.*, 15 ; on the catechism, 33 ; letters to Buzot, 241
Rolla, De Musset's, *v.*, 103–104, 105, 112, 120
Rollinat, François, *v.*, 146, 147, 149

Roman Catholic Church in Prussia, *vi.*, 9
Roman Catholicism, tendency of Romanticists, *ii.*, 114–115 ; and French Romantics, *v.*, 253
Roman Elegy, Goethe's quotation about knitting, *ii.*, 77
Roman law supersedes Germanic, *i.*, 187
Roman Magician, The, Gutzkow's, *vi.*, 263
Romance Nations, their view of Heine and Goethe, *vi.*, 141
Romancers, Heine's, *vi.*, 155
"Romances of the Rosary," Brentano, *ii.*, 244, 247 ; *vi.*, 155, 156
Romano, Guilio, *v.*, 158
Romans et Contes, Gautier's, derived from Hoffmann, *v.*, 57
"Romantic," *v.*, 23, 45 ; Romantic authors and religious mysticism, *ii.*, 256 ; Rugé on Christianity, *ii.*, 292 ; defiance of the "bourgeois," *v.*, 266, 288 ; duplication, *ii.*, 152–180 ; literary theory of independence of manner of matter, *ii.*, 315 ; period reviewed, *v.*, 370, 371, 372 ; phase in Scott's works, *iv.*, 114 ; poetry, *ii.*, 73 ; *vi.*, 151 ; psychology, *ii.*, 159–180 ; School, *i.*, 55, 169, 173, 178, 179 ; *vi.*, 388 ; School of France, *i.*, 197 ; pomposity of style of French School, *v.*, 21–22 ; Sénancour's renown in, *i.*, 55, *School in Germany, The*, 74 *n*, 75 *n* ; Spain of young Romantic School, *v.*, 265 ; *Romantische Schule*, Haym's, *ii.*, 88 *n* ; Die Romantische Schule, Hettner's, *ii.*, 109 *n* ; De Hauranne *On the Romantic*, *v.*, 46
Romanticism defined, *v.*, 24, 45, 46 ; programme of, 46 ; in its first period non-political and acknowledges authority, *ii.*, 293 ; later tendency, 309 ; as finally condensed in Immermann's mind, *v.*, 211, 217–218 ; transition to modern liberalism, 220 ; regarded as a support of ecclesiasticism, *iii.*, 289 ; of the generation of 1830, *v.*, 8 ; attacked by Gutzkow, *vi.*, 241 ; as reaction, *v.*, 314 ; its unreality, *vi.*, 302 ; developed into realism, *v.*, 337 ; religious *iii.*, 79 ; Byron's Radical campaign against, *iv.*, 355 ; Lake School oriental, 90 ; British, 102 ; and Denmark, *ii.*, 7 ; origin in France, *i.*, 31 ; *v.*, 43 ; French, *iv.*, 364 ; classicism of French, *v.*, 23–24 ; fantastic in French, *v.*, 42 ; goodness in French, *v.*, 58 ; influences on French, *v.*, 390 ; perfection of form in French, *v.*, 58–59 ; programme of French, *v.*, 46 ; tendencies in French of, *v.*, 58–60 ; truth in French, *v.*, 58–59 ; historical tendency of, *v.*, 390 ; trend, its devotion to art, *v.*, 291— *see* French, *also* German

Romanticists, Ruge's definition of a, *ii.*, 292 ; French, *i.*, 49 ; independence of French, *v.*, 107–108 ; picturesqueness of style of French, *v.*, 21, 22 ; German hatred of utilitarianism, *v.*, 300 ; of Germany, *i.*, 49, 103 ; and Denmark, 103 ; principle in relation to art, *vi.*, 305 ; Shakespeare their rallying cry, *v.*, 43
Romantisme, Histoire de, Gautier's, *v.*, 386
Romanzen vom Rozenkranz, Die, Brentano, *ii.*, 244
Rome, *i.*, 124 ; St. Peter's, 175 ; Raphael's paintings, *iv.*, 229
Rome, King of, *i.*, 110 ; *iii.*, 115
Romeo and Juliet, Shakespeare's, *iii.*, 231 ; A. W. Schlegel's translation, *ii.*, 49, 55, 56, 57 ; wife's collaboration, 49
Romische Reise, Tieck's, *ii.*, 120 ; parody by Ruge, *ib.*
Romilly, Sir Samuel, *iv.*, 30 ; Journal of, 29
Ronde du Sabbat, La, Hugo's, *iii.*, 250 ; *v.*, 42
Ronsard, Pierre de, *v.*, 17, 68, 70, 312, 373
"Roquairol," character in Jean Paul Richter's *Titan*, *ii.*, 66, 68, 161, 162
"Roquantin," in Mérimée's *Vase Étrusque*, *v.*, 277–278
Rosalind and Helen, Shelley, *i.*, 38 ; *iv.*, 235
"Rose," Sainte-Beuve's poem, *v.*, 312
"Rose Fairy," Hans Andersen's *iv.*, 141
Rosen, Kunz von der, *vi.*, 204
Rosetti, William, *iv.*, 213
Rossini, G. A., *iv.*, 182, 183, 338 ; *v.*, 350
Rothschild of Frankfort, *vi.*, 42, 46, 47, 62, 119 ; of Paris, *vi.*, 101
Rouge et Noir, Beyle's, *iii.*, 278 ; *v.*, 209–210, 226, 228, 231, 233, 234, 235
Rousseau, Jean Jacques, *i.*, ix., 5, 43, 52, 63, 72, 74, 98, 116, 193, 197 ; *ii.*, 4, 19, 72, 100 ; *iii.*, 24, 25, 26, 30, 54, 58, 63, 68, 69, 90, 103, 106, 117, 222, 232, 269 ; *iv.*, 10, 271 *n*, 346 ; *v.*, 20, 55, 76, 134, 153, 157, 226, 227, 260, 263, 319, 320, 350 ; early life, *i.*, 189 ; political doctrines, 190 ; his *La Nouvelle Héloise*, 15 ; *iii.*, 120 ; standpoint in his characters differ from predecessors, 15–17 ; Voltaire his watchword, 16 ; influence on history, *i.*, 29 ; influence on French Literature, 6, 9, 10, 14, 24 ; *iii.*, 18, 58 ; influence on Châteaubriand, *i.*, 29 ; virtue his watchword, 16 ; charges against him, *iii.*, 64 ; political theories, *iii.*, 65 ; social theories, 66, 117 ; place in the religious reaction, 63, 64, 90, 266 ; and nature, *i.*, 17, 18 ; influenced by scenery of his exile, *i.*, 18–19 ; returns to

37

INDEX

INDEX

INDEX